"Rivlin's valuable book is among the first to relate, in clear and scrupulous detail, the decisions that have brought us this far, and to identify those who made them. . . . Rivlin is a sharp observer and a dogged reporter. He is unerringly compassionate toward his subjects. . . . But Rivlin's most valuable journalistic skill is his acute sensitivity to absurdity. He is particularly piqued by the absurdity of racial and economic injustice."
—*The New York Times Book Review*

"Deeply engrossing, well written, and packed with revealing stories . . . a magnificently reported account of life in a broken, waterlogged city. . . . Rivlin's exquisitely detailed narrative captures the anger, fatigue, and ambiguity of life during the recovery, the centrality of race at every step along the way, and the generosity of many from elsewhere in the country."
—*Kirkus Reviews* (starred)

"*Katrina* is an important book. It's important not because it's brilliantly reported or well-written, not because it uncovers everything from political maneuvering in the White House to despicable acts of selfishness, and not because it also tells stories of courage and tenacity that give meaning to the word 'inspirational.' It's important as a case study of both how not to handle a disaster and how to survive one. There are real lessons here."
—John M. Barry, author *Rising Tide* and *The Great Influenza*

"One of the must-reads of the season. . . . Rivlin offers a good report of what happened during the storm, the bureaucratic snarls and blockages that followed and, most of all, the human cost to all New Orleanians."
—*The New Orleans Advocate*

"[A] carefully researched, beautifully written book."
—*San Francisco Bay View*

"The once-great city of New Orleans wasn't destroyed just by a force of nature. Along with the hurricane came a category-5 tsunami of racism, operating at every level from armed encounters in the streets to serene indifference in the White House. Gary Rivlin, one of our finest journalists, chronicles it all in superb and riveting detail. This is something we have to know, discuss, and absorb—before the next storm comes along."
—Barbara Ehrenreich, author of *Nickle and Dimed*

"A sprawling, epic tale, filled with cold numbers and heartbreaking scenes of loss and devastation. It's also an insightful, accessible saga that follows a wide cast of participants—including politicians, businessmen, and everyday residents—over the course of many years. . . . [Rivlin] doesn't pull punches as he looks at the political, economic, and social aspects of New Orleans's struggle to recover, nor does he shy away from the complicated racial themes that have always been a part of the city's history . . . he skillfully balances out the human elements with concrete details of the devastation and the reconstruction that has followed. For those interested in how New Orleans came to the brink of destruction and slowly fought its way back to become a thriving, even improved, metropolis, this is certainly a work worth checking out."

—*Publishers Weekly*

"A fascinating lesson in urban planning in the face of calamity and financial shenanigans about what has been deemed 'the most expensive disaster in history.'"

—*Booklist*

"Journalist Gary Rivlin sweeps from street to boardroom in this history of the aftermath. . . . As Rivlin sharply reminds, overcoming disasters is very much an issue of governance."

—*Nature* magazine

"Sweeping and searching, *Katrina* is a category-five exposé of disastrous disaster relief."

—*Florida Courier*

"A gem of a book—well-reported, deftly written, tightly focused. It's a book that will appeal to the urban planner and the Mardi Gras reveler. . . . *Katrina* is a genuine success, and is a starting point for anyone interested in how The City That Care Forgot develops in its second decade of recovery."

—*St. Louis Post-Dispatch*

"Painstakingly researched . . . Rivlin's reporting allows him to paint deep portraits of his characters and explain relationships . . . Rivlin does an admirable job keeping the political personal and helping readers understand how deeply and devastatingly Katrina affected everyone in the city. . . . The book is timed to come out a couple of weeks before the 10th anniversary of Katrina, but the timing this summer is equally important as part of the conversation America is currently having on the subject of race relations."

—*Miami Herald*

"A riveting, wide-ranging but detailed account of Katrina's immediate impact and its aftermath."

—*The Tampa Tribune*

"Gary Rivlin is one of our nation's most sharp-eyed cultural observers, and one of our most gifted social historians. *Katrina* is a provocative and beautifully rendered book that reminds us that the subject of race is always percolating below the surface. The vividly told and haunting *Katrina* is vital, not only for understanding New Orleans and what happened there over the last ten years, but for understanding how divisions of race and class are perpetuated across America today."

—Michael Eric Dyson, author of *April 4, 1968*

"It is in large part because race lately imposes itself upon our national consciousness with even greater force than usual that Gary Rivlin's vital, comprehensive account of Hurricane Katrina's long-term impact on the city of New Orleans comes across less as a 10-year-anniversary marker of an indelible calamity and more as an up-to-the-minute microcosm of our larger society . . . manages to pack into a lean, taut narrative the heartbreaking setbacks, thwarted dreams and the confounding, repeated inability of anybody in power to either get things done or transcend festering social divisions. . . . As with the finest works of journalism, Rivlin's book deploys the tools of his trade to illuminate the segment of history he examines—and make us wonder about the things we all have in common with those in New Orleans."

—*USA Today*

"[Rivlin] constructs his narrative to give readers unfamiliar with the terrain a cohesive back story and illustrates the aftermath through a cross-section of people."

—*Chicago Tribune*

"This blow-by-blow account of the months and years after Katrina brings back the frustration felt by so many who watched the devastation unfold and raises important questions about the role of race in the response to natural disasters."

—*Library Journal*

"A clear-eyed account . . . Rivlin weaves in powerful personal accounts from a cross-section of survivors—black and white, working class and affluent. . . . A skillful storyteller, Rivlin delivers a fascinating report on a city transformed by tragedy."

—*BookPage*

"Gary Rivlin's sharp eye for detail, grasp of the big picture, and thorough reporting reveals the endless errors, egregious official conduct, and exploitation that compounded the misery of Katrina victims long after the storm. It's a helluva a book that should arouse every American to demand reform before disasters strike their communities."

—David Cay Johnston, Pulitzer Prize winner and author of *Divided* and *Perfectly Legal*

"As harrowing as it is riveting . . . a balanced and comprehensive chronicle."

—*New York Daily News*

"A riveting account of the disastrous results of the storm, starting from the preliminary evacuations to the present day . . . skillfully blends personal comments with investigative journalism, presenting readers with a well-rounded view of the social, economic and emotional impact the storm had on hundreds of thousands, in the first days after the hurricane and over the ensuing decade."

—*Shelf Awareness*

"Gary Rivlin's *Katrina: After the Flood* is as raw as the title. . . . *Katrina* carries you from the days before the disaster through an aftermath so tumultuous and chaotic you can scarcely fathom it happening in a developed country. Rivlin's careful storytelling won't let us escape, however, as he confronts us with testimonials from streets that remain uninhabited 10 years later."

—*Sierra* magazine

"*Katrina: After the Flood* succeeds as a lucid and sympathetic account of a vital American metropolis crushed by natural forces and beset by issues of race and class in its ongoing attempts to recover."

—*Highbrow Magazine*

"In the last decade, few tales equal that of Hurricane Katrina in proportion or the amount of media devoted to it, yet nonfiction writer Gary Rivlin has woven a narrative so fresh in perspective and focus, his new book reminds us of how many personal accounts of this monumental event still beg to be told."

—*New Orleans Living*

"A *New York Times* reporter who covered the Katrina aftermath, Rivlin became a freelancer, kept coming back, and in a fair-minded way captures the struggle of ordinary people remaking their lives, or losing what they had, amid the complex politics. . . . Rivlin uses a deft hand, orchestrating a dramatis personae of politicians, planners, activists, policy advocates and grassroots change-agents across the narrative stage. . . . Rivlin casts a wide net without losing focus on the deep injustices borne by poor blacks, particularly those with valid leases in well-built housing projects the city chose to demolish."

—*America* magazine

"A deeply reported, character-driven procedural, not unlike the classics of its kind, such as *And the Band Played On* or *The Warmth of Other Suns*."

—*Virginia Quarterly*

ALSO BY GARY RIVLIN

Broke, USA

Fire on the Prairie

Drive-By

The Plot to Get Bill Gates

The Godfather of Silicon Valley

KATRINA

AFTER THE FLOOD

Gary Rivlin

SIMON & SCHUSTER PAPERBACKS

New York   London   Toronto   Sydney   New Delhi

For Daisy

Simon & Schuster Paperbacks
An Imprint of Simon & Schuster, Inc.
1230 Avenue of the Americas
New York, NY 10020

First Simon & Schuster trade paperback edition August 2016

SIMON & SCHUSTER PAPERBACKS and colophon are
registered trademarks of Simon & Schuster, Inc.

For information about special discounts for bulk purchases,
please contact Simon & Schuster Special Sales at 1-866-506-1949
or business@simonandschuster.com.

The Simon & Schuster Speakers Bureau can bring authors to
your live event. For more information or to book an event contact
the Simon & Schuster Speakers Bureau at 1-866-248-3049 or visit
our website at www.simonspeakers.com.

Interior design by Lewelin Polanco
Maps by Paul J. Pugliese

Manufactured in the United States of America

10 9 8 7 6 5 4 3 2 1

Library of Congress Cataloging-in-Publication Data is available.

ISBN 978-1-4516-9222-8
ISBN 978-1-4516-9225-9 (pbk)
ISBN 978-1-4516-9226-6(ebook)

CONTENTS

They say that in New Orleans is to be found a mixture of all the nations. . . . But in the midst of this confusion what race dominates and gives direction to all the rest?

—Alexis de Tocqueville,
1832

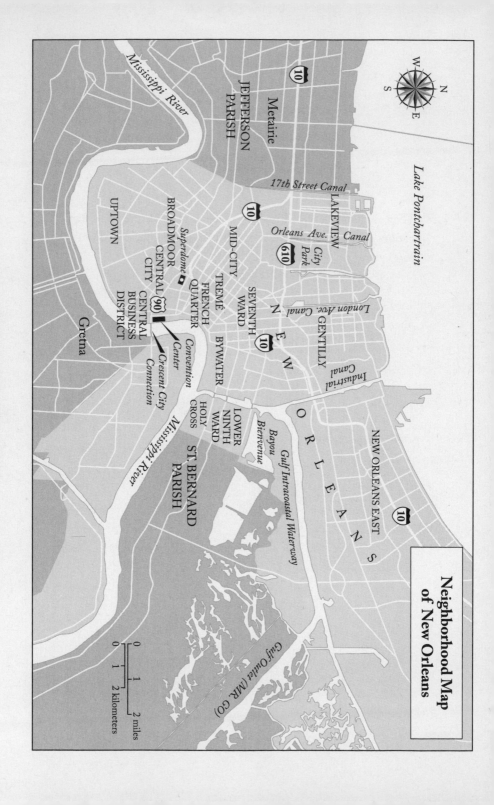

**Neighborhood Map
of New Orleans**

Lake Pontchartrain

Mississippi River

JEFFERSON
PARISH

Metairie

10

17th Street Canal

10

Orleans Ave. Canal

610

City
Park

LAKEVIEW

Canal

UPTOWN

BROADMOOR

Superdome

CENTRAL
CITY

MID-CITY

TREMÉ

FRENCH
QUARTER

SEVENTH
WARD

London Ave. Canal

GENTILLY

N
E
W

90

CENTRAL
BUSINESS
DISTRICT

Convention
Center

Crescent City
Connection

BYWATER

Industrial Canal

Gretra

Mississippi River

HOLY
CROSS

LOWER
NINTH
WARD

Bayou
Bienvenue

O
R
L
E
A
N
S

NEW ORLEANS EAST

10

ST BERNARD
PARISH

Gulf Intracoastal Waterway

Gulf Outlet (MR GO)

0   0
    1
1
    2 kilometers
2 miles

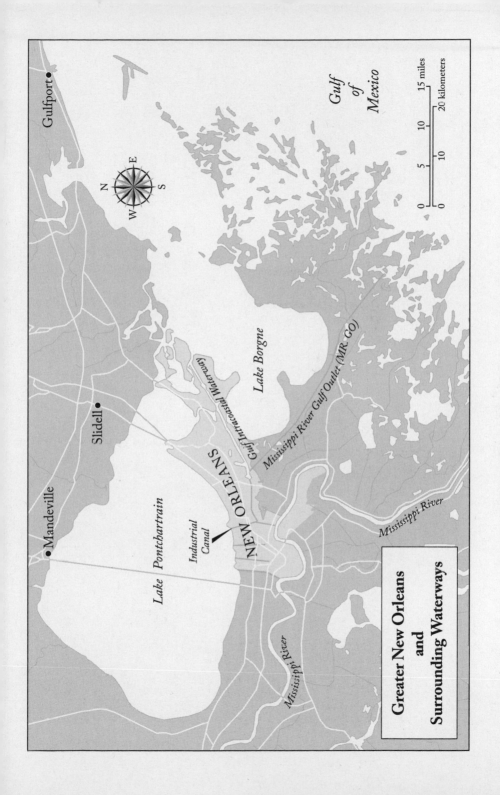

Gulfport

N
W E
S

Mandeville

Slidell

Lake Pontchartrain

Industrial Canal

NEW ORLEANS

Gulf Intracoastal Waterway

Lake Borgne

Mississippi River Gulf Outlet (MR. GO)

Mississippi River

Mississippi River

Gulf
of
Mexico

15 miles

20 kilometers

5   10

10

0   0

Greater New Orleans
and
Surrounding Waterways

AUTHOR'S NOTE

Water still covered much of New Orleans the first time I saw the city after Hurricane Katrina. Armed soldiers were stopping cars at roadblocks set up on the perimeter of the metro area. I had hitched a ride with a Republican state senator anxious to get to her flooded home and her then husband. My press credentials got us through one checkpoint; her legislative ID convinced the National Guard to allow us to pass through another. The highway was empty when, once inside the city limits, we hit an elevated stretch of road offering a panoramic view. This was the flooded city the world was seeing on television, but even there on the highway it still seemed unreal, like a special effect ordered up by Steven Spielberg. Eighty percent of the city lay underwater—more than 110,000 homes and another 20,000 businesses.

A week earlier, I had been sitting in the San Francisco bureau of the *New York Times* writing about Google, Facebook, and Silicon Valley's next crop of underage billionaires. My New Orleans was the New Orleans of tourists: Bourbon Street, Mardi Gras, the Jazz & Heritage Festival, po' boys. I had no connection to anyone living there. But an all-hands mentality prevailed at the *Times* given a disaster that displaced more than one million people.

My editor asked if I could help out, and a few days later I was picking up car keys at a rental counter at the Baton Rouge Metropolitan Airport, around an hour north and west of New Orleans. My new office was whatever patch of free space I could find at a place my colleagues had already dubbed "the plantation"—a white-columned, antebellum house in Baton Rouge normally rented out for parties that the *Times* had transformed into a makeshift newsroom and barracks. We'd take turns in New Orleans, sleeping in a trio of rooms the paper had booked at the Sheraton there, which, as one of the few functioning hotels in the center of town, also served as the city's main meeting place.

Most everyone around me was looking backward in those earliest weeks after Katrina. Teams of scientists were exploring how and why the levees around New Orleans had failed on the morning of Monday, August 29, 2005, when Katrina struck the Louisiana coast. Medical examiners around the region still had no idea what the final death count might be. There were reports of euthanized patients inside a New Orleans hospital. Three dozen elderly patients had supposedly been left to die at a nursing home. Reporters were assigned to each of those topics, but most were focused on the botched rescue, which had played out live on television. Thousands waited helplessly on elevated sections of the interstate, hungry and thirsty and looking skyward for the help that was not coming. It took the government four days to send the buses needed to rescue the twenty-five thousand people stranded inside the Superdome. Another twenty-four hours passed before buses were dispatched to pick up people at the Ernest N. Morial Convention Center, where another twenty thousand had taken refuge. The most powerful nation on earth had failed its citizens so miserably. Blame needed to be assigned.

Yet even before getting on that plane to Baton Rouge, my instincts had me looking forward to the mess ahead. Eventually, the floodwaters would recede. How would New Orleans go about the complicated task of rebuilding? The majority of the city's police and fire stations had flooded. So, too, had most of the city's schools. Flooding had destroyed the city's electrical system and disabled its sewer and water systems. Even the weight of all that water on the streets proved catastrophic, cracking gas lines and underground pipes and, in some cases, the roadways themselves. Most of the city's buses had been destroyed along with dozens of its streetcars. Meanwhile, powerful voices in Washington were saying the city shouldn't be rebuilt—that a low-lying delta was no place for a city (except if there wasn't a New Orleans at the mouth of the

Mississippi to serve as a port of entry to the thirty-one states and two Canadian provinces that are part of the Mississippi River Valley, they'd have to build a city there given its geographic significance).

The storm meant New Orleans would be without most of its revenues. All those shuttered businesses represented millions in lost sales tax revenues each month. Collecting property taxes, the city's second-largest source of revenue, seemed unrealistic in a city 80 percent underwater. Five weeks after the storm, the city laid off nearly half its workforce, including most of its Planning Department. New Orleans had long been one of the country's poorest and most violent cities. The Orleans Parish schools had been through eight superintendents in seven years, and off and on the New Orleans Police Department (NOPD) had been among the country's most notorious. And racial tensions were never far from the surface in New Orleans. "Our celebratory culture and accepting nature conceals a city with a troubled soul," Silas Lee, a well-liked black commentator, had written two years before Katrina. For two decades, Lee, a pollster with a PhD in urban policy, had been studying the socioeconomic makeup of the city. During that time, the portion of black New Orleanians earning a high school or college degree had dramatically increased, yet the income gap between black and white had widened. "Behind the mask," Lee wrote, "resides a divided city."

My temporary posting became more permanent when, around one month after Katrina, I was assigned to the "storm team" assembled to handle the paper's coverage of Katrina. My center of gravity shifted from the plantation to the Sheraton in New Orleans, where my neighbors included the president of the City Council and other elected officials who had lost their homes in Katrina. New Orleans then felt more small town than big city—home to maybe twenty thousand people where it wasn't uncommon to run into the mayor several times a week.

Any journalism endeavor has an element of luck. I wasn't in Baton Rouge twelve hours when I sat across the desk from Louisiana lieutenant governor Mitch Landrieu, who would play a central role in the story I tell here. That night, I racked up a bar bill of nearly $200 at a restaurant popular among political insiders, collecting names and cell phone numbers—the only digits that would count for months in a city of shuttered businesses and flooded homes. That's how I was able to reach the personal friend of George W. Bush who served as Karl Rove's eyes and ears in New Orleans and also Alden McDonald, a savvy, well-connected black banker whom the mayor would invite to shape the rebuilding plan as a member of the Bring New Orleans Back Commission.

"Bring a map of New Orleans" was McDonald's only precondition when he agreed to meet with me eleven days after Katrina. The talk then was of an equal-opportunity storm that had hit black and white alike, but he was having none of it. Sitting in the makeshift office his people had set up for him in the back of a bank branch in Baton Rouge, he drew a line down the middle of the map. He pointed to the western half of New Orleans. That's the New Orleans you know, he said: the French Quarter, the Superdome, the Warehouse District, the Garden District, St. Charles Avenue. Then he pointed to the eastern half of the map. That's where he lived, McDonald said, and also most of his customers. "Where you saw water up to the rooftops?" he said. "That's where most of the city's black people lived."

WATER RISING

Overtime pay was never enough. The bosses running the city's transit agency needed to offer more than money to convince the bus drivers, streetcar operators, mechanics, and others they needed to stay in town through a big storm. So in August 2005, with a hurricane named Katrina bearing down on New Orleans, they did as they had in the past ahead of previous scares: they opened up the agency's headquarters, a three-story brick fortress on Canal Street on the edge of the city's central business district. "To get the volunteers we needed, we'd allow them to bring their spouses, their children, grandmothers, grandfathers, girlfriends, nieces, nephews, whoever," said Bill Deville, then the general manager of the New Orleans Regional Transit Authority.

The A. Philip Randolph Building—what RTA employees called the "Canal Street barn" or simply "the barn"—was hardly the Hilton. People slept on air mattresses and needed to bring their own food. But the barn was also a veritable fort, stocked with military food rations and water and with its own backup generator. Most important, it was in a part of town that everyone knew never flooded. "People really want to be together in a protected facility," Deville said.

Around the region, the traffic on the highways out of town ahead of Katrina was heaviest on Sunday. The storm wouldn't hit New Orleans until early on Monday morning. Yet the city's bus drivers and others needed to work on Sunday, picking up people at evacuation centers around the city and dropping them off at the Superdome. Thus, on Saturday the RTA employees, their families, and their friends started showing up at the barn, dragging with them their suitcases and carrying coolers, and the occasional large silver pot heavy with gumbo. By Sunday night, somewhere around three hundred people were taking refuge there. The group, around 90 percent black, included grandparents and a couple of babies. Only around one-third worked for the RTA. People plugged in hot plates to heat up their food and shared the flasks and bottles they had brought with them. By 10:00 p.m., the winds sounded like a jet engine roaring. By midnight, the pounding rain echoed through the building. Why not a party when there was nothing to do except wait?

MONDAY

Gerald Robichaux, the RTA's deputy general manager for operations, was up early Monday morning. He saw water in the streets and immediately regretted his decision to leave the agency's three big dump trucks parked at the Uptown facility a few miles away, along with the big rigs they used to tow disabled buses. These trucks with tires as tall as the average-size man, Robichaux realized, might prove to be their chariots of escape if the water in the streets kept rising. Robichaux ordered a small crew to take the single high-wheeled vehicle they had at the Canal Street barn and pick up the other rigs on Napoleon Avenue. Robichaux also asked Wilfred Eddington to join them. Eddington was a member of the New Orleans Police Department, and part of the RTA's transit police unit.

The wind was still blowing at around fifty miles per hour when they pulled out of the barn at around 10:00 a.m. Eddington remembered a blue Chevy parked at the Chevron station a block away. The water, maybe curb high, reached the bottom of the Chevy's hubcaps. The water was halfway up the car's windows when they returned ninety minutes later.

Back at the barn, the men told Robichaux what they had seen. They had headed west and south of downtown expecting to see at least some flooding in Uptown, which often gets an inch or two of water after a hard rain. But Uptown was dry. Only closer to their building had they hit any real flooding. Needing to see for himself, Robichaux called out the names of a few of his top people and jumped into one of the big trucks. Bill Deville decided to join his number two and almost immediately regretted his decision. The fifty-eight-year-old general manager was taking medicine for a bad heart. He took another pill to manage his high blood pressure. Just getting to the rig meant walking through foul, brackish water up past his knees. Only once it was too late did Deville remember a cut on his leg.

Robichaux was anxious to see the large facility the RTA operated in the eastern part of the city, in New Orleans East. With water starting to leak into the ground floor of the Canal Street barn, that might need to serve as their temporary base for running the city's transit agency. Once on the interstate, Robichaux realized he had bigger problems than figuring out what day they might restart bus and streetcar service. Water was in every direction, sometimes up to the eaves of one-story homes. The I-10 became impassable after a couple of miles of driving, forcing them to turn back.

At some point on Monday the toilets stopped working—no small concern in a building housing around three hundred people. Landlines weren't working and cell phone coverage was spotty. They weren't completely cut off, however. The police scanner was still working, which is how they learned about the levee breaches. Bill Deville called everyone together late Monday afternoon to relay the bad news. He reminded them of the dozens of pumping stations the city operated around town and how effectively these miracle machines soaked up excess water. "It will probably take another day or so for the water to subside," he said.

TUESDAY

Gerald Robichaux and several supervisors were up early on Tuesday making rounds. So much water had gotten inside the building overnight that the emergency generator was submerged, rendering it useless. They were low on food and almost out of water. Walking around the building, they could feel the rising panic. Older people were running low on medicines. Mothers needed clean diapers. Robichaux went looking for his boss.

Deville had gone straight to his office after delivering the bad news about the city's broken levees. He had lain down on the couch, but who could sleep in the stupefying heat and with his cut leg feeling as if it were on fire? In the middle of the night, Deville grabbed a flashlight and headed to his car, parked in the employee parking lot. He turned on the engine, set the air conditioner to high, and fell asleep.

Robichaux rapped on the roof of Deville's car. Deville's first feeling was confusion, then shame. It had been dark when he'd closed his eyes, but he was squinting against the brightness. How long had he been asleep? he asked himself groggily. Three hours? Four? "We need to leave," Robichaux told him. He gave Deville a grim update and then laid out the plan Robichaux and a few others had hatched. We'll give people a choice, Robichaux said. They were maybe a dozen blocks from an entrance ramp to an elevated portion of the I-10. They could wade or swim to that ramp. They knew from listening to the radio and police scanners that the streets were dry on the other side of the Mississippi River. Those who felt up to it could walk a few miles on the elevated I-10 to the Crescent City Connection, the bridge that took traffic over the Mississippi River to the West Bank. With some luck, they could contact the drivers of the big coaches they had parked in LaPlace, a town halfway between New Orleans and Baton Rouge, and arrange to be picked up at the park 'n' ride commuter lot the RTA operated on the West Bank. Those who did not feel up to the long walk could remain in the barn while a small scouting party searched for boats to ferry them to safety.

A meeting was held on the roof parking lot later that morning. Deville asked Robichaux to explain his idea, but this no-nonsense manager who was so adept at making the buses run more or less on time wasn't necessarily the best messenger in the midst of a crisis. Robichaux admitted they had no idea how deep the water was to the ramp. He then told the group to split into two. He asked those who could swim to gather on one side of the roof and those who couldn't on the other. "They're leaving us to drown," some of the nonswimmers called out.

Deville stepped up on the back of a pickup truck. "No one is leaving anyone behind," he assured them. They had air mattresses, he said. They would float people who couldn't swim. He also made a promise: "I'll stay with anyone who doesn't feel up to the walk." Afterward, people patted him on the back for his bravery, but he felt like a fraud. "I was scared to death," Deville confessed. "People thought I was a hero for volunteering to stay behind, but I can't swim. Plus there was no way I was stepping another foot in that water." While still standing on the flatbed, Deville told the crowd of a conversation he had had that morning with someone in the governor's office. He'd promised to send helicopters as soon as any were available. Maybe those who remained at the barn would be the first ones rescued.

A LITTLE PAST NOON on Tuesday, August 30, 2005, the first RTA employees dropped themselves into the dark, murky waters that were chest high on a six-foot man. Around two-thirds of their group—two hundred people—chose to walk rather than remain. Children were hoisted on air mattresses, along with most everyone standing under maybe five feet five inches tall. Those tall enough to walk sloshed through the smelly, oily water, guiding the others on the makeshift rafts. Sharon Paul, a fifty-year-old RTA dispatcher, was a diabetic who had already gone more than twenty-four hours without her insulin. But Paul was a strong swimmer. She helped a pregnant woman heft herself onto an air mattress along with a pair of toddlers. Paul then tied a rope around her waist and towed the three of them. "I'm done," she said, collapsing once they reached the elevated highway. She'd need to walk another six miles to make the park 'n' ride on the West Bank.

Some had thought they were strong enough to make it the half mile to the interstate but were not. Others froze in place. Ruben Stephens, an NOPD lieutenant who headed up the RTA's police unit, helped with the stragglers. "People were petrified of the water," Stephens said. Wilfred Eddington was already sitting on top of the interstate with his boots off when Robichaux asked him and another officer to help coax people to the interstate. He laced up his boots and headed down the ramp and into the muck. "Our job was to make sure that we got everybody to that bridge," Eddington said.

Staying together was a challenge. They had imagined walking as a single group toward the twin cantilevered bridges looming a couple of miles away. Ruben Stephens, the police lieutenant, ordered Eddington to the front of the line. Stephens and several other officers retreated to the back of the group to wrangle any strays. People passed the Superdome, standing like a giant spaceship next to the highway, and stared. Some in their contingent had been at the dome as recently as Sunday, where orderly lines of people were waiting to be patted down (people were being checked for weapons) before they were admitted to this "shelter of last resort." Now thick crowds of people milled everywhere while nearby the National Guardsmen stood holding weapons. Pieces of the Superdome's roof had peeled off. The giant Hyatt Regency next door—where the mayor and his top people were—looked worse. Almost every window on the northern face of the hotel was shattered.

They passed clots of five or ten people, but no other contingent was nearly as large as theirs, and none seemed to be walking with the same purpose. The temperature was in the nineties and the humidity high. From the interstate they had an expansive view of watery New Orleans—a perfect vantage point for contemplating a drowned-out home. A torpor took over all but the strongest among them, but they kept walking. The bridge ahead led to Algiers, the New Orleans neighborhood on the other side of the Mississippi. Only later did they appreciate that it was also the route to white-flight suburbs such as Gretna, the first town they would reach once they had crossed the Crescent City Connection. At least one of them was in a wheelchair, and their ranks included grandmothers, toddlers, and several police officers. None seemed to be thinking about what it meant that theirs was an almost all-black group heading into a predominantly white community.

A bus driver named Malcolm Butler and his wife, Dorothy, were among the first to notice the blockade. Initially, Malcolm Butler thought his eyes were playing tricks on him in the hot, midday sun. Butler was set to retire, after thirty-three years on the job, on August 31—the next day. Their home in New Orleans East had most certainly flooded, and then there were the fresh horrors of their walk from the Canal Street barn to the interstate. Butler, who is not tall, had walked through greasy water up to his neck, his nose and chin pointed upward, guiding Dorothy, who clung to an air mattress. They had probably been on the interstate for less than an hour—enough so that their clothes had dried out even if the stink of the water remained—when Butler stopped and asked Dorothy if she was seeing what he was: a pair of police officers brandishing weapons, blocking their passage. "They was standing up there with their automobiles blocking the bridge with shotguns and M16s and told us we couldn't go no further," Butler recalled.

Wilfred Eddington, the police officer assigned to walk point as they headed toward the West Bank, figured he was around one thousand yards from the foot of the bridge when he saw the two police cars parked nose to nose, forming a wedge to block their passage. Eventually, he heard them yelling, "Go back! Go back! Get off the bridge!" He noticed their black uniforms—they were members of the small force responsible for policing the bridge.

Eddington was dressed in jeans but wearing a dark T-shirt stamped with the word POLICE in large letters. He wore a holstered gun on his belt. He asked the others to slow down while he approached his counterparts. The smaller of the two bridge cops, a young black woman, didn't seem to care what it said on Eddington's shirt. The closer he got, the louder she seemed to scream. "She was out of control," Eddington said. "She was irate."

"You gotta bring it down a few notches," Eddington said, looking at the female officer. "You're now at around ten. We need you to bring it down to three." He was a cop with two decades on the job, counseling a less experienced officer. "But she remained belligerent," Eddington said.

Ruben Stephens, the police lieutenant, jogged up from the back of their ranks. He introduced himself and explained that a group of city workers on duty at the time of the storm had gotten trapped by the flooding. They were only trying to reach their facility in Algiers, where some buses would be picking them up.

"You're not crossing my damn bridge," the female officer responded.

"You better get your rank," Stephens snapped.

"Pedestrians are not permitted on the bridge at any time!" she countered, as if this was any other Tuesday.

"She was hollering, 'I lost my house, I lost everything,'" Wilfred Eddington said. But she was also adamant. "You all ain't going nowhere," she repeated.

At the back of the line, Sharon Paul, the diabetic dispatcher, looked uncomprehendingly at the police cruisers parked to block their way until someone told her, "Police say we can't cross."

"Don't they know we've got water where we came from?"

A SUPERVISOR FOR THE bridge police arrived at the scene. So did Gerald Robichaux, who had been preoccupied tending to those at the back of the line needing help. A stalemate lasting between thirty and sixty minutes ended when several suburban-line commuter buses arrived to pick them up at the foot of the bridge. For the moment, everything seemed a crazy misunderstanding, and the RTA people boarded the buses. Sitting at the front of the bus, Lieutenant Stephens assumed they were heading to the RTA's park 'n' ride in Algiers. The coaches had instead brought them to the bus depot in suburban Gretna.

Stephens heard the Gretna police officers before he saw them. "Don't get off that bus," they barked. "Don't get off the damn bus." Stephens stepped down the stairs, thinking he could talk to them, cop to cop. "I'm a police lieutenant," he tried to say. But they were yelling too loud to hear him. Each pointed a weapon at him.

"Where the fuck y'all think you're going with all these people?"

"Who the fuck told y'all to bring these people here?"

"Y'all need to get the hell out of here."

Stephens had grown up in the Desire housing project in New Orleans's Upper Ninth Ward. He had served in the army and worn a police uniform for more than two decades. For the last five years, that uniform had been dressed with a lieutenant's star. He had probably five or six feet of water sitting in the modest place he owned in New Orleans East—a single-story ranch home—which guaranteed that most everything he owned had been ruined. "I ain't going nowhere," Lieutenant Stephens said. He had a gun strapped to his belt and told himself he was ready to use it, if necessary. "I feared one of them might start shooting," Stephens said, "and then you'd have a massacre."

People walked off the bus, despite the threats. Gail Davis, a fifty-three-year-old grandmother whose husband, Woodrow, worked for the RTA, was on that first bus with her daughter and three grandchildren. Davis found herself staring at guns as she got off the bus. "They was putting them in our faces and saying, 'If you move, if you breathe, we're going to shoot you,'" Davis said. "I'm trying to hold on to my grandchildren because they was nine, ten, eleven years old." Mary Ann Ruth, a forty-nine-year-old cashier at the Boomtown Casino just outside New Orleans (her fiancé was a driver for the RTA), was also on that first bus. She, too, was a grandmother, there with her fiancé's nine-year-old son and a two-year-old granddaughter. "We were hungry, we was wet after walking in that nasty water," Ruth said. "We wasn't trying to harm nobody. They had their guns cocked. They say, 'If they move, shoot them.'"

The second and third buses pulled up, and they, too, disgorged their passengers there at the Gretna bus terminal. There, on this large patch of sidewalk under a highway overpass, the police pointed shotguns and other long guns, yelling "motherfucker this" and "motherfucker that." On her bus, said Sharon Paul, the diabetic, people felt a sense of relief when out the window they saw all the police. "We really thought they was coming to assist us," Paul said. And why not? Gretna, a town of eighteen thousand whose official motto is "Small City, Big Heart," had lost electricity but still had plenty of food and water on stock. Its roads were passable, providing people a path to safety. Paul said she heard one cop yell, "Get on the curb *now* or we're gonna shoot," but she couldn't take the command seriously. "They cocked their guns," Paul said, "and then everybody paid attention.

"They was being ugly and all rough and rude with us," Paul said. "And it ain't like we was throwed-away people. We was working-class people trying to get where we had to go."

GRETNA POLICE OFFICER DWIGHT Dorsey was on patrol when he heard a staticky message over the single emergency channel available to all first responders in the area. "It was a call for assistance over the radio saying that they had a large group of subjects loitering," Dorsey said.

Dorsey says six to eight police cars were at the Gretna bus terminal that afternoon. Louis Alvarez, another cop on the scene, said there were five patrol cars, but allowed that the number might have been higher. Mary Ann Ruth, the casino cashier, said at least ten cops were watching over their klatch of grandmothers, children, and civil-service lifers. Wilfred Eddington, the longtime NOPD cop, put the number of officers who "semicircled around us" at between eleven and fifteen.

Chris Roberts also responded to the call for reinforcements. Roberts was a Jefferson City Councilman, not a sworn peace officer, but he later described himself as eager to help protect his town from looters and other bad elements from New Orleans. "He was this little, short white guy getting into people's faces," Brandon Mason, an RTA supervisor, said. "He's yelling at people, 'This is my city,' telling us how it's martial law and we have no business being in his city."

Wilfred Eddington was the first person Roberts encountered at the scene. The police officer had removed himself from the group and was sitting on the curb, smoking a cigar he had secreted away.

"Who in the hell ordered this?" Eddington heard the man's high-pitched, loud voice before he saw him. "Who said these people could get off here?" Eddington turned and saw a short white man walking his way, jabbing his finger at him.

"I'm like, 'Dude, what are you talking about? I'm just sitting smoking a cigar.'"

"I want to know right now who ordered this."

"Who ordered what?" Eddington stood up. He towered over Roberts.

"Who told you to bring these people over here under this bridge?"

Eddington asked who was asking, and Roberts identified himself. "Okay, Chris Roberts of the Gretna City Council, you have a few seconds to back off and just get out of my face."

"I'm not going anywhere."

"Get the hell out of my face," Eddington yelled, then heard the unmistakable crack of someone racking a shotgun. A Gretna officer, apparently, did not like the manner in which this black cop from New Orleans was talking to an elected official. Roberts kept jabbering at him ("He was this little gnat," Eddington said of the councilman, "a pain in the ass"), but Eddington was no longer listening. "I mean, I was tunnel vision, looking at this one particular police officer." He stomped over to confront the cop holding the shotgun. "As I'm walking to him, I'm breaking leather," Eddington said. "I'm coming out." He had a police revolver on his right hip. And he was unholstering his weapon.

Ronnie Harris, the longtime Gretna mayor, arrived and demanded to know who was in charge. All eyes turned to Harris and also to Gerald Robichaux, who was talking on a cell phone, seeing if he could find any buses and drivers to get them out of there. Robichaux had run the transit agency on this side of the bridge before taking the number two job at the RTA. He and Harris knew one another. If Harris had not shown up when he did, Lieutenant Stephens said, "God only knows where it would have went." The mayor promised a few Porta Potties and ordered someone to get some water for their "guests." Stephens ordered Eddington to the other side of their group to put distance between him and the shotgun-wielding Gretna cop.

The Gretna police still didn't holster their guns. "We had weapons pointed at us the entire time," Lieutenant Stephens said. The violation of the blue-brotherhood code seemed to aggravate Stephens more than anything else. "I would never have treated a fellow police officer the way they treated us," he said. "We felt like hostages."

Some part of the RTA contingent refused water when it was offered, including Brandon Mason, the RTA supervisor, and Cindy Crayton, Gerald Robichaux's executive assistant. For Crayton, the declined water was her small protest over how they were treated. "Mr. Robichaux was trying to explain that we were there doing a job and helping the city of New Orleans, not folks coming over to loot," she said. Yet they were treated as nothing but a mostly black group invading a predominantly white enclave. A pair of older black women, each in a wheelchair, arrived not long after the others. The women had been rescued by boat from the Canal Street barn and transported across the bridge on the back of a flatbed liberated from the agency's Napoleon Avenue facility. With no way to secure the wheelchairs on the flatbed, a pair of RTA employees gripped the legs of the chair with all their might, including Charlie Veal, the sixty-five-year-old assistant director for rail operations. "Nobody off!" the police yelled at them when they arrived in Gretna. "Nobody gets off this truck."

Rather than risk another confrontation, the driver was told to drop everybody off at the RTA's park 'n' ride in Algiers, which had been their original destination.

After a couple of hours of forced detention for the RTA contingent, several RTA coaches—between three and five, depending on who is telling the story—pulled up at the Gretna bus depot. They stopped by the park 'n' ride to pick up anyone who had ended up there. Their caravan then headed to Baton Rouge. A few, including Sharon Paul, would be dropped off at a hospital, but most were brought to an evacuation center. There they were reunited with many of those rescued from the Canal Street barn by the boats Bill Deville and his people had scavenged up. The group of them slept on canvas cots that week in a huge auditorium crowded with hundreds of other evacuees. But they also had access to a bathroom when they needed it. Their shelter had electricity and plenty of food and water. They were among the lucky ones.

WEDNESDAY

The Gretna police brass split their force into two. Those on the early shift began work at 7:00 a.m. Those on the late shift took over at 7:00 p.m. An ex-marine named Scott Vinson, a sergeant on the late shift, was responsible for patrolling that first exit ramp people would reach on the West Bank side of the bridge. For anyone in the vicinity of the New Orleans central business district, the Crescent City Connection—a pair of steel bridges stretching across the Mississippi, the fifth-longest bridges of their type in the world—pointed the way toward freedom. Vinson's job was to see that people didn't walk aimlessly through Gretna in search of an escape route.

Tuesday night had been quiet at the bottom of the exit. But all Wednesday evening and into the night, a steady procession of people in clusters of twos and threes and fives walked down the ramp. Vinson stationed two patrolmen at the bottom of the highway. They lined people up and kept order while he used his radio to scrounge up buses— anything to transport people to an evacuation point. He did the same shortly after daybreak on Thursday, when a "second wave" of evacuees, Vinson said, came trudging over the bridge.

Vinson worked past the end of his shift and into the early afternoon, "till that last person was loaded on a bus." A tired Vinson arrived at the Gretna police station, where he bunked that week, exhausted but feeling good about what he and his people had accomplished. "The three of us were able to help in excess of a thousand people. Closer to fifteen hundred," Vinson said.

THURSDAY

It was past 1:00 a.m. when Raymond Blanco—the husband of Louisiana governor Kathleen Blanco—showed in Gretna. He arrived with a state legislator and a Louisiana trooper. "We was just killing time, really," Blanco said. They were in the area to deliver medical supplies and waiting for a boat that would bring them to a flooded area south of the city. With nothing else to do, Blanco, who liked to call himself the First Guy, paid a courtesy call on Gretna's mayor, Ronnie Harris, whom Blanco had known since Harris was a teenager.

It was easy to find Harris. The police station was about the only building in town with lights. "By all appearances, they were in control of their situation," Blanco said. He remembered their giving him something to eat and recalled talk of all the people walking across the bridge. He told them FEMA was promising buses and that his wife, the governor, was trying to secure others from around the state. None of them, Blanco said—not the mayor, the police chief, or anyone else in the Gretna police station that night—brought up the idea of a bridge blockade.

The boat that was supposed to give Blanco and his entourage a ride never materialized. A frustrated First Guy slumped in the backseat of the car that took him home to Baton Rouge that morning. On either side of the interstate were parked dozens of buses, all of them idle. The drivers, he would learn when he got back to the state capital, had been scared off by reports of gunfire and looting out of New Orleans. "With all the drama in the media, the bus drivers said, 'Here are the keys, you can use the bus, but I'm not going in there,'" Kathleen Blanco said. Between the Superdome, Convention Center, and people stuck up on the highway, tens of thousands of people needed to be rescued. Raymond Blanco didn't give his visit to Gretna another thought until he heard that this small town of eighteen thousand had shut down a state-run bridge—the main escape route out of New Orleans.

CHARLES WHITMER, GRETNA'S DEPUTY police chief, expected to see mobs when he drove up on the bridge at 8:30 a.m. on Thursday. Instead he saw smaller groups of "one, two, three, here and there, with two or three behind them. Sporadic." But he also told his boss, Chief Arthur Lawson, that he could see people "just continuously as far as I can see into New Orleans." That was enough for Lawson. He ordered his number two to track down the chief of the bridge police. "Tell him we need to talk about the pedestrian situation on the bridge," Chief Lawson instructed.

Chief Lawson and several of his people were at the meeting on Thursday morning where they decided to shut down the Crescent City Connection. The head of the bridge police was there; the meeting was in his office, inside the small administrative building located on the West Bank side of the bridge. That was technically Orleans Parish, yet no one on their side of the bridge even tried to contact their counterparts in New Orleans. "The radios were out," Whitmer explained. "The phones were out." Yet somehow their group included a deputy representing the Jefferson Parish sheriff's office. NOPD had set up an impromptu headquarters at the foot of Canal Street, just on the other side of the bridge, under the entrance to the Harrah's casino—as anyone listening to a police scanner or even CNN would know. Including New Orleans in their multijurisdictional decision would have required just a ten-minute drive across the river to extend an invitation.

The chief of the bridge police, Michael Helmstetter, when asked to explain his rationale for voting to shut down the Crescent City Connection, said, "I guess to protect the pedestrians that were crossing." Chief Lawson cited any number of explanations for his decision. He needed to think about his men, he said, who were on their fourth or fifth day working twelve-hour shifts. The city had ample food and drink, but not if they had to share it with every person who crossed its city limits. "We aided as long as we could," Lawson said.

No notes were taken during the meeting, but by all accounts there wasn't much dissension. Mainly the talk was about the logistics of shutting down the bridge. The bridge police would block anyone already on the interstate from walking toward Gretna. Jefferson Parish posted several deputies at a ramp near the Superdome, while Gretna took responsibility for blocking the entrance ramp at Tchoupitoulas (pronounced "chop-a-two-liss") Street, also on the New Orleans side of the bridge and a short walk from the Convention Center. At around 10:30 a.m. on Thursday, September 1, 2005, with the thermometer near ninety degrees on a day that promised to be as hot and humid as the one before, the first three Gretna patrol officers took their post at the top of the Tchoupitoulas ramp. The Crescent City Connection was now closed to any pedestrian seeking a way out of New Orleans.

KATHLEEN BLANCO WAS AT the state's emergency operations center in Baton Rouge when she learned about the bridge closing. The governor was furious. "They had no authority to do what they did," Blanco said. The Crescent City Connection fell under the jurisdiction of Louisiana's Department of Transportation. Blocking pedestrian traffic from crossing the bridge would have been her call and a decision she would not have made.

"Nothing needed to be shut down," Blanco said. "It was totally unnecessary and a horrible reaction based on fear."

Ray Nagin might have been even angrier than Blanco—if he knew what was happening. On Thursday morning, Nagin was angry at Blanco, not anyone in Gretna. The governor had been promising buses for at least two days, yet now he was hearing reports of buses picking up people on the roadways *before* they even reached the city. Reports came as well of buses skipping past the city to pick up people in the suburbs. In protest, Nagin called for a "freedom march" across the Crescent City Connection. Tap out a press statement on your BlackBerry, he instructed Sally Forman, his communications director. "We said, 'If you want to walk across the Crescent City Connection, there's buses coming, you may be able to find some relief,'" the mayor wrote in a self-published memoir based on those few weeks when he was the most famous mayor in America. He also instructed his police chief to spread word among officers working near the Convention Center: the buses are just on the opposite side of the bridge.

KEVIN FERNANDEZ, GORDON MCCRAW, and Lawrence Vaughn were the first Gretna officers assigned to the Tchoupitoulas entrance ramp. Their orders had been minimal. "You're to stop people," their sergeant, James Price, had told them, "and tell them they weren't going to be allowed to cross." On their own, the three decided not to allow through even pedestrians carrying an ID showing they lived on the West Bank. Each carried a department-issued Glock .45 and a pump-action shotgun. Sergeant Price had not instructed his men to use the shotguns, but then, he had not forbidden them from using them, either.

The police felt for the people they couldn't let pass. "I would have tried to get out, too," Kevin Fernandez said. Instead they repeated the same few things. There was no food or water for them on the other side of the bridge. There was also no way out. "We kept explaining," Officer Fernandez said, "that there were buses going into Orleans Parish to evacuate them, that if they would wait, they'd shortly be evacuated." Lawrence Vaughn, who was black, suggested that people find a ride across the bridge. People were not permitted to walk to the West Bank, Vaughn said, "but I told them that they were welcome to use any other means of conveyance, a vehicle."

The three Gretna cops had been stopping people for around two hours when the mood, Officer Vaughn said, turned "a little more hostile." Somewhere around eight hundred to a thousand people were gathered by the Tchoupitoulas on-ramp on a hideously hot day that again saw temperatures in the nineties. It fell on him, Vaughn decided, as the only African American, to calm people down.

Instead, Vaughn's race gave people a focus for their frustrations. People in the crowd called Vaughn an Uncle Tom. He was a traitor. A black man holding a child around two years old was particularly cruel. Why was he doing the white man's business, he asked Vaughn, when so many of his own were in need? "Where are we supposed to go?" the man with the small child pleaded. Sit tight, Officer McCraw advised people. The buses were on their way. Others in the crowd yelled that they'd heard the opposite from NOPD.

The heckler handed off his child. As Vaughn told it, "The one doing all the talking says, 'We'll bum-rush them two white boys and jump this nigger here—we can get across this bridge.'" At that point, Vaughn had worn a badge for more than twenty years, including a stint in the military police in the US Army. "There was too many of them against the three of us," he said. Scared, he pointed his shotgun over the water "and fired off a round to get their attention."

"You Uncle Tom," the man who had been doing most of the talking said.

"Yessir."

"You stupid fucking nigger."

"Yessir."

"I'm going to whup your fool ass."

"Yessir. But you're still not crossing the bridge."

"THE THING THAT DISAPPOINTED us a great deal were the canceled flights," Kathleen Blanco told CNN a few days after Katrina. Continental Airlines had heroically continued to fly people out of New Orleans through 3:30 p.m. on Sunday, but Delta discontinued its passenger air service out of New Orleans at just after midnight on Saturday. "A lot of people got stranded like that," Blanco said. It fell to the city's hotels to care for those who couldn't get out of New Orleans ahead of the storm.

Plenty of lodgings booted lingering guests on Monday or Tuesday, pointing the way to the Superdome or the Convention Center before shuttering their doors. The staff of the Hotel Monteleone, in contrast, acted valiantly in those first days after the storm. This stately building in the heart of the French Quarter housed and fed around five hundred people—a group that included a mix of tourists and locals seeking refuge. By Thursday, though, the hotel was running out of water and food and also the fuel needed to operate its generator. Here are some maps, management told people. Go to the Convention Center. There'll be buses for you there.

Larry Bradshaw and Lorrie Beth Slonsky of San Francisco were among those who had gotten stuck at the Monteleone. They were in New Orleans for a conference of EMS (emergency medical services) workers, of all things, and were among those unable to catch a flight out of town ahead of Katrina. Now they were part of a group of around two hundred, the majority tourists, on the streets of New Orleans, left to fend for themselves.

The group ran into National Guardsmen a few streets from the Monteleone. They were no longer letting people inside the Convention Center, the soldiers told them, but didn't have an answer when people asked where they should go. "The guards told us that this was our problem—and, no, they didn't have extra water to give us," Bradshaw and Slonsky wrote in an article about their experience published in the *Socialist Worker* eleven days after Katrina. A few blocks later, they came across the impromptu command center the New Orleans police had set up in front of Harrah's. No one there could tell them where they were supposed to go, so as a group, they decided they would camp out across the street from Harrah's. By that time, their group numbered around three hundred. Maybe their size would make them impossible to ignore.

Their gambit worked—after a fashion. A police commander crossed the street to talk with them. Walk across the bridge, he advised. "I swear to you that the buses are there," he supposedly told them.

With "great excitement and hope," Bradshaw and Slonsky wrote, they headed toward the bridge. They passed by the Convention Center, where their determination to find a way out of New Orleans must have been infectious. "Quickly our numbers doubled and doubled again," the couple wrote. "Babies in strollers now joined us, as did people using crutches, elderly clasping walkers, and other people in wheelchairs." A torrential downpour drenched the lot of them, but the group, now a majority black, kept walking.

Their group made it onto the highway but were stopped before they reached the bridge by a barricade of police cruisers and "armed sheriffs," according to Bradshaw and Slonsky. The deputies "began firing their weapons over our heads." Most of their group ran, but Bradshaw and Slonsky, among others, tried talking to the deputies. "They responded that the West Bank was not going to become New Orleans, and there would be no Superdomes in their city," the couple wrote.

Bradshaw, Slonsky, and a small band of others set up camp on the roadway, not far from where they had been turned away. An elevated highway seemed safer than the streets. From their perch they watched others attempt to cross the bridge. Sometimes the police deterred would-be crossers with shouts. Other times they used gunfire to turn people around. Either way, no one was walking across that bridge.

OLIVER THOMAS, PRESIDENT OF the New Orleans City Council, noticed the blockade after a long day in and out of the water on a rescue boat. ("I had sores on my feet for two months," he said.) "Let's talk basic human rights," Thomas said. "You've got these people on the governor's bridge—stopping Louisiana citizens from crossing the bridge? Old people, children, people peacefully walking through a route literally that's the only way out of a city covered by water. By whose authority? And let's talk jurisdictional issues. This is an outside force telling our people they can't walk across the bridge? By what right?"

1

THE BANKER

The plan was to evacuate vertically. That's what the Uptown blue bloods did when a hurricane took aim at New Orleans, and so, too, would Alden J. McDonald Jr., president of the city's largest black-owned bank. With Katrina bearing down on the region, McDonald had his assistant book a block of rooms at the Hyatt in the city's central business district. That's where the mayor would ride out the hurricane and where Entergy, the local electric and gas utility, was setting up its emergency center. The Hyatt, a thirty-two-story fortress made from steel and cement, was wrapped in fortified glass. Rising high above its next-door neighbor, the Superdome, just off Poydras Street, the hotel had its own generator and would be stocked with extra provisions. Theoretically, it promised its guests a safe berth above the chaos.

McDonald woke up early in his home on that last Sunday in August 2005. He had slept maybe three or four hours. The National Hurricane Center categorizes every storm based mainly on the strength of its winds. When McDonald and his wife, Rhesa, had gone to bed on Saturday night, the center had rated Katrina a powerful Category 3. By early the next morning, the storm had been upgraded to Category 5. There is no Category 6.

The sixty-one-year-old bank president drank his coffee and readied himself for his day while a radio blared dire warnings. A lifelong New Orleanian, McDonald knew hurricanes could be fickle brutes. They shift in direction without warning. Their winds pick up speed or deflate in strength depending on the warmth of the waters over which they pass, among other factors. But as of Sunday morning, the radio was reporting that Katrina was a Category 5 storm expected to hit the New Orleans region within the next twelve to twenty-four hours. Scientists warned its winds could top 175 miles per hour. The storm surge—a giant tidal wave, essentially—might reach twenty-five feet. This storm looked like the Big One that experts had been warning about for years.

Home for McDonald was "out in the East"—more formally, New Orleans East, swampland that had decades earlier been drained and converted into a series of subdivisions housing a large portion of the city's African-American middle class, along with a large share of its black elites. McDonald was the son of a waiter whose annual wages had never topped $15,000. McDonald now lived on a quarter acre in Lake Forest Estates, one of the pricier enclaves in this sprawling appendage to New Orleans whose ninety-six-thousand-plus residents represented around one-fifth of New Orleans's population. His bank, Liberty Bank and Trust, had financed a sizable share of the homes and businesses in the East. Its headquarters were located in New Orleans East, as was its computer center and storage facility. The majority of the bank's employees lived in the East as well.

At a little past 8:00 a.m., McDonald slipped behind the wheel of his red BMW convertible. Only later would McDonald understand this drive around New Orleans East as a kind of farewell to his home of more than thirty years. "These are my people," McDonald would say of the residents of New Orleans East after Mayor Ray Nagin, a month after Katrina, appointed him to a blue-ribbon commission charged with determining which portions of drowned-out New Orleans should be rebuilt and which parts might more wisely be returned to marshland in a city certain to lose residents. "These were my neighbors." McDonald had been twenty-nine years old and a college dropout when, in 1972, Liberty opened in a trailer in a sketchy part of town. Thirty-three years later, with a massive storm gathering over the Gulf of Mexico, McDonald was readying for yet another storm. At that point, Liberty ranked sixth on a list of the country's largest black-owned banks.

The air already felt oppressive, heavy with humidity. The car radio blared ominous warnings about the potential for calamitous flooding that could damage half the city's homes and leave New Orleans without power for weeks. McDonald's first stop was Liberty's headquarters, a rectangular-shaped, six-story glass box gleaming in the morning sun, with LIBERTY spelled out in large white letters across its top. This building, only a few minutes from McDonald's house, was so new that not every department had yet moved over from the old headquarters on the opposite side of the I-10, the freeway that bisected the East. A few days earlier, the bank had taken delivery on a new mainframe computer that had cost around $500,000. Brand-new desktop computers matched the new furnishings. He parked his car and walked around the building, giving each door a tug to make sure it was locked. Inside was a man the bank had hired to ride out the storm. Accompanied by a pair of dogs and outfitted with several days of food and water, he would serve as a last line of defense against looters.

The percussive sound of nails pounding through plywood accompanied McDonald's pre-storm tour. Everywhere he looked, people were boarding up windows and loading cars. Despite the dour newscast, his spirits were lifted by the sight of so many of his neighbors taking warnings about the storm so seriously. He crossed to the opposite side of the I-10, parked in front of one of his bank branches, and again jumped out of his car. Standing just under six feet tall, McDonald is a courtly, light-skinned black man with a doughy face, wavy white hair, and matching mustache. Peering through the glass, he saw that his branch managers had placed Saturday's deposits on top of the filing cabinets—exactly as he had asked them to do.

Next McDonald visited the low-slung bunker next door, the old headquarters his people were vacating. The building housed the mainframe they were using to run the bank until the new machine could be brought online. Most of the bank's paper records were stored there as well. McDonald was frugal and sometimes questioned the wisdom of writing a $5,000 check each month to a Philadelphia-area disaster-relief company that promised to keep his bank online if ever his central computers went down. Now the decision seemed wise. As he had done in advance of past storms, he had his people make four backup tapes of the bank's computer files so they had up-to-date depositor records. One he sent to a Liberty branch in Baton Rouge, another he sent to a Jackson branch. The other two were with a pair of bank employees who had evacuated the area. Let people make fun, but a cautious streak had him creating backup plans for his backup plans. "Without those tapes," he said, "I'm dead in the water."

MCDONALD'S WIFE, RHESA, WAS also out of the house early that Sunday morning. She had wanted to leave town rather than ride out the storm at the Hyatt, but her husband and their twenty-four-year-old son, Todd, who worked for the bank as a loan officer, outvoted her. Her job was to pick up her parents on Park Island—a small, genteel community of good-size houses on the Bayou St. John closer to the center of town. Her father was eighty-two years old and her mother only a few years younger. Rhesa was an only child. Her parents would go wherever she was.

Rhesa McDonald's husband was a big deal in New Orleans. He had had his picture taken with every president stretching back to Ronald Reagan and had met a pope. He was one of the few African Americans who had ever been honored with what the city's once-daily newspaper, the *Times-Picayune*, called its Loving Cup—a person-of-the-year award given to someone in honor of his or her public service. But Rhesa's father, Revius Ortique Jr., represented black royalty in New Orleans. Ortique, a civil rights attorney, had been the first African-American justice elected to serve on the Louisiana Supreme Court. Whereas Alden McDonald had shaken hands with presidents, Ortique had been named to five presidential commissions, including the Commission on Campus Unrest that Richard Nixon had created after protesters were gunned down at Kent State and Jackson State Universities. As president of the National Bar Association, an organization of African-American lawyers, he had sat with Lyndon Johnson in the Oval Office, where he pressed the president to name more black attorneys to the federal bench. Several months later, Johnson appointed Thurgood Marshall to the US Supreme Court.

Rhesa crossed the short bridge that brought visitors to Park Island and pulled into the driveway of the home her parents owned directly across the street from Ray Nagin's. Thirty minutes later, she was at the Hyatt. The time was 9:00 a.m.

At the front desk, Rhesa picked up the keys to four rooms to accommodate not only themselves but Todd and their thirty-year-old daughter, Heidi. Rhesa helped set up her parents in their room on the twenty-third floor before entering the room she reserved for herself and her husband.

Thirty minutes later, she was knocking on the door of her parents' room. "We're leaving," she announced. She knew they would put up an argument, but on TV they were warning of mass blackouts. The image of her parents walking down twenty-three flights of stairs made her stand her ground. "You can't check out, you just checked in!" the clerk said when Rhesa reappeared at the front desk. "Oh, yes, I can," she responded. She phoned her husband. "I'm picking you up wherever you are. You're getting in the car and we're leaving town." After thirty-one years of marriage, her husband knew better than to argue. Besides, the car radio continued to impress on him the might of Katrina. The line that stuck with him was one the broadcasters kept repeating: *Only three Category 5 hurricanes have hit the continental United States in recorded history.*

Talk of flooding caused the McDonalds to take several extra precautions before leaving town. McDonald drove one of their cars, a gold-colored Lexus sedan, to Liberty's headquarters, where the bank had a two-story parking structure. McDonald parked the car on the second floor, where the Lexus would at least be above the flood line if the streets filled with water. He locked the sports car he had been driving in the garage of his house. That at least would protect it from falling debris and hide it from potential looters. At 10:00 a.m. on Sunday, as the McDonalds were preparing to take off, Mayor Ray Nagin declared a mandatory evacuation—the first in New Orleans history.

McDonald got behind the wheel of Rhesa's dark blue Lexus and pointed the car east. Heidi and her dog pulled in behind them, followed by Todd and a friend. The McDonalds had just said good-bye to houseguests, a couple visiting from Atlanta, who had cut their trip short because of the storm. "Come stay with us," the couple had suggested.

They were both physicians in Atlanta with a home large enough to accommodate a crowd. So with Revius and Miriam Ortique in the backseat, Alden and Rhesa McDonald headed to Atlanta, followed by two of their three children.

NORMALLY THE DRIVE FROM New Orleans to Atlanta takes around six hours. That Sunday, the McDonalds were on the road for twice that long—and they might be counted among the luckier ones. Ward "Mack" McClendon made the same trip from the Lower Ninth Ward several hours after the McDonalds. McClendon, who would eventually sacrifice everything in his fight to save the Lower Ninth, was already playing hero, rounding up a couple of his neighbors he knew had no other way out of town. McClendon was hoping to make the Atlanta home of his eldest daughter, but gave up past midnight, when they were still in east-central Alabama. There in the town of Opelika, in a cheap motel whose name none of them can remember, McClendon and the others would learn about the fate of New Orleans while watching a small television someone had set up in the corner of the lobby.

Safe in Atlanta, McDonald flopped on his friend's couch, watching the increasingly bleak storm coverage on a big flat-screen TV. The first burst of news out of New Orleans on Monday morning had left him breathing easier. As advertised, Katrina was on par with a Camille or a Betsy—a hurricane people would be talking about for decades to come. But the storm had jogged in the middle of the night. The destruction in towns such as Biloxi, Gulfport, and Bay St. Louis, along the Mississippi Gulf Coast, dominated the news that Monday, not New Orleans. A twenty-eight-foot tidal wave had destroyed properties along one hundred miles stretching from western Alabama to the southeastern corner of lower Louisiana. Where once thriving communities had dotted the coast, the TV cameras found little beyond empty foundations, broken-off pipes, and brick stairs leading to nowhere. "I can only imagine that this is what Hiroshima looked like sixty years ago," Mississippi governor Haley Barbour said after taking an aerial tour of the devastation. By the time the storm reached New Orleans, Katrina's winds were blowing at 125 mph, making it a Category 3 storm. To the extent newscasters talked about New Orleans on Monday, they all seemed to repeat the same cliché: New Orleans seemed to have "dodged a bullet."

For years to come, people would speak about the collapse of the New Orleans levee system as if it happened twenty-four hours after Katrina made landfall in Louisiana. That's how the president and his top aides saw it even weeks after Katrina; it's a mistake people still make today. But the city's 911 operators knew better. Early on Monday morning, the city's emergency switchboard was deluged with calls from frantic residents. At first almost all the requests for help were from the Lower Ninth Ward, but soon dispatchers were hearing from other parts of the city. Later, the LSU Hurricane Center figured out that the first few levee breaches occurred at around 5:00 a.m. on Monday. It just took time for the wider world to catch up to what was happening in New Orleans.

The city's flood-protection system had been devastated. One major breach was along the Industrial Canal, a man-made waterway that separates the Lower Ninth Ward (and also New Orleans East) from the rest of New Orleans.[1] The storm surge spilled over the top of the floodwall protecting the Lower Ninth, creating a trench so deep that by 7:30 a.m., two segments of the wall had collapsed. The propulsive force of the water pushed homes off foundations and devastated the northwestern edge of the Lower Ninth closest to the breach.

Other sections of the city flooded not because of breaches in the outer flood-protection system but due to failures in the drainage canals the city used to collect water after a heavy rain. Giant electric motors in two dozen pumping stations around New Orleans sop up excess rain and dump it into Lake Pontchartrain via one of three major canals that the Corps of Engineers had rebuilt in the 1970s. There were major breaches in two of these three canals, the Seventeenth Street and London Avenue

---

1. The Inner Harbor Navigation Canal, as the Industrial Canal is formally known, was built in the 1920s as a shortcut between Lake Pontchartrain, the enormous body of water lying just north of New Orleans, and the Mississippi River.

Canals, and more flooding because a section of a levee along the third, the Orleans Avenue Canal, had never been completed. The brackish waters of Lake Pontchartrain, the country's second-largest saltwater lake, flowed into Lakeview, a prosperous white enclave on one side of City Park, and Gentilly, a mostly black middle- and working-class community on the other. There were dozens more breaches in the New Orleans flood-protection system. That proved fatal in a city that geographically resembled nothing so much as a giant bowl that sits 50 percent below sea level. By the time the lake and the city reached equilibrium, 80 percent of the city was covered in water.

Television couldn't get enough of the images of devastation and despair once its producers learned of the flooding late Monday or early Tuesday morning. Sitting in Atlanta, Alden McDonald remembers seeing those first images out of New Orleans—of people stranded on rooftops and on elevated highways and on small strips of high ground, of entire neighborhoods underwater. No one was talking about New Orleans East, but the longer McDonald watched, the more certain he felt he was doomed. He had loaned tens of millions of dollars out to homeowners and entrepreneurs in the East, and now their properties were probably lying under four to six feet of water, unless it was under eight to ten feet. "The only thing I could think of is, All of these people lost their real estate, which I had as collateral," McDonald said. He began tallying up what else had probably been destroyed, starting with the bank's paper files. Most of the bank's most essential documents—the deeds for houses, the titles for cars—were still at the old headquarters and would be underwater. Sitting in his friend's home, he wondered if his bank's days as an independent institution were over. "I'm wiped out," McDonald told himself.

McDonald could have called a hundred people to commiserate. On his BlackBerry he had the private numbers of fellow bank presidents and a long list of elected officials. He had close friends he had known since childhood. Yet he kept redialing Russell Labbe, a Liberty employee whose tenure dated back to when McDonald's office was a small room with cheap paneling in a trailer. Labbe, who grew up on the edge of a bayou, had been piloting boats since he was a child. He had also worked as a general contractor prior to taking a job as a kind of Mr.

Fixit, jack-of-all-trades, at Liberty in the 1970s. Labbe had celebrated his seventieth birthday shortly before Katrina, but he was a sturdy man who stood six feet two inches tall.

"He was calling me every hour," Labbe said of McDonald. In McDonald's memory "it was probably more like every half hour." Sometimes McDonald was phoning to talk through strategies for getting into the city. Other times it was to ask Labbe what he might have heard about specific neighborhoods since they had last spoken. Mainly it felt good, McDonald acknowledged, to talk solutions rather than to stare helplessly at the television. They spoke countless more times over the coming weeks, especially while water still covered much of the city. "I must have taken fifteen boat trips in," Labbe said. "It was always something. Something that had to be done right away. Because that's Alden—if he needs it, he needs it now."

McDonald was eager to get back to New Orleans. If not the city itself, then at least Baton Rouge, which was seventy miles to the northwest and a lot closer than Atlanta to his drowned-out life. If anything were to happen to their New Orleans operations, the bank's doomsday plan called for key bank personnel to rendezvous in Baton Rouge, where the bank operated three branches. (They operated another two in Jackson, Mississippi, 180 miles due north of New Orleans.) On Wednesday, with barely more than the clothes on his back, McDonald flew from Atlanta to Baton Rouge. "Fortunately," he said, "I took four pairs of underwear."

Finding a hotel room in Baton Rouge was impossible. For those first few days he was in town, McDonald couch-surfed. Even when providence delivered a house in Baton Rouge to use indefinitely, the well-connected bank president continued to live like a much younger version of himself. This house that in normal times might comfortably have slept five or six more resembled a youth hostel during the summer high season. Several people from the bank, including his son Todd, took up more or less full-time residence there. And what was he supposed to do when someone such as Ronnie Burns, an old family friend who also sat on the Liberty board of directors, called to say he needed to be in Baton Rouge for a few nights? "People were sleeping on floor space wherever they could find it," Burns reported. "There must've been like twenty people staying there." At least McDonald usually managed to keep a bedroom for himself.

EVERYONE CALLED IT THE "Southern branch," this Liberty outpost in Baton Rouge across the street from Southern University, a historically black college that sits along the banks of the Mississippi. The branch wasn't much to look at—a tan-brick building with a corrugated-tin roof damaged in one corner. McDonald even had considered tearing it down and rebuilding something nicer. But this functional facility had a set of back offices that would serve as a temporary command center. Long before Katrina, McDonald had thought to install extra T1 lines and store extra phones and other backup equipment on-site. For the foreseeable future, this modest-size branch housing a single ATM machine would serve as headquarters for a bank with $350 million in assets and thirty-five thousand customers.

McDonald could list a hundred things he needed to do to save Liberty, and then another hundred things after that. But nothing preoccupied his attention like his lack of a centralized computer. Tuesday came and went and still the disaster backup firm had not received a backup tape. No package arrived on Wednesday or Thursday, either. Liberty owned two mainframe computers. Yet one was underwater and the other was useless in a city without electricity. Until the computer tapes showed up in Philadelphia, no interbank networks such as STAR or Plus could monitor how much money a Liberty customer had in his or her account.

The satellite imagery the cable networks broadcast in the hours before Katrina made landfall showed a giant white pinwheel of angry clouds stretching some five hundred miles across. That was McDonald's mistake; he had not counted on the storm's vastness. Airports across the Southwest were affected by Katrina and packages were stacking up in Memphis, where FedEx had its main hub. Both packages McDonald had sent for overnight delivery were being stored somewhere on the grounds of FedEx's sprawling facility. McDonald spent upwards of $15,000 to charter a plane to ferry someone first to Memphis and then to Philadelphia, once he had located one of the missing tapes.

Yet that wasn't enough. On Friday, McDonald's IT chief broke the bad news: the backup firm needed more from the bank before Liberty could be back on the interbank network. Worse, what was needed was inside the bank's New Orleans headquarters. McDonald could only laugh over the tens of thousands of dollars he had paid to the recovery company about the years. "It was that or cry," he said. Did a customer who had temporarily relocated to Tallahassee, Florida, have the money to cover the $300 she was requesting from an ATM? Who could say until the bank was back on the interbank network.

Russell Labbe didn't flinch when McDonald asked him to go into New Orleans and pick up what they needed. "I knew this had to happen or we had no bank," Labbe said. Discretion dictated they wait for the authorities to empty New Orleans of most of those trapped there. On Saturday, Labbe decided he would head into the city early Sunday morning. He would bring a gun, he said, because "you'd be crazy to go into that scene without one. When you have a hurricane like this, they'll steal your boat. They'll steal your truck. People will shoot you."

2

AIR FORCE ONE

Sally Forman was asleep when her BlackBerry rang for the first time in several days. It was 5:30 a.m. on the Friday after Katrina. Forman, who was Mayor Ray Nagin's communications director, was lying on a mattress on the floor of the Hyatt, across the street from City Hall. She had been dreaming that she was drowning when the ringing phone woke her up. Her husband, Ron, who would in a few months announce he was running for mayor against her boss, was lying next to her and still asleep. "Sally?" It was a woman's voice. "This is Maggie Grant from the White House."

Instinctively, Forman jumped to turn on a light. Then she remembered the hotel had no electricity. "You're the first call to come through on my BlackBerry," she told the caller, her tongue thick and her mind fuzzy. She asked Grant to repeat her name and had the presence of mind to ask her title. Grant identified herself as director of intergovernmental affairs.

"We understand that the mayor has not been saying very favorable things about the president for the last twenty-four hours," Grant said.

Of course. Forman's boss's rant was on the radio the day before. "It's not personal. It's been terrible."

"That's exactly why I'm calling. The president realizes he may not have gotten accurate information this week and wants to hear directly from the mayor." On the fifth day of the still-unfolding disaster, George W. Bush was coming to New Orleans to see the devastation for himself. Could the mayor meet the president at the airport that afternoon?

GEORGE BUSH WAS IN Crawford, Texas, nearing the end of a month-long stay at his ranch, when Katrina slammed the Gulf Coast. The vice president, Dick Cheney, was fly-fishing and the president's chief of staff, Andrew Card, was on vacation with his family in Maine. Michael Brown, director of the Federal Emergency Management Agency, had ordered every FEMA employee must be on the job, whether or not he or she had a planned vacation, but that sense of urgency was apparently not shared by his bosses.

On Sunday—when the highways out of New Orleans were thick with people trying to escape the storm—Bush logged on to the daily videoconference FEMA initiates when preparing for a potential disaster. Normally, only state and local emergency response officials listen in, but this time the guest list included, in addition to the president, Michael Brown and also Brown's boss, Michael Chertoff, head of the Department of Homeland Security. "I don't have any good news," Dr. Max Mayfield, the director of the National Hurricane Center, began. He compared Katrina to Hurricane Andrew, the 1992 colossus that destroyed or damaged more than 125,000 homes in southern Florida and killed at least twenty-six people. "Right now, this is a Category Five hurricane," Mayfield said of Katrina, "very similar to Hurricane Andrew in the maximum intensity." But the ominous difference, he added, was that "this hurricane is much larger than Andrew ever was." The president spoke near the end of the call: "I want to assure the folks at the state level that we are fully prepared to not only help you during the storm, but we will move in whatever resources and assets we have at our disposal after the storm to help you deal with the loss of property." Hearing how that might sound, he added, "And we pray for no loss of life, of course."

Bush kept to his regular schedule on Monday. The White House talking points that week called for the president to focus on immigration reform and the new Medicare prescription-drug benefit, scheduled to go into effect that January. In the morning, the president flew to Arizona, where his first task was political. August 29 was John McCain's sixty-ninth birthday, and Bush arrived with a cake. There on the tarmac, in the 110-degree heat, the president posed with his former political rival before the two politicians went their own ways. The president's motorcade drove to the Pueblo El Mirage RV & Golf Resort, where Bush touted his drug plan in front of an invitation-only audience of around four hundred. He spoke at length about the war in Iraq but offered only a few words about Katrina. It was more of the same after a quick flight to Southern California. The president spoke about Medicare at a senior center that afternoon and again that evening in a town-hall-style meeting in the town of Rancho Cucamonga in San Bernardino County. Only at this last stop did he address the images people were seeing on TV all day.

"For those of you who are concerned about whether or not we're prepared to help, don't be," he said. "We're in place." The president and the first lady spent the night in the Hotel del Coronado, where Bush was scheduled to give a speech the next morning.

In New Orleans, Marty Bahamonde was not feeling nearly as confident as the president. FEMA had sent Bahamonde, a regional external affairs director in its Boston office, to New Orleans ahead of the storm. Bahamonde was planning to ride out the hurricane in a hotel near the airport, but at 4:00 a.m. on Sunday someone had knocked on his door to tell him that he had two hours to vacate the premises. Bahamonde phoned the emergency operations center in Jefferson Parish, but when no one there answered, he called the one in New Orleans. He jumped when Ray Nagin's people invited him to ride out the storm inside City Hall. On Sunday night, he watched the head of the city's emergency operations order his people to scavenge every last roll of toilet paper they could find and get it to the Superdome as soon as they could. What else hadn't they thought of? he asked himself.

Bahamonde was in the emergency operations center on Monday at around 10:30 a.m. when the city learned of a major breach in a floodwall along the Seventeenth Street Canal. Using his BlackBerry, Bahamonde texted the news to his colleagues. Two hours later, the agency's deputy director of public affairs was circulating an e-mail reporting the breach. "Water flow bad into New Orleans," she wrote, adding Bahamonde's estimate that parts of the city were under eleven feet of water. All day, the city's emergency operations center was receiving reports of more failures in the area's storm-protection system. Late Monday afternoon, Bahamonde insisted room be made for him on a Coast Guard helicopter so he could assess the damage. From his vantage point in the air, he estimated that 75 percent of New Orleans was underwater. By 7:00 p.m. he was on the phone with Michael Brown, who promised to immediately phone the White House. Back at the city's emergency operations center, Bahamonde ran into Ray Nagin, where he told the mayor that most of his city was underwater. "Nagin was stunned," Bahamonde said. "He had this vacant expression as he listened to me that said everything." Bahamonde slept that night under a desk in City Hall. He used a rolled-up shirt as a pillow.

Brown was already in Baton Rouge when he briefed the president by videoconference early on Tuesday morning. The vice president was on the call, as were other top officials. "What's the situation?" Bush began. "Bad," Brown responded. "This was the Big One." Brown confessed it was more than FEMA could handle and raised the idea of sending troops to New Orleans. Speaking from his vacation home in Wyoming, Cheney assured Brown that they would reach out to Defense Secretary Donald Rumsfeld. After that call ended, a Black Hawk helicopter flew Brown to New Orleans for a quick tour of the disaster zone, along with Governor Kathleen Blanco and Louisiana's two US senators, Mary Landrieu and David Vitter. They landed on a helicopter pad atop a parking structure adjacent to the Superdome. Bahamonde pulled Brown aside to speak privately. "It's critical, sir, especially here at the Superdome," Bahamonde warned his boss. Barely twenty-four hours after the city started filling up with water, they were already out of food and low on water. Medical personnel were overwhelmed.

The president kept to his schedule on Tuesday. It was the sixtieth anniversary of the Japanese surrender in World War II, and Bush was at the North Island Naval Air Station in San Diego to talk about the war in Iraq. The president compared the fight in Iraq with the struggle to repel the German fascists and Japanese imperialists. "The terrorists of our century are making the same mistake that the followers of other totalitarian ideologies made in the last century," Bush said. After his speech, the country singer Mark Wills gave the president a guitar stamped with the presidential seal and Bush pretended to strum a few chords. It made for an odd juxtaposition, the historian Douglas Brinkley wrote in *The Great Deluge*, this "photograph of Bush playing air guitar while Americans were seeing agony in pictures from the Gulf Coast." The president stopped at the Naval Medical Center in Balboa Park, where he awarded a Purple Heart to a wounded corpsman and met with another two dozen soldiers injured in Iraq. Bush slept that night in Crawford and the next day flew home to the White House, several days earlier than planned.

The last massive hurricane to hit New Orleans was Betsy in 1965. A Category 4 storm, Betsy flooded parts of the city and caused widespread power outages. The next night, President Lyndon Johnson showed up at a shelter, stood on a crate, and, with people shining flashlights on his face, promised to help the city any way he could. Forty years later, another president from Texas demonstrated his concern for those swept up in a disaster by ordering Air Force One to detour over New Orleans and dip below the cloud canopy so he could see the damage for himself. A White House photographer snapped pictures as Bush stared out the airplane window. Even Karl Rove, the president's top political adviser, would dub the photo op a "big mistake."

A few hours after landing in Washington that Wednesday, Bush addressed the nation. For the past forty-eight hours, the viewing public had heard about little else except the government's lack of a response to the human suffering they could see on television. But rather than offer a mea culpa, the president boasted of all the federal government was doing to help. In the Rose Garden, standing flanked by members of his cabinet, he recited statistics: four hundred trucks had been used to deliver 5.4 million meals and 13.4 million liters of water to the stricken area. The *New York Times* editorial page described this halfhearted, stilted address as "one of the worst speeches of his life." Before going to bed on Wednesday night, Bush spoke to Nagin for the first time. "We're trying to come and see you real soon," the president assured him. "Everything is going to be all right."

Bush didn't help his cause when, during an appearance on ABC's *Good Morning America*, he said, "I don't think anyone anticipated the breach of the levees." No statement seemed a more transparent statement on how poorly the president had been briefed. Even Karl Rove felt obliged to contradict that claim in his 2010 memoir, titled *Courage and*

Consequence. "Computer models," Rove wrote, "had long anticipated a horrific disaster if a Katrina-like storm ever hit the city."

"WHERE THE HELL IS the cavalry?" Kate Hale, the emergency-management director in Dade County, Florida, asked during a 1992 press conference three days after Hurricane Andrew. "For God's sake, where are they?" Congressional hearings were held, followed by a report condemning FEMA as a kind of "turkey farm" for political donors and bureaucrats past their sell-by date. Jimmy Carter had created FEMA in 1979 through executive order. Barely a decade later, no shortage of voices inside and outside government were calling for its abolition.

James Lee Witt, Bill Clinton's choice to head the agency, saved FEMA. At first his appointment seemed more of the same: a friend of the president dating back to when they were children. The son of an Arkansas sharecropper who had never finished high school, Witt's background proved easy fodder for partisans seeking to stir trouble for the new president. But Witt also had a résumé that distinguished him from every past FEMA chief: having served as director of the Arkansas office of emergency services for nearly half of Clinton's twelve-year tenure as governor, Witt was the first director of FEMA to have actual emergency-management experience.

Witt's first priority after taking over the agency was to spend less time on "continuity of government" plans for after a nuclear attack and other doomsday scenarios and focus instead on what he called "real-life disasters" such as floods and tornadoes. He put his people through customer-service training and pushed them to help locals with emergency preparedness. Witt championed the idea of prepositioning supplies and first responders so they were closer to where they would be needed after a disaster, and he convinced Clinton to raise the FEMA director to cabinet level. "I've got to pay the administration a compliment," George W. Bush said to Vice President Al Gore during one of the 2000 presidential debates. "James Lee Witt of FEMA has done a really good job." Witt was that rare public servant who had champions among both Democrats and Republicans.

Bush's first FEMA director was Joe Allbaugh, a party operative who had moved to Texas in 1994 to work on Bush's first gubernatorial campaign. Allbaugh served as Governor Bush's chief of staff until resigning to become the campaign manager of his 2000 presidential run. A grateful president-elect asked Allbaugh, the son of an Oklahoma wheat farmer, if a job as agriculture secretary interested him, but he said he would prefer to be head of FEMA. That way, he said, he could at least occasionally play hero on the public stage. "You're not always in the limelight," he said, "but when you are, it's for all the marbles." Although Allbaugh had no disaster-management experience, the Senate confirmed his appointment, 91–0.

Incompetence hurt the Bush administration after Katrina, but so, too, did ideology. The Bush administration slashed FEMA's budget under Allbaugh, who pulled the plug on Witt innovations such as Project Impact, which helped communities become more disaster-resistant. Following the September 11 attacks, money grew even tighter as Allbaugh revived some of the doomsday-preparedness projects that Witt had shut down. FEMA would lose more of its clout when in 2003 it was merged into the new Department of Homeland Security the Bush administration created after the terrorist attacks. Allbaugh objected to the change, arguing that the move would rob FEMA of both independence and bureaucratic clout. He tendered his resignation soon after losing that fight. In his place, the president nominated Allbaugh's number two, Michael Brown—the man Bush famously referred to as Brownie.

Like Allbaugh, Brown had no disaster-management experience prior to arriving in Washington. He had been an Oklahoma-based lawyer who worked for the International Arabian Horse Association when Allbaugh, a longtime friend, hired Brown as FEMA's general counsel, then elevated him to deputy director. At the time of Katrina, FEMA's top three appointees had worked as political operatives for the president. Five of FEMA's top eight officials had negligible disaster-management experience, the *Washington Post* found, and nine of the agency's ten regional chiefs were either serving as an acting director or filling two jobs at once.

Yet one didn't need to be an expert in disasters to know that a Category 5 storm aimed at New Orleans had the potential to overwhelm first responders. When shortly after its creation the new Department of Homeland Security drew up a list of the fifteen worst disasters that could confront the country, the detonation of a nuclear device made the list, as did a biological attack. But so, too, did a tropical storm making a direct hit on New Orleans. Even a hurricane of moderate strength, study after study showed, could cause more loss of life and property in this low-lying coastal city surrounded by water than even a major earthquake on the West Coast. "When I have a nightmare," said Eric Tolbert, who served as FEMA's disaster-response chief until leaving the agency several months prior to Katrina, "it's a hurricane in New Orleans."

Yet the country was waging a pair of expensive wars in Iraq and Afghanistan, creating pressure to shrink the size of government. Not only FEMA but the US Army Corps of Engineers, which had built and maintained New Orleans's flood-protection system, were feeling the financial squeeze. In 2004, the Corps said it needed at least $22.5 million to shore up the levees in the New Orleans metro area. The Bush administration budgeted $4 million for New Orleans and compromised with Congress on a final outlay of $5.5 million. Yet somehow the government found $14 million to dredge a man-made canal known mainly by its local nickname, MR. GO (Mississippi River Gulf Outlet). For years coastal experts had been calling on the federal government to close down this underused and fragile seventy-six-mile waterway that the Army Corps of Engineers had so arrogantly built forty years earlier to save ships from the twists and turns of the Mississippi through southern Louisiana. Critics called MR. GO a "hurricane highway" that could amplify the storm surge—exactly what happened during Katrina. The water from MR. GO caused severe flooding in the eastern half of New Orleans and also St. Bernard Parish to the south and east.

Brown was not the complete incompetent he was made out to be in media accounts. He could be smug and arrogant, but he was also bureaucratically adept and could be tenacious, especially when fighting his superiors on behalf of the agency under his charge. He even managed to pry a few million dollars from his tightfisted bosses to run a series of war-games-like exercises so they were better prepared for natural disasters. The first of these was Hurricane Pam, a hypothetical storm that planners imagined hitting New Orleans.

Pam should have been the lucky break that saved FEMA's reputation post-Katrina. Its designers imagined a powerful, slow-moving Category 3 storm—Katrina. The city's flood-protection system was rated as strong enough to withstand a Category 3 storm, but computer simulations paid for by FEMA showed that the levees would breach with catastrophic consequences: as much as 90 percent of the city would flood even in a Category 3 storm, and an estimated fifty thousand would seek shelter in the Superdome or another refuge of last resort.

Incredibly, Hurricane Katrina had not only been imagined in July 2004, thirteen months before the storm actually hit, but the hundreds of government employees FEMA brought together in New Orleans for the exercise had practiced their response. They imagined everything from the number of boats they would need to conduct search-and-rescue to the truckloads of bottled water needed to hydrate the survivors. The government was supposed to spend a few hundred thousand dollars more on follow-up discussions and meetings, but most of those slated for the first half of 2005 were scrapped due to a lack of funds. The government spent around $800,000 on the Hurricane Pam simulation but left the project unfinished. Brown blamed his boss, Michael Chertoff, the federal judge whom Bush had named to run Homeland Security at the start of 2005, and other top administration officials for cutting off the money.

Some presidential historians argue that the Bush presidency died in New Orleans that week. If so, ego is, in part, to blame. The FEMA directorship was no longer a cabinet-level position with direct access to the president and his top people, but Brown, claiming he didn't want to waste precious time going through proper channels, contacted the White House directly in those first hours after the levees broke. By Tuesday night, Michael Chertoff had had enough. Brown was on a military plane heading back to Baton Rouge when the Homeland Security secretary reached his insubordinate underling. He grounded Brown, ordering him not to leave Baton Rouge. As Brown told the story to Chris Cooper and Robert Block, the authors of *Disaster: Hurricane Katrina and the Failure of Homeland Security*, when he pointed out that he was supposed to meet Mississippi governor Haley Barbour on the Gulf Coast, Chertoff said, "I don't give a shit," and hung up. After that, Brownie ran the rescue operations from his hotel room.

Brown was the designated face of FEMA's stunted response to Katrina, but plenty of people deserved blame. First on that list might be a former marine general named Matthew Broderick, who ran Homeland Security's operations center during Katrina. Broderick's job was to synthesize the snippets of intelligence the government was receiving and keep Chertoff and top people in the White House up-to-date. Broderick had Bahamonde's report of a major levee breach Monday morning and his firsthand observations from a Coast Guard helicopter by that evening. At 1:15 p.m. on Monday, the Coast Guard sent out an e-mail reporting on a levee breach that caused at least eight feet of flooding in the Ninth Ward. As Broderick drove to work from his Virginia home on Tuesday morning, radio reports declared New Orleans a flooded city. Yet not until later in the afternoon on Tuesday did he send out a bulletin confirming that most of the city was underwater. Asked to explain the delay, he cited a television report he had glimpsed Monday evening on a TV in the agency's break room. On the screen, people were being interviewed inside a French Quarter bar. How bad could it be, Broderick thought, if people were drinking and carrying on in the center of town?

Broderick and his people never seemed to catch up. Their Wednesday intelligence report told of the twelve thousand to fifteen thousand people stranded at the Superdome when the true number was closer to twenty-five thousand. That same report also failed to note that, in an act of desperation, the city had opened its Convention Center as a second refuge of last resort, despite a lack of provisions there. On Wednesday morning, the Louisiana state police were estimating that another twenty-five thousand were inside the Convention Center. Yet not until Thursday did Broderick's intelligence report even mention it. "Actually, I have not heard a report of thousands of people in the Convention Center who don't have food and water," Chertoff said during an appearance Thursday night on NPR, though by that time the cable stations were doing stand-ups in front of the building. Talking to Ted Koppel later that night, Brown estimated that around five thousand people were in the Convention Center. In the first several days after Katrina, the average cable news viewer seemed to know more about the catastrophe than the people running the show from Washington.

"THIS IS GOING TO get real ugly real fast," FEMA's Marty Bahamonde wrote in a text message he sent to his bosses the Sunday night before Katrina even reached New Orleans. They had been expecting fifteen trucks loaded with bottled water but only five arrived. They had also received 320,000 fewer MRE ("meals ready to eat," which the military uses on the battlefield) than requested. After the Pam exercises, FEMA had promised to pre-stage four hundred buses and eight hundred drivers just outside the storm zone to be ready to cart people out of the city. For days, everyone from Governor Blanco down was yelling for buses, but the answer was always the same: tomorrow. "Even if the FEMA buses had come on Wednesday, George Bush would have looked like a hero," Kathleen Blanco said. The promised buses wouldn't start arriving en masse until Friday morning.

"We need to get people out of here," Blanco told Brown when the two were in New Orleans on Tuesday morning. "We need buses." Nagin also stressed the need for buses when he met Brown that same morning. At Bahamonde's suggestion, the mayor had arrived with a list. "Be as specific as possible to help FEMA do its job," Bahamonde had coached the mayor and his people. Maybe it's only an apocryphal story meant to underscore the government's ineptitude, but one well-traveled report had Brown or one of his people misplacing the mayor's list after receiving it Tuesday morning.

"Sir, the situation [in the Superdome] is past critical," Bahamonde wrote to Brown on Wednesday morning. Yet once grounded in Baton Rouge, Brown seemed focused more on ensuring that he still looked to be in charge than on managing his team. "In this crisis and on TV, you need to look more hard working," a handler wrote to Brown in an e-mail that eventually would be made public. "ROLL UP THE SLEEVES!" When Brown's press secretary asked people via e-mail to leave her boss alone for a couple of hours so he could enjoy a proper meal before an appearance on MSNBC, Bahamonde had had enough of the e-mail string he was reading. "Tell her," Bahamonde pecked out on his BlackBerry, "that I just ate an MRE and crapped in the hallway with 30,000 other close friends so I understand her concern about busy restaurants."

Hundreds of New Orleans police officers went AWOL in those first few days after the flooding. By midweek, Eddie Compass, the chief of police, announced that his people would no longer help in the rescue efforts because he didn't believe he had enough of a force to maintain order in dry parts of town. Blanco requested that troops be sent to New Orleans, as did

Nagin and Michael Brown. The White House at first indicated that Defense Secretary Donald Rumsfeld was unavailable (he was spotted sitting in the owner's box at a San Diego Padres baseball game Tuesday night). Days of delays followed as lawyers inside the White House argued over lines of authority and paperwork rather than ordering the military to the region and sorting out the legal technicalities later. By Thursday—three days after the levees broke—the police were running out of ammunition, and Chief Compass, a friend of Nagin's since childhood, breathlessly told the mayor a story about how he was nearly taken hostage inside the Convention Center. "People are shooting at officers there," Compass said, "but we can't shoot back because we don't want to hit innocent people." The chief "was clearly shaken up," Nagin concluded, but he didn't know what to tell his old friend except to suggest that he get some rest. Turning to longtime aide Terry Davis, Nagin said, "This thing looks like it could blow. It'll take a miracle for us to hold it together."

RAY NAGIN HAD FIGURED on riding out the storm on the large leather couch in his office on the second floor of City Hall. But someone woke up the mayor at around midnight the Sunday before Katrina hit. The winds were causing the building to sway, and people were nervous about staying inside the cement structure. So in the middle of the night, the mayor and key staff moved across the street to the Hyatt. That first night Nagin chose to sleep on a cot in a fourth-floor ballroom, where the city had set up an auxiliary command center, rather than in a suite that had been reserved in his name on the twenty-seventh floor. "Raindrops so large they sounded like gunshots as they hit the building," Nagin wrote in a self-published memoir. Winds that screamed "louder and crazier than a wild banshee," and a "constant drone like sci-fi possessed Gods chanting ominous incantations." The night's most frightening moment came when the windows on the northern face of the hotel blew out, forcing the occupants of hundreds of rooms to flee to safer quarters. Nagin figured he got maybe two hours of sleep that first night.

On Monday morning, Nagin spoke with the deputy police chief overseeing the city's 911 system. During one twenty-three-minute period, he told Nagin, the system received six hundred calls. To learn what was going on, the deputy had listened in on a sampling of calls. He told the mayor, "It was people begging and screaming for help. 'The water's up to my neck. Please come now.' 'My husband has blown off the roof.' 'My children are drowning.'" All day Nagin learned about more levee breaches, but his meeting that night with FEMA's Marty Bahamonde underscored for Nagin the tragedy in the making. Water was covering three-quarters of the city. Thousands of people were stranded on rooftops, and thousands more wading through the waters to get to the Superdome, which was already nearing capacity. Alone in his suite that night, Nagin told himself that nothing mattered more in the coming days than his appearing calm.

Around midday Tuesday, Nagin got his first glimpse from inside a Black Hawk helicopter of the watery Atlantis over which he now presided. The mayor fixated on the Seventeenth Street Canal, where Lake Pontchartrain was pouring through a large gash in the levee wall. To his eye, the city would continue filling with water until they plugged this breach that measured 450 feet. From the air, he saw the restaurant in the middle-class enclave of Lakeview where he and his wife and the youngest of his three children had dined on the Saturday night before the storm. Ten feet of water now covered it.

"What do you need, Mr. Mayor?" Bush asked Nagin when the two spoke by phone on Wednesday night. By that point, Nagin and his people had calculated that they needed more than one thousand buses. A small caravan of trucks carting water and food rations would have helped make a terrible experience a little less miserable for thousands of people. The city needed military medevac teams at both the Superdome and the Convention Center. Nagin instead chose to make a single request of the president: plug the Seventeenth Street Canal. His communications director, Sally Forman, jumped on him as soon as he was done talking to the president. Nagin cut her off, snapping, "Let him do this one damn thing, Sally, and then we'll move to the next set of needs."

In some ways, Wednesday was the week's low point for the mayor and his people. "Absolutely brutal," Nagin said of the weather that day. "It felt like it was at least one hundred and ten degrees with one hundred percent humidity." The hotel's bathrooms had stopped working, so people started using the stairwell when they needed to relieve themselves. Every day Nagin, a former athlete hobbled by a bum knee, and his staff used those same overheated stairwells to reach their rooms on the twenty-seventh floor. "I worked hard not to step in the excrement," Sally Forman said of her regular treks from their fourth-floor command center to her hotel room down the hall from the mayor's. Nagin described the experience as "stiflingly putrid."

The Superdome next door was becoming a bigger worry. The cavernous indoor stadium had several large holes punched in its roof. The facility was without electricity or working toilets and was critically low on water, food, and medical supplies. It also connected to the Hyatt via a second-floor pedestrian bridge. The National Guard, who were responsible for security there, had been asking for reinforcements, but none were coming. They were vulnerable, Chief Eddie Compass told the mayor and others. From an informant inside the Superdome, the chief claimed, he was hearing that a small cabal was plotting a kind of insurrection. It would start with a diversionary action, the informant said. They would then overwhelm the National Guard, rush the pedestrian bridge, and take over the command center the city had established on the hotel's fourth floor.

Compass's wife was eight months pregnant and staying with him at the Hyatt, along with their three-year-old daughter. The chief didn't hesitate when he heard a gunshot in the parking lot outside the Superdome on Wednesday afternoon. He burst into the city's fourth-floor emergency command center and ordered people upstairs for their own safety. "We all ran up twenty-three flights of stairs to the twenty-seventh floor," said Nagin. Others stayed behind to barricade the second-floor walkway. "Yes, we boarded ourselves into the Hyatt," said Greg Meffert, a top city official at Nagin's side that week. "There was this real fear that there was going to be this mass break-in." That night, lying in a hot hotel room with windows that did not open, Nagin heard gunshots on the street. "I really didn't think we'd make it through Wednesday night," he wrote, "without an Armageddon-like war occurring in the total darkness."

Thursday brought more of the same. There were no convoys of supplies and no buses, only the occasional coach pulling up in front of the Superdome. Nagin was livid with Bush and even angrier with Blanco. On a hand-cranked radio in his suite, surrounded by staffers, Nagin caught a snippet of a Blanco press conference on the one local station still broadcasting, WWL-AM. Mainly what he heard was a governor boasting about all that the state was doing to help New Orleans. "I've had it with all this bull-shit," he told people around him. "I'm calling in to set the record straight." They had given up trying to get their satellite phones to work, but Greg Meffert, the city's chief technology officer, figured out a way to make an analog phone work over a computer line. They reached Garland Robin-ette, the well-regarded talk-show host, in WWL's studios. On air, Nagin mocked the president for his Air Force One flyover and then lit into both the governor and the president. Maybe it's Bush's fault, maybe it's Blanco's, Nagin told Robinette, but either way the president needs to get his "ass on a plane" so he can sit down with the governor and figure things out.

"Get off your asses and do something," he implored both Blanco and Bush, "and let's fix the biggest goddamn crisis in the history of this country."

NAGIN FINALLY WOKE UP to some good news on Friday morning. Looking out the window, he saw several buses on the interstate, headed toward the Superdome. He also spotted a convoy of military supply trucks. He called out and people came rushing in. That's when Sally For-man shared the news about her early-morning call. "So buses just happen to start arriving the day the president makes his first visit," Nagin said.

Air Force One left Washington at around nine o'clock on Friday morning. The president's first stop was the Mississippi Gulf Coast, where he held an airport press conference. He was joined by a pair of Republi-can governors, Bob Riley of Alabama and Mississippi's Haley Barbour.

"I want to thank Mike Brown and his staff," Bob Riley said. "FEMA has absolutely been great."

"I want to join with Bob," Barbour said. "The federal government is great—FEMA and all of your people who are on the ground." When it was his turn to speak, the president used those compliments to give a public pat on the back to his beleaguered FEMA director: "Brownie, you're doing a heck of a job!"

Maggie Grant had asked Sally Forman to have Nagin at the airport about an hour before Bush's scheduled arrival at around 1:00 p.m. For security purposes, the government flies two Air Force Ones, one as a con-veyance for the president and his entourage, the other as a decoy. They would have Nagin wait in the second Air Force One, Grant had said, until the president's arrival, which gave Forman an idea. It had been days since any of them had bathed. "Forgive me for asking, but is there any way the mayor could take a shower while he waits?" Forman asked. The president's trip was in part to make a friend in Ray Nagin. Grant seemed pleased to provide so easy a deliverable. "Absolutely!" Forman remembers her enthusing. Nagin would be able to use a bathroom on the decoy plane.

The chief flight attendant was named Reggie, whom Nagin described as a "brother from New York." "I'm not sure who you are," Nagin remembers Reggie telling him as he ushered the mayor to the president's private quarters, "but it's very rare that someone other than the president uses this part of the plane." Nagin figured he was in the shower barely ten minutes when Reggie knocked on the door to warn him of the president's imminent arrival. Rather than finish up, Nagin soaped a second time and then a third for what he described as a "triple-lather shower." He took his time shaving and waxing his head for the coming photo ops. "We had waited for the president for several days," he said, so "he could at least wait a few minutes for me." For his meeting with the president, Nagin wore a pair of dress slacks and a clean white T-shirt stamped with the word DESIRE.

Kathleen Blanco was sitting at a table in the belly of the president's plane when Nagin arrived. So, too, were Senators Mary Landrieu and David Vitter and several congressmen, including Bobby Jindal, the thirty-four-year-old Republican whom Blanco had defeated for governor, and Bill Jefferson, a black Democrat who represented New Orleans East. Michael Chertoff and Michael Brown were also there.

The president entered after Nagin, who was struck by the president's "swagger"—a "cowboy-type walk with slight bow legs." Bush took a seat at the head of the table and lunch was served. The elected officials took turns sharing their frustrations with FEMA. Nagin, sitting to the president's immediate left, went last. Some around the table felt as if they were watching a man unglued. By several accounts, his eyes grew wider the longer he spoke, and he began to tremble. Senator David Vitter remembered Nagin angrily slamming down his hand and barking at Bush and Blanco. Blanco thought the mayor was on the verge of a breakdown. "My adrenaline was flowing, and my pulse was a bit elevated," Nagin said.

After their meeting, Bush and Blanco met in private. There in the Oval Office in the sky, the president pressed her to sign a document that would allow him to federalize the National Guard troops, which otherwise fall under a governor's jurisdiction. The governor, whose staff opposed the idea, asked the president for twenty-four hours to consider the proposal. She knew that even without her signature, the president had the authority to take over the National Guard. (Bush's father had done so after the Rodney King riots in Los Angeles in 1992.) Bush also had the power to send military forces to an area that Blanco had declared to be in a state of emergency even before Katrina made landfall. But Blanco's staff feared that by making a big show of the governor handing control to the president, Bush and his people could later cast her as not up to the task of command—a woman paralyzed by fear.

Senator Mary Landrieu, a Democrat, cornered Nagin while Bush and Blanco met. You're being played, she warned the mayor. Landrieu thought she was stating the obvious: the president's people were hoping to use Nagin to help discredit Blanco and distract attention from their own failures in the days after Katrina. Nagin saw Air Force One as bringing to their disaster the worst of Washington politics. "She was going on and on about us not smiling if we stood beside the president," according to Nagin. "I remember telling her, 'You've got to be kidding.'" In an air-conditioned mobile unit parked on the tarmac nearby, Blanco's staffers were delivering a similar warning to their counterparts from New Orleans: don't allow yourselves to be used by the Bush administration.

Three helicopters were parked near Air Force One to take the presidential entourage on a tour of the city. The president walked a little ahead of the pack and called for Nagin to join him. Nagin remembers the president slipping an arm around his shoulder and asking him if he was still angry. "My staff said you used some strong words yesterday on the radio," Bush said. Nagin apologized but asked the president what he would have done if he were in the same spot. "Mr. Mayor, I know we could have done better," Nagin quotes Bush as telling him. Blanco joined Bush and Nagin on Marine One, the presidential helicopter. The other politicians rode the second helicopter, followed by the media documenting the president's tour of the flood-ravaged city.

As they flew over New Orleans, Bush peppered Nagin with questions. The helicopters landed near the breach in the Seventeenth Street Canal. Where there had been no activity the day before, crews of soldiers were now working with trucks and sandbags.[1] Nagin walked off to get a closer look, but a Secret Service agent jogged over to fetch him. "Apparently, the president had been calling for me," Nagin later wrote. The two spoke for another fifteen minutes. Blanco and Landrieu were fuming, Nagin said, because "the president's people kept them out of all the key photo shoots." Back at the airport, Bush looked into the television cameras and said, "I believe that the great city of New Orleans will rise again and be a greater city. I believe the town where I used to come to enjoy myself, occasionally too much, will be that very same town, that it will be a better place to come."

THAT NIGHT, AFTER A debriefing with his staff, Nagin stood by the window in his suite with several of his top people. He looked over his darkened city. Ever since the levees had broken, he had been asking himself, "Why me?" Today he had spent time with the president of the United States and watched buses clear people from the Superdome. Things were progressing more slowly at the Convention Center, but at least people there had food and water. Finally the Army Corps of Engineers was working to seal the Seventeenth Street levee breach. The mayor's face brightened as he stared at his reflection in the glass. He had his answer.

"Are you okay?" asked Sally Forman, who noticed the strange look on the mayor's face.

"This is God's plan for me."

"What is?"

"To rebuild a new New Orleans." They smiled at him in quiet agreement. At least that's how the mayor imagined it when he re-created the moment years later.

---

1. Mary Landrieu later swore that when she flew over the Seventeenth Street Canal breach the next day, there was no longer much to see. "All the dump trucks were gone. All the Coast Guard people were gone. It was an empty spot with one little crane," she told the journalist Paul Alexander, author of *Machiavelli's Shadow: The Rise and Fall of Karl Rove.* "I could not believe that the president of the United States, staged by Karl Rove himself, had come down to the city of New Orleans and basically put up a stage prop."

3

BEHIND ENEMY LINES

Lance Hill wasn't leaving town just because Ray Nagin had decreed it. If anything, a mandatory evacuation order from Nagin was a reason to *stay* in New Orleans through Katrina. "A black man playing front man for the white establishment," Hill said of Nagin, and one who hadn't bothered helping those without means remove themselves from harm's way. That July, city officials had distributed a DVD in low-income communities around the city. Its purpose was to let people know New Orleans was too broke to help even the infirm or the disabled in the event of a major hurricane. Our main message, the DVD's producer told the *Times-Picayune*, "is that each person is primarily responsible for themselves."

Hill, who is white, worked for Tulane University as an adjunct history professor and executive director of the Southern Institute for Education and Research, a center devoted to better race relations in the South. His wife, Eileen, was a public school teacher. They were graying empty nesters with enough spare cash to get themselves out of town and seemingly the good sense to make it happen. But Hill, who had moved to the New Orleans area in the early 1980s, had embraced the local

machismo that dictated that real men stay put when a hurricane threat-
ens a community. "You don't leave until everyone leaves," he said. "You
take care of the little old lady down the street. You take care of anyone
needing help."

One in four families in New Orleans was living on less than $20,000
a year at the time of Katrina. That same proportion of the population
did not own a car. The storm came at the end of the month, when
people living paycheck to paycheck are typically low on funds. It also
hit just prior to the start of school—an expensive time of the year for
parents. An estimated seventy thousand people—nearly 15 percent of
the population—remained behind in New Orleans during Katrina for
many reasons, but money played a big role. According to a study of the
thousands of evacuees who ended up in Houston-area shelters, 67 percent of those who needed to be rescued from New Orleans had a job,
but 68 percent had neither cash in the bank nor a usable credit card.
Two in every five evacuees indicated that they were either physically
disabled or were caring for someone who was. Eighty percent were renters and their median income was under $15,000.

The rich would have no problem leaving ahead of Katrina. They
jetted to Aspen or Deer Valley or, on Saturday morning, they pointed
their luxury sedans east and decamped to Destin, Florida, the preferred
beachfront playground of Uptown's elite. They flew to Dallas, where they
had a satellite office, or they remained because they could. Some New
Orleanians were so rich that they faced almost no risk in staying in town.
They lived on the high ground in homes along St. Charles Avenue or in
Audubon Place, a gated community where the average home goes for a
few million dollars. Their homes were well-constructed fortresses that
had survived prior storms. Many had a generator powerful enough to
keep at least one air conditioner running and the ice cubes frozen. That
week in New Orleans, even as families camped on highway overpasses or
stood stranded on rooftops, the occasional helicopter flew over Uptown
to the green expanse of Audubon Park. That was the area's makeshift
heliport for any of the city's well-heeled burghers who decided it was
time to get out of town.

Lance Hill didn't have helicopter money, but he lived Uptown not
far from Audubon Park and St. Charles Avenue. He was another white

man on the wrong side of fifty, pear-shaped and bald, walking the streets dressed in shorts and a T-shirt. "If you were Uptown and white right after Katrina, people assumed you were rich," he said. "People let their guard down. I got to talk to everyone that way. To cops, to Guardsmen, to anyone I'd meet on the street." So this former activist turned scholar who ran a center dedicated to the ideal of a more equitable, racially inclusive world passed among the city's barons and its princes, its eccentrics, and its captains of industry.

"I was in the middle of people who were openly planning for a city that was whiter and more affluent than before Katrina," Hill said. His newfound friends were the city's blue bloods with roots stretching back multiple generations. Membership to the topline Mardi Gras krewes such as Comus and Rex—those mysterious pleasure clubs that helped establish the social order in New Orleans—and also the Boston Club, where city business was often worked out over tumblers of bourbon, was theirs by birthright. Hill eavesdropped on their conversations that week and concluded their vision was of a New Orleans a lot like the one their ancestors had enjoyed, long before the city's black community came to dominate local politics. Katrina was their pretext for ridding New Orleans of enough blacks, Hill said, so that whites were once again in the majority, "and I was sitting at the table, literally on occasion, sipping cocktails while they were discussing how they were going to accomplish this."

LANCE HILL, BORN IN the Midwest, was twelve years old when he wrote a poem about black and white living together in a color-blind world. While still in high school, he worked as a busboy at a local college. There he organized a strike for higher pay. In 1968, Hill, then eighteen, the son of a mechanic and a nurse, led an unsuccessful push to integrate the town's swimming pools. He matriculated at Kansas University but was expelled after one semester for organizing demonstrations in opposition to the Vietnam War. He joined a revolutionary group, read Karl Marx, and went to work in a factory with the aim of politically awakening its employees.

"In the early to mid-1970s, a lot of people in the antiwar student movement started to look at the industrial working classes as the agents of change," Hill said. "That's where I ended up." Hill worked a series of jobs in Kansas City—as a machinist, a welder, a printer—all in the name of inspiring a broader movement among the country's blue-collar masses. At night and on the weekends, he read books about labor history and other social movements, including those on the right. That's when he started reading about the Ku Klux Klan and other white supremacist groups that together would become the focus of his scholarship.

In 1979, Hill and fellow political activist Eileen San Juan arrived in Louisiana. The couple's first stop was Hammond, a blue-collar town sixty miles north of New Orleans, where Hill found work as a welder in a local shipyard. The job served as a harsh introduction to some of the differences between the Midwest and the Deep South. In Kansas City, he had always enjoyed lunch at the welding shop where he worked. The neo-Nazis and the black nationalists and the lunch-bucket whites sat at the same long table, eating and arguing and ribbing one another over their beliefs. In Hammond, black and white ate separately. In a shipyard that employed hundreds, he never saw a black person in a supervisory position. Whites still casually used the N-word. Hill stood six foot three and weighed almost three hundred pounds. People who didn't like his politics just left him alone, but it didn't go unnoticed when he started giving a ride home to a black coworker.

After two years in Hammond, Eileen was offered a job teaching in the Orleans Parish schools. The couple, along with their son and Hill's two stepchildren, moved into a trailer park in the New Orleans suburbs. Hill said he had lost faith "in this grand theory that socialism would come through the working class." He started a grass-cutting business to bring in extra money and returned to school to earn his college degree.

Back on a college campus, Hill threw himself into any number of popular causes, including the nuclear-freeze movement and the fight against apartheid in South Africa. His obsession, however, remained white supremacists, and the New Orleans metro area proved fertile ground for study. A neo-Nazi group was based in Kenner, near the airport. In nearby Metairie, a white-flight suburb that saw its population soar in the 1960s and 1970s, he found a group calling itself the National Association for the Advancement of White People—a name chosen as a deliberate jab at the NAACP. Hill subscribed to the newsletters of each group and even visited the offices of the NAAWP. Posing as a sympathizer, he met the group's leader, David Duke. A budding historian, Hill would save and catalog the materials sent to him by Duke's group.

Hill began working toward his PhD at Tulane in 1987. The next year, David Duke announced that he was running for a seat in the state legislature. Duke had been a Grand Wizard in the Ku Klux Klan, and his new group, the NAAWP, preached racial superiority. Yet in seeking to represent the western suburbs in the Louisiana House of Representatives, Duke fashioned himself as a mainstream Republican, opposed to affirmative action and higher taxes and in favor of the mandatory drug testing of welfare recipients. Duke won that election and two years later shocked pundits when he captured 58 percent of the statewide white vote in a run for the US Senate. Duke lost that election but was again in the national spotlight a year later when he ran for Louisiana governor. Duke made the runoff in the race. Hill was among those behind a group called the Louisiana Coalition Against Racism and Nazism, created to pressure mainstream Republicans into opposing Duke. Duke lost his bid for the governorship but again won a majority of the state's white vote.

The years following Duke's failed gubernatorial run were gratifying ones for Hill, even if not quite as glamorous. He earned a doctorate in history and cofounded, in 1993, the Southern Institute for Education and Research at Tulane. At this center dedicated to the improvement of race relations, Hill and others developed a tolerance curriculum used to train teachers throughout the Deep South. A dozen years later, Hill, fifty-four, was preparing for a heavy calendar of training sessions for the upcoming academic year when Katrina hit.

FOR MOST PEOPLE IN New Orleans, the days after Katrina were a harrowing experience. In Broadmoor, a mixed-race community in the western half of the city, a lawyer named Bill Hines was trapped in his home, surrounded by water, with his son, his brother-in-law, and a Tulane law student. They numbered eleven by the time a boat rescued them four frightening and sweltering days later. "You had the guns going off at night and looters were coming by in boats," said Hines, the managing partner at the city's largest law firm. "It was *Lord of the Flies.*" Yet Hines knows they were among the lucky ones. In the Lower Ninth Ward,

Robert Green Sr. was trapped with his family in a home that the flood-waters had pushed off its foundation. He lost his mother and three-year-old granddaughter. "He had to watch both of them die right in front of him," his pastor later reported.

Yet for Hill, who had no idea of the disaster taking place elsewhere around the city, those first days after Katrina were more a swashbuckling adventure. "We were completely cut off," Hill said. "I basically ended up adopting this group of nice old ladies who didn't want to evacuate because they had pets." On Wednesday, the National Guard and other outside police agencies started going door-to-door in Uptown, encouraging anyone still in town to leave. "That caused old people to think they needed to hide," Hill said, "which was the last worst thing you could do with midday temperatures in the nineties." At the homes of people who had shuttered themselves in, he would blow a whistle, yell, "I'm leaving water on your porch," before heading to his next stop.

Hill learned about the travesty unfolding at the Convention Center while chatting with people he met on the street. On Friday morning, he drove to this massive facility only a few miles from his apartment, where he found several blocks of people standing five and ten deep, looking in vain for help. "People tried to get me to take older folks and children not doing well to the hospital," he said. "I had to explain that all the hospitals were closed, even those Uptown." Seeing the phalanx of armed soldiers who had stationed themselves across the street infuriated him. The soldiers stood at a distance, as if there only to keep order rather than to help. Hill remembers one white Guardsman standing in the middle of the street, refreshing himself with a long slug of water. The soldier, in full uniform and carrying a heavy rifle, was no doubt thirsty, but he seemed oblivious of the people, nearly all of them black, watching him. "He's drinking in front of all these parents with babies and young children screaming from extreme dehydration," Hill said. He doesn't see the hordes of dark-skinned people as quite human, Hill thought to himself.

The sight of so much suffering caused Hill to shift into a high gear of superactivism. He couldn't save the sick, but at least he could distribute water. He drove his family's venerable Oldsmobile to the western suburbs, where the main thoroughfares were clear and some of the big-box stores were open. The car was a wide boat with a massive backseat and large trunk—perfect for ferrying cases of bottled water. Hill spray-painted the word AID on the doors and added a few red crosses (and later had to phone his father: How do you remove spray paint from a car?). The challenge was getting back into the city. He had his laptop with him, along with a portable printer and a voltage converter, allowing him to set up a veritable office in the backseat. Using official Tulane-issued stationery, he said, "I wrote a letter addressed to myself giving myself permission to be in the city tending to property damage." Arriving at a checkpoint behind the wheel of an older car with a throaty muffler, missing hubcaps, and leopard-design seat covers, Hill aimed for nonchalance. He pretended to be chatting on his cell phone as he handed over his made-up letter and ID to a boy soldier. The Guardsman didn't know what to make of the scene and phoned his commander: "Captain, I think we have the president of Tulane here." Hill was allowed back in the city.

Hill made several runs to the Convention Center, delivering around twenty gallons of water at a time. A contingent of rifle-wielding soldiers tried to stop him from emptying his load. They backed off, he said, only after confronted by shouts from the crowd. He had just finished emptying his fourth load when a pair of officers driving a civilian truck pulled behind him a block or two from the Convention Center. One was a New Orleans cop, the other a Louisiana state trooper. "They're yelling for me to stop but I'm pretending not to hear them and just drive faster," Hill said. He stopped only after one of the cops fired a warning shot. Hill bolted out of his car as if ready for a fight.

"What the fuck you think you're doing?" the state trooper yelled.

"What the fuck are *you* doing?" Hill yelled back. In the suburbs, Hill had passed a fleet of ambulances sitting idle while at the Convention Center hundreds of hungry and thirsty people surrounded him. Some seemed in dire need of medical attention. "There's twenty thousand people that you're supposed to protect and serve," he yelled, "and you're sitting in an air-conditioned truck doing nothing." They let him go but with a warning. "Don't let me see you here again," one of the cops barked at him.

ALMOST A PARTY ATMOSPHERE prevailed along St. Charles Avenue after the flood, a bubble inhabited by people tromping around in cutoffs and flip-flops. It wasn't uncommon to be offered a cold beer despite a citywide blackout. Each day Hill made it a point to stop by Audubon Place, where he spoke to the black-clad Israeli commandos that the Audubon Place Homeowners Association had helicoptered in for protection. "They kept me up-to-date on what was going on in the rest of town," Hill said.

Sometimes the comments Hill heard while making the rounds were overtly racist. He watched as two white men thanked a white National Guardsman for helping to protect their city. "Now if you can just keep the blacks from coming back," one called out. But mainly Hill's time passing as a member of the tribe revealed more of a general good-riddance as they learned details of the disaster taking place in the eastern half of the city. "It was impossible not to pick up on this sentiment that this was our chance to take back control of the city," Hill said. "There was virtually a near consensus among whites that authorities should not do anything to make it easy for poor African Americans to come back."

People eventually figured out that Hill wasn't one of them. Maybe it was the way he elongated his words or his habit of averting his eyes upward as he spoke, as if delivering a lecture in the classroom. Yet rather than shunning him, "they made more of an effort to make me feel comfortable," Hill said. For some, his association with Tulane increased his stock. Others no doubt noticed this adopted member of their tribe caring for some of their older neighbors. It helped, too, that Hill was handy with tools and comfortable around machinery. One prominent lawyer, Ashton O'Dwyer, who owned a big house on St. Charles, even stopped by Hill's apartment building, where he left a message with Hill's wife. O'Dwyer was having trouble with his generator and had heard that Hill might be able to help. Could Hill stop by his place on St. Charles?

O'Dwyer was hard to miss after Katrina—the "silk stocking lawyer," wrote Jed Horne, then the city editor of the *Times-Picayune*, who had "taken up a sentinel's post" on St. Charles Avenue. O'Dwyer had dragged a black wrought-iron table to his driveway, and there, with a shotgun visible, he sat watching a small portable television. A jowly man with short-clipped, steel-gray hair and thin lips set into a permanent frown, he offered visitors ice cubes for their drinks. That was where

Hill found him around a week after Katrina hit. Christopher Cooper of the *Wall Street Journal* was also there the day Hill showed up to fix O'Dwyer's generator.

"OLD-LINE FAMILIES ESCAPE WORST of Flood and Plot the Future," read a headline on the front page of the *Wall Street Journal* ten days after Katrina. Cooper, who had spent a decade in New Orleans working for the *Picayune* before going to the *Journal*, began the article by describing O'Dwyer, dressed in nothing but a blue bathing suit, dipping a pair of plastic milk jugs into a neighbor's swimming pool for water to flush his toilet. "The mostly African-American neighborhoods of New Orleans are largely underwater," Cooper reminded his readers, and its residents scattered across the country. Yet the people living in "the fashionable district surrounding St. Charles Avenue"—the Kings and Queens of Carnival, many who "have ancestors who arrived here in the 1700s"—were maneuvering to play a central role in the recovery.

"New Orleans is ready to be rebuilt," O'Dwyer said. "Let's start right here." O'Dwyer uttered those words, Cooper wrote, "standing in his expansive kitchen, next to a counter covered with a jumble of weaponry."

The next person Cooper quoted was Jimmy Reiss. "I might've spoken to the guy for all of two minutes," Reiss said of his conversation with Cooper. But that was enough. In the months and years ahead, it wouldn't be the image of O'Dwyer in his swim trunks, nor his words, that Hill and the drive-time hosts on black talk radio would repeat but those few thoughts Jimmy Reiss shared with Cooper about the recovery. "He told us everything that was going to happen before it did," Hill said.

Like O'Dwyer, Reiss was a product of old-money New Orleans, except Reiss was wealthier, better looking, and enjoyed a higher perch on the city's social ladder. He was New Orleans royalty invited into the family business after earning his MBA at Tulane. A charming rapscallion with twinkly blue eyes and a well-earned reputation within his social set as a ladies' man, Reiss had taken a bachelor pad in the French Quarter and seemed determined not to follow his father and his father's father into the wholesale candy business that his great-grandfather had started a century earlier. "I was trying to drink and fuck myself to death and doing a pretty good job of it," Reiss said. "And my father asked me to leave."

Reiss and a fishing buddy started a business selling fire-suppression equipment to offshore oil rigs and shipbuilders in the area. Eventually they got into the electronics business, selling specialized automation and control systems to large businesses. A large multinational bought their company, and then Reiss, who had stayed on as a division president after the sale, bought back the company with a loan from the Whitney Bank, which had been taking care of the Uptown elite since his great-grandfather's time. "That's when I made the bulk of my fortune," Reiss said. Reiss had elected to ride out the storm at a second home he owned in Aspen, Colorado. A week after Katrina, he hired a helicopter to fly him into the city.

Reiss was in his mid-sixties when Katrina hit. Yet his friends all said it: he was the same Jimmy they knew growing up, naughty and outspoken, the man at the cocktail party who made people laugh by uttering what decorum dictated be kept to oneself. But this Jimmy owned a big house on Audubon Place and was one of the best connected people in New Orleans. Sally Forman was a young mom when she volunteered for an organization Reiss cochaired called Dollars for Scholars. Forman watched with awe at Reiss's gift for convincing the wealthy of Uptown to write big checks for their cause. Reiss sat on the Tulane Board of Trustees and ran the Business Council, an organization made up of most of the city's top CEOs. He was even nominally a member of the Nagin administration as the chairman of the city's Regional Transit Authority, an agency with thirteen hundred employees and a $110 million budget.

Reiss and Nagin had met late on the Friday night before the storm. In retrospect, they should have been talking about running more buses that weekend to shuttle people out of town, but they stuck to the agenda: the city's crime problem. Only Camden, New Jersey, had a higher homicide rate than New Orleans in 2004. Property crimes had soared under Nagin. Yet rather than offer any solutions, Reiss said, the mayor vented about the city's substandard schools and an unemployment rate among black men that hovered around 50 percent. Their meeting broke up at around 8:00 p.m.

Reiss started phoning friends and other members of the Business Council in the days after Katrina. The city's crime rate, the lousy schools, the unemployment, and maybe even the mayor's lackadaisical attitude toward these social ills were a topic of almost every conversation. By the time Cooper phoned, Reiss figured he had probably spoken to forty business leaders. They were all fed up, Reiss told Cooper. New Orleans would need to be a city with fewer poor people and better-run services if people such as himself were going to participate in the recovery efforts.

"Those who want to see this city rebuilt want to see it done in a completely different way: demographically, geographically, and politically," Reiss said. "I'm not just speaking for myself here. The way we've been living is not going to happen again, or we're out."

In time, Hill would dub it the "exclusionist movement"—the efforts by some within the white community to prevent the city's poor from returning. A large portion of the city's black community had been given one-way tickets out of town to places hundreds, if not thousands, of miles away, often with nothing but a garbage bag of belongings. "You had this old-line economic elite reassert their position of dominance the moment the city flooded," Hill said. "It was like I was watching them revert to their original state."

4

A FIRST BURST OF OPTIMISM

At 9:00 a.m. on the first Sunday after Katrina, Liberty Bank's jack-of-all-trades, Russell Labbe, pulled into the parking lot of an International House of Pancakes just outside Baton Rouge. Labbe had driven from Lafayette, one hour to the west, in a brown 2005 Ford pickup truck he had bought a couple of months earlier. At IHOP he met Joe James, who had driven from Abita Springs, one hour to the east. The two men had known each other for years, but if they said ten words by way of greeting on this morning, Labbe would be surprised. "We were anxious to get going," he said.

James oversaw Liberty's computer operations and would be going with Labbe into the city. James buckled himself into the passenger seat of Labbe's truck and the two drove south and east to New Orleans. Water still covered much of the city, but they also both knew that the bank's odds of survival depended on their picking up the computer tapes and other items they needed to get the bank back on the interbank network.

They made their first stop at a McDonald's on the other side of

Baton Rouge to meet Arthur Morrell. A black legislator and a friend of the bank's, he represented the black, middle-class enclave of Gentilly. Morrell would ensure that Labbe and James had no trouble getting through the checkpoints set up around New Orleans. A deputy sheriff rode shotgun next to Morrell. Both were carrying a gun, as was Labbe but not James. "Follow me," said Morrell, who was towing the boat they would need to reach the bank's headquarters.

The interstate was quiet. They encountered water on their drive but only when the highway dipped. The first checkpoint they encountered was at the Bonnet Carré Spillway, a dozen miles west of New Orleans. The soldiers had parked their vehicles to pinch traffic to a single lane. Morrell flashed his credentials and explained that the people in the truck behind him were with him. They encountered no trouble at that roadblock or any other along the way.

The first detour came at the split in the highway that would take them to the eastern half of the city. Several feet of water prevented them from taking the turnoff for the East, forcing them to take a circuitous route. They encountered their first long delay a couple of miles east of downtown: the elevated highway was being used as an impromptu landing pad to refuel rescue helicopters. Labbe and Joe James stepped out of the truck, walked to the highway embankment, and looked at the water still covering much of the city. "What's that over there?" James asked, pointing at the water. A body was floating face down, and then they noticed that the National Guardsmen were fishing bodies out of the water. "They had four or five bodies stacked up and ready to be shipped out," Labbe said.

Their contingent reached the edge of New Orleans at a little past noon. The police had set up an impromptu marina at the edge of the water, with a small armada of borrowed boats. Morrell knew several of the cops. "Take your pick," one offered. Abandoning the smaller boat they had towed, the four of them rode in a sixteen- or eighteen-footer piloted by a New Orleans police officer.

The water was as deep as twelve feet, but they still needed to follow the road grid to avoid rooftops and second stories. When they reached Liberty's headquarters, Labbe navigated them to the back of the building. There, a set of metal stairs led to a back door a few feet above the waterline. In different circumstances, Labbe might have tried phoning the man they had hired to stay with the building to let them in, but cell phones were not working. Labbe grabbed the two-by-four he had brought with him and smashed the glass part of the door. They tied the boat to the staircase and everyone except the police officer went inside.

There was no power. The sun outside was bright, but inside the building it was gloomy and dark. Labbe's eyes were still adjusting to the change in light when he heard breaking glass. He looked over to see the deputy sheriff who had accompanied them on their journey smashing windows with the two-by-four. "What are you doing?" Labbe yelled. The deputy asked Labbe to feel the moisture in the air. "You need to get some cross-ventilation going or you're losing this building," the deputy said. Labbe later said the deputy had probably saved them from writing off the building as a total loss.

Labbe and James headed for the third-floor computer room, relieved to find it dry and the mainframe looking pristine. James found the computer tapes they needed and grabbed other equipment that he thought they might need in Baton Rouge. Labbe left him and checked the rest of the building. Except for some water damage near a few windows broken by the wind, everything seemed as it should be. The guard they had hired to watch the building had somehow made it out on his own.

Back on the boat, the group headed a couple of miles deeper into New Orleans East to check on the bank's old headquarters and the branch next door. They could do nothing but shake their heads over a pair of buildings with six feet of water inside. Doubling back the way they had come, the police officer motored through Lake Forest Estates—Alden McDonald's subdivision. There, the water was still so high that the only clue that cars were parked along the street was the occasional antenna poking up.

Once back on dry land, they doubled back the way they had come. After a few miles, they jogged north and west to look at Gentilly. Liberty had another two branches in the area. It was also where Labbe lived.

They found water inside both of Liberty's branches in the area, but Labbe discovered that he and his wife were among the lucky ones. Their house was built on a slight ridge. Their home, set up a few feet on a foundation, had been spared.

DURING THOSE FIRST WEEKS after Katrina, Alden McDonald worked when he wasn't sleeping. He arrived at the Southern branch before 9:00 a.m., driving the putty-colored minivan that he chose from the scant inventory the car-rental company was offering. He sometimes had cell phone coverage in those first days after the storm but often he didn't, which made for a frustrating half-hour drive each morning. That was prime time to call the East Coast, where it was one hour earlier, or to steal a few private moments with Rhesa. The workday ended well after 9:00 p.m., if not later.

Nothing proved easy during those first weeks. McDonald may have had the foresight to outfit the Southern branch with an extra ten phone lines to handle diverted customer-service calls, but he had not counted on the telephone company's being overwhelmed by service calls. So many businesses and people had relocated to Baton Rouge that it took BellSouth until the second Thursday after Katrina—ten days after the storm—to rerate the bank's customers to its 1-800 lines.

Putting together even a skeletal crew meant finding a place to live for each additional employee McDonald brought on—this in a city where every hotel was sold-out. "In some cases, it wasn't just employees but entire families," McDonald said. And it wasn't just a matter of finding them housing but also paying them an extra stipend to cover their costs. Post-storm, even a modest apartment could cost a displaced employee thousands of dollars a month. "You need to worry about how they're going to cover their expenses," McDonald said. "You have to make sure their families will be all right."

McDonald had around twenty people helping him in those first weeks after Katrina. Most worked in the open office space in back of the Southern branch. The bank's loan department comprised two people sitting in mismatched chairs at a folding table. Next to them sat the one-person department assigned the task of figuring out which home-owners with a Liberty loan had flood insurance and which did not. Four tables pushed together in the middle of the room served as a makeshift call center. Even with the extra phone lines, customers had to listen to busy signals for hours before getting through. Some callers were worried about past-due bills (Liberty granted every customer affected by the storm a four-month grace period on home and car payments), while others called to see about a bump in the limit on a Liberty-issued credit card. Desperate to know how much money they had, many phoned for an account balance, not realizing the bank itself didn't know. Several times a day, a car pulled into the parking lot driven by someone coming from Houston or Dallas or somewhere else far away. They were customers worried about the large sum of money they still owed on a seemingly worthless house or car or business who had driven a half a day or more in the hope that someone could answer their questions.

McDonald himself set up shop at a small table in a windowless conference room. Piles of cardboard boxes lined the floor in this space, which doubled as the bank's records room. McDonald had a door but it usually remained open. Every minute or two, someone else would be seeking guidance or passing along a message. He had two cell phones, and often one would ring while he was already talking on the other. The bank's chief operating officer had resigned earlier that year, and Liberty was without a chief financial officer. McDonald, who was doing the job of three people, seemed to be in perpetual motion, bouncing between the main room, the branch lobby, and his own office, where only occasionally did he allow himself to sit exhausted in his chair and do nothing before the inevitable next request for his attention.

At around 7:00 p.m. each evening, McDonald convened a small group in his office for what he called "my daily crisis-management meeting." McDonald, a practicing Catholic, prayed. "I said to myself, 'Lord, you have to help me out here because I'm not one hundred percent sure we're going to make it.'"

THE BANK STILL HADN'T heard from a large portion of its employees. In the silence it was hard not to think the worst. One week after the flooding, the mayor speculated on the *Today* show that about ten thousand of his fellow citizens had likely perished—and Liberty's people generally lived in the city's hardest-hit areas.

Finding the employees wasn't easy. People's home phones didn't work and of course work extensions were worthless. The bank had some cell phone numbers but that usually meant listening to the rapid busy signal everyone in the 504 area code was hearing. Weeks passed before anyone heard from Pete, an appraiser for the bank. He had been rescued from his roof in New Orleans East. Others had endured the hell of the Convention Center or the Superdome. A month passed before McDonald was able to say with certainty that no Liberty employee had perished in the storm.

CELL PHONES STARTED WORKING more reliably nine or ten days after the storm. That made communication easier, and as people's phones chirped to life, a corresponding burst of hope occurred among the city's business leaders. That only brought into greater relief the disparity between McDonald's life and that of most of his corporate peers.

On Thursday nights in Baton Rouge, the well-connected gathered at Gino's, an Italian restaurant with a large bar area popular with legislators, lobbyists, and other local power brokers. Over copious glasses of wine on the second Thursday after Katrina, the mood was almost triumphant as good news finally started to arrive via newly revived phones. The French Quarter was dry. So, too, was the core of the central business district and Uptown—or at least the Uptown of old New Orleans. "Things have really started to turn for the better in the past forty-eight hours," said Stephen Perry, a Gino's regular and CEO of the New Orleans Convention & Visitors Bureau. Perry, who had served as chief of staff to Blanco's predecessor, was hearing that power would be restored to the core city within three weeks. The water and sewer systems should be functioning in key parts of New Orleans by then as well. Perry predicted the Quarter could be ready to greet visitors in less than ninety days. In a town where tourism was the number one industry, the areas that visitors would care most about, including the Warehouse and Garden Districts, were the least affected by the flooding. That, Perry said, would provide the city a base on which to build.

Uptown hadn't escaped unscathed. Fallen trees and downed utility poles were everywhere. Falling limbs had destroyed much of the catenary that powered the streetcars that run up and down St. Charles. Many Uptown homes suffered roof damage. Yet optimism coursed through this well-heeled, mostly white crowd. A well-connected corporate attorney talked about the possibility of holding Mardi Gras that February as usual. An executive with a major oil company saw no reason his coworkers couldn't be back at their desks inside a few weeks. He had been on the phone with his employees all day. Not a single person he spoke with owned a home that had taken on water.

In many ways, the men and women gathered at Gino's that night were McDonald's peers. He served on the same boards and commissions and knew them from meetings of the Chamber of Commerce, where McDonald was the presiding officer. Like McDonald, most seemed to be doubling up in satellite offices or working at borrowed desks. "Alden is one of the city's five or ten most prominent movers and shakers," said Patrick Quinn, a prominent developer and hotelier in town who, along with his wife, a state senator representing the western and northern suburbs, had taken up temporary residence in Baton Rouge. Perhaps it went without saying that few, if any, other blacks were on Quinn's list.

The contrast was not lost on McDonald. In much of the western half of town, where the majority of whites lived, Katrina was proving a severe inconvenience more than a tragedy. Most of the white businesspeople at Gino's that night were frustrated that they couldn't get home, but they knew they would have a home and belongings, and a job, to which to return.

McDonald, however, lived in the black half of town, where everyone he knew was staring into the abyss. Their homes and businesses were in ruins. "You're looking at the television and seeing water up to the street signs," said Arthur Johnson, an administrator in the New Orleans school district at the time of Katrina who lived not far from McDonald. "And we're all thinking, We'll never go back. There's no reason to go back. Everything is gone."

RUSSELL LABBE AND JOE James were hailed as heroes for their water journey into New Orleans to retrieve the software and equipment Liberty so desperately needed. But another week of phone calls followed with the emergency-backup company, who always told McDonald and his people that the problem was on their end. In the months to come, no topic—not his interminable fights with insurance firms or utility companies or even a final bill on all the money the looters stole—irritated McDonald quite like his disappointments with a backup company that had him running the bank blind for nearly two weeks. Not until 4:00 p.m. on Friday, September 9, 2005—eleven days after the flood—was Liberty back on the interbank network.

Initially, McDonald had put a $100 daily limit on all ATM withdrawals. But imagining his customers in hotels around the country, racking up expenses, he upped the daily maximum to $500 and hoped his customers had the money to cover the cash they were withdrawing. In a catastrophe, he was intent on playing Jimmy Stewart's George Bailey and not Lionel Barrymore's Mr. Potter. "A banker is someone who gives you an umbrella when the sun is shining and takes it away when it starts to rain," McDonald said, repeating an unflattering adage about his profession. But he added, "We try not to be that banker." The decision cost Liberty close to $1 million.

That was nothing compared to the bank's other losses. A no-questions-asked, four-month grace period on any home, business, or auto in a flooded area might have been the right thing to do, but it also represented millions of dollars in checks the bank wouldn't be cashing in the months to come. And even once January 1 came, then what? Could he expect most people to resume payments on properties and cars and businesses that had been wrecked in a once-in-a-lifetime flood? Pre-Katrina, Liberty generated $150,000 in loan fees and another $70,000 in charges from checking accounts every month. But the bank wasn't originating many loans in the months after Katrina, and Liberty had suspended checking fees for most of its customers. The $100,000 a month the bank generated leasing out space in its headquarters also disappeared. Liberty had frozen interest charges on credit card balances, representing more lost revenues, and there would be no late fees for four months. In the long run, it would be good for Liberty's business that people carried larger balances on their credit cards, but first the bank needed to survive the short run. "Everywhere I look," McDonald said six weeks after the storm, "I'm losing money."

Layoffs were inevitable. "I'm going to have to give severance packages and try to help people get to where they're going to get," he told a reporter around an hour after Liberty was back on the global financial grid. "I need to balance income and expense." Eleven days after Katrina, he offered a few halfhearted words of optimism and then confessed, "I'm running against time."

He knew the regulators were watching him closely. State examiners in Baton Rouge were coming by his temporary offices, and another set were checking in from Dallas, where the FDIC has its regional office. "They understand we're losing a certain amount of money now," McDonald said. "But regulators are not going to let us lose too much before they step in." Six of his eight branches in New Orleans had flooded. Several had been battered by looters, including one of the two that hadn't taken on any water. The ground floor of his new headquarters was a complete loss, and what was happening with the rest of the building remained a mystery. If nothing else, he would need to replace every window. He had insurance on the building, but what his policy would cover and what it wouldn't was another unknown.

The Whitney, where the city's blue bloods banked, was off the ATM network in the days after Katrina. So, too, were other local banks. "Regulators were worried about the whole system in New Orleans collapsing," McDonald said. "But I think it's fair to say they were more worried about me than anyone else."

It would have been an overstatement to say that as went this one bank, so would go New Orleans. But it didn't seem too much of a stretch to claim that Liberty's success and the future of the city's black neighborhoods were entwined. McDonald would need a healthy black middle class if he hoped to revive the bank. In turn, the black middle class would need a bank like Liberty to help it thrive again.

At the moment, it looked as if the French Quarter, the Garden District, and other parts of New Orleans precious to locals and visitors alike would survive. The prognosis for New Orleans East and Gentilly, however, and the smaller, black or Creole neighborhoods such as the Seventh Ward, St. Roch, and the Lower Ninth Ward, was far from clear. Dennis Hastert, the Speaker of the House of Representatives, was openly suggesting that at least some of these neighborhoods didn't have a future. "It looks like a lot of that place could be bulldozed," said Hastert, a Republican from Illinois, two days after Katrina. Through his own contacts in Washington, McDonald knew Hastert was speaking on behalf of many inside the Beltway. A great deal of recovery money would be set aside for New Orleans, McDonald's Washington contacts assured him, but it would be nowhere close to the multiple tens of billions the city needed to rebuild after the most expensive disaster in US history. After thirty-three years spent building Liberty into one of the country's biggest black-owned banks, McDonald was asking himself whether he would outlast the bank examiners to celebrate a thirty-fourth.

5

THE SHADOW GOVERNMENT

Mayor Nagin woke up early on Saturday morning. It was barely sunrise on his sixth day of presiding over a waterlogged city, and finally he had gotten four or five hours of sleep. Clots of people were still at the Superdome, but he was pleased to learn the buses had been running all night. Convoys of buses were finally starting to clear out the Convention Center, which would be empty of people by Sunday night.

Sunday was the day Nagin started talking to the media. First up was Oprah Winfrey, who was due in the city at noon.

The early part of the Winfrey interview proved disastrous. At first the problem was Eddie Compass, the police chief, who, Nagin said, "verbally exploded in front of the cameras." Compass himself had told the *Guardian* newspaper that his people had yet to substantiate any rapes at either the Superdome or the Convention Center. The article appeared the night before the Winfrey interview. There was also no evidence of the violent crimes that had supposedly been committed in either refuge. Yet Compass, who kept butting into Nagin's conversation with Winfrey, blurted out, "We've got babies being raped." The mayor asked for a small break and pulled his chief aside. "Pull yourself together!" he hissed. Yet

Nagin proved no less reckless a spokesman for his city. "People in that frickin' Superdome for five days," Nagin told Winfrey, "watching dead bodies, watching hooligans killing people, raping people." For days there had been apocryphal talk of slit throats and even the rape of a seven-year-old girl inside the Superdome. Now New Orleans's mayor and its police chief were repeating unsubstantiated accounts of unspeakable crimes to the afternoon audience watching *The Oprah Winfrey Show*.

Winfrey was dressed in jeans, a lime-green blouse, and rain boots. Nagin asked if she'd like to go inside the Superdome but immediately regretted the invitation. Too late to say no, he made Winfrey look at the camera and repeat after him, "I, Oprah Winfrey, promise not to hold the city liable financially or otherwise as a result of me going into this doggone stinky-ass Superdome." All week Nagin had avoided talking to people inside the dome out of fear for his own safety, but now with Winfrey, walking into the empty facility, he was assaulted by a smell so malodorous, he said, "I could taste funk." Tears filled Winfrey's eyes as she scanned the dank building lit up by shafts of light from the big holes that Katrina had punched in the dome's roof. "How could the richest country in the world let Americans suffer the way they did over the past week?" Nagin asked. The two hugged when they said their good-byes.

Nagin sat down with John Donvan of *Nightline* after Winfrey. Immediately, Sally Forman knew she had made a mistake pushing the mayor into the spotlight when he was describing himself as "mentally and physically drained." Donvan opened with a soft-ball question about Nagin's house. The mayor's home had not flooded and only suffered minor roof damage, yet she watched as the mayor told Donvan, "I know it's gone. I don't want to see it." The mayor seemed surprised when Donvan asked if race was the reason it took so many days to come to the city's rescue. Call it race or call it class, the mayor said, but "I don't think this type of response would have happened if this was Orange County, California." The mayor ended his Sunday with Scott Pelley of *60 Minutes*, where his exhaustion expressed itself as pessimism: "When you see a city that you love so much and you see it devastated and almost dead, you wonder what the future looks like."

Nagin was up early the next morning talking with Matt Lauer, who spoke with him via satellite from the *Today* show studio in New York.

The mayor gave Stone Phillips of *Dateline* a flyover tour of the city, then opened up to CNN's Soledad O'Brien. "What the state was doing, I don't friggin' know," Nagin told O'Brien. "But I tell you, I'm pissed. It wasn't adequate." Off camera, Forman was frantically slashing her finger across her throat, but the mayor ignored her. "She said she needed twenty-four hours," the mayor continued, referring to the governor's confrontation with the president on Air Force One. "And more people died." When Diane Sawyer asked Nagin about Bush, the mayor gave the commander in chief the benefit of the doubt: "I don't think the right information got to the president."

Sally Forman was with Nagin when she received the expected phone call from the governor, early Tuesday morning. The mayor and his communications director were on Canal Street. Post-storm, the media had parked satellite trucks, RVs, generators, and tents where normally streetcars would be running. Nagin and Forman were sitting under the big top NBC had set up, waiting for the mayor to talk live with Katie Couric. Nagin nodded an emphatic no when Forman mouthed that the governor was on the line. So Forman absorbed Blanco's fury at being accused of making a decision that cost lives. "If the mayor wants to go toe to toe, I'll go toe to toe with him," Blanco warned. The governor's voice was cracking, Forman said, and she thought Blanco might be crying (Blanco said she wasn't). Forman mimed tears and gave her boss a pleading look. He wouldn't take the phone.

The conversation ended when the connection was lost, causing Forman to utter an audible "Thank you, Jesus."

"MAN, I GOTTA GET out of Dodge." Ray Nagin made it no secret how badly he needed a break that second week after Katrina. Thousands of Guardsmen were now patrolling New Orleans, along with another twenty-two hundred soldiers from the Eighty-Second Airborne Division. The city was safe and he wanted to see his wife and kids, who had flown to Dallas the day before the storm. In the command center that the city and Entergy were still operating on the fourth floor of the Hyatt, he asked Dan Packer, Entergy's CEO, for a ride to Dallas on Entergy's corporate jet. On Thursday, September 8, ten days after the city flooded,

Nagin flew to Dallas, forcing Packer to make the trip as well given a company policy that an Entergy officer be aboard. "I was very much in need of rest and recuperation," Nagin wrote of his decision to leave New Orleans for five days after Katrina.

The mayor's time in Dallas was uneventful. His two boys, Jeremy, twenty-one, and Jarin, eighteen, were there, as was his daughter, Tianna, who was six. The mayor caught up on sleep, but otherwise they spent their days like other well-off New Orleanians needing to relocate, at least temporarily. The Nagins went to the mall to buy the mayor some new clothes. They visited potential schools for Tianna and found a town house that would serve as their temporary home base. Nagin told his wife that the family should figure on staying there for "at least the next six months."

The mayor did have city business in Dallas. Just before leaving New Orleans, Jimmy Reiss had phoned. Reiss was an important ally and Nagin's RTA chief, but he was also the one who told the *Wall Street Journal* that New Orleans would become "demographically" different after the storm or he and the other old-line families wouldn't be moving back. Now Reiss was insisting that Nagin make time to meet with him and other members of the Business Council. The mayor's being out of town made everything simpler. Dallas had an operating airport and hotels with working toilets. That Saturday, the mayor drove himself to the giant Loews Anatole Hotel just north of downtown Dallas for what he later described as "my meeting with the shadow government" of New Orleans.

RAY NAGIN WAS NINE years old in 1965 when Hurricane Betsy battered New Orleans. His family stayed in New Orleans through Betsy, he wrote, because "we just couldn't afford to leave the city for an unplanned 'vacation.'" Levee failures after Betsy caused mass flooding in the Lower Ninth and other parts of the city, but not in the Seventh Ward, where the Nagins lived.

Nagin's father worked as a bricklayer and a truck mechanic. Eventually, he'd secured a job as a garment cutter and earned extra money moonlighting as a City Hall janitor. The mayor described his mother as

a homemaker who did seamstress work to supplement the family's income. The future mayor would be born at the city's Charity Hospital in
1956. His parents named their only son Clarence, but only Nagin's wife,
Seletha, seemed to call him that. Officially, he was C. Ray Nagin, but to
most everyone he was Ray.

The Seventh Ward was a community of cottages and shotgun
houses filled with the city's barbers, waiters, and factory workers. The
Nagins were a religious family, Catholic, and Nagin was an altar boy at
the church a block from their house. That's also where Nagin attended
elementary school. He earned good grades without having to work too
hard. Mainly he focused on athletics. His curveball won him a baseball
scholarship at Tuskegee University, where Nagin earned a degree in accounting. After graduation, he bounced around in various jobs that sent
him first to Los Angeles and then to Dallas. In 1985, at age twenty-nine,
he landed a good-paying job that brought him back to New Orleans as
a controller for Cox Communications, the cable company.

Nagin flourished at Cox. Its books were in horrible shape when he
arrived, Nagin said. Somehow the franchise was losing money despite
having a monopoly and ninety thousand customers. Nagin was steadily
promoted and was soon a Cox vice president, overseeing its New Orleans operation. While at Cox, Nagin launched a live call-in show on
the community-access channel and served as cohost of this once-a-
month program that gave unhappy Cox customers a forum to complain.
There he learned the skill of talking to the general public via a television
screen—or, as he put it, "honed my skills on 'romancing the camera.'"

Bill Hines, a prominent attorney in town, recalled the night that
Nagin announced he was running for mayor. A year earlier, Hines,
who is white, helped to inaugurate what participants tended to call the
"black-white dinner": ten black business leaders and ten white had a
standing invitation to a monthly dinner that was ostensibly about improving race relations in New Orleans. At one of their regular dinners
in the fall of 2001, Hines said, "Ray Nagin clinks his glass and says, 'I
have something to tell everybody.' We ask what's that, and he says, 'I'm
going to run for mayor.' We all started laughing." If Nagin harbored any
political ambition, he had done a good job of concealing it. Even his
wife confessed bafflement over her forty-five-year-old husband's sudden

interest in local politics. "My initial reaction," Seletha Nagin wrote in an e-mail exchange with Sally Forman, "was that of shock."

Nagin made it official in December 2001, on the final day of candidate registration. Two months before election day, he was joining an already crowded field of fourteen, nearly all of them black. Polls showed him drawing less than 3 percent of the vote. He fashioned himself as a crusading outsider vowing to take the "for sale" sign off City Hall, but others were also claiming the reformer's mantle. "Had Ray Nagin started this eight months ago, it would have been very interesting," said Stan "Pampy" Barre, a local businessman and political fixer. "I gave him money. . . . [But] I just don't see this happening."

FOUNDED IN 1718, NEW ORLEANS is one of the older US metropolises. In the early nineteenth century, it was the country's third-most-populous city. Its port opened the city to a cosmopolitan assortment of characters, but it also made New Orleans the center of the slave trade. The city was home to the largest slave market in North America at the same time more free black people walked its streets than anywhere else in the Deep South. The country's largest slave revolt took place just north of New Orleans, in 1811.

A former French colony, New Orleans lived by the infamous "code noir," which spelled out the rules for slave ownership. If a slave struck his or her owner or anyone else in his master's family, the law dictated that the slave be executed. An escapee should have his or her ears cut off (and their hamstrings severed if gone for two months). But slaves in New Orleans also had the right to earn money and, during Spanish rule, they secured the right to buy their freedom. Both French and Spanish law recognized that freed slaves—"free people of color," they were called—and those who had never been enslaved had the same rights as any other colonial subject. In time, many free people of color settled the Faubourg Tremé, or simply Tremé (pronounced "truh-may"), just across Rampart Street from the French Quarter. Tremé has been described as the "oldest black neighborhood in America." Its cultural center was Congo Square, which some music historians point to as the birthplace of jazz.

The country's first black-owned daily newspaper was founded near the end of the Civil War—the *New Orleans Tribune*. This paper, begun as a bilingual broadsheet, had a mixed-race staff that sought to help shape the new, post–Civil War South. The *Tribune* called on government to divide the southern plantations and grant plots to former slaves and advocated equality under the law. Closer to home, the paper also demanded the integration of the city's streetcars, which occurred in 1867. That was during Reconstruction, when the federal government exerted its might to guarantee that newly enfranchised blacks could vote. One-fifth of the city's schools were integrated; Louisiana could even boast of the country's first black governor (the country's next would not be elected until 1990).

The federal government withdrew its troops from the South in 1877—twelve years after the Civil War ended. The schools in New Orleans resegregated. Congo Square was renamed Beauregard Square in honor of a Confederate general who had lived in New Orleans.[1] A statue of Confederate hero Robert E. Lee was erected near the bottom of St. Charles Avenue, and in 1884 Tivoli Circle was renamed Lee Circle. Taking direct aim at New Orleans, the state legislature, in 1890, passed the Separate Car Act, which reinstated segregation on public transportation.

The black population fought back. In 1892, a half century before the 1955 arrest of Rosa Parks helped to spark the modern civil rights movement, a black man from New Orleans named Homer Plessy took a seat in a train carriage reserved for whites. The resulting legal case made it to the US Supreme Court, which, in 1896, used *Plessy v. Ferguson* to establish the doctrine of separate but equal. *Plessy* remained the law for six decades, until it was overturned in 1954 by *Brown v. Board of Education*. *Plessy* was a cruel blow to all African Americans, but the loss was more deeply felt in New Orleans, where the dream of equality had seemed closer at hand. Following *Plessy*, Louisiana purged 95 percent of the state's blacks from its voter rolls, and the city stopped offering schooling past the fifth grade to black children. The Klan took hold in the area and lynchings in the city became more commonplace.

---

1. The city would officially restore the Congo Square name in 2011.

The integration of the schools—more accurately their reintegration—proved the bitterest, most hard-fought battle. In 1956, two years after *Brown v. Board of Education* and the year Ray Nagin was born, a federal judge ordered the Orleans Parish school board to adopt a blueprint for desegregating its schools. Four years later, the Orleans Parish school board finally unveiled its plan—limited to a single grade in two of the city's hundred-plus schools. The governor, an avowed segregationist named Jimmie Davis, called an emergency legislative session to forestall the implementation. The state even tried to have November 14—the date the board's plan was to take effect—declared a school holiday.

The names of the affected schools were kept secret until the morning of the fourteenth, but that just added to the spectacle. Four black girls were chosen to enter the first grade in a pair of whites-only schools in a working-class section of New Orleans. (Could anyone be surprised that the board was choosing to integrate first in the neighborhoods where the city's laborers and factory workers lived?) As news spread, white parents descended on the schools. By day's end, every white child but one had been removed from the two schools. That white girl, Pam Foreman, whose father was a minister, would complete the year at her assigned school—but in a classroom by herself.

"Don't wait for your daughter to be raped by these Congolese," Judge Leander Perez, an organizer of the Citizens' Council of Greater New Orleans, a local white-supremacist group, said at a rally held the day after the schools were integrated. "Don't wait until the burrheads are forced into your schools. Do something about it now." The *Times-Picayune* declared integration a "tragedy," and the school board president left it no secret what he believed: "As an elected official, I feel it is my duty to provide public education, if possible on a segregated basis, but, if not, on an integrated basis." He was only following the law, but people shunned him and his business.

IN RACE RELATIONS AND in other ways, New Orleans has always been a city apart from the rest of America. This port city that served as a gateway to the rest of the Americas has always had a strong Caribbean flavor. Creole culture defines New Orleans—its food, its music, its dance—and

its African traditions date to even before the Revolutionary War. Over
the centuries, control of the city shifted from the French to the Spanish
to Anglo Americans, and all of them left their imprint on the city's culture. The city was famous for an annual Mardi Gras celebration, which
stretched for weeks and featured seemingly endless parades. Black?
White? Who cared in this laid-back, good-time city where the phrase
laissez les bons temps rouler, "let the good times roll," is seen and heard so
often it might as well be the city's motto.

Yet the white community's reaction to school desegregation
showed that attitudes toward race in New Orleans were no different
from in other American cities. Seventy thousand whites fled the city
in the first ten years after school integration. Another ninety thousand
moved out during the 1970s. Those who could afford it found a place
in Jefferson Parish, west or south of the city, or they bought a home on
the other side of Lake Pontchartrain, in St. Tammany Parish. Those of
more modest means chose to start over in St. Bernard Parish, just south
and east of New Orleans, where a major thoroughfare was named in
honor of the judge warning about "burrheads" in the schools. At the
same time, tens of thousands of blacks moved into the city. In 1960,
New Orleans had a population of just over six hundred thousand people, nearly two-thirds of whom—63 percent—were white. By the time
Katrina hit, in 2005, the city's population had shrunk to under five
hundred thousand and a full two-thirds—67 percent—of its people
were black. The suburban parishes saw a corresponding explosion as
the population of the metro area remained steady. White flight re-
shaped the New Orleans metropolitan area as profoundly as any in the
United States.

In 1962, white business leaders in New Orleans pressured the
eateries on Canal Street to desegregate—a kind of preemptive strike
against the sit-ins just starting to take place in the city. In 1963, the
city's white mayor removed the WHITE and COLORED signs from the
restrooms in all city-owned buildings. In 1970, the city elected Moon
Landrieu, a white liberal, as mayor. Landrieu, who had been the only
legislator to oppose the state's attempts to thwart the integration of
the Orleans Parish public schools, captured 90 percent of the black

vote in a city then equally divided between black and white. Landrieu appointed a black man to serve as his number two and filled a vacancy on the City Council with an outspoken pastor who had called for a boycott of any store that didn't hire black clerks. Landrieu's eight years in office won him the enduring love of the city's black community and turned the Landrieu name into a curse word inside more conservative circles.

Ernest "Dutch" Morial followed Landrieu into office. Morial's life was a series of firsts: first African American to receive a law degree from LSU, first African American since Reconstruction to be elected to the Louisiana legislature, the state's first black juvenile-court judge and the first elected to an appellate-court judgeship. In 1978, Morial became the city's first black mayor by capturing 95 percent of the black vote and 20 percent support among whites. An astonishing 76 percent of the black electorate turned out to vote, as did 75 percent of the parish's registered whites. Four years later, Morial easily won reelection against a white challenger, though he received only 13 percent of the white vote the second time. A majority of the city's workforce was black by the end of Morial's second and final term (mayors in New Orleans are limited to two terms in office). Black-owned business accounted for $17,000 in contracts at the start of Morial's tenure, but $11 million by the time he left office in 1986. That figure was paltry but worrisome to all those construction barons and bond underwriters and lawyers who had for years feasted on City Hall contracts.

White New Orleans wasn't without influence. Much of the city's white populace had disappeared to the suburbs, but not its gentry— those upper-class burghers who traced their New Orleans bloodlines back at least to the nineteenth century and awaited their turn as king of Mardi Gras. They lived on St. Charles and the side streets around Audubon Park in the same sturdy, two-story manses as their ancestors. They still ate and drank at the same private clubs. "I'll give people Uptown credit," said Paul Beaulieu, the programming director for WBOK, a black-oriented talk-radio station. "Just a few blocks from these nice, stately homes you've got all these little shotgun singles and doubles. There's a lot of people of modest means in those small houses, black people, but the old-money white people stayed."[2] (A shotgun home is one without hallways, where one room leads to another.) It helped that those with enough money could send their children to private school, thereby sidestepping the integration issue.

Uptown still retained its economic clout despite the shift in majority from white to black. Its people were still the city's CEOs, top lawyers, bankers, and real estate developers. Whites controlled the business community and dominated philanthropic circles. One member of their club, Ashton Phelps Jr., owned the *Times-Picayune* (the fourth generation of his family to run the paper). They had deep reservoirs of cash and other means of political influence. If they couldn't elect one of their own, they'd elect someone willing to do their bidding.

After Morial, the white elite backed Sidney Barthelemy for mayor. Barthelemy was a black member of the City Council more moderate in both his politics and demeanor. Barthelemy was elected with 88 percent of the white vote and only 25 percent of the black vote, but disappointed his white backers by supporting the affirmative action policies of his predecessors. Two terms of Barthelemy were followed by his predecessor's eldest son, Marc Morial, who won only 7 percent of the white vote in his first run for mayor. Marc Morial, too, would serve for eight years, leaving the city in 2002 with no incumbent in the race and also no favorite for mayor.

DESPITE HIS INEXPERIENCE, NAGIN proved an appealing candidate. He had been born at the city's public hospital and was a graduate of its public schools. He lacked experience—"Like most citizens," Nagin would say when it was revealed during the campaign that he had only sporadically bothered to vote, "I was basically making the best of my

---

2. Beaulieu continued, "That's New Orleans at its best. Shotguns next to big houses, and black people next to white people, somebody making five hundred thousand dollars a year and somebody making fifty thousand dollars a year, but they're taking care of their fifty-thousand-dollar shit just like you're taking care of your five hundred. The gumbo that is New Orleans."

time while consciously ignoring the declining state of my city"—but his outsider status proved an asset in a city more than a little fed up with the drumbeat of news stories about politicians in the pockets of wealthy contributors. ("We don't tolerate corruption in Louisiana," the homegrown James Carville once quipped. "We demand it!") Nagin was a good-looking candidate whose plainspoken manner had its own charm. "Man, I think we need to sell that sucker"—that's how he had described his idea during one debate for putting the city's airport on the auction block to pay to fix the city's crumbling infrastructure.

Nagin had a few big names in his corner, including Ashton Phelps of the *Times-Picayune* and Jimmy Reiss. Yet barely a month before the election, he was already out of money and polling at an anemic 5 percent. "Ray was basically running his own campaign at that point," said his friend David White, a local black businessman who served as campaign treasurer. "There was a group of us who made all the strategic decisions, but there wasn't what you'd call a campaign manager." What began as a campaign against waste and fraud broadened into a run against the black establishment. Rather than seeking the endorsements of the existing black political organizations, Nagin openly mocked them. He came out against a living-wage ordinance and signaled his intention to eliminate the city's set-aside program for minority- and women-owned businesses.

Uptown money poured into his campaign, turning an also-ran into an unlikely front-runner. The slick, new brochures and radio and TV ads the campaign could now afford cast him as a fresh-faced, reform-minded businessman who would turn around New Orleans. The *Times-Picayune* endorsed him. ("He thinks on his feet," the paper's editorial board wrote. "He is focused and innovative.") So, too, would the *Gambit*, the city's alternative weekly. Nagin proved the top vote getter in February and then glided to victory in the runoff one month later, when an 86 percent share of the white vote was more than enough to make up for only 40 percent of the black vote.

6

LOOKING THE PART

Nagin's first summer as mayor was about spectacle. To show he was serious about snuffing out under-the-table payoffs and other forms of graft, the new mayor had initiated a sting operation. In a single day, arrest warrants were issued for eighty-four people. "The biggest crackdown on municipal corruption in the modern history of the city," the *Times-Picayune* enthused, and even the national news picked up on the story. Most of those arrested were cabdrivers who felt obliged to make payoffs to stay in business. The local district attorney dropped two-thirds of the cases, citing weak evidence. Yet Nagin was the new mayor who even had a cousin among those who had been indicted. His approval ratings soared to 80 percent.

Nagin's self-assuredness and confidence—what Jed Horne, then city editor of the *Times-Picayune*, described as the mayor's "loose-limbed affability"—served him well in his first few years of office. His communications director, Sally Forman, spoke of the shift she felt when the mayor walked into a room. Her boss, she said, would "captivate onlookers with his polished style, muscular build, and trademark shaved head." Once a month, Nagin got into a Rambo-looking black SUV he nicknamed Big

Daddy, and the two of them would tape a show on his old cable-access channel. He always looked great, Forman said, dressed in a crisp white shirt, silver cuff links, and a dark pinstripe suit.

Yet governing meant more than looking and sounding a part. Nagin's decision to make a radical break, seeking out top people who had little or no government experience to help him run City Hall, was principled, maybe even admirable. But he was also on his third chief of staff when Katrina hit, and she had been on the job for less than a month. Sally Forman, who had started as the city's chief of protocol before being promoted to communications director a year into Nagin's tenure, was one of the more seasoned members of his team.

Nagin had big ambitions for New Orleans that could be summed up by a story he repeated often when he was still a candidate. He was sitting at the kitchen table talking about the future with his two sons and a few of their friends. They all loved New Orleans—its music and food and the good-time vibe that gave the city its big-easy pace and "indolent charms," as *Newsweek* once put it. But all assumed they would need to leave New Orleans to build the career and life they had in mind for themselves. The city had fallen behind other southern cities such as Atlanta and Houston, and even Birmingham and Mobile were perceived as offering more economic opportunities. Reversing this "brain drain," the mayor would say, meant doing something about a horrifically high murder rate, the city's failing schools, and other social ills. "Someone once said a small band of revolutionaries can change the world," the mayor wrote in an early e-mail to Sally Forman. "Let's change New Orleans for the better." As usual, he signed the e-mail *MN*, for "Mayor Nagin."

"RAY NAGIN WAS A man who didn't have allies," offered Oliver Thomas, president of the City Council. Thomas was a good-natured political natural who, pundits and pollsters said, could be the next mayor. A burly, six-foot-six-inch, light-skinned black man with a lumbering gait, Thomas is a soft-spoken giant as likely to throw an arm around a shoulder as shake a hand. "We went to school together, man," Thomas said of Nagin. "We were friends before he became mayor. But he pushed me away, just like he pushed everyone away." Thomas's apparent sin was

his association with one of the black political organizations in town.
Nagin wanted to show himself above the old ways of narrow partisan-
ship and cliques. "After he became mayor, our families never got together
anymore," Thomas said.

Sally Forman was always pushing Nagin to act more like a politician.
"Give him a call," she'd say about one elected official or another. "He only
wants to hear from you." So, too, were others around the mayor, including at least one of the chief of staffs whom he had fired. You need friends
in the City Council, they'd counsel; you need friends in Baton Rouge to
get anything done. Nagin had built up considerable political capital yet
didn't know how to use it or simply refused to do so. "Let them come to
me," he'd tell people. "I'm the mayor." People nudged him to do a better
job of promoting his ideas, even when it meant sitting down with people
he didn't like or respect. He acted as if they were asking him to grovel or
act in a way that cheapened the office. Instead he'd float a proposal in the
media and hope the pundits and others saw its inherent wisdom.

Nagin felt frustrated by the racial balancing act in being a big-city
mayor in the modern era. "If I do something the white community likes,
the blacks get upset," he complained during his weekly Friday lunch with
top staffers. "And when I do something to help the black community,
the whites get upset." This "constant tug-of-war between the races," as
Nagin described it, had come up as recently as the Friday before Katrina.
The primary topic at that lunch was not the impending hurricane but
the upcoming mayor's race in February. With the election less than six
months away, no big-name opponent had yet to step forward, but Nagin
was asking his staff to help him deliver a mandate, not just a victory.
Around the table people floated ideas that would help the mayor win
more support among black voters, but others invariably pointed out how
that could alienate the mayor's white supporters. "Race, politics, and economic development had become a part of every major executive-staff decision," Sally Forman said of that last Friday gathering before the storm,
"and this day was no different."

One exasperating case that had Nagin grumbling was the death
of Levon Jones, a black college student killed on Bourbon Street nine
months earlier. On New Year's Eve 2004, Jones tried to enter a popular
Bourbon Street club. In an argument over the way Jones was dressed,

four bouncers surrounded him, and he was strangled to death. After protests by the local NAACP and other civil rights groups, Nagin responded by announcing a "secret shopper" study: the city would send white and black males of roughly the same body type and dress to the Bourbon Street clubs and see if they were treated differently. Despite signaling his intentions, 40 percent of the street's twenty-eight clubs charged black patrons more for the same drink than white customers. Some also charged blacks a higher cover charge, and a few applied different dress codes depending on the race of a customer. The bar owners should have been ashamed. Instead, they criticized the mayor for putting an unflattering spotlight on Bourbon Street.

By the final year of his four-year term, Nagin's "Relax, I've got this in hand" act was starting to grate. On the campaign trail, he'd spoken about building a new City Hall and merging departments to save money, but that turned out to be just talk, just like his idea for selling the sucker to contend with a crumbling infrastructure. "Let me percolate on that," Nagin would say—and then weeks, if not months, would pass before the mayor might be ready to make a decision. He was a CEO, Forman said, "who did not like the burden of timelines or deadlines." He had vowed to end minority set-asides but hadn't, just as he had yet to streamline the permit process or follow through on any number of campaign promises.

Nagin could point to accomplishments prior to Katrina. The city's website was good enough to win the notice of other municipalities, and the city was moving forward with a Nagin proposal to install crime cameras around the city. Yet even a straightforward promise to give the city a digital upgrade was proving far more difficult than it had looked from the outside. "The bureaucracy couldn't be reasoned with," complained Greg Meffert, the city's technology chief and eventually one of the mayor's closest aides. "It didn't care about the merits of an idea. It was this leaderless half human, half machine that kept coming. It was their way or nothing happened."

NAGIN'S RTA CHIEF, JIMMY REISS, was already fed up with Nagin. Reiss had helped to create Nagin, opening doors for him among his Uptown friends. But the crime rate was worse than it was at the start of

the Nagin administration, and the schools were in such a poor condition that the state was moving to take them over. "I didn't care if it was
someone black in that office or someone white," Reiss said. "We needed
results." Katrina only added urgency to the need for action.

The Business Council members met with Nagin that Saturday in
Dallas at a suite Reiss had reserved for them at the Anatole. By Reiss's
count, fifty-seven members had shown up. Almost everyone in the room
was white, but to Reiss that was irrelevant. "I was just looking for concerned citizens willing to give their time and their soul to help the city,"
he said. While waiting for the mayor, Reiss, a slight man with wavy gray
hair, offered a sly grin when anyone brought up the *Wall Street Journal*
article, which had been published just two days earlier. "Don't regret it
one bit," he'd offer, or "It had to be said." The mayor, dressed casually
in a pale yellow, short-sleeved pullover and dark pants, showed up with
Entergy's Dan Packer and several others.

Later, Nagin would cast Dallas as the scene of his political liber-
ation. In his telling, he let these people "intent on engineering a very
different New Orleans" talk for a few minutes and then, after drawing a
deep breath, let them know he wouldn't be doing their bidding. "Look,
I'm aware of what some of you have been saying to the national media,"
he quoted himself as saying in the memoir he wrote after leaving office.
"But if you're thinking about rebuilding the New Orleans of the 1850s,
I'm definitely not interested." Being there, he would write, was "like I
had been invited to a private, secretive meeting of the Rex and Comus
organizations."

Others there tell a different story. Bill Hines, the attorney, had
served on Nagin's eight-person transition team and was still part of
Nagin's unofficial kitchen cabinet. He sat with the mayor and remembered him saying little. Certainly he didn't offer anything like the speech
he included in his memoir. There was no talk of making New Orleans a
whiter or less poor city, Hines said, only a lot of dry talk of the best way
to dewater the city, fix the infrastructure, and rebuild the city's battered
business community. Dan Packer also didn't recall any speeches. "I remember the mayor sitting and listening a lot," Packer says.

Jimmy Reiss also remembered the mayor saying little—and being
quite perturbed by it. An investment banker friend of his asked, "Mr.

Mayor, what recovery plan do you have for us?" Reiss and others in Dallas that day quote Nagin as responding, "I don't have a plan." The investment banker asked more gently, "Then what resources do you have to call upon to help us draw up a plan?" An expressionless Nagin offered a single-word response: "Nil."

They were still meeting when the mayor excused himself to take a call. Joe Canizaro, a wealthy white real estate developer and financial supporter of Nagin's, was on the line. Canizaro lived in Old Metairie, a leafy suburb just over the city line. Canizaro was a personal friend of the president's and had been in regular contact with Karl Rove since shortly after the storm. "Now take this down, Mr. Mayor," Canizaro said in his gravelly voice. Cradling the receiver in one ear, Nagin pulled pen and paper from his pocket. Canizaro repeated the words Rove had shared with him: "Tell your mayor not to give us a list of everything he's ever wanted. Let's focus on getting government back and operating." Rove had also stressed the need for a blue-ribbon panel of businesspeople and other community leaders—a group who could vouch for a rebuilding plan before the federal government committed to spending the tens of billions of dollars New Orleans would no doubt be requesting.

Jimmy Reiss lobbied for a similar commission when he and the mayor spoke after the meeting. It didn't need to be just businesspeople, Reiss counseled. Add people like Scott Cowen, the president of Tulane, and maybe a couple of religious leaders. The mayor seemed receptive, but then Reiss was frustrated that one week passed, and then a second, without any announcement from the mayor's office.

THE CITY HAD A visitor while Nagin was still in Dallas. Ten days after Katrina, Vice President Dick Cheney arrived for his first look at New Orleans. With the mayor out of town, it fell to Greg Meffert, the city's chief technology officer, to greet the vice president. "A portly techie with blazing blue eyes hidden behind blowing bangs," Sally Forman said when summing up Meffert, a "left-brain genius" with a "garbled delivery" that made her and the mayor nervous. But with the mayor away and his chief of staff and other top aides in Baton Rouge, Meffert was also the highest-ranking city employee in New Orleans.

Meffert greeted Cheney at Harrah's, where NOPD had set up temporary quarters. "Mr. Vice President, I'm Greg Meffert, the senior on the ground, welcoming you to New Orleans."

The vice president was dressed casually in a blue dress shirt and tan slacks. Meffert, by contrast, was wearing whatever he'd found on the floor. He was still at the Hyatt and had not showered or shaved since the storm.

"Where the hell did you come from?" were the first words out of the vice president's mouth, Meffert said. "And then the next thing he says is something about the way I smelled." Meffert can't remember the vice president's exact words, but he's certain of what he said next: "Fuck. You."

He left the vice president to find his own way while he was in town.

7

CASSANDRA

The people of New Orleans had plenty to complain about. They made that much clear to the eminent geographer Peirce F. Lewis when he arrived in New Orleans in the early 1970s. A major port city at the "entrance to the richest valley on earth" may have been inevitable, Lewis wrote in his seminal book, *New Orleans: The Making of an Urban Landscape*, published in 1976, but it also required its residents to live in a subtropical city surrounded by swampland. The summers were brutal, the mosquitoes were omnipresent, and the streets flooded after even a moderate rain. Hurricane season lasted six months each year. Yet the people Lewis met couldn't imagine living anywhere else. Their native town was the Big Easy, a beguiling city home to costumed parades, brass bands marching through the streets, and jambalaya. New Orleans, Lewis found, was a city that didn't work at selling itself because it didn't seem to dawn on locals that someone might prefer to live somewhere else.

Lewis taught geography at Penn State, more than a thousand miles away. But he had shown up in New Orleans because he felt he had no choice. There was little geographical scholarship about New Orleans, yet could there be a more fascinating city in the United States? Or one more preposterous from a geographer's point of view? "The Mississippi River demands a city at its mouth," Lewis offered, "but fails to provide any place for one." New Orleans is a "transplanted Mediterranean city," he wrote in his book, but he also described it as the globe's northernmost Latin American one. Sugarcane grows in the area along with banana plants and bougainvillea, and at least until the advent of air-conditioning, people sensibly took midday siestas. The United States had annexed New Orleans nearly two centuries earlier as part of the Louisiana Purchase of 1803, but in many ways it was still a foreign land. In New Orleans, a county is called a *parish*, the median bisecting a boulevard is the *neutral ground*, and (like the rest of Louisiana) the legal system is based on the Napoleonic Code. Its libertine spirit set it apart, as did its celebration of both the sacred and the profane in a stretch of the United States sometimes called the Bible Belt.

Like others before and after him, Lewis labeled New Orleans the country's most "eccentric city." But unlike his counterparts, he did not fixate on the city's voodoo priestesses or drag queens or the Mardi Gras Indians—the legions of black men in New Orleans who devote an inordinate amount of their spare time stitching together feathers into intricate costumes they'll wear only a few times. Instead, Lewis found the city's eccentricities in the Garden District's "flamboyant mansions," the cast iron and pastels of the French Quarter, even people's accents, which he heard as more Brooklyn than Vicksburg.

Technology is the villain in Lewis's book. Through most of its first two hundred years, the citizenry of New Orleans harbored a healthy fear of floods. Most of the population confined themselves to the high ground and avoided parts of the city that lay below sea level. Then, early in the twentieth century, a local engineer named A. Baldwin Wood invented a pump powerful and reliable enough to drain the swamplands and keep them dry even after a heavy rain. Land once off-limits was now open to settlement. "Just as high speed elevators changed the geography of New York City by making skyscrapers possible," Lewis wrote, "the Wood pump revolutionized the urban geography of New Orleans."

The large tracts of marshy land that sat between the central business district and Lake Pontchartrain to the north were the first parts of the city to experience a metamorphosis. Wood's invention allowed speculators to develop Lakeview in the 1910s, among other communities there. That part of the city was off-limits to black home buyers, but the Wood pump was also used to drain the back-a-town swamps (those downriver from the French Quarter) to expand the Lower Ninth Ward, among other communities. The Wood pump allowed New Orleanians to spread out and also cut themselves off from one another. Technology, Lewis found, accelerated racial segregation rather than slowed it down.

The Wood pump made New Orleans East possible, but first came the interstate, which did nearly as much to reshape the geography of New Orleans. It would have been unthinkable to build an elevated highway above St. Charles Avenue or Magazine Street. Yet that's what happened on the other side of town in the 1960s, when city fathers mapped the I-10 through the center of Tremé. "A white man's highway through the black man's bedroom," said one critic on the losing end of that fight. The interstate was built directly over Claiborne Avenue, the commercial center of black New Orleans. In its day, Claiborne was a handsome boulevard of large oak trees, lined with businesses, most of them black owned. By the time of Katrina, it was a strip of vacant storefronts under a thick slab of elevated concrete thrumming with traffic. Lewis judged it as nothing short of "murder."

Lewis was still researching his book when billboards sprang up on the I-10 advertising the newly christened New Orleans East. Speculators were homesteading large stretches of cypress swamp on either side of the interstate just past the new High Rise Bridge that carried people over the Industrial Canal, heading east toward the Gulf Coast. The pitch was simple: a small patch of suburban paradise inside the city limits and only a twenty-minute drive from downtown. Yet the geographer read in horror the promotional materials used to sell this large swath sandwiched between two giant bodies of water—Lake Borgne and Lake Pontchartrain. On twenty square miles of spongy, low-lying, flood-prone land, developers imagined a community of 250,000 people. Advertisements played up the golf courses and nearby marinas "but remain strangely quiet about hurricanes," Lewis wrote. The East had been inundated with water after Hurricane Betsy in 1965. It had flooded again four years later after Hurricane Camille. Yet both those storms had supposedly delivered only glancing blows to the city.

Coastal erosion added to Lewis's worries about a city he judged as having "deficient land controls." The marshy wetlands of the Louisiana coast were a natural buffer against storm surge—the tidal wave of water that accompanies a strong hurricane.[1] Yet the wetlands were disappearing at a rate of twenty-five to thirty square miles per year. The US Army Corps of Engineers was partly to blame, starting with the choices it had made decades earlier when it first designed the area's flood-protection system. The same levee system that protects New Orleans from the Mississippi River also prevents the wetlands from replenishing themselves. The sediment the river would otherwise be depositing at the mouth of the Mississippi was now ending up on the bottom of the Gulf of Mexico. The Corps also built the MR. GO shipping channel, which caused more deterioration. Another culprit were the navigation lanes the oil and gas interests carved through coastal Louisiana to construct pipelines and move their heavy machinery to and from the area. These man-made canals caused salt water from the Gulf of Mexico to spill into the freshwater wetlands, killing freshwater plants that held the soil in place, causing more erosion. No longer were a hurricane's high winds the greatest threat, Lewis concluded, but the "murderous tidal wave" that one of these blasts off the Gulf Coast could provoke.

When Lewis returned to New Orleans in the early 2000s to work on a sequel to *New Orleans*, he was disheartened. Everywhere he looked, the geographer saw a long list of afflictions: crime, declining schools, a "grinding poverty, especially among black citizens." He found a city even more segregated and more intolerant than when he'd left it. "As in most other big American cities," Lewis wrote, "New Orleans's main malady is racial."

Yet physical threats to the city were the ones that most alarmed Lewis. He had left New Orleans in the mid-1970s hoping that more rational voices would defeat what he called the "unrestrained greed by land sellers and house builders," but by the start of the new century,

---

1. A common rule of thumb among environmental engineers holds that a surge will lose at least one foot of its height for every three miles of marshland it encounters.

nearly a hundred thousand people lived in New Orleans East. To drive home his point about the vulnerability of those living in the East and other low-lying areas, he cited an article appearing in *Scientific American* near the end of 2001, "Drowning New Orleans." "New Orleans is a disaster waiting to happen," its author, Mark Fischetti, wrote. "If a big slow-moving hurricane crossed the Gulf of Mexico on the right track, it would drown New Orleans under 20 feet of water."

MIDDLE-CLASS WHITES WERE THE first to settle into the early sub-divisions being built in New Orleans East. A couple could purchase a four-bedroom, three-bath home with a nice expanse of backyard for less than half of what it would cost Uptown. Lakeview was closer to the center of town, but the homes there were more expensive and generally smaller.

Inevitably, blacks with money visited those model homes develop-ers had built for prospective home buyers. The passage of fair-housing laws in the 1960s reduced aggressive discrimination, and mortgages—in part because of Liberty and the two small black-owned competitors that followed—were becoming easier for African Americans to se-cure. "Black people were testing the rules, testing the market," Alden McDonald said. "First it'd be one house in a community, then a sec-ond, then a third." The McDonalds moved to New Orleans East right after they were married, in 1974.

New Orleans East in the late 1970s was a kind of racial nirvana. There the middle class and upper-middle class, black and white, lived side by side and seemed to want more or less the same thing. "It was like suburbia on steroids," said Beverly McKenna, a black woman who moved to a subdivision called Lake Willow Estates in 1977. "You could fish in the lake. There was a beautiful shopping center. Everyone not black. Everyone not white. Life." A graduate of Indiana University, McKenna had taught high school English before quitting to raise a family. Her hus-band, Dwight, was a surgeon. Their neighbors, whatever their race, were lawyers and accountants and junior executives commuting each morning to a downtown office tower. "That's what makes me so sad and angry," McKenna said. "It was such a beautiful little community."

McKenna and her husband started noticing the FOR SALE signs shortly after they moved in. The tipping point, McKenna eventually figured out, was when nearly as many black families lived in a subdivision as white ones. Alden McDonald called it a "round two of white flight"—the transformation of New Orleans East into an almost all-black community.

"We were people moving in who had as much money as they did," said McKenna, who within the decade would revive the *New Orleans Tribune* as a monthly newspaper. "We were as well educated. We spoke the same English. We drove the same cars. But these people were moving because of us." She thought of a neighbor, a white man, who lived in a large, white antebellum home that made McKenna, a northerner, think of a southern plantation. A good-natured man, he stayed longer than most, but that only meant she had more time to eye him mistrustfully. "I barely said hello to him," McKenna said. "It was a defense mechanism. I didn't feel very welcome and so I wasn't very welcoming myself."

Yet a new and more modern New Orleans was the animating idea that gave life to the East, not integration. The area was "still a magnet for strivers and achievers," according to J. B. Borders, who after Katrina wrote a long feature about the East for the *New Orleans Tribune*. "The outlines of an Afropolitan utopia could be glimpsed." There was an ice-skating rink where Beverly McKenna and the other moms would bring their children. There were upscale restaurants and "whatever you wanted to buy, you could find out in the East," McKenna said. The former teacher praised the local schools. The city's successful black entrepreneurs and some of its ballplayers and even a televangelist moved into Eastover, a gated community of McMansions boasting its own golf course. Meanwhile, the city's postal workers and clerks and truck drivers bought in Little Woods and Pines Village, where the homes tended to be small, tidy cottages. They were the children of the hotel and restaurant workers who made the city run, the offspring of its elevator operators and custodians. The East, Alden McDonald said, meant that for "the first time in New Orleans history, the African-American community had seen significant wealth creation that they could hand down to the next generation."

Yet other changes came to the neighborhood once its population shifted from white to black. Landlords who once only rented to aspiring young professionals were now happy to accept the government's Section 8 vouchers and house lower-income residents. Eventually so many poor people were living in the apartment buildings along the service roads and main arteries that, at the time of Katrina, according to one community group, 40 percent of the city's government-subsidized housing was located in New Orleans East. The retail face of the community also changed. Pawnbrokers and check cashers and payday lenders opened storefronts at the bottom of the off-ramps. So, too, did Dollar General, Family Dollar, and the Dollar Tree. The East had a Maison Blanche and a D. H. Holmes, two of the area's frillier department stores, but both shut their doors. A Sears closed down, and so, too, did a Dillard's. Lake Forest Plaza was open when Katrina hit but was already dying before it was drowned under eight feet of water.

McDonald was part of a group that organized to fight for the East in the early 2000s. On Wednesday nights, people would meet in a conference room at Liberty Bank, trying out their ideas for bringing higher-quality restaurants, better stores, and amenities to the East. Liberty funded a study to document the great sums of discretionary income sloshing around New Orleans East. A second one showed how the East had become a dumping ground for the city's problems. McDonald, who often pitched the businesses they were trying to lure to the East, had even put up some of his own money to open a twelve-screen movie theater on the site of the old Sears parking lot. The city put up several million dollars in federal redevelopment money as well in what McDonald characterized as a "risky venture" to prove that New Orleans East was a community worth investing in. "We were very close to getting some national restaurants out here," McDonald said. "We were getting close on some big retail. And then Katrina hit."

CASSANDRA WALL WAS AS shocked as anyone else that she bought in New Orleans East. Wall had always seen herself as an Uptown girl even if technically she grew up in Central City, on the woolly fringes of the Garden District. Central City suggested black and low income, but though there was no denying her skin color, she had not grown up poor.

Her father was a contractor who made good money buying and restoring dilapidated properties, her mother an English teacher who taught all her girls to enunciate and drilled them in good grammar. Wall grew up a few blocks from St. Charles and attended the Xavier University Preparatory School, a fancy Catholic girls' high school on Magazine Street. Even the grand, two-story Victorian home they grew up in set the Walls apart from most of their Central City neighbors. This 150-year-old jewel had been restored by their father, who had kept the original chandeliers, the flocked wallpaper, and the crown moldings. Like any good Uptown family, they ate on china and drank from crystal during formal meals.

"I've always appreciated the finer things in life," Cassandra said. "We're all that way." Yet she was a public school teacher who earned extra money teaching composition and literature at Xavier and the University of New Orleans. She had married a hospital technician. The finer things in life would mean a two-story, three-bedroom, two-bath home in New Orleans East for under $200,000.

Cassandra Wall was the oldest of four girls—or five if you included her cousin Robyn Braggs, whom they all referred to as a fifth sister. Growing up, Cassandra was the child in the corner reading a book, the rule-follower who never got into trouble. All the girls heard it growing up: Why can't you be more like Cassandra?

"The perfect pill," cousin Robyn said of Cassandra.

Cassandra attended Xavier University, a ten-minute drive from their house, and then moved West when offered a fellowship to the University of Oregon. There she earned a master's in English literature and secured teaching jobs at Portland State and a local community college. Cassandra moved back to New Orleans in the 1980s after an eight-year stint on the West Coast that included a first marriage that ended in divorce.

Cassandra's sister Tangeyon—Tangee—was the first Wall sister to move to New Orleans East. In 1982 Tangee and her then husband, both still in their twenties, bought a three-bedroom, two-bath, in Little Woods. A decade later, they traded up to Eastover—a gated community where for $400,000 or $500,000 you could buy the same-size house that would cost $2 million Uptown. The black aristocracy lived in Eastover.

Cassandra followed Tangee to the East in 1990. She lived briefly in a three-bedroom, two-bath house she bought for $65,000 before re-marrying and moving to Tamaron Estates, a more upscale subdivision that ranked somewhere between Little Woods and Eastover econom-ically. Her youngest sister, Talmadge, whom they called Petie, followed her sisters when a year later she and her husband bought a home near Cassandra's. The final Wall sister, Contesse, bought in the East a year after that. Robyn followed a few years later when she bought around the corner from Petie.

Petie, the baby, was more of a party girl. "She could've excelled if she pushed herself a little harder," Cassandra tsk-tsked. The sisters had the usual assortment of resentments, tensions, and buried feelings that form among any group of siblings. The others loved Contesse, but she could also be exhausting. "It's always been Contesse against the world," Petie said. Tangee, the second born, had always been the intrepid one. She was the leader who had the others following her even when they were small. That was also the role Contesse sought for herself. "Contesse wants to be in charge," Robyn said. Corrected Petie, "She *thinks* she's in charge."

Yet it would be challenging to find a group of five women any closer or more similar in their likes and habits. New Orleans East stretched along a half dozen highway exits, yet the five sisters all chose homes off the same one. None lived more than a few minutes' drive from the others. All of them lived what Petie called "the Big Easy lifestyle: if you have the money, you spend it and enjoy it." You saw it in the $400 shoes they sometimes bought or the cars they drove ("We only act like we're rich," said Robyn). Sunday nights meant dinner back in Central City, where their mother always used the good china and the heavy silver-ware. They had their standing Thursday-night dinners, and after Cas-sandra remarried, Petie's three kids had a younger cousin. Almost every day, or so it seemed, some combination of them were coming together. The husbands got along, and the sisters and their cousin also had en-tanglements through a variety of partnerships they'd formed. Cassandra helped Tangee with an art business she ran on the side, which required the occasional trip to Europe together. Petie illustrated a children's book Contesse wrote and self-published through a company she named Four Walls of Success. And it seemed practically every week that at least several of them would get together for one of their epic shopping expeditions. "That's when we really had fun," Petie said.

CASSANDRA DIDN'T WANT TO leave ahead of Katrina. None of the sisters did. They spent Saturday evening phoning one another, each at home watching the storm coverage and hoping for consensus. "We're leaving," "We're staying"—they changed their minds all night. The old maps of New Orleans described the area as "cypress swamp," but it had never come up that they lived at least several feet below sea level. They decided to leave only after Nagin on Sunday morning declared the city's first-ever mandatory evacuation order. "I'm thinking, Wait, this is unprecedented? I'm outta here," Robyn said. They broke into two groups. Cassandra, Tangee, and Contesse formed one caravan, Robyn and Petie another. They would head west and north and reconnoiter in Baton Rouge.

Petie had been the last holdout. She had a two-year-old Doberman in heat and a pit bull puppy she was training. Her husband, who worked on a ship that ran supplies to the oil rigs, was at sea and motoring toward safe waters. "You all can take Garrett," Petie said of her son, then fifteen years old. "I need to stay." The sisters took turns calling to talk sense to Petie while Robyn stuffed the backseat of her Honda with half her closet. "You're packing all this stupid stuff," Petie told her. Petie eventually relented but then only brought a nightgown, a single pair of pants, a couple of shirts, the sandals she had on, and, inexplicably, a pair of ridiculously impractical and expensive beaded shoes she had just bought. Robyn had been hoping to hit the road by 1:00 p.m. but punctuality isn't a Wall trait. It would be closer to 4:00 p.m. when Robyn pulled from the curb, followed by Petie, her son, a dog in heat, and a puppy in a Toyota 4Runner. Facing terrible traffic, they tried to take a shortcut that had them, six hours later, stopping for the night on the outskirts of Jackson, Mississippi, hundreds of miles from where they were supposed to be.

The other three sisters left New Orleans at around 1:00 p.m. yet didn't reach the outskirts of Baton Rouge, seventy miles away, until 10:00 p.m. It was a little past midnight when the group of them arrived to take the last two empty rooms in a charmless Microtel at the crossroads of the city's two busiest highways. Eventually, they'd take up almost an entire floor as Petie and Robyn joined them later in the week, along with their mother and stray members of their extended family. For at least a few of them, the Microtel would be home for more than six months.

THEY STARED BLEARY-EYED AT CNN. Those first few days were an enervating drone of anchors, a miasma caused by the same few images playing in an endless loop. They didn't dare turn off the TV out of fear of missing something. With the rest of the country they learned that Uptown (and their mother's home) had largely been spared, and also the Quarter and the central business district. They learned that big sections of the Lower Ninth Ward had been destroyed and that Lakeview was covered by water. Eventually they started turning channels, but not once did any of them hear a newscaster mention New Orleans East. A well-off black community did not fit television's narrative about poor blacks and well-off whites. They constituted one-fifth of the city's population, Tangee said, "but it was as if our community didn't exist."

The sisters ran into neighbors they knew or at least recognized at the Walgreens and at the Walmart buying cheap clothes. "You hear anything?" they'd ask, but no one knew anything. A couple of the sisters even ran into their state legislator while visiting the mall. "She had the same weird look on her face that we all did," Robyn said. All they had were rumors of government plans to bulldoze the East and a plot by the government to seize people's land to build a new airport. "There was even talk of entire subdivisions sinking back into the swamp," Contesse said.

Ten days after Katrina, Tangee and Robyn ran into a neighbor named Mack Slan at the Shoney's near their hotel. Slan was eating breakfast with his wife and mother. The group of them were having the same conversation nodding acquaintances were having in Baton Rouge and all over the country until one of them brought up the idea of organizing a meeting. Slan knew a local Baptist minister, who agreed to let them hold a meeting in his church's community center. "Are You from New Orleans East?" read the handwritten flyer they posted at every Days Inn, La Quinta, and Super 8 they came across driving the area's highways.

People were invited to show up that coming Monday, September 19—three weeks after the storm—at the True Light Baptist Church.

The first meeting was "more like a reunion," Tangee said. At least seven hundred people, the sisters and Slan agree, showed up at a gathering marked by a lot of hugging and crying. Hundreds more showed up the following Monday, when Tangee surprised even herself by proposing that they defy the blockade keeping New Orleans East off-limits even to residents. "Tangee would shut down the I-10 if she thought it would bring attention to our issues," Mack Slan said. "She was always ready to rumble. Cassandra, too—though she'd show up wearing high heels."

The next day, a convoy of more than seventy cars, many of them luxury sedans with a new-car sparkle, took off in the early-morning hours from a Lowe's parking lot just south of Baton Rouge. "As a group, we decided that it was our constitutional right, that there was no law in the land that could prevent us from seeing our homes," Tangee said. In the end, they'd get an escort into the city from a police commander.

8

HE SAID, SHE SAID

Ray Nagin had coffee with Minister Louis Farrakhan, the controversial leader of the Nation of Islam, his last morning in Dallas. The two had first met a few months earlier, when Farrakhan was in town to give a series of talks. Nagin had sought out Farrakhan. Nagin had attended the Million Man March in Washington, DC, ten years earlier, in 1995, and had been surprised that he felt as moved as he did when all those black men stood together on the Mall and recited, in unison, their commitment to improving "myself, my family, and my people." Nagin remembered the experience when he saw on one of the city's intel sheets that Farrakhan was coming to New Orleans. He had enjoyed their first meeting and was pleased when he heard the peripatetic minister's voice on his BlackBerry. They met at the Dallas airport before Nagin flew home to New Orleans.

Nagin had been monosyllabic with Jimmy Reiss and friends that Saturday. With Farrakhan on Monday morning, Nagin spoke as an intimate. Farrakhan, Nagin said, was keen to hear about how the levees had

been breached. They had been dynamited before[1]—was there any wonder some in the black community suspected it had happened again? "Did
they bomb the levees?" Farrakhan asked Nagin. Rather than offer an emphatic no, Nagin repeated the official story as he had heard it: the loud,
explosive noise people had heard in the Ninth Ward was most likely the
sound of water, mud, and debris roaring through the community and
demolishing homes. "We've yet to see any evidence to the contrary," the
mayor said carefully.

The two spoke for about an hour. Their meeting ended with Farrakhan offering a friendly warning. You're now a high-profile black man
in America, he said, and therefore a target. "Be very careful," the minister
advised, adding, *"Salaam alaikum"*—"peace be unto you" in Arabic. *"Salaam alaikum,"* Nagin repeated, adding a "sir."

That night the mayor ate dinner with George Bush.

NAGIN NEVER CALLED KATHLEEN BLANCO back. Blanco only learned
the mayor was in Dallas because her people were picking up chatter
about a big, invite-only meeting there. "Five days with my family at that
point would have been nice," she said.

The two would see one another face-to-face if the president or
some other notable was in town and protocol demanded that the
mayor and the governor both be there. But otherwise there was little
direct contact. "It wasn't just me," Blanco said. "He stayed holed up
in that hotel room, scared to death . . . having no idea what to do."
Through intermediaries, she offered a helicopter to bring him to the
state capital. She passed word that she was in New Orleans a few times
a week, helping to oversee the state's part of the disaster recovery. "If
he had gotten himself into Baton Rouge," Blanco said, "if he would
just agree to meet with me." Eventually, Blanco hosted a lunch for
Nagin at the executive mansion, but that meeting had been arranged

---

1. In 1927, the bankers and businessmen running New Orleans conspired to blow
   up the levees south of the city to relieve pressure on the levees protecting the city.
   The decision left thousands of downriver citizens homeless.

by their respective communication directors for the television cameras and photographers.

"It hampered their recovery," Blanco said. "It meant everything took longer." And it also harmed the reputation of a governor for whom New Orleans's fate was also largely her own.

IN A DIFFERENT WORLD, Blanco might be seen as a kind of superwoman. She alone had taken Katrina seriously among top leadership in the Gulf Coast. That Thursday, Blanco was supposed to be in Atlanta for a meeting of the Southern Governors' Association. Though she was slated to be sworn in as the group's chairwoman, she canceled the trip to stay closer to home. By Friday night, Blanco had declared a state of emergency. That was a day ahead of both Nagin, who was worried about the impact of a mandatory evacuation on the city's tourist trade, and Haley Barbour, the governor of Mississippi, where an estimated three hundred people died in the storm and thousands were left homeless. It was two days ahead of Bush.

The president mentioned Iraq eight times in his weekly radio address that Saturday but did not bring up Katrina. The National Hurricane Center was doing its job by warning emergency-response directors across the region about the monstrous Category 4 or 5 storm bearing down on New Orleans, yet in Washington, a FEMA supervisor with twenty-five years' experience bemoaned a lack of urgency inside the agency's Washington headquarters. "They weren't ordering buses for [an] evacuation," he would tell a pair of reporters from the *Wall Street Journal*. "They weren't . . . into the fray as FEMA has the power to do." Nagin spent much of Saturday—five hours—on the set of *Labou*, a kids' film being shot on location in New Orleans.[2] Afterward, he had dinner in Lakeview with his wife and daughter.

Blanco, in contrast, was counting down the hours to a massive storm. On Saturday, she put both her staff and the Louisiana National Guard on alert and set herself up in the state's Emergency Operations Center.

---

2. Nagin was there as an actor, to play the part of a corrupt mayor.

Concerned that the storm wasn't being taken seriously enough in New Orleans, she pestered Nagin and instructed her people to enlist the help of any legislator representing a New Orleans district. Her staff also pushed some of the city's better-known ministers to encourage people to evacuate during their Sunday-morning sermons. On Sunday, George Bush reached Blanco on her cell phone to tell her that New Orleans needed to be under a mandatory evacuation order. She told the president he had reached her at a press conference in the city where Nagin was doing just that.

Blanco had grown up with hurricanes in Cajun country in the southwestern corner of the state. Born Kathleen Babineaux, she was from Grand Coteau, Louisiana, a tiny hamlet where French was still the primary language. Her grandfather owned the area's country store, and her father sold and cleaned carpets. She grew up hunting (in her run for governor, her campaign would release photos of her dressed in camouflage and holding a rifle to burnish her bona fides among rural voters) and attended an all-girls Catholic school that included group prayer several times a day. When she earned a degree in business education from the University of Southwestern Louisiana in Lafayette, she became the first Babineaux to earn a four-year degree.

Raymond Blanco was the head coach of her brother's high school football team. In 1961 when they first started dating, she was nineteen and Raymond twenty-six. He showed up three hours late for their first date, but she recognized that he had a big heart so there was a second. "He was everybody's caretaker," she said. He had gotten a job as defensive coordinator for the University of Southwestern Louisiana football team by the time he proposed with a $500 engagement ring he could buy only because he had gotten hot playing blackjack at an illegal casino along the highway. The newly married Kathleen Blanco took a job teaching high school, but that lasted less than a year. She was pregnant and the rule was that a public school teacher couldn't be showing in the classroom. She would remain a stay-at-home mom for the next dozen years, raising six children. The family finances improved when, in 1969, to help quell campus unrest, Raymond became the university's dean of students. To earn extra money, Raymond, whom everyone still called Coach, did political commentaries for a local Lafayette television station and worked as an adviser on political campaigns.

The governor-to-be first got involved in politics in the early 1970s, when the couple still had kids in diapers. At first it was short commitments, such as the time she volunteered to work on Jimmy Carter's 1976 presidential run, but by her late thirties, she was working as regional deputy director for the US Census Bureau. When the incumbent state representative announced his retirement in 1984, Blanco, with Coach's encouragement, started passing out candidate petitions. She won, and at the age of forty-one, Kathleen Babineaux Blanco (the maiden name was added to remind locals of her Cajun roots) was representing Louisiana's Forty-Fifth District in Baton Rouge. Four years later, she won a seat on Louisiana's powerful Public Service Commission, the first female commissioner atop this statewide agency that oversees everything from utility and garbage-collection rates to towing outfits and bus companies. She was still halfway through her six-year term when she announced her intent to run for governor, but then suspended her campaign three months later. She wasn't ready, she declared. Four years later, in 1995, she was elected to serve the first of two terms as lieutenant governor. She'd take over as governor after a close election against Piyush "Bobby" Jindal in 2003.

Jindal was practically half Blanco's age when the two faced off. A Rhodes Scholar, he had been only twenty-four years old when the Republican governor picked him to head the state's health and hospitals department. By twenty-eight, he had been appointed president of the Louisiana university system, and at twenty-nine Bush nominated him to be an assistant secretary of health and human services. With Karl Rove's blessings, Jindal resigned his post in the Bush administration in early 2003 to return to Louisiana to do his part to hold the governor's mansion for the Republicans in November. He was thirty-two years old.

Blanco was a politician easy to underestimate. She is short, thickset, and soft-spoken. But she was also politically shrewd and used Coach to pass along her threats. Winning wouldn't be easy in a state that leaned conservative. Jindal's dark skin might hurt in some of the state's more conservative precincts, but then so would her gender. It would be a close election—and winning meant everything had to go right in New Orleans, where she would need a big turnout to win.

Nagin was a "lifelong Democrat," or so he described himself. And

Blanco was not just a Democrat but a fellow centrist representing the same moderate, pro-business wing of the party. She had cast herself as the good-government reformer who would disinfect the statehouse much as Nagin had done when seeking to take over City Hall. Blanco was calling for universal pre-K across the state, which would only help a parish whose public schools were 94 percent black and failing a frighteningly high percentage of its students. Another of her campaign pledges was to beef up funding for public hospitals and clinics around the state after Jindal had slashed budgets as secretary of the state's health department. Yet rather than endorse his fellow Democrat, Nagin asked both her and Jindal to write why they thought they deserved his support. Jindal responded within forty-eight hours with what Nagin described as "an elaborate, well-thought-out response." Two weeks passed before Blanco sent him a two-paragraph letter that stressed their shared party affiliation.

Nagin phoned Blanco just before the press conference he held to endorse Jindal. He described Blanco as "ranting and raving" and quoted her as telling him, "You're making a big mistake and there will be hell to pay." (She said she was angry but made no threats.)

The endorsement ended up meaning next to nothing. Nagin had no organization to help Jindal produce votes. Blanco won with 52 percent of the vote in no small part because she trounced Jindal in New Orleans. She was sworn in as governor in January of 2004, which gave the state's new chief executive and the mayor of Louisiana's largest city another twenty months to dislike one another before Katrina hit.

FOR THE WHITE HOUSE, a bad week turned into two. Bush was supposed to be the compassionate conservative who was several notches more progressive on race than the typical Republican. As president he had given the country its first African-American secretary of state in Colin Powell and its second with Condoleezza Rice. Yet following Katrina, commentators spoke of a president who had said no every time he was invited to address the NAACP and were dissecting a record on race that left many blacks wishing for a Republican more like his father. "George Bush doesn't care about black people," the rapper Kanye West said on network television during a hurricane-relief telethon held on the Friday after Katrina, while people were still stranded in New Orleans. Even the president's mother caused him headaches during a photo op at the Houston Astrodome. There, where thousands of rescued New Orleanians were living temporarily, Barbara Bush said of a crowd who had lost their homes, possessions, and perhaps even a loved one or two, "So many of the people in the arena here were, you know, underprivileged anyway. So this is working out for them."

Polls revealed that the White House had a problem. Maybe it was no surprise that 85 percent of black respondents said the administration could have done more to help the relief efforts, but 63 percent of white respondents in a Pew poll agreed. Fidel Castro had volunteered to send fifteen hundred doctors and twenty-six tons of medicine to New Orleans. Russia offered four planes stocked with food, medicine, and rescue equipment. Around the globe, people were questioning the administration's basic competency given the bad news out of Iraq and Afghanistan. Now, the United States of America, the most powerful nation on earth, the lone remaining superpower and the first country a foreign leader might call if in need, was the globe's biggest charity case. It would fall to Karl Rove, the political mastermind whom some insiders dubbed "Bush's brain," and Dan Bartlett, the White House communications director, to devise a strategy that would contain the damage and perhaps rescue the remainder of the president's second term.

That first weekend after Katrina, Rove and Bartlett established a war room inside the White House. Coached emissaries were offered to all the Sunday news shows, and the pair devised a schedule that had cabinet secretaries showing up regularly on the Gulf Coast. The administration's commitment to the people of the region would be punctuated by frequent visits by the president. Over the weekend, Rove and Bartlett assembled top congressional Republicans to work on talking points. One attendee told the *New York Times* that Rove admonished them not to take the bait from Democrats. This is no time to play the "blame game," they were told to say, when a great American city was facing ruin.

The administration dumped Michael Brown while Nagin was still in Dallas. One week after the "heckuva job, Brownie" pat on the back, the FEMA director was summoned to Washington and stripped of responsibility for the Katrina-relief efforts. In his place the president appointed Vice Admiral Thad Allen, the Coast Guard's chief of staff. Three days later, Brown resigned.[3] Bush's job approval stood barely at 40 percent—and seemed in free fall. (Gallup found that Bush's approval rating was down to 25 percent in October 2008, a few months before the end of his second term.) "It was the darkest period of the presidency for those of us in the White House," Dan Bartlett said.

Was it any wonder with a president sinking in the polls that Republican operatives were whispering in the ears of reporters, pundits, and other parts of the chattering class that if you wanted to know who was to blame for this mess, you should take a good look at this woman Rove described "as simply not up to the challenge." Kathleen Blanco had beaten a good man, Bobby Jindal, for governor. Let her share in the misery of a PR disaster that was big enough for more than a single politician to be at fault.

BLANCO MADE HER MISTAKES after the flooding. On the Monday Katrina hit New Orleans, FEMA hosted a noontime videoconference for officials who were part of the rescue efforts. By that time, Blanco's chief counsel had told her about the collapse of part of the Seventeenth Street Canal levee, yet she dismissed it as an "unconfirmed report" and then emphasized, incorrectly, "We have not breached the levee at this point in time." Yet she also stressed that overtopping—rather than any breaks in the defense system—meant flooding so severe in some New Orleans neighborhoods that "we have people swimming." Midweek, at a press conference to announce that three hundred National Guardsmen from Arkansas were joining the fifteen hundred Guardsmen already in the city, she reminded everyone that these soldiers had recently returned from Iraq. They were there, she stressed, to prevent looting, not aid in the rescue. "They have M16s, and they're locked and loaded," she said.

---

3. Brown remained on the federal payroll for several months after his resignation, Chertoff would claim, because the department needed his "expertise."

"These troops know how to shoot and kill, and they are more than willing to do so if necessary, and I expect they will."

Yet Blanco performed admirably that week. She ordered any and all available employees working for the state's Department of Wildlife and Fisheries to New Orleans, which meant around two hundred boats working the floodwaters in and around New Orleans. She assigned one of her top people the job of recruiting shrimpers, oystermen, tour operators, and anyone else who might have a craft that could help reach people trapped by water. By midweek, the city needed buses more than boats, but that wasn't for a lack of effort on Blanco's part, who brought up the issue incessantly in conversations with federal officials. On Monday night, she called the president and told him, "We need everything you've got." By Wednesday, she was asking the White House for forty thousand troops. Seeing that the state's shelters were overflowing, she convinced Texas governor Rick Perry to open the Astrodome as an emergency shelter. Maybe her savviest move was the decision several days after Katrina to hire James Lee Witt—the man who had remade FEMA under Bill Clinton—to help Louisiana navigate the opaque byways of the Washington bureaucracy in the months ahead.

Blanco blamed Karl Rove for the beating her reputation took in the weeks after Katrina. She saw his fingerprints all over the president's gambit on Air Force One when the president told her she would need to stand down from her command before he sent in federal troops. Within days, Bob Mann, Blanco's communications director, was receiving phone calls from reporters repeating unflattering quotes about his boss. Each was attributed to "unnamed senior White House officials." Even her play-it-down-the-middle chief of staff, Andy Kopplin, who had held that same position for her Republican predecessor, saw partisan politics at play. "There was an unfortunate attempt to politicize the response to Katrina to help a president getting terrible press," Kopplin later said.

Nagin, too, saw Rove playing politics with the disaster. For days the mayor was worked up over his appearance on *Meet the Press*, when Tim Russert flashed an aerial photo of a hundred Orleans Parish school buses underwater. "This was classic Karl Rove," Nagin complained to people around him. And how do you think Russert learned that the city ignored Amtrak's offer to send extra trains to help with the evacuation? The last five Amtrak trains to leave New Orleans on the Sunday evening before Katrina carried no passengers—"ghost trains," the *Washington Post* called them. "Karl Rove is good, real good," Nagin said.

Yet isolated in the Hyatt, Nagin imagined that Blanco was his true tormentor. He fumed when he learned around a week after Katrina that the sandbag-carrying helicopters he had ordered to plug the Seventeenth Street Canal breach had temporarily been hijacked by the governor's people so they could save a politically connected pastor and members of his congregation. Nagin described it as "diverting helicopters from plugging levee breaches to perform political favors." The New Orleans police desperately needed help, but Blanco, Nagin said, was "secretly assigning" National Guard troops "to areas in the state not in crisis." Sometimes he blamed Blanco for failures that were the federal government's fault if not a consequence of one of his own blunders.

"I kept hoping and praying the governor would snap into action," Nagin said. "Unfortunately, she never did." He accused Blanco of using Katrina to fulfill the threat she had delivered during the governor's race.

For her part, Blanco didn't know what to do about Nagin. "I won," Blanco said. "I don't care what happened in the past. I'm the governor and all I want is a good working relationship with the mayor of the state's largest city." Yet short of ordering her counterpart into intensive therapy, what could she do? To the monumental challenges confronting postdiluvial New Orleans, add a governor and a mayor who were barely speaking. Said Blanco, "Nagin had a long-standing problem with trust. Way before the storm."

NAGIN ACCUSED BLANCO OF costing lives because she hesitated when the president tried to convince her to federalize the state's National Guard. Yet no effort was made to federalize the Guard in Mississippi, despite the chaotic conditions there. The governor of Mississippi was Haley Barbour, the ultimate GOP insider. He had served as chairman of the Republican National Committee in 1994 when the party won the House for the first time in forty years and then cashed in as a big-time

Washington lobbyist with a client list that included R.J. Reynolds, Philip Morris, and United Health. Of all the southern states, only Louisiana had a Democratic governor.[4]

A House committee, chaired by a Republican, concluded that there was no advantage in "federalizing" the disaster. Indeed, troops were deployed to New Orleans the next day without Blanco's signature. But it gave the White House a talking point that could at least help muddy the waters and maybe shift the blame. "The president will not let any form of bureaucracy get in the way of protecting the citizens of Louisiana," the White House's Dan Bartlett told the *Washington Post* for an article appearing on the paper's front page on that first Sunday after the flooding. As of Saturday, a "senior Bush official" claimed, Blanco *still* had not declared a state of emergency. The *Post* needed to print a correction noting that the governor had done just that nine days earlier.

Nagin proved an integral part of the White House strategy. The "ultimate pimpmobile," an impressed Nagin had said of Air Force One. That one long shower seemed to have bought the White House endless goodwill to the point Nagin was repeating their talking points. "She's putting politics ahead of people," Nagin said when asked about the disagreement between Bush and Blanco over the deployment of troops. Karl Rove couldn't have written the script better himself. The South's sole Democratic governor was feuding with the high-profile black mayor at the center of the Katrina story. A little more one-on-one time between Nagin and the president, and they might ensure that Blanco was a one-term governor. Louisiana was a purple state that they could turn solid red.

Including that first meeting on Air Force One, Bush visited New Orleans five times in five weeks. The second visit came ten days later and on the same day that Nagin flew home from Dallas. The White

---

4. Speaking to a group of graduate students at the Metropolitan College of New York seventeen months after Katrina, former FEMA director Michael Brown said, "Unbeknownst to me, certain people in the White House were thinking, 'We had to federalize Louisiana because she's a white, female Democratic governor, and we have a chance to rub her nose in it. We can't do it to Haley because Haley's a white, male Republican governor.'"

House arranged for Nagin to join Bush for a briefing on the USS *Iwo Jima*, a giant naval assault ship now docked a few blocks from the Convention Center. After that, Nagin and the president stood on the back of an open-top military truck for a three-hour tour of the ravaged city. The two had dinner together on the *Iwo Jima* with Thad Allen, FEMA's new point man in the Gulf, and Lieutenant General Russel Honoré. The White House had sent Honoré, Louisiana-born and the Pentagon's second-highest-ranking African American, to New Orleans to coordinate military efforts in the Gulf region.

After dinner, Bush invited his companions to join him on the top deck for some fresh air. Bush offered them Dominican cigars and nonalcoholic beer. In return, Nagin said nothing, but instead gave the president a self-satisfied, happy nod. "He knew he was working a brother," Nagin wrote in his memoir of those first couple of weeks. "First I got to take a shower on the ultimate pimpmobile. And now I was smoking a cigar and sipping a cold beer in the mild night under the stars." Rather than talk about Katrina, Nagin remembered, "We just talked about life. We all formed an interesting bond."[5]

THE PRESIDENT WAS BACK in New Orleans three days later, this time to address the nation. The backdrop the White House advance team had chosen was the St. Louis Cathedral, a triple-spired architectural masterpiece that towers above Jackson Square in the French Quarter. The Quarter still had no electricity, but the president's people flew in generators, klieg lights, and communications equipment (and then carted it away the next day, to the chagrin of the city's Greg Meffert, who was still scrambling for equipment). During the speech, the Eighty-Second Airborne Division patrolled the Quarter's darkened streets. "I am speaking to you from the city of New Orleans, nearly empty, still partly underwater, and waiting for life and hope to return,"

---

5. "They met a bunch of times and always got along fantastic," Greg Meffert, the top mayoral aide, said of his boss and Bush. "Ray got along better with George Bush than he did Barack Obama."

President Bush began. The effect was stunning. The president was wearing a blue dress shirt but no jacket or tie. The podium was positioned so that the television cameras captured the full effect of the iconic white cathedral gleaming against the black sky.

The bold speech was as strong as Bush's Rose Garden press conference two weeks earlier had been weak. "As all of us saw on television, there is also some deep, persistent poverty in this region," Bush said. "And that poverty has roots in a history of racial discrimination, which cut off generations from the opportunity of America. We have a duty to confront this poverty with bold action." Hard decisions lay ahead as communities needed to devise realistic rebuilding plans, Bush warned, but he assured state and local officials that they could rely on Washington. "We will do what it takes, we'll stay as long as it takes, to help citizens rebuild their communities and their lives." He was speaking about the entire Gulf region, but he also added, closer to the end, "And all who question the future of the Crescent City need to know, there is no way to imagine America without New Orleans, and this great city will rise again. . . . We will not just rebuild, we will build higher and better."

Nagin had no doubt what tack he would take. "To hell with the state," Nagin told Sally Forman. From where the mayor sat, the president was offering them the keys to the Treasury. Bush himself had asked Nagin for regular briefings, and Bush's top people had offered the mayor a back channel that allowed him to bypass Blanco. "Mr. Nagin has emerged as the leading advocate for the Bush administration's post-Katrina agenda," the *Wall Street Journal* reported a few months after the storm. Nagin had a pinch-me attitude over the access he was getting, but that same article, by the *Journal*'s Corey Dade, noted that the federal government's aid package favored Mississippi by a ratio of around five to one.

9

RITA

Ray Nagin was in an expansive mood three weeks after Katrina. For the first time since the storm, he was again the relaxed CEO whose communication style sounded more DJ than elected official—doing his "Ray-Ray thing," as some locals described it. When he spoke without notes and felt confident, his speech had a musicality; he was jazzbo Nagin, the hepcat scatting his words, adding a little snare and brushwork to his sentences. "Man, I'm tired of hearing these helicopters," he told the reporters gathered for a press conference after he returned from Dallas. "I want to hear some jazz." The mayor was thinking about all those New Orleanians temporarily living in Atlanta or Dallas or San Antonio. "The last thing we need is people putting down roots somewhere," Nagin said. "We need to get them back to town." That would require that the city have lights and drinking water, along with some semblance of police and fire departments.

Technically, New Orleans had had at least some electricity since the Wednesday or Thursday after Katrina. Several days after Katrina, Nagin had asked Entergy CEO Dan Packer to give him lights somewhere in the city to show the world New Orleans was still standing. It meant jury-rigging fifty miles of wire and diverting power from two parishes away, but that week Entergy lit up the trim lights on the Crescent City Connection bridge, of all icons, lighting up its path across the Mississippi. Yet that was nothing but a parlor trick by a utility unable to turn on the lights even in dry parts of New Orleans. Entergy operated twenty-two substations scattered around the city, and nearly every one had been flooded. So, too, had two of its power plants. "The important thing was getting all the water out of the system," Packer said, "so we could turn things back on without blowing everything up." Entergy's parent company shipped pumps and other equipment to New Orleans, and other utility companies pitched in. Within a few weeks, the utility was delivering electricity to the West Bank, the French Quarter, the central business district, and Uptown. Gas lines in those areas would work, too, at least once Entergy could dispatch a repairman to restore service at a home.

Water proved a more complicated issue. The quality of the water in New Orleans wasn't anywhere near its pre-Katrina levels, but it was still better than what was coming out of the faucets in places like Mexico City. Some around Nagin were telling him that if water was the only reason for not reopening the city, he should lift the evacuation order. People would do just as any of them would do if a tourist in a third-world country—drink bottled water—but otherwise the tap was fine for showers and boiling. State inspectors, however, were reluctant to certify the city's drinking water. Nagin saw it as another example of Blanco's missing the urgency of the crisis.

Despite the state, Nagin announced a phased-in repopulation that started with anyone living in a section of the city with electricity and running water. The White House, which didn't need any more bad news out of New Orleans, sided with the state. The mayor is being "extremely ambitious," said the White House's Thad Allen, who also called Nagin's plan "extremely problematic." How would they get out the message that people should avoid drinking from the tap? And what if people ran out of bottled water in a city with no functioning local economy? In response, Nagin sarcastically referred to Allen as the "federally appointed mayor of New Orleans."

A confrontation over repopulating the city was avoided only when another megastorm formed off the Gulf Coast: Rita. Forecasters were predicting Rita would hit west of New Orleans, but with another storm seemingly as large as Katrina aimed at the general area, no one was moving back to the city. Instead of inviting people back to dry parts of New Orleans, Nagin encouraged anyone still inside the city limits to leave.

Rita was enough to make a heretic think the religious fanatics might have a point that a divine power had it in for New Orleans. It was the eighteenth tropical storm of the season, a Category 5 hurricane that ranked as the Gulf Coast's fourth most powerful storm on record. The country might have been talking about a storm that ended up causing $15 billion in damage—a dollar figure that placed it among the most expensive disasters in US history—except people were already predicting that Katrina's price tag might exceed $200 billion.[1]

Rita caused widespread flooding in low-lying areas along the coast. It wiped out several smaller towns in southwestern Louisiana and east Texas. A half a million Houstonians would be without power. But in New Orleans they rejoiced over the tragedy that had been averted. At a press conference after the rain and wind had died down, Nagin said, "Rita set us back about three to five days, but we're very much on schedule," as if an actual timetable existed against which New Orleans could measure its progress.

RAY NAGIN HAD ALWAYS been too conservative for Greta Gladney's tastes. "Ray Reagan," she and other activists had dubbed the mayor because of his moderate, generally business-friendly policies. But anyone wanting to know why she would run against him for mayor a few months after Katrina could start with that first phone call the mayor had with the president on the Wednesday after the storm. Nagin had the leader of the free world on the line but only spoke about the breach in the Seventeenth Street Canal levee—the breach pouring water into Lakeview and the surrounding neighborhoods—when holes were everywhere in the city's flood-protection system. Helicopters hadn't dropped masses

---

1. Katrina caused an estimated $135 billion in damages.

of sandbags to plug holes in the breaches that had flooded the Lower Ninth. Rita had pushed a modest seven-foot water surge through the Industrial Canal, but that was enough to topple the rickety, makeshift solution that the authorities had cobbled together. The flooding in the Lower Ninth was as bad on September 24, the day after Rita, as it was on August 30, the day after Katrina. It would take at least another week to pump out the new floodwaters.

"It was like the Lower Ninth didn't matter," Gladney said. "It was like people in power were already writing us off."

Three bridges connected the Lower Ninth to the rest of New Orleans. It had been that way since the early twentieth century, when construction of the Industrial Canal cleaved the Ninth Ward into two. Downriver from the rest of New Orleans, the Ninth Ward had always been a place apart. Yet the Industrial Canal and those bridges meant the Lower Nine, as residents tended to call the neighborhood, seemed its own village, not one neighborhood among many. Large swaths of New Orleans, including Lakeview and large sections of New Orleans East, sit lower than the Lower Ninth Ward. Only around half the Lower Ninth is included in the federally designated flood zone, and most of the area lies within eighteen inches of sea level. It's "lower" in the same sense as lower Manhattan or the lower forty-eight states. But the split of the community into an Upper and Lower guaranteed that most of the world, including a great many native New Orleanians, would assume the Lower Ninth represented some of the city's lowest-lying land. The soon-to-be-ubiquitous red shirts printed up by ACORN, the community-organizing group, which had its national field office in New Orleans, read I'M FROM DAT NINE AND YOU AIN'T TAKING MINE! The phrase seemed aimed at the rest of New Orleans more than state or federal officials.

That's not to say the Lower Ninth was a safer place to live than other spongy, low-lying parts of New Orleans. It sat at the mouth of what scientists called the Funnel. The giant Lake Borgne—more an extension of the Gulf of Mexico—sat just east of New Orleans, at the top of the Funnel. Lake Borgne was bordered by MR. GO on one side and the Gulf Intracoastal Waterway on the other. These two man-made shipping channels pinched together right above the Lower Ninth Ward. It was an "excellent storm-surge delivery system," said Ivor van Heerden, deputy director of the LSU Hurricane Center, that the "federal powers-that-be had inadvertently designed."

The visuals were one reason the Lower Ninth dominated the news in the early days after Katrina. The water had pushed homes off their foundations and turned some into splinters. Homes ended up on top of other homes. At least a few ended up in the street. More people died in the Lower Ninth than in any other community after Katrina. The Lower Ninth's demographics were another reason this small patch of New Orleans came to dominate the early news coverage. The average resident of the Lower Ninth Ward earned $16,000 a year, and more than one in every three residents lived below the poverty line. Sections of Washington, DC, Newark, or Los Angeles—or rural California or Mississippi— were just as poor. But it had been New Orleanians whose forlorn images had been beamed to the world, dressed in tattered clothes and looking dehydrated, famished, and pitiful, and it would be the city's impoverished blacks who dominated the narrative in the early days of Katrina. The country will be "forever scarred by third-world horrors unthinkable in this nation until now," Shepard Smith told Fox viewers several days after the flood. The Lower Ninth Ward, for better or worse, served as a proxy for poverty in New Orleans, if not the entire United States. And it would be the Lower Ninth—a mixed-race community before school desegregation but 98 percent black at the time of Katrina—that stood as a synecdoche for anyone debating the rebuilding question starting to dominate the discussion a few weeks after the storm.

The Lower Ninth is relatively small, a compact neighborhood twenty blocks long and twenty-five blocks wide. Prior to Katrina, it was home to just under twenty thousand people—a fraction of the ninety-five thousand who lost their homes in New Orleans East. The Industrial Canal that cut the Lower Ninth off from the rest of New Orleans forms its western border, and the streets bleed into St. Bernard Parish, an almost-all-white suburb just east of the neighborhood. The Mississippi forms the Lower Ninth's southern border. Locals call the corner of the Lower Ninth closest to the French Quarter and bordering the river Holy Cross. The houses there tend to be bigger and have more New Orleans–style frills. The northern border—back-a-town in back-a-town—was the Bayou Bienvenue. Before the federal government built MR. GO, the Bayou Bienvenue was a thriving wetlands thick with cypress trees and high grass. But MR. GO caused salt water from the Gulf of Mexico to leach into the Bayou Bienvenue, killing the bayou and the area's last line of defense. By the time of Katrina, the bayou, separated from the Lower Ninth by a short levee, was basically a giant puddle with little vegetation or wildlife.

No big housing projects were in this part of town, where almost everyone seemed to live in a house built by a parent or a grandparent if not ancestors dating back further than that. Homeownership was high in the Lower Ninth—higher than most other places in the city. Most people had a job, even if a low-paying one at one of the city's hotels or kitchens. The place was more hardscrabble working class (with a ghastly high crime rate: its homicide rate was twice that of a city that ranked as one of the country's most murderous), but to the wider world, the Lower Ninth might have seemed little different from a run-down slum on the edge of a third-world city. "It was just distasteful being called a 'refugee' on American soil and 'the poor, poor people of the Lower Ninth Ward,'" said Ronald Lewis, a retired streetcar repairman from the Lower Ninth who lost his home in Katrina. "We weren't even given credit for being working-class people."

After Katrina the area's residents were scattered around the country and reeling. "Nothing out here can be saved. At all," said New Orleans's homeland security director, Terry Ebbert, a former colonel in the Marines, of the Lower Ninth Ward two weeks after Katrina in an interview with the *New York Times*. Even the mayor piled on when he incorrectly said of the Lower Ninth, "I don't think it can ever be what it was, because it's the lowest-laying area." A week later, Housing and Urban Development Secretary Alphonso Jackson delivered the area's death sentence after a meeting with Nagin in New Orleans. "I told him I think it would be a mistake to rebuild the Ninth Ward," Jackson said. Most of New Orleans had flooded, yet the world fixated on the future of this small, two-square-mile patch.

Charmaine Marchand, who represented the Lower Ninth in the state legislature, was among the few people sticking up for the area. Marchand was a child of the Lower Ninth, raised by a schoolteacher and a mailman, a single mother who had put herself through law school working as a paralegal. Standing not quite five feet tall, she had been representing the area in the state legislature since 2004. Marchand had been behind the wheel driving her son, her parents, a brother, and other family members to Houston the day before Katrina. She then had ordered everyone back in the car once she learned about the Lower Ninth flooding and headed to Baton Rouge.

Marchand spent those first days in the state's Emergency Operations Center, helping organize the efforts to rescue people trapped in the Ninth Ward or surrounding communities. "We've got people calling from a rooftop and I'm guiding the helicopters," she said. Her next big job was helping residents find missing family members. People who had been rescued from the Superdome or Convention Center were put on airplanes or buses. Often they didn't know where they were headed until they were in transit. "I asked FEMA who was keeping the names of people in the different shelters, and FEMA said Red Cross," Marchand said. "When I asked Red Cross, they said FEMA."

Marchand needed to find a school for her son, who was about to start high school. Her father had Parkinson's and was exhibiting the early signs of dementia. He needed specialists, as did her brother, whom she described as bipolar and depressed. "I'm figuring out doctors for everybody," she said. "I'm finding us a place to live." But she was also the only elected official who lived in the Lower Ninth at the time of Katrina.

Marchand had too much to do in Baton Rouge when one day a couple of weeks after Katrina she pointed her car toward New Orleans. Like everyone else, she was hearing talk about giving up on the Lower Ninth. "I literally sat outside Mayor Nagin's room at the Hyatt, with the windows blown out and everything, until he'd meet with me," Marchand said. "To get him to confirm our right to rebuild our community, just like everyone else." She'd get enough of a promise out of him to get on television "and tell everyone of the commitment the mayor had just made." Then she watched in the coming weeks as the mayor flip-flopped on the future of the Lower Ninth, depending on his audience.

WITH RITA BLOWN OVER, Ray Nagin again pushed to repopulate. This time, though, he avoided another confrontation with Washington by initiating a more gradual plan. "We're not asking people to come back who have a lot of kids, a lot of senior citizens," the mayor said at a press conference. "That's going to be the reality of New Orleans moving forward." He urged all business owners to come home, but otherwise he would re-open New Orleans neighborhood by neighborhood by zip code. The city would start by welcoming people back to Algiers. Once the mayor and his people had a chance to assess progress, they'd give a date for officially reopening the French Quarter, Uptown, and other dry patches of the city. Those living in parts of the city that had flooded would be allowed in the city under a program Nagin called Look and Leave. These residents would be permitted to work on their homes but not sleep on their property overnight. In another nod to Washington, the mayor announced a daily dusk-to-dawn curfew—a mandate that went largely unenforced, just like his staged repopulation of dry parts of New Orleans.[2]

The city distributed brochures so that people knew the risks they were taking. It recommended that people get a tetanus shot before returning to a city that had little medical care to offer and advised them to drink bottled water until further notice. "Standing water and soil might be seriously contaminated," the city warned, so one should wash as soon as possible with an antibacterial soap if exposed. The sewer system, the brochure said delicately, was "compromised" (most of the city's toilets were still not working), and federal authorities were quoted as suggesting people limit their exposure to mold by wearing masks, gloves, and other protective gear.

---

2. Or selectively enforced the curfew laws. Five weeks after Katrina, Robert Davis, a sixty-six-year-old former teacher, black, was walking on Bourbon Street at around 8:00 p.m. He approached a small clot of police officers to ask about the curfew, and when he received no response to his question, he called them "unprofessional and rude." A cameraman working for the Associated Press captured on video a trio of policemen, all of them white, punching and kicking Davis until they had him on the ground and in handcuffs—and still one officer delivered two more blows to his face. The police said they were detaining Davis on suspicion of public drunkenness (Davis claimed he hadn't had a drink in twenty-five years) and for violating the city curfew. Two of the officers were fired and a third received a four-month suspension. The city would settle with Davis for an undisclosed amount.

Police headquarters had flooded. So, too, had the crime lab, the evidence room, and the local jail. The police brass moved its operation from the driveway of Harrah's to the Royal Sonesta, a stylish Bourbon Street hotel with marble floors and a lobby fountain. Until further notice, the city's bus and rail station served as the city's makeshift jail. The state dispatched flatbeds of chain-link fencing to the city, and where buses would normally be loading and unloading passengers, the National Guard built a series of makeshift holding cells, each topped with razor wire. Camp Greyhound, the guards and inmates dubbed it.

The city's police force was in shambles. About one-third of the force went AWOL during Katrina, the department acknowledged. Hundreds faced disciplinary charges. Yet New Orleans in those first months after Katrina might have been one of the safest spots on earth. In normal times, about fifteen hundred police officers patrolled a city of 450,000. Post-Katrina, somewhere around fifteen thousand National Guardsmen were in a largely deserted city.

Cops who had lost their homes, like other essential city and parish personnel, were generally assigned to one of two cruise ships docked on the Mississippi near the Convention Center. FEMA had agreed to pay Carnival Cruise Lines $236 million to borrow for six months a pair of ships named *Sensation* and *Ecstasy*. The police were assigned cabins on the latter of the two ships, which meant endless jokes about cops on ecstasy. "It was weirdly an okay experience," said Linda Santi, who worked for the city. Those months they spent together had a communal feel something like college, except everyone had a private berth and the food was better. The bosses were mainly still in Baton Rouge, where most of the directors, assistant directors, and top City Hall aides retreated pre-storm. Inside the Capitol Annex, a handsome, six-story building across the street from the capitol, New Orleans had set up a kind of government in exile. They were there at the invitation of Mitch Landrieu, the state's lieutenant governor and also son of Moon Landrieu and younger brother to Senator Mary Landrieu. Mitch Landrieu worked on the building's top floor. The city's chief administrative officer was given an office near Landrieu's, while other department heads worked wherever they could find an empty desk. Economic development set up shop on the second floor, finance on the third.

New Orleans had few residents, but it was anything but a ghost town. The center of the city could seem crowded, with soldiers in uniform, countless government officials, and virtual battalions of middle-aged white men wearing tucked-in polos bearing the name of their cleanup company or demolition business. By Sally Forman's rough count, three weeks after Katrina more than a thousand media people were in town. Yet to venture out beyond the central business district was to encounter a dead city. There were no people and no cars and none of the normal ambient sounds, such as the rumble of a passing bus or children playing. The view at night was even more stark. The streetlights were working in the French Quarter, the central business district, and Uptown, but the rest of the city was a black void.

A permanent stench infected New Orleans, even parts that had remained dry—like a seaside community near the end of summer, except that the brackish smell was mixed, not with the odor of rotting alewives, but with hints of oil, sewage, rancid meat, and death. Decaying human bodies were cooking in the intense New Orleans heat along with those of cats, dogs, and other animals that had been caught in the flooding. The surviving dogs only added to the strangeness of the city back then. These weren't roaming bands of mangy beasts but abandoned pets looking emaciated. Cars routinely drove the wrong way down one-way streets, sometimes because people didn't care or because a tree blocked the way. Often it was because people didn't know where they were going in a city that had lost many of its street signs. Around town, blue-and-white newspaper boxes that had not been destroyed by the flood displayed the August 28 *Times-Picayune*, with its prescient front page: "Katrina Takes Aim."

The airport reopened to commercial flights fifteen days after Katrina, but where once Louis Armstrong International boasted nearly two hundred departures a day, it was down to thirty. The few open hotels seemed like armed fortresses. Typical was the Sheraton, a giant rectangle rising forty-nine floors above Canal Street. Though often it felt as if more soldiers were on the streets than civilians, for security the Sheraton hired Blackwater USA, which placed hulking slabs of beef dressed in black at its entrances, armed with AR-15 assault rifles. Rooms were cleaned only sporadically, but in other ways it was still a Sheraton, including a twenty-four-hour hotel channel advertising restaurants and clubs that sat boarded up and closed to the public.

Meals tended to be utilitarian. A town known for its food had virtually no restaurants. At the Royal Sonesta, for instance, those first weeks after Katrina, dinner tended to be from the jars of peanut butter the management left out, along with bread, green apples, utensils, and paper plates. For the FBI agents, FEMA workers, and other government employees, the Salvation Army truck was another option. The bars of Bourbon Street opened immediately after Rita (and stayed open late, despite the curfew orders), followed by the strip clubs. Rarely was a city as overwhelmingly male as New Orleans was following Katrina, and never more so than on Bourbon Street, crowded with disaster specialists and construction workers and muscular US marshals with guns strapped to their waist.

THE CITY'S NUMBER ONE priority was dewatering. Only then could officials remove the remaining dead bodies and assess the damage. New Orleans had a wondrous system for pumping water out of the city, but its giant pumps, each around the size of a locomotive engine, were useless without electricity.

The Army Corps of Engineers had estimated that it would take eighty days to drain the 250 billion gallons of water the experts estimated covered greater New Orleans. In that timetable, the city wouldn't start cleaning up the worst-hit areas until at least Thanksgiving. But the Corps' engineers had made their calculations based on the capabilities of the portable pumps the federal government had shipped to the area. The chief engineer of the Sewerage and Water Board of New Orleans, the agency responsible for the interconnected network of drainage canals and pumping stations that kept this low-lying city livable, dismissed them as "Tinkertoy pumps." They were so small, he said, that it was like "going to the seashore with a soda straw and trying to empty it."

The city would drain in just under three weeks rather than the almost three months the Corps had said it would take.

The Corps deserved some of the credit. Their main task after Katrina was fixing breaches in the levees, but some of its people had experience cobbling together electrical systems on a battlefield, which proved invaluable. Water agencies from around the country also pitched in, loaning the city pumps and personnel. The Water Bureau of Portland, Oregon, alone sent sixty employees to New Orleans after Katrina. Luck was also a factor. The city's largest pump stood at the edge of the flood zone and close enough to the neighboring parish for a team to jury-rig lines to a working electrical switching station. Eight days after Katrina, the first pumps coughed back to life. There was always some burp—large chunks of storm debris, a leaky gearbox—but the city was slowly draining.

Yet mainly credit goes to the ridiculously named New Orleans Sewerage and Water Board. "Ours is an agency with a storied past," said Marcia St. Martin, who had taken over as executive director of the Sewerage and Water Board two years earlier. Some of its pumps ran on aging motors designed by Thomas Edison, and A. Baldwin Wood had been among its employees. "We have people whose fathers and grandfathers worked here. It's in their blood," said St. Martin, who is black. The agency stationed people inside pumping stations and other facilities around the city, but despite the flooding, not a single one abandoned his or her post.[3]

About half of St. Martin's staff of three hundred slept in the bunk rooms of pumping stations or power plants around the city. The rest stayed on the other side of the river at the big water-purification plant the agency operated on the West Bank. They had large stores of food and other supplies there, along with backup generators and plenty of fuel. To help it feel more like a base camp, St. Martin dispatched trucks and crews to the homes of anyone living in a dry part of town. They picked

---

3. Several days after the flooding, the National Guard forced an exhausted pump operator named Ricky Ray to leave his post running a pumping station that sat astride the Orleans Avenue Canal, near Lakeview. He returned a few days later. The city's pumps were so old and idiosyncratic that some still operated on Edison's direct-current electrical system and were therefore incompatible with the alternating-current electrical system that the rest of the city used. Ray, who told his story to the *New York Times'* John Schwartz, knew the sound and the feel of these ancient warhorses. He stayed until the city was dry.

up barbecues and sleeping bags along with refrigerators and washers and dryers. They'd set up one area for washing clothes and another for cooking. By the second week, FEMA had driven in food-service trucks along with tents and a laundry trailer.

Salt water was poisonous to a storm-drainage system that needed to produce its own power. But pump operators needed water to both operate and cool their machinery, and without power there was no way to siphon river water from the freshwater Mississippi. Employees painstakingly disassembled all the system's electrical equipment, then baked it dry, to remove even traces of salt water. They then used the only available coolant to get the pumps working again—the salty, corrosive waters covering much of the city. "I made the decision to destroy everything again," St. Martin said. "Our mission was to dewater the city, so that's what we would do." Once they got the first few pumps thundering again, the city would drain in eleven days. They would worry about what a second dose of salt water would do to their equipment once the city was dry.

WHOSE JOB WAS IT to remove the dead after a disaster such as Katrina? Normally, the coroner would be responsible for collecting bodies, but those offices, too, had been flooded. The coroner would swim through muck and spend two days outside the criminal courts building on Tulane Avenue until he was rescued. FEMA had its Disaster Mortuary Operational Response Teams, or DMORTs, but they identified victims, performed autopsies, and stored the remains until they could be claimed. They did not retrieve the bodies. A colonel with the Eighty-Second Airborne volunteered his troops, but he was overruled by a commanding officer. A colonel with the National Guard offered his people, but higher-ranking officials inside the Defense Department in Washington said they were worried about risk of infection. A state police commander was also told to stand down. Finally, the state hired a British-based private firm called Kenyon International Emergency Services. They carted bodies to a collection point near the Convention Center, where they were loaded into a refrigerated tractor-trailer and brought to St. Gabriel, Louisiana. In this small town about an hour west of New Orleans, FEMA had leased a giant warehouse that it converted into a makeshift morgue. Blackwater, the security firm, patrolled the grounds, and black tarp covered the chain-link fence FEMA had installed to block the prying eyes of the media.

The grisly task of searching for bodies inside homes fell on the National Guard, which fanned out across the city to conduct a house-by-house search. They'd use boots and rifle butts to open doors, and then, once a team had looked around, they spray-painted a large X on the front of the house—the famous "Katrina X" still visible on the occasional home even years after the storm.[4] They discovered far fewer human remains than they feared. The number of dead in New Orleans would end up closer to a thousand than the ten thousand Nagin and others were predicting.

ENTERGY NEW ORLEANS FILED for bankruptcy protection twenty-three days after Katrina. It accounted for less than 7 percent of the revenues of Entergy Inc., but its parent company sought to protect itself from $325 million to $425 million in estimated storm-related costs. "When do you ever hear of a utility company going bankrupt?" Dan Packer would ask once he had stepped down as Entergy New Orleans CEO. "It just doesn't happen." Packer had been assuring people the company was "ahead of the game," but bankruptcy also required the utility to terminate any contracts it had for outside workers. In the early months after Katrina, Entergy had a repair crew of roughly two hundred divided between electric and gas repairs. It would be up to them and the goodwill of outside agencies willing to lend volunteers to fix the crippled systems.

The National Rifle Association presented another distraction. The organization sued the city because the police were confiscating any gun

---

4. The number inside the top of the X told a passerby the date that a home had been searched. A unit identified itself on the left (*TXO*, say, for the Texas National Guard), and the right was reserved for identifying any hazards the soldiers had encountered. On the bottom a soldier would identify the number of bodies found inside.

they came across following Katrina—a blatant violation of the Second Amendment, the NRA charged. "With looters, rapists and other thugs running rampant in New Orleans, Ray Nagin issued an order to disarm all law-abiding citizens," the NRA's Wayne LaPierre declared in a press statement. "With no law enforcement and 911 unavailable, he left the victims vulnerable by stripping away their only means of defending themselves and their loved ones."

New Orleans's reputation was another casualty of Katrina and represented one more mess that needed cleaning up. LaPierre's comments, while harsh, underscored that challenge: to recover, the city would need to resurrect its $5-billion-a-year tourism industry, yet who would want to visit a city where even the mayor and the top cop had suggested their residents had acted like barbarians terrorizing a darkened city. In those first days after the storm, the cable stations had little concrete to report, and they often repeated rumors and half-truths to fill out their round-the-clock coverage.[5] So much of what was reported in the early days of the coverage turned out to be false. Babies weren't being raped at the Superdome, despite what Eddie Compass, the police chief, told Oprah Winfrey. People didn't sit in "that frickin' Superdome for five days watching dead bodies, watching hooligans killing people, raping people," as Nagin claimed. Six people died in the Superdome that week. One man threw himself off a balcony, another perished from a drug overdose. The other four died from natural causes. Two rape attempts but no rapes were reported. The crimes committed tended to be the petty thefts of people who broke into vending machines and concession stands in search of food.

Tales about what happened inside the Convention Center had been similarly overblown. The police were largely absent from inside

---

5. And it wasn't just television. "Rumors of gang rapes and wanton murder needed to be repeated only two or three times before reporters decided the rumors had been corroborated and repeated them in print," according to the *Times-Picayune*'s Jed Horne.

the building,[6] but the scene wasn't so much *Lord of the Flies* as a made-for-TV movie. As reported, bands of young black men, many of them armed, roamed the corridors of the Convention Center. However, they acted as self-deputized sheriffs rather than gangs of marauders. Teams of scouts were dispatched to search for food and water. Others collected luggage carts from nearby hotels so they could move the trash into big piles. Once the buses started to arrive, these same young men organized the crowds so that the older people were placed at the front of the line, followed by women with children.

The stories of widespread looting were real. Anyone out on a boat long enough was bound to encounter someone breaking into a store or someone's home. City Council president Oliver Thomas was on the water with members of the Kentucky National Guard when they came across three young people on a raft going into the second floor of someone's home. The trio claimed to be helping out with the rescue, but Thomas, a streetwise pol who had grown up in the Lower Ninth, knew better. "They were breaking and entering, plain and simple," Thomas said. Liberty Bank was hit by looters as were scores of businesses, including an Uptown Walmart.

Some of the worst perpetrators, though, ended up being those who were supposed to be keeping the peace. Police in uniform appeared in a video taken inside the Uptown Walmart after Katrina. One cop was shown in the shoe section pushing a loaded cart. Prior to the storm, Nagin had signed an emergency order giving law enforcement the right to commandeer private property—yet even before the levees broke, witnesses saw cops driving Cadillac Escalades with dealer plates. The president of Sewell Cadillac Chevrolet told a reporter that he lost more

---

6. The police showed up in force at least one time that week. A Jefferson Parish deputy sheriff, after learning that his wife and a female cousin had ended up in the Convention Center, reached out to a friend inside NOPD. A SWAT team of thirteen, Wil Haygood and Ann Scott Tyson reported in the *Washington Post*, burst into the facility on Thursday morning, along with the deputy sheriff. They found his wife and relative, both of whom were white, and then backed out the way they came in.

than two hundred cars during the storm—many because the cops were in so much of a hurry, they failed to properly secure the lot before driving away.

Yet even the looting was overblown by an overzealous media. There's no doubting that the person walking off with a flatscreen television in a city with no electricity is guilty of looting (though at least one man used a pilfered TV to buy a spot on the back of a truck headed out of town). Someone taking clothes or shoes from a Walmart presented a trickier ethical question. But nothing seemed complicated about the morals of a man stepping into a darkened store to get food for his hungry family. The press, however, seemed to judge a person's behavior based on race rather than the immediate need for the item taken. Van Jones, an environmentalist and civil rights activist, juxtaposed a pair of wire-service photos he had found online. The caption on one picturing a young white couple: "Two residents wade through chest-deep water after finding bread and soda from a local grocery store after Hurricane Katrina came through the area." The caption accompanying a photo of an African American: "A young man walks through chest-deep floodwater after looting a grocery store in New Orleans on Tuesday, August 30, 2005." Apparently, "black people 'loot' food," Jones concluded, while "white people 'find' food."

Eventually, Eddie Compass, the city's top cop, would help clear the record—sort of. Sally Forman was in a borrowed house in Baton Rouge, spending a couple of days with her family, when Compass came on the TV. He spoke during a press conference carried live on CNN and MSNBC about the "vicious rumors" of children being found murdered and other wild claims made in the days after Katrina. Forman couldn't help herself. "Chief," she yelled at the television, "this would be a perfect time to apologize for perpetuating those rumors!" Four weeks after the storm, Nagin announced that he had accepted Compass's resignation.

The department's number two, Warren J. Riley, was now in charge.

RON FORMAN, SALLY'S HUSBAND, was thinking a lot about his late-night conversations with Ray Nagin in those first days after Katrina. His wife would be there, of course, and also a couple of others. The mayor would be in the corner of his suite, fiddling with his hand-cranked radio, pumping its handle, seeing if he could pick up any bits of news. Eventually, the hotel would send up some food. At first it was sandwiches and a few pieces of fruit, but then it was the military-issued MRE. "We'd eat by candlelight or flashlight and talk about what needed to be done to rebuild the city," Forman said. "At that point, I would've said Ray was focused on what needed to get done. I was still a believer."

Ron Forman tried not to feel frustrated when a week later the mayor had still failed to act on some of the ideas they had discussed. Between the zoo and the aquarium, Forman had plenty to keep him busy as head of the city's Audubon Nature Institute, but it was hard not to think the mayor was procrastinating. The two had talked about the idea of a citizens' commission that would oversee the rebuilding plan, and the mayor had even told Forman that he would give him first consideration as chairman. Yet there had been no movement on that idea, nor any progress on a more pressing project that the mayor had asked Forman to spearhead. CEOs of some of the globe's best-known companies were offering help. So, too, were the famous and fabulous, from pop stars to Prince Charles to Bill Gates. The mayor said it was a great idea when Forman volunteered to take on coordination of that. Forman had even found a New York–based firm willing to log the offers and help the city sort through them all. "I'd call for follow-through," Forman said, "but he'd just do his whole Ray-Ray thing: 'Hey, man, what's up, how you doing?' Then he'd tell me he'll need to get back to me."

Forman had enough sense to avoid Dallas and the Business Council's meeting with Nagin. "I stayed away from that mess," he said. But plenty of the participants had described for him the petulant mayor who made no effort to reassure them that he was in control. Forman's Uptown neighbors started calling him. "Where's Ray?" neighbor after neighbor asked, and Forman would respond in a way both loyal and disloyal to a mayor he also described as a friend. He shared his own frustrations with a man who didn't seem to want his help—who seemed to vanish when his city needed him most. But then Forman gave each the same spiel: He's our mayor. He understands the central role business can play. He must recognize that he can't do this by himself. "He knows he has to include us in any recovery efforts," Forman would reassure people.

DAVID WHITE, THE FRIEND who had served as the mayor's campaign treasurer, was in Houston when Nagin called. White didn't hesitate when his friend asked for his help. White waited for the National Guard to gain control of the city and then headed to New Orleans. Ten days after Katrina, White set himself up in a room in the Hyatt near Nagin's.

White was from Cleveland and had spent much of his career in Memphis, where he worked as a logistics executive for Federal Express. He didn't arrive in the New Orleans area until the late 1980s, when he bought a pair of McDonald's franchises in Central City—a part of New Orleans as poor as the Lower Ninth, if not as well-known. The stores were so profitable he bought two more, then sold them for a lot of money a few years before Katrina. Nagin and White had met only a couple of years before Nagin became mayor, when both joined a group of black and white businessmen working to bring professional hockey to New Orleans.[7] The two had started a car-rental company together while Nagin was still running Cox in New Orleans, but the business never panned out. "I was the unofficial guy the mayor bounced ideas off of," White said. People in City Hall described him as the mayor's closest confidant, but that's not to say, White said, that they were close. "Ray is a very private person," he said. "I'm not sure he had anyone he was really close to when he was mayor." At the Hyatt, the group around Nagin was basically his bodyguards, White, and a few key aides, such as Greg Meffert, who described his boss as "hermetically sealed." Meffert noted, "Ray isolated himself big-time. It got very bin-Laden-in-the-cave there for a while."

White, a practical man, figured that as bad as things were in New Orleans, they weren't unprecedented. He researched other cities that had experienced calamity. He spent time reading up on Kobe, Japan, a city

---

7. The group bought a minor league franchise that they renamed the Brass. Despite a few successful years, the team folded after five seasons.

that used a catastrophic earthquake to redesign itself, but he zeroed in on New York after September 11. The physical damage in New York was limited to a small corner of the city, whereas New Orleans saw damage to more than one hundred thousand of its homes, but he had found his template. New York had used special "Liberty" bonds, tax credits, and other tax incentives to fund its recovery. "I told Ray that's the way I thought we should proceed, and he agreed," White said.

But White went one step further with an idea he thought would push the bureaucrats to the side and put entrepreneurs like himself at the center of the recovery. Rather than follow the expected route and fight with the federal government over the proper size of a bailout check, he asked Nagin, why not suggest a ten-year tax holiday to any individual or business willing to move into the city limits? That represented billions in lost revenues for the US Treasury, but, as White saw it, it would short-circuit a process that otherwise would take months, if not years.

"I thought that we could get the rebuilding moving quicker than if we had to wait for an infusion of money through a government bureaucracy," White said. The mayor loved the idea, White said, but despite pushing it hard among his new friends in Washington, his pitch never got anywhere.

White lived on the North Shore, in Mandeville, thirty-five miles north of the city. The mayor's other key adviser early on was also a suburbanite, Joe Canizaro, who was the personal friend of the president and had Nagin scribbling over the phone while others waited in Dallas. To Canizaro, Nagin would delegate primary responsibility for putting together the blue-ribbon panel Karl Rove had said was needed to win the Bush administration's sign-off. Jimmy Reiss, too, recommended names for what would become the Bring New Orleans Back Commission. But it was Canizaro's commission to shape. "It was very clear to us that Joe knew what we had to do and he had the connections to do it," Meffert said.

JOE CANIZARO WAS NOT yet thirty years old in 1965, a relative newcomer to the city, when he caught a glimpse of New Orleans that changed his life. He was working as an $800-a-month junior appraiser for a real estate company who somehow talked his way to the thirty-third-floor observation deck in a tower being built on Canal Street near the river. Most people, when atop the International Trade Mart (now the World Trade Mart), take in the views of the Mississippi and the Quarter to the north or east. Canizaro fixated on the view west. Canal and Poydras Streets converged just below him but where Canal was lined with stores and office buildings, Poydras was a narrow street of warehouses, bars, and low-rent buildings. Two years later, Canizaro had convinced the New Orleans–based Lykes Brothers Steamship Company to partner with him on a twenty-two-story building on Poydras they would call the Lykes Center. Canizaro built several towers on Poydras and also the massive— and massively successful—Canal Place at the foot of Canal Steet.

Canizaro had grown up in Biloxi, an outsider in a city that can be parochial. Even once he had made a name for himself, he still needed to go to Baton Rouge or Jackson, Mississippi, to raise funds for a new project. In some lean years Canizaro felt so overleveraged that he feared everything would crumble. Alden McDonald and Liberty were among those who over the years helped Canizaro stay afloat. By the mid-1990s, though, Canizaro was charging some of the city's highest rents on a street crowded with high-rises. Canizaro bought a bank and funded his own venture-capital outfit. He sold two of his office towers for $133 million and made another $25 million on a suburban office park he owned. "The grandest palace in Old Metairie," the *Times-Picayune* said of the house Canizaro and his wife, Sue Ellen, had built a few doors down from the Metairie Country Club. A "magnificent neoclassical mansion influenced by Palladio's sixteenth-century Italian villas," said the couple's interior designer. The couple moved into the home Christmas of 2004—nine months before Katrina.

The Canizaros had talked about retreating to Crawford ahead of the storm, where they owned a spread only a few miles from George W. Bush's ranch, but they thought it would be too hot in late August. The couple decided to ride out the storm in a $400-a-night hotel in Dallas. They told Curtis, their house manager, to expect them home as early as Tuesday. Curtis, who was black, doubled as Canizaro's valet and driver.

Curtis called midmorning on Monday when he noticed water in the street. He called again a couple of hours later to say the water was at the front door, and then again a few hours after that to tell them he was on the second floor because the first had taken on two feet of water. The wealthier suburbs of New Orleans had remained dry; the exception was a large stretch of Old Metairie, which sat just west of the Seventeenth Street Canal. The Canizaros decided to continue west to the Utah mountains, where they also owned a home. That would be the couple's home base for the next four months. Canizaro's fractional ownership of a private jet helped cushion the hassles of the repeated trips he would make between Utah and Louisiana.

Canizaro spoke directly with the president in those first weeks after Katrina. Canizaro had been one of Bush's earliest financial supporters when the then governor was first creating a presidential exploratory committee. Canizaro had attained Ranger status—that of someone who raised at least $200,000—during the president's reelection campaign. In 2008, Canizaro would rank as one of John McCain's top bundlers, raising more than $500,000 for the Republican nominee. In 2012, Canizaro hosted a $50,000-a-plate fund-raiser at his home for Mitt Romney, the evening's special guest.

Yet it would be a mistake to dismiss Canizaro as just another wealthy white businessman serving as a banker to the Republican Party. Maybe it was because of his daughter, whose struggles with addiction he spoke about so openly. "It makes you humble," Canizaro said. "It makes you stop and realize it's not just the problems of these 'other people.'" Perhaps it was because of his experiences as a developer in a majority-black city, which had made him recognize that if you wanted to get anything done in modern New Orleans, it helped to have allies in the African-American community. "Joe has proven a good friend to our community," Alden McDonald said.

Canizaro's first big foray into the civic arena came five years before Katrina. He put up the seed money for a group he called the Committee for a Better New Orleans. The old Canizaro would have put himself in charge, certain he knew what was best for the city. He still named himself chairman, but added two African-American cochairs—Norman Francis, the president of Xavier University of Louisiana, the nation's only historically black Catholic university, and the founding chairman of Liberty Bank; and also Barbara Major, a local community activist. "We had

serious problems in this city," Canizaro said. "Education. Crime. Housing. I came to appreciate that no way were we going to get to a solution
unless we included everyone." To round out the group, he appointed a
long list of local African-American leaders, including Alden McDonald, as well as Uptown blue bloods and downtown business interests.
"We have enough people in here who hate each other," Major said at an
early meeting, "to make sure this process works." The resulting report,
"Blueprint for a Better New Orleans," released in 2002, was impressive
in its breadth and specificity, even as it was ignored by the new Nagin
administration. For his efforts, the majority-black City Council declared
September 10, 2003, "Joe C. Canizaro Day."

Nagin and Canizaro met around two weeks after Katrina in Baton
Rouge at the executive center where Canizaro would stay when he was
in town. The rich white Republican from the suburbs seemed to care
more about getting a diverse mix on the citizens' commission Nagin
would soon be naming than Nagin himself. Nagin's initial list seemed as
if it had been drawn up by Jimmy Reiss—predominantly white with a
few token blacks. "Mr. Mayor," Canizaro counseled, "you need to better
reflect the community if this group is going to have any legitimacy." It
would be a struggle, Canizaro said, "because the mayor was allowing
himself to be pulled by these other interests." A final decision came "at
least ten days later than it should have," by Canizaro's reckoning, but in
the end eight African Americans were on the seventeen-member commission and eight whites, with a single Latino. The list included David
White, who said he was "chosen to be the mayor's eyes and ears on the
commission." Ron Forman would not make the cut, though the mayor
acknowledged he had told Forman he would give him "first consideration" as chairman, but Jimmy Reiss, persona non grata in some circles
after his comments to the *Wall Street Journal*, was included. "I'm not
one to throw people off because they're controversial," Nagin said of the
Reiss selection. "You need some edginess, especially in this town."

There was no edge to Mel Lagarde, whom Nagin chose as one of
two people to cochair the commission. Lagarde—or, more formally,
Maurice L. Lagarde III—was a top executive at HCA, the health care
giant. He was a member of the Uptown royalty, a blue blood in good
standing with a big house on St. Charles. He was a Nagin ally and a

friend of Canizaro with a seat on his bank's board of directors. With his bland good looks, Lagarde was a chubby-faced son of Uptown who never uttered a controversial word if he could help it. "Mel," said a fellow member of the commission, "was the white rice you throw into a gumbo to cut the spice."

The other cochair of the mayor's Bring New Orleans Back Commission was Barbara Major, a Canizaro favorite. The two had met in the late 1990s during the pitched fight over a housing project in the lower Garden District. A local developer named Pres Kabacoff had proposed that it be torn down and replaced with a mixed-income housing project. Major, who ran a low-income health clinic in the area, was among those leading negotiations for the tenants. Canizaro got involved because he owned an adjacent parcel and stood to make a lot of money if the city approved Kabacoff's proposal. Major sought out Canizaro after growing fed up with Kabacoff, the son of a local liberal champion, who kept talking about all the benefits to the community of a plan that would see a large portion of the project's residents lose their homes. "Pres Kabacoff wanted to come and save the black folk," Major said. "And Joe Canizaro came and said I want to make money. So we said, 'That's the one we want to talk to.'"

Canizaro was blunt at their first meeting. "People tell me you're difficult to work with," Canizaro said to Major.

"I can be."

"You might hear things about me."

"Yeah, what's that?"

"Well, because my last name is Canizaro, you might hear I have some affiliation with organized crime."

"Well, I'll tell you what. I'd love some organized crime because this disorganized shit is driving me crazy."

Through contacts in the social service world, Major learned about Canizaro's generosity—the bikes he bought for underprivileged kids for Christmas, the help he gave families in need. "Stuff he never talked about but stuff I knew he had done. Christian things," she said. Major, who was raised in the Ninth Ward by a great-aunt who stopped going to school after the fourth grade, saw a little of herself in this local mogul. He would become her champion.

The Bring New Orleans Back Commission included an archbishop, the City Council president, and the president of Tulane University. Yet because of Canizaro, it was co-led by this woman who had spent part of her youth in a housing project and seemed to accept lip from no one. "People tell me, 'You have a New York attitude,'" Major said. "I tell them, 'No, I have a Ninth Ward attitude.'"

Alden McDonald was an obvious choice for the commission. McDonald didn't have time to sit around talking in New Orleans for several hours every week, but he also couldn't afford to pass up a seat. "I always tell young people, 'You want to be on the design side, not the behind side. Because when you're on the behind side, you get shit on,'" McDonald said. The mayor asked him to serve and he agreed.

The mayor unveiled the Bring New Orleans Back Commission at a press conference held at the Sheraton Hotel on September 30—one month and a day after the flooding. The seventeen-person panel included two women: Major and a corporate attorney with a big downtown firm. Of the fifteen men, no fewer than seven were CEOs, and three were bank presidents, including McDonald. From the start, Nagin reflected the comfort level of a mayor who had spent his career inside corporate America. "The importance of this group," said J. Stephen Perry, the head of the New Orleans Convention & Visitors Bureau, "is that it will give the federal government the confidence that the city is harnessing the private sector to do a lot of its work." Barbara Major wasn't nearly as impressed. Blacks represented two-thirds of the city's population, not half. "I think some people don't understand that an equal number of black and white isn't the same as equity," Barbara Major said on the day the commission was announced. "But I tell you what, I give them credit, at least it's fifty-fifty."

10

BRICK BY BRICK

Alden McDonald was alone the first time he saw his house after Katrina. Rhesa was still in Atlanta. She didn't want to fly to Baton Rouge to join him for a drive into New Orleans just to have her heart broken. "I knew I'd be a wreck," she said. That was one task she happily delegated to her husband.

McDonald was on edge by the time he reached his exit on the I-10. He saw destruction everywhere once he passed over the High Rise Bridge and crossed the Industrial Canal into New Orleans East. For years all people saw of the East while whizzing by at sixty or seventy miles an hour were rickety two- and three-story wooden apartment complexes built on the cheap and housing a disproportionate share of the city's working poor. Post-Katrina, they'd see these same buildings except with corners caved in and rooftops exposed. McDonald had to remind himself of the names of the inexpensive motels along the highway. The signage atop the Motel 6 a half dozen blocks from his home had blown out, just as it had at the nearby Days Inn, Clarion Inn, and the Shell station at the bottom of the ramp. He made a right and took in the strip malls that lined either side of the street. The plate-glass windows fronting nearly every store had been destroyed. The innards of each lay scattered across the asphalt.

There were no traffic lights. Not that any cars were on the road. More than once McDonald needed to reverse down the street because of a fallen tree. Once even a boat blocked his way. He flinched when passing a car crushed by a falling tree, but then remembered that practically every car he saw had been ruined by floodwaters. His car, the BMW two-seater that he had parked in the garage, was ruined, but so, too, was the gold Lexus—Rhesa's favorite—that McDonald had parked on the second floor of his bank's parking lot. It had been smashed by falling debris.

McDonald's house was a solid, two-story, brick split-level with a two-car garage. The grass was the color of dried dung as were the shrubs, but at least some green was in the trees. The roof would need patching and the gutters were at crazy angles, but the house didn't look too bad from the outside. It was probably a good sign that he still needed a house key to get inside. Maybe the idea of rebuilding wasn't so far-fetched.

McDonald opened the front door. The odor knocked him back. The pungent, swampy stench was of a home soaking in dirty salt water for weeks of scorching, subtropical heat. The sodden furniture and carpeting in the living room gave off its own fusty perfume, but nothing compared to the kitchen. By that time, McDonald knew better than to open the refrigerator door. He had heard the stories from friends and friends of friends of odors so overpowering they couldn't dislodge them from their sense memories. One had made the mistake of opening a freezer full of rancid meat, fish, and fowl and was haunted by the maggots that had spilled out onto the floor.

McDonald needed to step carefully on floors slick with a thin film of left-behind muck. It was daylight, but without lights it was hard to see in places. He felt disoriented. He looked to where the big couch and chairs should be but instead saw random items on the floor. The furniture sat scattered and overturned around the room, wherever the water had left it. Swirls of mud were everywhere.

Some greeted their drowned-out homes with tears. They'd see a favorite chair or an heirloom handed down from a grandparent and sob. That wasn't McDonald, who fell into that category of New Orleanian who was numb rather than overwrought as he took in the destruction. His mouth agape, his chin thrust forward, his eyes bulging, McDonald stared. The emotion, it seemed, had been shocked out of him.

The McDonalds had become empty nesters shortly before Katrina. Heidi, their oldest, had studied at Spelman College and then gone to Harvard to work on her master's. Chip, their second-born, attended Harvard undergrad and then graduated from Harvard Medical School. He was doing a surgery residency in Dallas in 2005. Todd, the baby of the family, had recently graduated from Morehouse and was living on his own.

The McDonalds had thought about downsizing but they loved the old place, rich with good memories. Another advantage in staying put in this house that had been their home for nearly twenty-five years was a master bedroom on the ground floor. That meant never having to worry about getting up and down the stairs once they were older. Instead of selling, they decided to give the home an upgrade. Now the hardwood floors that had a year earlier cost a fortune were warped and ruined. The light-colored silk couch they'd spent more on than either would care to admit was a muddy, waterlogged, smelly mess. Rhesa had always thought the dining-room set that they had moved from their prior home was wrong for the new place. A year before Katrina, she had finally replaced it with a handsome wood table large enough to accommodate fourteen, along with matching chairs. McDonald found the table sitting outside in the street.

Once McDonald's eyes adjusted to the poor light, he noticed the mold crawling up the walls, great blooms of green and red and black, nasty and evil looking. The wooden furniture looked swollen, the finishes blistering and cracking. A bottle of Chivas sat on a counter, as did jugs of Cheer and Woolite in the laundry room. That was part of the strangeness of Katrina, which left a dirty bathtub ring in houses around the city (for McDonald it hit at around the five-foot mark). Anything below that line was ruined. Anything above probably escaped the water.

McDonald was thankful for some small miracles. Two decades earlier, in 1987, McDonald had served on the executive committee that had welcomed Pope John Paul II to New Orleans. He and Rhesa had met the pope, who gave them a rosary as a gift. The McDonalds displayed the rosary, along with a communion bowl and plate the pope had eaten from, in a china cabinet they had assumed had been destroyed in the flood. But apparently the water hit the cabinet in such a way that it sealed its doors and pinned it to the wall, protecting the contents. The miracle McDonald found in the backyard was even more incredible. A huge oak tree had fallen across the lawn. Yet somehow the statue of the Blessed Mother the couple had put at the base of the oak had gone untouched. McDonald found it where it was supposed to be, except now it was standing between the cleaved halves of the tree, as if this stone rendering of the Virgin Mary had been protected.

The final miracle was their bed. Rhesa McDonald always made the bed first thing every morning, arranging the pillows just so. The rushing waters had settled the bed in the middle of the room, but it otherwise looked untouched. McDonald, always the jokester, told his wife, "You'll be happy. The bed is still made."

Others in a subdivision like his—places where most people had a second floor—invariably ended their visit by stuffing the backseat and trunk with belongings retrieved from the upstairs bedrooms. Owning a home with a first-floor master bedroom was a disadvantage: closets and dressers had for weeks been soaking in the oily, dark waters of the Gulf of Mexico. Only the few items the McDonalds had brought with them to Atlanta would survive Katrina.

Back at his car, McDonald scanned the block. He thought about the doctor next door and the pediatrician who had recently bought a home around the corner. Nearly a month after Katrina, each was no doubt already associated with a hospital if not a practice wherever they had ended up. McDonald had just driven past Methodist Hospital, one of two hospitals in the East. It looked so battered that he couldn't imagine its opening for at least one or two years. He thought about the doctors in his social circle. Their offices were in flooded professional buildings around the East. They had privileges at shuttered hospitals; their patients lived in a hundred different zip codes. New Orleans seemed destined to lose a large portion of its black physicians to cities such as Atlanta, Houston, and Memphis. The neighbor who ran his own plumbing company would have plenty of business to keep him busy, as would the contractor who lived a few houses away. But what about the guy down the block who ran his own insurance office? Was he doomed given the catastrophic losses? Or the funeral director? Would it be worth it for him to rebuild or would he just need to start over somewhere else?

"I don't know if this place is ever coming back," McDonald told more than one friend.

THE THIRD TUESDAY NIGHT of every month, the Liberty board of directors would convene to talk bank business. It had been that way since the earliest days of the bank, when they were still in a trailer, and the tradition had continued in the new headquarters. It had been an extraordinary moment the first time they gathered on the bank's top floor, sitting around a polished dark-wood conference table in a spacious conference room that offered soaring views of the East. Liberty's executive offices were modest compared to the hushed palaces some bankers build for themselves. The furniture was high-end Home Depot, the chairs comfortable but not leather. The splurge was in the art that covered the cream-colored walls. McDonald was in his early forties when he bought his first piece, a Jacob Lawrence limited print for $1,000 that sold for closer to $20,000 when Katrina hit. By 2005, McDonald and the bank owned a trove of artwork by Lawrence, Elizabeth Catlett, and other renowned African-American artists. They lined the hallways and conference room on the building's sixth floor.

Twice the board of directors had the pleasure of gathering in Liberty's new boardroom before Katrina. Their next meeting was held around several mismatched tables pushed together in the back room of a bank branch on the outskirts of Baton Rouge, one month after Katrina.

McDonald couldn't sugarcoat his presentation to the board. To raise cash, McDonald had started selling some of the $40 million in fixed securities Liberty held on to for emergencies. Already the bank had taken a $1 million loss on the first batch of bonds it had sold. Liberty was looking at severance for maybe a hundred employees and no telling yet how many tens of millions of dollars in real estate losses. Ronnie Burns, who had been with the bank since the beginning, had been visiting the Southern branch when a set of regulators came around to poke into some of Liberty's records. "They were as kind as they could be," he told his fellow board members, "but they had this tone, 'I don't know how this is going to work out.'"

Liberty carried insurance, including flood insurance, on its headquarters and branches, McDonald reassured them. The bank also had business-interruption insurance. But that only meant they were in a position to negotiate a settlement that would come nowhere near their true losses. The more critical question was what portion of the bank's loan portfolio was backed by flood insurance. From the insurance industry's perspective, Katrina was less a hurricane and more a flood, and while a homeowner policy would theoretically cover damage caused by the winds, it wouldn't cover anything destroyed by flooding. That's why any borrower living in a flood zone was required to buy flood insurance, yet who knew how many people had allowed their coverage to lapse after they had closed on their loan. Without flood insurance, the remaining balance on any residential or commercial loan was a write-off. The magic number, McDonald told the board, seemed to be around 90 percent: unless 90 percent of their borrowers carried flood insurance, the bank might not survive without a government bailout.

More pressing was the question of whether there would be a New Orleans East or a Gentilly or a Lower Ninth Ward moving forward. Kathleen Blanco had asked Norman Francis, Liberty's founding chairman, to chair the Louisiana Recovery Authority, the state equivalent of the Bring New Orleans Back Commission. Both Francis and McDonald were hearing from influential voices inside the business community about the need to "shrink the footprint"—to right-size a city once home to more than 600,000 that had lost one-quarter of its population even before the city flooded. "Three of our branches I don't see coming back for a long, long time," McDonald warned the board. As for the rest of the bank? That was anyone's best guess.

"If we were going to survive," Ronnie Burns said, "Alden was going to have to rebuild this thing brick by brick."

"WHERE DO PEOPLE SLEEP?" Rhesa asked the first time her future husband had brought her around to meet his family. "On the walls?" She had grown up the only child of a prominent lawyer, the princess whose corner of the house included a private bathroom. The McDonalds, by contrast, were a family of seven living in a two-bedroom shotgun, and that didn't include the set of grandparents who lived with the family throughout much of McDonald's childhood or the stray his sisters occasionally brought home.

McDonald's parents had the back bedroom. The other bedroom had a pair of bunk beds for him and his two brothers and a double bed for the grandparents. The two girls slept on a sofa bed in the living room and made room for a third when necessary. In a pinch, the small space between the living room and the first bedroom could fit a rollaway. Maybe the biggest challenge was managing with a single bathroom. "We came up hard," said the middle brother, Byron.

Their father worked as a waiter at the Boston Club, a place so exclusive no sign was on its building, only an etched *B* on its frosted-glass door on Canal Street. At this whites-only redoubt, Alden McDonald Sr., thin, dark-skinned, and standing over six feet tall, worked his way up to headwaiter during a fifty-two-year career. Aaron McDonald, the baby of the family, described his father as "real smooth." He worked lunch, the cocktail hour, and dinner at the Boston Club and often stayed late for private parties or to serve when Rex met there. On the weekends, he was usually Uptown working the parties of Boston Club members. "He was very highly regarded," Alden McDonald said of his father, though hardly well compensated. This job never paid more than $15,000 a year, including tips, and never included health insurance or retirement benefits. If anyone in the family fell sick, he or she saw a doctor at Charity Hospital.

McDonald's mother always worked. She was a short, stout, good-natured woman who devised any number of ways for bringing extra money into the house. She sold burial insurance to neighbors, most of whom paid by the week, and hired herself out as a kind of community taxi service. First in the family station wagon but then in the van she bought to accommodate more passengers, she carted old people needing to do errands and added extra pickups in the morning when taking her own children to school. She made and sold pickles and candy and, in the warmer months, sold a frozen, sugary concoction the kids called a huckabuck. The family never wanted for food, but had plenty of nights of "stewed wieners"—hot dogs and peas cooked in the same pot.

Everyone started working at an early age in the McDonald household. Two of their mother's brothers were bricklayers who ran their own company. By ten or eleven years old, the boys were working "on the pile," as Byron put it, cleaning and sorting bricks, mixing mortar, and dragging the cinder blocks they could not lift. By thirteen, they joined their father on weekends at the houses of the wealthy white people whose parties the senior McDonald worked. They'd make themselves handy doing yard work or mopping the kitchen floor or helping set up chairs for a party.

All the kids worked hard growing up, but none more so than the oldest son, who always seemed to be doing *something* to make extra money, whether collecting bottles and cans on the street or getting the siblings into car washing. One Christmas, a thirteen-year-old McDonald convinced his younger siblings that what they all wanted was a movie projector for Christmas—and then used it to get them into the movie business. He draped a white sheet over a clothesline he had set up in the empty lot next door and then charged kids a nickel entrance fee. It was the mid-1950s. A movie cost thirty-five cents a day to rent back then, but he'd pick it up on a Saturday because the rental shop was closed on Sundays and that way he got a free day. He also set up a concession stand to sell popcorn and lemonade. He split the take with his siblings, who, as part-owners of the projector, were his business partners. "He always took care of us that way," Byron said. "He was a good older brother."

McDonald wasn't a brilliant student or a standout athlete. He had friends, but not so many or so few that people talked about it. Through his father's Uptown connections, he entered a fancy Catholic prep school, but he didn't study hard and they asked him to leave. He graduated from the local high school, where he continued to post average grades. "I was always more interested in making money than books," McDonald said. He delivered prescriptions for a local drugstore and started a grass-cutting business. He took a job for a local electronics company selling batteries, flashlights, and transistor radios to area stores.

McDonald was from the Seventh Ward, a working-class enclave. His uncles had done well for themselves, so he figured he'd work as a bricklayer after graduating high school. At his parents' behest, he gave college a try, matriculating first to Xavier and then to Loyola University, an Uptown institution next to Tulane. But college proved a repeat of his high school days. The pest-control company that he and a childhood friend had started consumed him more than books. After only a few semesters, he dropped out of Loyola and signed up to study accounting and other more practical skills at a local business trade school.

McDonald's big break came courtesy of his father's Uptown connections. The senior McDonald was working a party Uptown when he heard about the new bank a prominent family in town was starting, the International City Bank and Trust, or ICB. They talked about hiring a few promising young black employees, and the senior McDonald recommended his industrious firstborn. McDonald was twenty-three in 1966 when he and two other African-American men became the first three black bankers in New Orleans history. By twenty-six, McDonald had moved up from part-time bookkeeper to vice president.

McDonald routinely worked eighteen hours a day. Eventually, he was a free-floating manager sent to help fix any underperforming department. McDonald was a vice president but also a black man without portfolio or pedigree working in an almost all-white industry. Yet what might have been a fraught situation was made easier by the manner in which the bank's president handled it. "He'd call a department head into his office and say, 'Alden is being brought in to clean up. So whatever he tells you to do, you'll do.'"

McDonald was twenty-nine when a group of black leaders started meeting to talk about establishing the city's first minority-owned bank. They included Xavier president Norman Francis and Dutch Morial, a former state legislator then serving as a sitting judge, and also a powerful white state senator named Michael Hanley O'Keefe. O'Keefe had been a classmate of Francis's in law school and helped them to secure a charter for their bank and to raise $2 million from a multiracial group of investors. "We couldn't have done it on our own," Francis said. And they couldn't do it without the right person to run their start-up operation.

McDonald said no the first time Francis approached him about going to work for Liberty. He had only been in banking for around six years. He was not ready to leave ICB. Francis laid it on thicker the second time they met. New Orleans needed a bank where all felt welcome, whatever the color of their skin or the size of their bank account. The black community needed a bank to spread homeownership and build a more robust entrepreneurial class. "You can be part of history, Alden," Francis told him. But again McDonald said no. He only said yes the third time because Francis didn't give him any choice.

MCDONALD WASN'T A ONE-DIMENSIONAL career man. He was indefatigable and still had the energy to enjoy himself on Saturday night even when he had been at the office since early that morning. "I had the party house Uptown, but it was Alden who had the party house downtown," said Bill Rouselle, a longtime friend. "You knew you were going late if Alden was putting on the party." There'd be music and dancing and the alcohol flowed. Shortly after the two met, Rhesa attended one of these legendary parties—a birthday bash McDonald was throwing for himself. "I decided to bake him a cake," she said. "When I arrived, I had to put mine next to the six birthday cakes that other ladies had made for him."

They had met at a fund-raiser being held for Rhesa's father, then a crusading civil rights activist running for district court judge. McDonald, who was still working at ICB, confessed he was there to network. Rhesa Ortique was there because she was twenty-two and her mother pushed her single daughter into attending an event certain to draw at least a few bachelors. One of McDonald and Rhesa's earliest conversations was about the new black-owned bank that people were asking him to run. "I think Alden was genuinely scared that he wasn't ready," Rhesa said. McDonald attended a part-time executive training program in Baton Rouge, on LSU's campus. Two years later, he had earned a certificate from LSU's Graduate School of Banking.

Rhesa had been a pioneer in her own right, albeit a reluctant one. In 1962, she had been looking forward to attending high school at Xavier Prep with the rest of her friends. But there was a price for being the only offspring of a crusading civil rights attorney who liked quoting Frederick Douglass's famous line "If there is no struggle, there is no progress." Her father and others were talking about integrating several of the town's more exclusive all-white private schools. So Rhesa and two others were the first blacks to attend Uptown's Ursuline Academy, an all-girls Catholic school that dated back to 1727. "Everyone was perfectly nice to me there, but I never felt that it was my school," Rhesa said. After Ursuline, she would earn a degree at Xavier University of Louisiana. She had just started teaching for the Orleans Parish school district when she met McDonald. The couple would marry two years after they met.

MOON LANDRIEU, THE CITY'S new, liberal mayor, attended Liberty's grand opening in 1972. A stage was set up next to the trailer on Tulane Avenue a few minutes from the central business district. That was the bank's first branch and where McDonald had set up his office. Landrieu addressed the crowd, as did McDonald and Norman Francis. A torch was lit that has been a fixture of the Liberty logo from the beginning. "This bank represents freedom of our community," McDonald said. "A light shining the way for a better New Orleans." They would accelerate black homeownership, speakers said, and provide the essential seed funding to would-be shopkeepers, restaurant owners, and other entrepreneurs in the black community. "We were starting to attain political power," McDonald said, "but not economic power." Two thousand people opened accounts that first day.

Liberty's early days were about survival. "I think of the racism still going on then," said Ronnie Burns, who was one of McDonald's first half-dozen hires. "I think of the odds against any small business." Back then Burns was the one-person accounting department, "but also janitor, courier, and the man who turned the lights on in the morning." Like everyone else, McDonald grabbed a broom if he saw a mess on the floor or picked up a phone if it was ringing.

With only $2 million in start-up cash, mortgages would have to wait, as would commercial loans. Instead McDonald started where he knew the need was great: fairly priced consumer loans for such items as refrigerators, bedroom sets, and home repairs. A lack of banks in the black neighborhoods gave rise to so-called hard moneylenders such as Household Finance and Beneficial that charged annual interest rates of 20 percent or more for loans that McDonald knew would be profitable at less than half that. His customers paid closer to 6 percent. "We saw ourselves as offering financial freedom in the black community," McDonald said. His parents never had much money, but they had faithfully met their financial obligations and so had their neighbors. "Credit score has always been on the bottom of the list for us," McDonald said. "We want to hear that person's story and judge eye to eye if we think they're going to pay us back."

That's not to say McDonald was anyone's soft touch. Once a week, the staff stayed late to work on delinquent accounts. Each staffer was given the same lesson from the young bank president. See if someone will work with you. "Even if someone is willing to pay you just ten dollars or twenty dollars a month, that shows a commitment," he counseled. But the flip side of that was no sympathy for anyone unwilling to agree to a payment plan. "Growing up poor, Alden knew what giving someone a break could mean, but he wasn't going to let anyone step all over him," Ronnie Burns said.

The banker who didn't like being taken advantage of was on display late one evening when a man owing the bank money on a car told McDonald he had no intention of paying what he owed and then hung up the phone. McDonald had his people call the New Orleans cop they kept on retainer for repossessions and then rode shotgun in search of the car. "It's like midnight when we find it," Burns said. The off-duty cop jumped out of the car brandishing a shotgun while another Liberty employee jimmied his way into the car. "I'd go along just to make sure no one does something stupid," McDonald said, but Burns wondered if it wasn't also for a bit of justice. "Alden worked hard each and every day, and he expected the people we did business with to do the same," Burns said.

It took two years to move out of the trailer and into a permanent building. At the same time, Liberty opened a second branch in nearby Gentilly, another predominantly black community. "With Alden it was all about perseverance," said Bill Rouselle. McDonald's old friend from the days when they had competing party houses had become the city's first on-air black television reporter in 1968 before cofounding a marketing company two decades later. McDonald was a natural at marketing, Rouselle said, but it was his "Eveready bunny" personality that was the difference. "He just kept pushing, pushing, pushing. And when there were obstacles in his way, he kept moving and eventually he got there." One clever PR gimmick that won the bank attention was what

McDonald called "five minutes with the president": anyone thinking he or she had unfairly been turned down for a loan could take the case to McDonald.

Most new banks lose money for a few years before they start to make money. Liberty was profitable from year one. "In the early years, Alden would scare me sometimes, but he understood the need for us to take risks more than I did," Norman Francis said. "Not willy-nilly risks, but the risks that would let the bank serve its core function helping the black community grow." Six years after it opened its door, in 1978, Dutch Morial, one of the Liberty's founders, was elected mayor. Soon the City Council majority shifted from white to black. "Liberty would become this test of black consciousness in the community," said Jacques Morial, who was ten when he opened a savings account at his father's new bank using the $20 he had earned working the opening-day festivities. The bank opened a third and then a fourth branch.

Liberty was able to start offering mortgages shortly before its tenth year. It helped that the competition was guilty of redlining—the practice of withholding loans to minority communities—in a robust economy. Oil prices spiked from under $10 a barrel in 1974 to more than $40 a barrel in 1980, and the same gushers that made the city of Dallas a perfect locale for a nighttime soap opera about avarice and lust had a big impact on New Orleans as well. The area's refineries and the offshore oil rigs meant opportunities for the ambitious Uptown blue blood looking to extend the family fortune (Jimmy Reiss, for instance, who made tens of millions of dollars selling them supplies and technology), but it also meant good-paying blue-collar jobs. Liberty also started offering college loans. Again credit score would prove only a small factor when evaluating someone's risk portfolio.

Liberty also started making business loans. The city's main newspaper, the *Times-Picayune*, dubbed chef Leah Chase, the co-owner of Dooky Chase's, "the Queen of Creole." Since first opening its doors in the 1940s, Dooky's was the only white-tablecloth establishment that served black customers. When it needed money in the 1980s to expand, Liberty loaned Chase and her husband, Dooky Jr., $120,000. "Before Alden McDonald, it was hard to even get a conversation with a banker,"

Leah Chase said. Liberty bankrolled other promising restaurateurs and also a former Pizza Hut executive who grew a chain of forty franchises in the area, creating hundreds of jobs.

Oil prices crashed in the mid-1980s. Crude had dropped to $14 a barrel in 1986, and remained in the teens or low twenties for a decade. People lost jobs, hours were slashed, the price of real estate plummeted. Liberty posted its first loss in 1987, then its second and third in 1988 and 1989. No local bank turned a profit during those three years, but unlike several others, Liberty stayed open. To save money, the bank organized systems to make sure the paper clip used at the front end of a process would be reclaimed in a box at the end. The bank went more than a year without spending a dime on rubber bands courtesy of a retired postal worker who told McDonald he could get as many as the bank needed from his old place of work. Liberty didn't lay off a single employee. "We were well seasoned in survival by the time Katrina hit," McDonald said.

The downturn caused heartache but also opportunity. Liberty had helped plenty of young professionals buy homes for $150,000 or $200,000 in burgeoning middle-class black neighborhoods, but McDonald thought of people like his parents who'd worked hard their whole lives but never had a chance at homeownership. The drop in oil prices meant that a wider range of the population could afford the monthly payment on a house. Liberty created a loan that could be had for a down payment as low as 3 percent. That way McDonald could underwrite plenty of mortgages for homes costing $50,000 to $70,000 in working-class enclaves such as the Seventh Ward. The program proved successful enough that Fannie Mae, the government-backed mortgage giant, flew McDonald to Washington so its people could learn more.

In the 1990s, the bank opened a branch in Uptown, on Magazine Street, and another across the river on the West Bank. It expanded to Baton Rouge and Jackson, Mississippi, and moved its operations to a larger space in New Orleans East. Liberty put up the money when a group of African-American doctors proposed a multistory professional building in New Orleans East. It funded small shopping centers and other sizable projects. The bank's original $2 million investment turned into $20 million, turned into $200 million. Liberty had $350 million in assets by the time of Katrina.

THE LAYOFFS POST-KATRINA WEREN'T as wrenching as McDonald had feared. People were in Atlanta or Houston or Chicago, and their children were already attending a school. Others felt incapable of getting themselves back to the region. They were in Tampa or Memphis or Oakland, California, because that's where they had people, and they were too traumatized to face all that they had lost. Some employees apologized to him that they weren't available to pitch in when the bank needed them. As of the one-month anniversary of Katrina, Liberty had 41 of its 150 employees back on staff. Of the rest, just under 40 percent said they wanted to return to work but couldn't through at least the end of the school year. Twenty-eight people—nearly one in five employees—still hadn't checked in.

McDonald seemed to have little trouble settling into his new Baton Rouge life. He replaced his rent-a-car with a silver minivan, and he started looking for a house. He figured it would be at least a year before he and Rhesa were living back in New Orleans. The drive down to the city from the state capital was usually a two-hour trek with so many people using Baton Rouge as a temporary base. Home in New Orleans became the RV he bought so at least he had a bed in town. It sat in the Liberty employee parking lot for three years.

On Mondays, McDonald was in New Orleans for the Bring Back New Orleans meetings. Often he stayed the night to take care of other business he had in the city, but the pull of Baton Rouge was still strong: That's where his staff was housed and for the moment the bank examiners felt more comfortable meeting someplace other than New Orleans. It wasn't uncommon for him to make a second trip to New Orleans each week as the center of gravity shifted back to the city. Every other weekend he tried to make it to Atlanta to spend time with Rhesa.

IN MID-OCTOBER, SIX WEEKS after Katrina, McDonald snuck away to Europe to join Rhesa and a group of their friends on a cruise of the

Greek islands. The launch point for the cruise, which had been organized before Katrina, was Rome, a city Rhesa had always wanted to see.
The original plan had them spending a week there before joining their
friends. McDonald begged off that part of the trip, so rather than enjoying a second honeymoon, Rhesa hung out with two girlfriends in the
$700-a-night suite that McDonald had booked months earlier as a gift
to his wife—another empty-nest splurge by a couple accustomed to far
more modest accommodations. McDonald nearly didn't make the second half of the trip, either. Arriving in Atlanta a few hours early for his
connecting flight to Rome, he headed to the plane's slated departure gate
and fell asleep. A last-minute gate change meant that a groggy McDonald was pleading his case to a gate agent ten minutes before the flight,
by which time the airline had given away his seat. His break came when
he looked down at her ID badge and saw that her name was Katrina.
"You're not going to believe this," he began. This kinder, gentler Katrina
secured McDonald a seat. From the airport in Rome he headed straight
to the ship—then fell asleep in the wrong cabin.

McDonald appeared rested and calmer after his return. He even
dressed differently, dropping the polos and short-sleeved cabana shirts
that had been his attire since the storm. After Rome, casual might be a
pair of gray slacks and a white dress shirt stamped with the green Liberty Bank logo that someone had found lying around the Baton Rouge
branch. Dressing up meant wearing the blue blazer he had bought for
himself after the storm and choosing from among the three new ties he
now owned.

The bank reopened its first branch in New Orleans in early October, six weeks after Katrina. Lines formed every morning outside
the doors of this Liberty outpost on Magazine Street in the Garden
District—its sole property inside the city limits that escaped Katrina
relatively unscathed. The wind had caused a bit of cosmetic damage
to the facade of this white-columned building, but nothing—neither
water nor looters—had harmed the marble floors or dark-wood decor.
"We have people arriving in from all over," said Anderson Williams, the
lobby guard. One day it was a couple who had driven from Atlanta and
another who had flown in from Los Angeles. People arrived to fill out
change-of-address cards and to order new checks, but mainly they were

eager to learn what was expected of them now that they had lost everything, including a weekly paycheck.

Barbara and Robert Emelle, the couple who had flown in from L.A., were retired after careers in the Orleans Parish schools. He had worked as a gym teacher, she as an administrator. These lifelong residents of New Orleans had been with Liberty since its days in a trailer on Tulane Avenue, but after visiting their home in New Orleans East, they were on Magazine Street to close their account. "Totaled," Robert said. "We concluded we'd be taking too big a chance rebuilding," Barbara said. Instead they would look to buy something in Atlanta.

The manager of the Magazine Street branch, Sheila Howard, had been with Liberty for nine years. On the Thursday after Katrina she had shown up at the Baton Rouge branch ready to work. She was living with family in Gramercy, a small town fifty miles west of New Orleans. Donna Walker, a thirteen-year Liberty veteran who had worked in New Orleans East prior to the storm, was staying with family in the West Bank. A pair of tellers fortunate enough to live in a dry part of the city handled deposits and withdrawals while Howard and Walker cared for customers arriving with more complicated issues. A sitting area that could accommodate a half dozen wasn't nearly big enough, so they brought in extra folding chairs and set them up wherever space was free. A meeting with either Howard or Walker meant waiting an hour or more.

"We'd bring on more employees, but housing is an issue," Howard said. Eventually, two more employees were dispatched to Magazine Street, but only temporarily. They would be needed across the river once repairs were completed on the West Bank branch, which opened at the end of October. McDonald then hired a marketing company. "I want to get out the word that we're alive and well," McDonald said.

The lines at Liberty's two New Orleans branches were welcome news, but more people in the city meant they were short-staffed in Baton Rouge. McDonald also had no idea when he might reopen a branch in a flooded part of the city. "Where will the jobs come from?" McDonald asked. "And if there's jobs, where will people live and where will their kids go to school?" Even McDonald himself couldn't say for certain he would rebuild. In November, he closed on a three-bedroom house he had found near Southern University in Baton Rouge for $150,000. Rhesa and her parents moved in with him during Thanksgiving week. Rhesa searched for doctors for her parents while shopping for the furniture and other items they needed to make Baton Rouge home.

Cash flow was a big worry. People needed capital if they were going to rebuild, and the bank needed to start lending again to make money. McDonald unveiled what he dubbed Katrina Investment Deposits, or KIDs. These were nothing but certificates of deposit, or CDs, offering a below-market interest rate wrapped in a feel-good package. The going rate for a CD then was 5 percent, but McDonald was offering interest rates of between 2 and 2.5 percent. "If I can get a hundred friends and banks and corporations from around the country to send me one hundred thousand dollars, that's ten million dollars," McDonald said. "If I get two hundred, that's twenty million dollars." By October 31, a friend of McDonald's who ran a big investment fund in Boston had secured roughly $5 million in commitments, primarily from other banks willing to help one of their own. That money would be used to jump-start home lending, Liberty's primary profit source.

Friends in high places could prove critical in the coming months. McDonald had met with Bill Clinton when the former president visited New Orleans a few weeks after Katrina. McDonald had spoken about his decimated bank with the Reverend Jesse Jackson and also with Andrew Young, the former Martin Luther King aide who served two terms as Atlanta mayor. His two most important allies, however, might prove to be a pair of white men who ranked as two of Washington's more successful lobbyists, Robert Livingston and John Breaux.

Former US senator John Breaux, a Democrat, had represented Louisiana in Congress for thirty-two years before retiring the year prior to Katrina and taking a position at lobbying giant Patton Boggs. Robert Livingston, a Republican, had represented New Orleans in Congress for twenty-two years. He was several days from taking over as Speaker of the House in 1998—until Larry Flynt, the publisher of *Hustler*, responded to the impeachment of Bill Clinton by offering $1 million to anyone digging up sexual dirt on a Republican member of Congress. Exposed as an adulterer, Livingston resigned from Congress in 1999 and opened his own lobbying shop called the Livingston Group.

Breaux and McDonald, who had known one another for at least

twenty-five years, spoke after Katrina. McDonald followed up their conversation with a list of items he wanted to see in any recovery package, including a provision dictating that a minimum share of federal aid must be funneled through smaller banks in the region. Breaux assembled a team inside Patton Boggs to work on what he dubbed a Financial Industries Working Group and offered comments that negated the happy talk dreamed up by the marketing firm McDonald had hired. "What we're trying to do," Breaux said, "is figure out how the federal government can help keep them open."

McDonald didn't know Livingston as well as Breaux, but the former Republican lawmaker offered to help. If ever McDonald doubted Livingston's influence, any disbelief was dispelled when a couple of weeks after Katrina, McDonald complained of some problem he was facing—and by day's end he was talking with someone inside the White House. Asked why he was offering his services at no charge to someone he didn't know well, Livingston responded, "This is a particularly acute situation given this is the largest African-American bank in New Orleans." He would push both the White House and Congress to require that at least $6 billion in federal aid flow through Liberty and the other community banks. "Without that," Livingston said, "I don't see how Liberty survives."

11

BLUE SKY

Boysie Bollinger settled into a conference room on the second floor of the Sheraton Hotel on the last day of September. Bollinger, the CEO of Bollinger Shipyards, had spent much of the past month overseeing the cleanup of a pair of wrecked facilities his company operated in the area. He arrived at the Sheraton for this first meeting of the mayor's Bring New Orleans Back Commission thinking he already knew how dire the city's situation was. Then he sat through the PowerPoint presentation the mayor's team had prepared. "The scope of the devastation was hard to comprehend," Bollinger said.[1] More than one hundred thousand homes in the city had been damaged, and most every business was shuttered.

---

1. Donald T. Bollinger struck many as an unusual choice for the commission. He lived in Lockport, Louisiana, fifty miles to the south and west of New Orleans (he also owned a pied-à-terre at the foot of Canal Street), but he was also a good friend of President Bush. His family had called him Boysie since childhood, but he said, "When the president of the United States started calling me Boysie, that's when the name really stuck."

Even the weight of the water on the streets for all those weeks meant broken roads all over the city—and an untold number of cracks in the sixteen hundred miles of waste- and drinking-water pipes beneath them.

"That was the meeting where we scared everybody so bad," Nagin said, "I felt obliged to tell them it was okay if they didn't want to come back for meeting number two."

The most daunting moment for Bollinger came when fellow commissioner Dan Packer, the CEO of Entergy New Orleans, rose to talk about the city's electric and gas systems. Packer told them about the ruined substations, switchyards, and power plants and confessed that the utility had no idea when they might be able to restore power in much of the rest of the city. He also said it was too early to tell how many tens of miles of cracked gas lines they would need to replace. First they needed to flush out the salt water corroding a system that was more than a century old.

Marcia St. Martin gave a similarly dire presentation. Her agency may have pulled off a miracle when it dewatered the city in three weeks, but that was only step one in fixing a devastated water and sewer system. Just prior to the storm, St. Martin had instructed her people to open the valves and dump raw sewage into the Mississippi. The decision, while controversial, was smart given the flooding, but one month later, sixty-six of the pump-and-lift stations her agency used to move wastewater were still not operational. Her people were installing temporary pumps and generators around the city, but meanwhile, whatever people flushed down the toilet—"untreated product," St. Martin called it— was still being dumped in the river. The agency's two waste-treatment plants had been badly damaged, and one of the agency's two giant water-purification plants was incapacitated. Even the water they were drinking that day at the Sheraton had been trucked from the West Bank.

One-quarter of the city's police cars had been destroyed in the flooding. More than half its fire engines were lost along with a large percentage of its ambulances. More than 200 of its 272 buses had been destroyed. Each bus would cost around $300,000 to replace unless the city upgraded to hybrids; then the cost would be closer to $500,000. The RTA didn't lose any of its St. Charles streetcars, but falling tree limbs had destroyed the overhead wiring that powered them. But the two dozen pristine streetcars used on the old Canal Street line the agency had revived only sixteen months before Katrina were damaged. All twenty-four would need to be refurbished at a cost of nearly $1 million apiece.

The city could count on FEMA to cover a large share of the damage. But the federal law that spells out the rules of disaster assistance, called the Stafford Act, stipulated that the federal government would only reimburse for overtime pay, not base salaries, and capped at $5 million the amount a municipality could borrow to cover its operating expenses. The city had an annual budget of around $500 million and six thousand people on its payroll. The city normally collected an average of $13 million in sales taxes each month, "but we expect that number to be closer to zero for the foreseeable future," Reggie Zeno, the city's finance director, told the group. The city's second-largest source of revenue, property taxes, was also unreliable. The tax was based on the assessed value of a property, but what was a person's home or business worth in New Orleans East or Lakeview? The parking tickets people wouldn't be paying in a near-empty city; the taxes New Orleans imposed on the utilities, which were largely out of commission—these and other fees added up to millions more in missing revenues. The city owed payments on more than $300 million in bonds. Yet its only reliable source of funds, Zeno told them, was the $1.5 million Harrah's was required to pay the city every month even as its casino doors remained closed. Widespread municipal layoffs seemed inevitable.

The bad news kept coming. More than 100 of the public school system's 128 buildings had seen flooding, including the district's headquarters. The commissioners also learned that the city was without a criminal justice system. The local courts were closed indefinitely and the evidence room flooded. The parish prison took on four feet of water at its main complex, rendering it unusable. Inmates awaiting trial had been dispatched to prisons around the state, where they remained in a holding pattern.[2] The city aquarium, one of New Orleans's leading

---

2. For months, defense attorneys, private investigators, and others were finding lost inmates. That included many doing what insiders dubbed "Katrina time," such as the woman picked up just prior to Katrina on a prostitution charge who was locked up for seven months on a charge that carried a six-month maximum, had anyone bothered to find her guilty of anything.

tourist attractions, had lost five thousand fish and other creatures in Katrina, and City Park, at thirteen hundred acres one of the country's largest urban greenspaces, had lost a thousand trees during the storm; another thousand were on the critical list. All trade shows and annual meetings scheduled for New Orleans had been canceled through at least March 31, 2006, in a city third only to Las Vegas and Orlando in convention business.

The city's damaged flood-control system barely earned a mention that day, but that didn't make it any less pressing a problem. "As far as I'm concerned, the levee system is the number one issue," Boysie Bollinger said. "Because if you can't protect what you're talking about rebuilding, what's the use of doing anything?" But Bollinger, a generous donor to the Republican Party, was nothing if not a realist. "In the last hundred years, we've had less than five Category Fives hit America," he said. Could the city reasonably expect the US government to pay for a system strong enough to withstand a Category 5 storm when the city's list of needs was so long?

Another question no doubt preoccupied many in the room that day: Should the city permit people to rebuild wherever they wanted, even if that meant they were putting themselves in harm's way again, or should the city ban rebuilding in the lowest-lying parts of the city? Even if they allowed people to rebuild wherever they wanted, would they have the money to promise police, fire, and other city services to the whole city? Once a city of 625,000, New Orleans was down below 500,000 people by Katrina—and who knew if and when the population would get back to even 300,000? "It will be a smaller New Orleans," Alden McDonald said. "Except no one has decided which part."

A KIND OF BLUE-SKY syndrome infected New Orleans after Katrina. To many, a flooded New Orleans meant a blank slate on which to create a new and better city. "Build up, not out" was a familiar mantra voiced in the weeks after Katrina. Entire neighborhoods were being reimagined as parklands, while other parts of the city would be transformed into mini-metropolises thick with condo developments. The mayor used the Bring New Orleans Back Commission to avoid voicing any opinion on the city's future. "We've put a process in place," he repeated. "Now let that process work."

For residents, though, the mayor's commission seemed one more irritant to endure. People's displeasure was a constant on WWL, which was still the only radio station operating in New Orleans. Ann Marie was on the line from Gentilly, carping to talk-show host Garland Robinette about the mayor's putting their lives on collective hold for at least three more months. One heard the frustration when the Wall sisters and their neighbors gathered on Monday evenings at True Light Baptist. "We're not pieces on a chessboard for people to play with," boomed a speaker at one early meeting at True Light Baptist.

Would Lakeview be included on a citywide "do not resuscitate" list? And even if not, what would the neighborhood be like if only half its residents chose to rebuild? Two people not waiting to find out were Artie Folse and Tonja Osborne. Every day, Folse and his eighty-year-old father showed up at their house in Lakeview. Working eight- and ten-hour days, they cleared out the ruined furniture and other debris before turning to the mold. "You scrubbed, bleached, and let everything dry out—and then did it again," Folse said.

Five weeks after they started, Folse and his father started to rebuild. Tired of driving back and forth across the bridge to their temporary perch in the West Bank, Folse, who was fifty-three, camped out in a bedroom on the second floor, though technically he was in violation of the mayor's look-and-leave policy. "The first thing we did was put in a hot-water heater so I could wash up," Folse said. Let some blue-ribbon commission tell them Lakeview should revert to swampland. By the time the mayor's commission would get around to making any grand pronouncements, Folse, Osborne, and other like-minded pioneers scattered around the flooded zone would have invested tens of thousands of dollars in their homes. Declaring any part of the city off-limits to redevelopment would mean destroying homes for a second time.

FREDDY YODER DIDN'T PLAN on giving a speech at the big rally some of his Lakeview neighbors had organized near the breach in the Seventeenth Street Canal. But even the elected officials who spoke that day weren't providing answers. "People were desperate for information," Yoder said. "They were desperate for some semblance of hope. And they were getting neither from their government." Would people need a city permit to start gutting their houses? The answer was no, but the question elicited an ambiguous response. Whose job was it to cart away the ruined insides of their homes? Yoder knew the Army Corps of Engineers was responsible for the cleanup, but the person posing the question was told, "I don't know." So in front of a crowd he estimated at five hundred people, Yoder stood up to share what he knew.

Yoder was president of Durr Heavy Construction, one of the largest construction companies in the New Orleans metro area. His firm laid the sewer and drainage lines in the city's public housing projects; they installed water and electrical systems in buildings throughout the region. In the aftermath of Katrina, no one needed Yoder for the kind of underground systems that were Durr's specialty, but his firm owned trucks and other heavy equipment. A call from Phillips & Jordan, one of the big multinationals hired by the federal government to help with the cleanup, proved a double payday for Yoder, a past president of the Lakeview Civic Improvement Association and still a member of the organization's board. "I was hired to do all of the storm-recovery work in Lakeview," Yoder said. "Helped with the dewatering, pushed aside debris, removed vegetation, picked up debris, hauled it to the landfill."

Yoder is heavyset with sleepy eyes and a matter-of-fact attitude even toward the eight feet of water that covered his neighborhood for weeks. "To me Katrina was just something you'd have to get past," he said. At the rally, he answered people's questions, but more important, he reminded the community that it had the resources, the pull, and the drive to survive. "Don't let anyone tell you Lakeview isn't coming back," he told his neighbors. "We're coming back and stronger than ever."

A WEEK AFTER THE city's finance director laid out the grim news for the Bring New Orleans Back Commission, Nagin held a press conference to announce he was laying off half the city's workforce—nearly three thousand people. Each of the laid-off employees would receive three months' pay, dating back to the day of the storm. "We've talked to local banks and other financial institutions, and we are just not able to put together the financing necessary to continue to maintain our City Hall staffing at its current levels," the mayor told reporters. Most of those laid off were clerical and support staff, so the city was cutting closer to one-third its personnel expenses rather than half. One exception was the Planning Department. At a time the city seemed desperate for experienced planners, the mayor shrank that department from thirty-six to eight.

All seven-thousand-plus employees of the Orleans Parish schools were placed on what the district called "disaster leave without pay" and then laid off en masse. That meant more than ten thousand public employees, a large portion of them black, were out of jobs at the same time most were also without a home. Layoff notices had been sent to people's pre-Katrina addresses and directed teachers seeking an appeal to show up at an office that had been closed since the flood. Teachers had contracts and most were tenured, yet the authorities maintained no recall list. Teachers were free to apply for a job when new schools reopened, but no one would be guaranteed a position, no matter what his or her seniority. A lawsuit filed by teachers would drag through the courts for years.

The city looked to Baton Rouge for help, but it was New Orleans's further misfortune to need the state when officials were reeling not just from Katrina but also Rita. The twin strikes meant disaster zones in both the southeast and southwest corners of the state that flooded a combined 125,000 homes. New Orleans would need to share whatever money the feds disbursed through the state with more than a dozen other parishes. Workers who had lost a job because of Rita or relocated to someplace outside the state meant tens of millions more in lost state income tax. Fewer cash registers operating in the southwest corner of the state meant millions more in missing sales tax money. Greg Albrecht, the chief economist for the state's Legislative Fiscal Office, calculated that the two storms added up to nearly $1 billion in lost revenue.

Citing a state statute that dictated that a governor must keep her budget in balance, Blanco, at the start of October, summoned legislators to Baton Rouge for an emergency legislative session. Then even before they arrived, she announced more than $400 million in unilateral cuts, including the entire budget of New Orleans's Charity Hospital. Charity had suffered relatively minor damage, but keeping the hospital closed saved the state tens of millions of dollars. "Charity's patients aren't in the city," Blanco rationalized. "They're in Houston or Philadelphia." Blanco proposed that the state cover the remaining $600 million deficit by dipping into its reserves and issuing bonds.

The emergency session proved another blow to a governor whose approval rating had already fallen from a pre-storm 55 percent to 38 percent. Blanco took flak from Republicans, who charged that she didn't go far enough in making cuts, but her left flank was what worried aides. The governor had good relations with the legislature's black caucus, but several days into the two-week special session, they sued, charging Blanco with breaking the law when she slashed the state budget without legislative approval. "In this tragic time, we can't balance the budget on the backs of poor people and the backs of the very people displaced," said Representative Cedric Richmond, who represented parts of New Orleans in the state legislature. No one questioned the governor's claim that Charity's patients were living elsewhere, but members of the black caucus and others argued many couldn't come home without a hospital for the working poor and others without insurance. Charity would remain closed while their suit worked its way through the courts.

The legislature and the governor agreed on at least one issue: a bill that stripped the Orleans Parish school board of control over most of the city's public schools. The schools in New Orleans had been a preoccupation of the governor's even before Katrina. Louisiana's school system was one of the poorest performing in the country, ranking as low as forty-sixth in student achievement, and Orleans Parish's scores ranked it second to last among the state's sixty-four parishes. The year before Katrina, school officials admitted they couldn't account for $60 million in expenditures. While the main culprit was sloppy accounting, not malfeasance, as a punishment an outside management team was put in charge of the district's finances. Shortly before Katrina, the state legislature had granted the governor the right to take over schools the state's Department of Education deemed "unacceptable," mainly as a tool for fighting school failure in New Orleans.

Two months after Katrina, the state took over more than a hundred schools in Orleans Parish, leaving the city's elected school board with control over only the eight schools whose test scores were too high to

permit a state takeover. A Recovery School District was formed, and
the state's superintendent of schools signed an "emergency suspension of
education laws" that helped ease the way for charter schools by stripping
teachers and staff of the right to vote on a school's fate. "The storm gave
us the perfect opportunity to rebuild the school system from the ground
up," Blanco said. "And I was intent on seizing that opportunity." Critics
accused her of using a crisis to overreach her authority, but to Blanco it
was possibly the flood's only silver lining.

"I TALKED A LOT with Karl and the White House in those early days,"
Joe Canizaro said. And Rove had always made it clear to Canizaro that
federal dollars for New Orleans were contingent on there being blue-
prints that they could underwrite. The president had said as much in his
Jackson Square speech. "The federal government will undertake a close
partnership with the states of Louisiana and Mississippi and the city of
New Orleans," Bush said, "so they can rebuild in a sensible, well-planned
way."

Whose plan would the president use?

The same day Nagin unveiled his blue-ribbon panel, the City Council announced that it was forming its own advisory group. Nagin had
given City Council president Oliver Thomas a seat on the Bring New
Orleans Back Commission, but that didn't stop Thomas and his council allies from championing their own panel. In contrast to the mayor's
commission, Thomas said, the council's panel would be populated by
people "who can roll up their sleeves and come out with some real recommendations. Concrete stuff that the city can act on." Three weeks later,
the governor caused more confusion with the creation of the Louisiana
Recovery Authority. This twenty-three-member commission, Blanco
announced, would set "a body of principles that will guide Louisiana's
long-range recovery efforts." Presumably, the governor didn't expect the
mayor's commission to put its planning on hold while her appointees
worked out those principles.

The mayor's panel included two Bush favorites, Canizaro and also
Bollinger. Nagin also had a budding friendship with the president.
That relationship may explain Bush's decision that October to meet

with the mayor's panel for a meal at Bacco in the French Quarter. Such was the chaotic state of New Orleans in the fall of 2005 that Boysie Bollinger used the president's decision to dine with them as a declaration of victory. "I'm thinking that him coming and having dinner with us and talking about what he needs from us differentiates us from other groups," Bollinger boasted.[3]

PEOPLE COMPLAINED ABOUT THE makeup of the mayor's commission. Where were the artists or writers or thinkers? the *Times-Picayune*'s Chris Rose asked in a column running under the headline "All the Wrong Visionaries." The mayor had the sense to include a musician among his seventeen picks, but inexplicably selected trumpeter Wynton Marsalis, a terrific musician from a highly regarded New Orleans family, but one who had been living in New York for two decades. The head of the city's Convention & Visitors Bureau questioned a panel that lacked a single restaurant owner or hotel executive in a tourist-oriented economy.

The commissioners themselves did their share of carping. Many were shocked when the mayor and his people moved them to a big ballroom inside the Sheraton. Hundreds of chairs were set up for spectators and cameras were brought in to broadcast the proceedings on local cable-access television. "I question that decision," Bollinger said publicly, echoing what other commissioners were saying privately. Their main concern after a couple of meetings was that the cameras were quelling honest debate among them. Already Bollinger was annoyed with Oliver Thomas, whom he described as "always worked up about something and up on his high horse, acting like the harmed party." Yet

---

3. The City Council's commission proved to be more press release than alternative effort. "The council pledged to provide the committee with adequate staff resources and set a date for the first meeting for mid-October," Robert B. Olshansky and Laurie A. Johnson, a pair of planning professionals, wrote in their book, *Clear as Mud: Planning for the Rebuilding of New Orleans.* "That meeting was never held, and there were no subsequent announcements regarding the existence or intentions for this committee."

Nagin needed the broadcasts to show the wider world that progress was being made. The cameras remained.

The public complained about the commission, but the commission also complained about the public. Its mandate was to have a viable rebuilding plan on the mayor's desk by year's end, but in anxiety-filled New Orleans, the commission served as a proxy for all levels of government. Vexed that no one at FEMA or the Small Business Administration would respond to your requests? Frustrated that city officials would still not let you see your home more than a month after Katrina? Angry that the cleanup crews and other contractors were out-of-towners when New Orleanians desperately needed jobs and the business? In a town where residents were desperate for answers, people knew that this group blessed by the mayor would be meeting in a Sheraton ballroom every Monday starting at 2:00 p.m. The first hour or so of every meeting would be devoted to housekeeping chores, and then the public would be invited to share their ideas for rebuilding New Orleans. Yet rare was the citizen taking a turn at the microphone who actually shared a concept related to the job at hand. "We were there to develop a plan for the city, not to talk about who would pick up their trash or to open the schools," complained Tulane University's Scott Cowen. The commission would endure two or three hours of public venting before adjourning until the next week.

To get some work done, the commission broke itself into committees. Cowen was put in charge of education, and Entergy's Dan Packer headed economic development. Given all he had to do running a bankrupt utility, Packer went outside the commission to choose Bill Hines, the high-profile lawyer and Nagin confidant, as his cochair. Jimmy Reiss led the committee on infrastructure, which would dictate the schedule for repairing the city's broken systems. Joe Canizaro, because he was either brave or foolish, volunteered to chair Urban Planning. Canizaro's committee would decide the fate of New Orleans East, Lakeview, and other low-lying neighborhoods.

Canizaro also went outside the commission when he named as his cochair a local architect named Ray Manning, who was black. And with the permission of his fellow commissioners, he sought to enlist the help of the Urban Land Institute, or ULI, a nonprofit research organization funded largely through developers like himself. Canizaro, who had served as ULI chairman, had seen firsthand how the organization mobilized teams to help after earthquakes, floods, and other disasters. "Mr. Chairman, they have the experience and they have the expertise," Canizaro said. They would also bring the more removed perspective of outsiders. In the first half of November, the best and the brightest from around the country would come to the city for what the ULI billed as a "summit" on dreaming up a smarter, better version of pre-flood New Orleans.

The anticipated summit gave the commission a reasonable excuse for putting on hold any discussion of the fate of the city's lowest-lying neighborhoods. Yet rather than wait for the ULI's diagnosis, Oliver Thomas proposed that as a body they commit to rebuilding the entire city, the Lower Ninth Ward and New Orleans East included. Every commissioner voted in favor of Thomas's resolution except Canizaro, who abstained. "I don't want to see people rebuilding on quicksand," Canizaro said during debate over the vote. "I think it's important that we make sure that all of the people in New Orleans East and the Lower Ninth Ward have an opportunity to live in a safe and secure area that is not susceptible to destruction in future disasters." The next morning, he was less diplomatic. Eating $25 scrambled eggs in a dining room graced by a chamber music orchestra, Canizaro shook his head over "Oliver's grandstand."

He groused, "I thought the whole idea here was that everything would be on the table."

12

SHRINK THE FOOTPRINT

Nagin was back in his City Hall office. His suits and dress clothes, like the rest of his home, had survived Katrina, but for months he continued to dress in his Katrina wear. No matter whom he might be meeting—the president, the governor, Larry King—Nagin wore a short-sleeved polo and dress slacks. The mayor chose not to move home and instead secured an apartment in one of the historic Pontalba buildings on Jackson Square, a pair of matching redbrick beauties with wrought-iron-lace balconies that had been built in the 1840s.[1] A common sight in small-town New Orleans was the mayor and a large bodyguard bouncing between his City Hall office, a meeting at the Sheraton, and his new digs in the French Quarter, just steps from Café Du Monde. "He always had this glazed look," said one city worker who ran into the mayor regularly.

A fragile Ray Nagin was overseeing the city's recovery in the fall of

---

1. Truman Capote described the Pontalba buildings as the "oldest, in some ways most somberly elegant, apartment houses in America." They would be declared a National Historic Landmark in 1974.

2005. In early October, the mayor arrived at the Sheraton to address three hundred people there for a meeting to help locals get work with the big outside firms descending on New Orleans as part of the cleanup effort. The NAACP, AFL-CIO, and others who had organized the gathering had invited the mayor, hoping he could use his pulpit to convince those outside the city to view the recovery as a vehicle for bringing people home. Instead the mayor chose that moment to take a swipe at the thousands of Latino laborers who had descended on New Orleans after the storm—people whom most locals, black or white, seemed to appreciate for their willingness to do the miserable work of gutting homes and cleaning out ruined, malodorous restaurants in a hot city. "I can see it in your eyes," Nagin began. "You want to know, 'How do I take advantage of this incredible opportunity? How do I make sure New Orleans is not overrun with Mexican workers?'"

At a press conference a few days after his Mexican workers comment, Nagin said, "Now is the time for us to think out of the box"—and Sally Forman flinched. He had been thinking about the gambling industry, he told the assembled reporters, and all those billions they had to invest. Why not create a casino district in the center of the city? He hoped to enlist the governor's support, he said, perhaps unaware that Blanco had campaigned on a moratorium on new casinos. "We're a cash-strapped city," Nagin said. "I know of no other way."

The casino proposal seemed to perturb the Uptown establishment as much because the mayor had failed to vet his proposal with them as because of the idea itself. As director of the city's zoo and aquarium, Ron Forman was a key member of the city's hospitality industry, yet he hadn't heard a thing about a proposal to build as many as six casinos in the center of town until Nagin floated the idea at the press conference. "It came from nowhere—and then the next week it was gone," Forman said. Another Nagin story that had Uptown talking was Nagin's trip to the capitol and the tongue-lashing he took from the city's black legislators. After the meeting, Nagin was spotted slumped against a wall, half sitting, half standing. "I did not sign up for this shit," the mayor cried out. "I did not sign up for this shit!"

Maybe it was just as well that the mayor was out of town when the Urban Land Institute's all-star team of planners, architects, academics, ex-politicians, and others convened in New Orleans that November. Greg Meffert, who prior to taking a job at City Hall had founded a pair of encryption-technology start-ups, had rented a place with his wife in Jamaica. Why not join us? Meffert asked Nagin. To further entice the mayor, Meffert made sure free first-class airplane tickets for Nagin, his wife, and his three children were part of the deal. Feeling he needed another break, Nagin told Meffert yes. He would be back in town by week's end, when the press would show up at the Sheraton to hear what the ULI had to say. When anyone asked, the mayor's people said their boss was in Washington on city business.

OF COURSE JOE CANIZARO was in town that week. He was glad that with his adopted city in crisis he was in the position to offer them this gift. "We need to hear how other people dealt with tragedies of this magnitude," Canizaro said. "We need the best minds in this nation on this."

Canizaro was back in his office on Poydras. By mid-October, he and Sue Ellen were living again in Old Metairie. The bottom floor of their house had been gutted, but generators had been trucked in so they had power. They limited themselves to the second floor, where Curtis, their houseman, had set up a microwave and a refrigerator for them. But a bad odor lingered in the house and Canizaro started to feel wobbly and run-down. The longer they stayed, the more convinced Canizaro became that the mold was making him sick. They lasted maybe two weeks at the old place before Canizaro moved them into a house he found nearby for $850,000.[2] That would serve as their base of operation for the next couple of years as they oversaw reconstruction. No one, of course, was suggesting that parts of Old Metairie revert to greenspace.

Jimmy Reiss wouldn't have to find alternative housing for himself. He was back in Audubon Place less than two weeks after Katrina. Bring New Orleans Back cochair Mel Lagarde also slept in his own bed every night. Indeed, his home on St. Charles would serve as the commission's

---

2. After selling the place several years later, he joked, "I lost a couple of hundred thousand dollars on it, but I kept a wife."

unofficial offices. "We were meeting at Mel's house almost every day," said Margaret Beer, hired to serve as the commission's communications person. It was mainly black members of the mayor's panel who needed to make do in temporary digs. Alden McDonald was living in Baton Rouge when he wasn't sleeping in his RV, and Entergy's Dan Packer, whose house had taken on eight feet of water, was living and working out of the Hyatt. Oliver Thomas was living at the Sheraton with several other members of the City Council rendered homeless by Katrina.

Barbara Major, the panel's other cochair, had gotten seven feet of water in the ranch-style home she owned in New Orleans East. Using her home even as a temporary base while in town wasn't an option. She also had her fourteen-year-old son and his schooling to consider. She was in Houston because she had a brother there. He had found her a house in a good school district that was big enough to accommodate her older son and his family, along with assorted in-laws and nieces and nephews needing a place to stay. "I tell folk I was a rich white woman for a year," Major said. "It was a gated community so rich the guards at the front gate wore gloves."

At first, Major made the weekly five-hour drive to New Orleans for the Monday meetings. But this woman chosen to represent the average New Orleanian was as financially stressed and overwhelmed as her constituents. She was perched in a strange city and spending most of her time, or so it seemed, either on the phone with an insurance company or waiting in one line or another for assistance. She wore donated clothes picked up at a giveaway arranged for Katrina survivors and was thankful for the $500 check she received from the Red Cross. FEMA was picking up the rent, but she and her family still had food and other expenses when none of them had paying jobs. Major's insurance company sent her a check for $2,500 for the loss of the use of her home. They sent another $25,000 to cover the contents of her house. "That's what we lived on for a long time," Major said. For a time, they were on food stamps.

Every trip to New Orleans took another bite out of the insurance check. She footed the bill every time she filled up with gas and the wear and tear on her truck. There'd also be the cost of a hotel room if she wasn't up to making the ten-hour round-trip in a single day. "No one gave me a free room when I came to New Orleans for the commission meetings," Major said. "No one was buying my meals. Folks don't believe me, but I never got no money from anybody over that." She was the mayor's single nod to the activist set, but she also declared that she didn't have the time or money to spend a week in New Orleans listening to the ULI's planners and architects. Instead she would show up on the last day of the ULI's visit to hear what they had to say. At that point, Major said, "I was seeing my job as stopping bad things from happening."

THE URBAN LAND INSTITUTE took over the Sheraton the week before Thanksgiving. The fifty or so panelists the ULI had flown to New Orleans were encouraged to take a half-day tour of the city to see the damage for themselves. ULI organizers set up interviews with three hundred people described as "business owners, decision makers, community activists, and citizens." Yet the organization's final report had the city flooding on Tuesday, August 30, rather than early Monday morning—as if the deluge had not happened until they saw the pictures on CNN.

The panel ULI assembled to help New Orleans were polite guests. They said all the right things about the city and its culture to the 250 people who showed up at the Sheraton on a Friday in mid-November 2005 to hear the group's initial assessment. (A more formal seventy-one-page report was submitted one month later.) The city was a "national treasure" in the words of one panelist; New Orleans was an "international treasure" to another. There were paeans to the city's people, its spirit, its resilience, and its neighborhoods.

Yet the ULI's message was harsh. New Orleans was doomed, panelist after panelist said, if it didn't overcome a political environment that several described as "dysfunctional." The panel chairman, Smedes York, himself a former mayor, chided city leaders for their lack of urgency. "Put aside your bickering," said another elected official. Several also brought up the city's notorious reputation for politicians on the take. The city should create an independent oversight board to control the city's finances for five years, the panel suggested, so outsiders were less hesitant about giving New Orleans billions in bailout money. Coastal restoration needed to be a priority. They also told the city to adopt a living-wage ordinance if people were serious about lifting up its poorest citizens.

Yet few in the audience that day seemed interested in what the ULI might have to say beyond the future of the lowest-lying neighborhoods. "There are areas of the city we're recommending not be rebuilt just now," Smedes York said early in the presentation. The room shifted. York and his colleagues named three categories of neighborhoods, ranging from the most damaged to the least. They recommended that, in the short run, the city only invest in neighborhoods in the least-damaged category. That way the city could revive its crippled economy and start rebuilding its tax base. The head of the ULI went one step further when she suggested that the city forbid individuals from rebuilding in the most damaged areas. The ULI imagined fingers of restored marshland in each low-lying neighborhood for better storm-water management. Greenspace in the city's most vulnerable neighborhoods should be mapped out before people were allowed to rebuild. Those owning property in areas to be reverted to a natural wetland needed to be compensated, they stressed, and also offered first dibs on homes of those choosing not to return.

The ULI didn't go so far as to draw up the maps themselves. It suggested that the city stage planning meetings in the affected areas. Provide residents with the same topography maps the ULI had been given, the panelists predicted, and they, too, would see the wisdom of giving the city thousands of acres in additional parkland, along with bike trails and natural wetlands inside the city's limits. The panelists didn't single out any neighborhoods that would need to shrink, but they didn't have to. An elevation map of New Orleans was flashed on a screen partway through the presentation. Areas that were at least two feet below sea level according to the US Geological Survey were depicted in red. Veins of red appeared in the Lower Ninth Ward and other parts of the city, but the communities of Lakeview, Gentilly, and New Orleans East looked like bloody masses.

Joe Canizaro smiled after the ULI's presentation. There would be no more dodging of the tough issues after today, he said. "This should get us talking frankly about some of the stuff we need to deal with, particularly extremely low-lying areas and areas where we have a low-income black population," Canizaro said. But he worried in private. His hope in those first weeks after Katrina was that a shared fate would unite a city split between black and white. But his expert panel had convinced him that was a fantasy. "The ULI told us that the number one determinant for how a city recovers is its history," Canizaro said. "If in fact a city was divided and not really working together, and not doing well economically, then it would take a whole lot longer to recover than if everyone was pulling together in the same direction." Katrina didn't mean a do-over for a city that had too many problems prior to the storm. Instead, the ULI said, history was destiny: the hurricane and the flood that followed would only amplify New Orleans's problems.

"POTENTIAL FOR MASS BUYOUTS" read the front-page headline in the next day's *Times-Picayune*. The City Council's "two Cynthias"—Cynthia Hedge-Morrell and Cynthia Willard-Lewis, who between them represented New Orleans East, Gentilly, and the Lower Ninth—slammed the ULI's "proposal to eliminate our neighborhoods from New Orleans." Exiting the ballroom after the ULI's presentation, Willard-Lewis told reporters that she and her neighbors were "not going to allow themselves to be shoved into the back of the bus." A few weeks later, the council approved a resolution requiring the city to invest in every part of New Orleans and not stagger its commitments based on damage assessments.

Cassandra Wall and her sisters viewed the ULI's recommendations as perversely cruel. Uptown and the Quarter and the central business district had survived Katrina largely intact, yet that's where the city should focus its efforts and resources? Terrel Broussard, an attorney with a downtown firm who owned in the East, had volunteered to monitor the mayor's panel for their organization, Eastern New Orleans United and Whole. At the next Monday meeting, Broussard spoke with scorn about the so-called experts. "Seven days," he said. "Seven days to pass a verdict on a lifetime of work. We deserve better."

The reaction was the same in flooded neighborhoods across the city, black or white. "The ULI is what really got us religion," said Al Petrie, a member of the board of Lakeview Civic. Petrie and others had been talking regularly by phone, but after the ULI passed its verdict, Freddy Yoder decided they needed to reach out to every connection they had. He invited all the former presidents of Lakeview Civic to a meeting at his offices in Harahan, right outside New Orleans. That included Martin Landrieu, son of Moon Landrieu and brother to both a US senator and Louisiana's lieutenant governor. "They wanted a war, we'd be ready for one," Yoder said.

"IT WOULD KILL THE black psyche if New Orleans East isn't rebuilt," Cassandra's sister Petie Wall said at a Baton Rouge Applebee's after one Monday-night meeting. "Think of what it would mean if the city successfully chased off so many African Americans who had money, its doctors and successful businesspeople and lawyers and such. People would no longer feel they had a chance." A sociology professor at Brown University released a study showing that the ULI was talking about land that housed 80 percent of the city's black population. Lakeview could trace its roots back to the 1910s. People in every affected community, black or white, rich or poor, spoke about the property rights they were supposed to enjoy as American citizens.

Yet what if the experts were right? What if the right thing to do for the Wall sisters and the people of Lakeview was to insist they live someplace safer and more practical? The Urban Land Institute had warned against what its experts labeled the "jack-o'-lantern" effect—partially occupied blocks that looked like the broken teeth of a carved pumpkin, littered with boarded-up homes and empty lots—and also spoke of the importance of geographically right-sizing the city so people weren't so spread out. As their experts saw it, a lot of people weren't moving back, and fewer people meant less tax revenue and therefore less money to spend on everything from police and fire to street repairs.

Geographers didn't seem to have any trouble reaching a consensus. Craig Colton, who taught geography at LSU, heard from colleagues around the country in the weeks after Katrina. To them the only question was whether 20 percent of the city's landmass should revert to wetlands or 40 percent.

"I don't know exactly where I would draw the line, but I assume that's what the city is trying to figure out right now," Colton said shortly after the ULI left town. Roughly half the city sat below sea level, Colton said, but that's not to say he would decree half the city out of bounds. A community sitting a few feet below sea level might be deemed an "intermediate zone," where people would be permitted to rebuild—so long as homes were jacked up high enough. "The city needs to choose some level below sea level and declare it economically unfeasible to build in areas that are at that elevation or lower," he said.

Bruce Sharky is a professor of landscape architecture at LSU. He, too, thought it would be irresponsible to rebuild all of New Orleans. A couple of months after Katrina, he ran into an acquaintance who told him he was already working on his home in Lakeview. Sharky knew he was supposed to praise the man's pioneer spirit, yet he viewed his colleague as selfish. "The government is going to spend, what, one hundred billion dollars or more to rebuild New Orleans—and for what?" Sharky asked. "If we don't do things differently, it can happen again next year."

Michael Liffmann was also affiliated with LSU. He was an economist working for a university-based program that promoted smarter stewardship of the state's coastal wetlands. He had lived in New Orleans East in the early 1970s. "There are parts of New Orleans that are not fit for human habitation," Liffmann declared. "They never were and never will be." The best use of the commission's time, he argued, would be to devise formulas for compensating homeowners unlucky enough to own a stretch of the city that would be returned to its natural state.

Some thought such ideas were a fool's errand in a town where most long-range planning meant deciding what to do that weekend. "There are only two things people around here plan for in an entire year, and that is what costume they're going to wear on Mardi Gras and which Friday they're taking off work to go to Jazz Fest," *Times-Picayune* columnist Chris Rose wrote that fall. "The rest just happens."

Yet Liffmann was confident that those in charge would force people to move "in the name of safety." As he saw it, the problem was one of timing. The city needed to settle some fundamental questions even as it was only partially through what might be called the Five Stages of New Orleans. Rather than grieving an individual, the city was collectively going through more or less the same phases Elisabeth Kübler-Ross had identified for a person who loses a loved one. Liffmann put New Orleans somewhere between denial and anger at around the time the ULI was in town, and somewhere between bargaining and depression in the final weeks of 2005.

13

ISLE OF DENIAL

Cassandra Wall and her sisters were still camped out at the Microtel in Baton Rouge. Various nieces and nephews migrated there, along with cousins and assorted significant others. Cassandra said, "We basically had our own floor" within a few weeks. Among them, they had four dogs and two cats.

Petie had what she called her "pantry": the dresser drawers of spices, red beans, and other dry goods. Cassandra's mother had a small refrigerator in her room and a hot plate. Between them they were good for at least a few home-cooked meals a week. A local church was still bringing food each evening to evacuees stuck at the Microtel, and Monday nights after their weekly meeting the family would treat themselves to a meal at the Applebee's down the street.

Cassandra was starting to like Baton Rouge. Or at least she wasn't disliking it as much as her sisters. You'd only have to mention their adopted town to Petie to get a lecture on proper hospitality. "They have a real attitude toward us," she would say. "We're these bad people who are going to destroy their community. We keep these crazy hours. No one sleeps." Over a Big Mac one night, Petie caught an unvarnished glimpse of the hostility when she overheard the workers complaining about the people from New Orleans. The McDonald's workers were even blaming the evacuees for the longer hours they were asked to work. "I'm sorry if our flood inconvenienced you," she told them. It didn't help her view of Baton Rouge that it had taken so long to find a place where her son Garrett could attend school. "They're telling me, 'Wait till you're called,' but I've got my kid running around at the Microtel," Petie said. "Of course I'm calling them." Not until the second half of October did they find a spot for him.

Cassandra defended Baton Rouge when she was with her sisters. Think of the church ladies still bringing food to the Microtel months after Katrina, she said. Think about the stresses the flooding was causing in their adopted city. Baton Rouge's population didn't quite double post-Katrina, as the locals thought, but there were an extra 100,000 people living in a city home to 228,000 prior to the storm. The traffic was horrendous and the wait for everything longer—in the grocery-store checkout line, at a favorite restaurant. The schools might have moved slower than Petie would have liked, but the academic year had already started when thousands of students arrived in need of a spot.

Yet a feeling of unwelcome wasn't just in the heads of Cassandra's sisters. A contingent of fifty-five Michigan state troopers had volunteered to help in the Gulf Coast after Katrina. They were asked to assist the police in Baton Rouge, where multiple officers said they were under orders: make life unpleasant for New Orleans evacuees so that they will relocate elsewhere. One trooper quoted a local cop's reference to blacks as "animals" who needed to be "beaten down." As a thank-you gift, another trooper said, he was invited to "beat down" a man in custody. A small squadron of state troopers from New Mexico also assigned to Baton Rouge told a similar story. A complaint the New Mexico commander filed with the city stated that his people had witnessed illegal searches, physical abuse, and other behavior that a top officer summed up as "racially motivated."

Petie was also hearing it from Garrett, her youngest, for whom the storm's timing had seemed especially cruel. When Katrina hit, he had just completed his first week as an upperclassman at St. Augustine, a storied all-boys Catholic school in town that counted the city's second

African-American mayor and other local African-American luminaries as graduates. Now he was attending some anonymous school in Baton Rouge, where his grades started to slip. That November, officials from St. Aug, which had taken on five feet of water, teamed up with St. Mary's Academy, an all-girls Catholic school that had also flooded. Both schools were partnering with Xavier Prep, the all-girls school that Garrett's mother and his aunts had attended, to open a school on Xavier Prep's campus Uptown, which had not flooded. The combined school would include faculty and students from St. Mary, St. Aug, and Xavier Prep and be called the MAX. "After that it was 'the MAX, the MAX, the MAX,'" Petie said.

Their mother, Daisy Wall, was also adamant about getting home to New Orleans. Pushing seventy-five, she had been diagnosed with cancer before the storm. The family home in Central City, on the edge of Uptown, had suffered modest roof damage but no flooding. She wanted to sleep in her own bed.

"My mom wanted to come back," Petie said. "My son wanted to come back. I was coming back."

It was too soon to think about moving back to New Orleans East. Entergy wasn't even giving a date for when it might restore power to the neighborhood. But they had the family home and also a small Uptown rental property her mother owned. Thanksgiving at a Baton Rouge restaurant had been "cheesy," Petie declared, and told her sisters, "I promise you a better Christmas." The next day, Petie began making daily trips to New Orleans to work on her mother's house and eventually the rental. By January 1, she had given up their room at the Microtel.

The pressure on Cassandra to move back to New Orleans was growing. The Friday after Thanksgiving was also the day that cousin Robyn moved back into the city. She earned a good living working as a paralegal for a local litigator, who put her back to work four weeks after Katrina. The room at the Microtel was free, courtesy of FEMA, but the commute to and from New Orleans was brutal. She found a condo for rent in the Warehouse District near work. The price was exorbitant for New Orleans—$1,250 a month for a small one-bedroom—but it was a nice place conveniently located and the best she could find in a city with an acute housing shortage. A week later, Tangee, who worked as an administrator at the University of New Orleans, rented a unit just down the hall. The university had lost use of its engineering building and also a dorm, but its administrative offices were reopening as of December 1.

In retrospect, the sisters and their cousin admit that they may have ganged up on Cassandra. But with three-fifths of them back in New Orleans, the center of gravity was shifting back home. They wanted their sister back with them in New Orleans. Cassandra spoke on behalf of herself and her husband, who worked as a medical technician. "We can't go back," Cassandra told them. "There's no hospitals. There aren't the schools. There's no shopping." They responded by throwing back at her the words she had said from the podium at their Monday night meetings, which they discontinued now that several of them were back in the city.

Cassandra reminded them that while at least a couple of them had jobs bringing them back to New Orleans, she was a tutor without clients in a city devoid of school-aged children. Her husband had secured work at a Baton Rouge hospital. It was a step down after heading the cardiovascular testing unit at a New Orleans hospital, but Cassandra was relieved he had found any job.

There was also their son Brandon to consider. He had started the seventh grade in New Orleans, and he was adjusting to the middle school they had found for him in Baton Rouge. What sense would it make to move him into a third school midway through the academic year? She thought about all the unknowns of life back in New Orleans. Would they have adequate flood protection? What kind of insurance settlement might they receive? Moving forward, would insurance companies even write policies in parts of New Orleans? "They moved back and said they'd figure it out," she said of her sisters. "That's the way they are. I need to see the big picture before I leap."

PEOPLE CALLED THAT PART of New Orleans built along the high ground that had remained mostly dry when the rest of the city flooded the "sliver by the river": Uptown, the French Quarter, the Marigny, and Algiers on the West Bank. By the time Petie, Robyn, and Tangee moved back to the city, an estimated seventy-five thousand people were living in this area, which others called the "isle of denial." It was anyone's guess what portion of the sliver's residents had lived in New Orleans prior to Katrina and were not newcomers there to help with the recovery.

A degree of normalcy was returning to this part of the city. Every day seemed to bring another mini-miracle. Mail service resumed in early October, and UPS trucks started delivering packages around that same time. The City Council was again meeting in its regular chambers. (It had held its first two meetings after Katrina at the airport.) A movie theater reopened, a grocery store carried fresh produce, the city's once-robust restaurant scene was springing back to life, one establishment at a time. Bill Hines baffled his law partners in Baton Rouge when in October he announced that he was giving up his borrowed room in a colleague's air-conditioned home to move back to a flood-damaged home still under repair in a town with few amenities. Yet that also meant he was back in New Orleans the day Red Fish, one of the city's more popular seafood restaurants, reopened. Red Fish offered a one-item menu that night, cheeseburgers and fries served on styrofoam plates. The drink choice was beer or bottled water. Yet this small taste of the familiar, Hines said, left him crying with joy.

Yet more common were the moments that left people in tears of frustration. Dry parts of town experienced frequent power outages in an overstressed system. Garbage pickup had resumed, but New Orleans often looked as if the city were in the third week of a sanitation workers' strike. Sure, UPS's familiar brown trucks were back, but the delivery company's main facility in the area had flooded, and now its entire New Orleans operation was being run out of a trailer in the western suburbs. And UPS driver James Conerly, who worked a small section of the central business district before the flood, was now covering almost the entire area by himself. Two months after Katrina, one-third of the city's office high-rises were still shuttered, Conerly estimated, "and I'd say there's only two or three buildings at least fifty percent occupied." The US Postal Service may have resumed deliveries, but the mail would show up for three days running and then there'd be nothing for a week.

The reminders that New Orleans was still broken were constant. In normal times, the Port of New Orleans ranked as the fifth busiest in the United States, yet more than two months after Katrina, it was still at only

30 percent of its normal capacity. The Saints were playing in another city, as were the Hornets, the city's NBA team. The Sugar Bowl would be played outside New Orleans for the first time in seventy years. The city got a boost at the end of October when the American Library Association announced its next annual convention would be in New Orleans—in June. The district attorney and his staff took over an old nightclub, the *PBS NewsHour* correspondent Betty Ann Bowser reported, conducting business "beneath the glare of a disco ball." The public defender was forced to lay off more than thirty of its lawyers, leaving only nine attorneys to handle thousands of cases.

"Life in Refrigerator City," the *Times-Picayune*'s Chris Rose labeled those first post-storm months in his book *1 Dead in Attic*, a collection of columns he wrote in the first eighteen months after Katrina. People thought they were leaving for a few days and returned weeks later to freezers full of putrefying meat. So even the dry parts of New Orleans were lined with ruined refrigerators that stood as a small, semipermanent billboard for voicing displeasure in frustrating times. When it seemed that Tom Benson, the owner of the Saints, might move the city's football team to San Antonio, Texas, discarded, duct-taped refrigerators around town announced TOM BENSON INSIDE.

Life along the river felt congested even in a city still missing most of its people. Traffic lights were out everywhere, turning busy intersections into a four-way stop. Rubble from the storm still blocked main thoroughfares. The St. Charles streetcar line remained shut down for more than a year. A refrigerator could sit curbside for months even in parts of town that had remained dry—and an estimated one hundred thousand wrecked cars littered the streets all over town.

People had small complaints about finding a doctor or a dry cleaner and larger-scale laments about a mayor many feared would not be up to the task of rebuilding the city. The consensus among those residing in this isle of denial was that the answer to the city's woes was simple: offer people buyouts in low-lying communities, starting with residents of the Lower Ninth Ward, and focus on fixing up dilapidated homes in parts of the city that had been blighted before Katrina. Anyone doubting the wisdom of that solution needed to look no further than the side-by-side maps the *Times-Picayune* had published on its front page that fall. One map showed the city as it existed in 1870. The other showed the areas that had flooded after Katrina hit. The area that remained dry and the city boundaries as they existed in 1870 were nearly identical. The city's Greg Meffert seemed to get it when he told CNN's Soledad O'Brien in early November, "The answers to our present are really in our past. All we've got to do is do what people were doing in the late 1800s." But then the mayor would speak as if he hadn't seen the front-page maps. "If the president follows through with his pledge to provide us with enough resources," the mayor said that same week, "we can rebuild New Orleans totally."

The graffiti on the refrigerators around town asked the question: WHERE'S NAGIN? "Each time Ray and I would talk, I would walk away more angry," Ron Forman said. Much of the city was still without electricity or drinkable water. Most of its residents were living scattered across the country. People were making do on couches and doubling up with relatives. Yet Nagin didn't seem to be working half as hard as Forman or any other chief executive he knew.

"There was this lack of engagement, this lack of urgency," Forman said. Finally, he couldn't take it anymore. "I told him, 'This is getting personal with me. We gave up everything to be behind you and you're not doing your job.' I was fed up."

RAY NAGIN HEARD IT all the time: Why couldn't he be more like Rudy Giuliani, the New York mayor who had acted so decisively in the days after September 11? Giuliani's star turn had produced a bestseller, followed by a lucrative speaking career, and even a short-lived run at the presidency. Nagin had a copy of Giuliani's *Leadership* on a bookshelf in his office, a freebie he had picked up at a charity golf tournament a year or two earlier. People around Nagin doubted he had even looked at it given the mayor's irritation when Giuliani's name came up. Nagin would offer the same response each time. He had been marooned on a small island of high ground and slept in a blasted-out hotel that had lost its power and had no working toilets. The death total was greater inside the World Trade Center than on the streets of New Orleans. But Giuliani slept in his own bed the week of September 11, left to worry about the significant but small corner of his city that had been destroyed.

"You've never had a city devastated like this," Nagin said repeatedly—to friends, to reporters, to anyone pressing him about the city's rebuilding efforts. Insurance companies were already declaring Katrina the most expensive disaster in history. Historians were labeling the dispersal of the city's residents the largest American diaspora in history, bigger even than the displacement caused by the winds and drought of the Dust Bowl. The American Water Works Association declared that New Orleans had experienced the most catastrophic multisystem failure by a US city in modern history. The destruction of the city's power grid and also its gas system were unprecedented, as was the blow to the New Orleans economy. "It's not going to be a pretty process," Nagin said two months after Katrina, "but I'm sure the *Harvard Business Review* will be doing case studies on this for years."

By early November, a team of fifty-plus city inspectors had graded 60,000 of the 110,000 homes in the flooded parts of the city. Two in every three they tagged with either a yellow sticker, meaning it was more than 50 percent destroyed, or red, indicating that the city thought it needed to be bulldozed. Contractors working for FEMA had removed an astonishing 1.3 million cubic yards of debris (fallen trees, wrecked cars, pieces of broken homes blocking a street, discarded furniture), yet that represented only a tiny fraction of the garbage that the authorities predicted they would need to clear. "Housing is probably our most pressing issue right now," the mayor declared—and yet every time he or one of his people approached FEMA about trailers, they were met with excuses. The same federal government that had moved too slowly right after Katrina, Nagin said, was now dragging its feet on the recovery.

Nagin phoned his new friends inside the White House. "I told them, 'I really can't wait until you figure out what the final deal number is,'" Nagin said. Let them work out inside the Beltway whether the region would receive $100 billion or $200 billion or $250 billion. He asked the White House to free up $100 million as a down payment on money that would eventually flow to the city, "to help us cover the cost of operations for the next three to six months." Officials promised to see what they could do, but nothing happened. While on the phone with someone from the White House, Nagin repitched a more modest version of the tax plan that David White had devised right after the storm. What if any business or individual agreeing to move back to New Orleans got a 50 percent reduction (rather than the 100 percent they had originally asked) in taxes for seven years (instead of ten) as a way of inducing people to rebuild? Nagin was turned down.

"I've thrown out some pretty creative ideas," Nagin told a pair of *Times* reporters he had invited into his office two months after the storm. The problem was that the bureaucracy couldn't see beyond its byzantine rules. Even the city's business community hadn't caught up to the reality of post-Katrina New Orleans, he said. He mentioned the casino idea he had floated and their reaction to it as if he had suggested carving out an Amsterdam-like red-light district in the center of town. "I have a tendency—and I'm not being bravado about this—but I have a tendency to see things probably a little quicker than others," Nagin said.

NAGIN WAS CAPABLE OF acting boldly. When, later that fall, FEMA announced it had thirty-one thousand trailers available to any Gulf Coast community needing them, Nagin invoked the emergency powers the City Council had granted him after the storm. He would have trailers delivered to parks and playgrounds around the city. He would set them up on the neutral ground in any community with the necessary utilities. Nagin also endorsed the idea of temporary tent cities in the city's parks. "We need to let people come back home," the mayor proclaimed.

Nagin stood strong when members of the City Council lambasted him for a plan that might mean black people would temporarily live in predominantly white neighborhoods. One white member of the council stressed the importance of parks and playgrounds in the life of a child—in a city without children. Another council member, also white, said she resented those who were insinuating that race played any role in her vote—and then said she could support putting trailers in her district if they were reserved for first responders. When the council passed legislation giving an individual council member final say over any temporary housing slated for his or her district, Nagin vetoed the bill, setting up a legal battle. Across the Gulf Coast, communities were receiving bulk shipments of FEMA trailers, but not New Orleans.

In Lakeview, people seethed over a mayor whom they had helped put in office several years earlier. Electricity had only recently been restored, and a few intrepid souls had started to work on their homes. Now Nagin wanted to put trailers on the neutral ground on West End Boulevard, a few blocks from the neighborhood's western border, and more trailers and possibly a tent city in City Park, which served as Lakeview's eastern border? "A lot of us agreed that the last thing that Lakeview needed was to be turned into a trailer park for the rest of the city," said Jeb Bruneau, then president of the Lakeview Civic Improvement Association. "The mayor was going to turn the park and our neighborhood into a dump"—without the courtesy, he added, of talking about it with anyone who lived in Lakeview.

Nagin backed down. He agreed to grant individual members of the council veto power over any housing built in his or her district—and fought FEMA when it attempted to set up trailers at sites his administration had already approved. The trailer parks would instead be set up on the grounds of New Orleans's public housing projects and other places where City Hall would receive no pushback. But while the mayor and City Council negotiated, the people of Lakeview weren't taking chances. People were emptying the waterlogged innards of their homes, and small mountains of discarded appliances, couches, and other detritus formed around the neighborhood. "We figured, why not take care of two problems at once?" Bruneau said. "So we started piling all our trash on the neutral ground on West End." How could the city set up trailers on a stretch of grass serving as the community dump?

NOTHING SEEMED EASY, EVERYTHING seemed to spark a fight. More than half of the city's inhabitants were renters. What about all those apartments around New Orleans filled with people's possessions even as their occupants were living a thousand or two thousand miles away? Landlords had plenty of motivation for rehabbing units in a market where $550 apartments were renting for $800 or more and cheap motels ringing the city were charging downtown hotel prices. The governor had seemingly done the humane thing when she placed a moratorium on post-Katrina evictions, angering landlords. Nagin, by contrast, was inclined to take the side of the landlords in a city desperate for housing. When in the last week of October Blanco, under pressure, lifted her ban, landlords inundated the courts with eviction notices. "That's somebody's life in there," a Legal Aid attorney told a Knight Ridder reporter. "You want a chance to save it." Under Louisiana law, a person could be evicted and his or her possessions tossed into a Dumpster within ten days. But Legal Aid sued, putting the matter on hold.

The city's pending elections precipitated another legal battle. New Orleans was slated to have its first round of voting for mayor and City Council on February 4. Any runoffs would be held one month later. The obvious question was whether the city could even pull off an election in its disabled state. Racial issues also had to be considered in a city that was majority white in the fall of 2005. Civil rights groups were threatening a lawsuit if the election was not postponed, while prominent voices Uptown were making the case that Louisiana's secretary of state, Al Ater, in whose hands this hot potato had landed, had no legal basis for ordering a delay. At the Bourbon House late one night, Greg Meffert admitted he'd probably had too much to drink when things turned unpleasant between him and a white legislator arguing that the election would be a chance for whites to grab back control of the city while most of the black community was scattered around the country. The woman's husband, Meffert said, needed to intervene before things turned ugly. "There was this big push to white-ify everything," Meffert said.

Al Ater asked FEMA for $2 million to replace voting machines damaged in the flooding. FEMA turned down his request, just as its people said no when the secretary of state asked the agency to underwrite the cost of sending notices to displaced residents to let them know they could vote by absentee ballot. The Bush White House even rejected Ater's request that FEMA share with the local election authorities the addresses of evacuees. Without help, Ater said, New Orleans would not be ready to hold an election by early February. To figure out what to do, Ater, who had been in office for less than two months when Katrina hit, assembled an advisory group. Members included both party leaders and civil rights advocates. The plan they devised included satellite polling places in Baton Rouge, Houston, Atlanta, and other cities home to a large number of evacuees. Based on their recommendations, Ater said the elections needed to be postponed for at least eight months.

A Republican mayoral hopeful sued. So, too, did the developer Pres

Kabacoff. A federal judge was sympathetic but emphatic. "Mr. Ater," she told him, "if you don't set a date in April, I'm going to do it for you." Shortly thereafter, the secretary of state announced that the election would be held April 22 with runoffs scheduled for May 20.

Dueling bureaucrats were the main combatants in the fight over Charity Hospital. Founded in 1736, Charity was the country's oldest public hospital,[1] built after the death of a wealthy shipbuilder whose will instructed that his fortune be used to finance a hospital for the city's indigent. Since the days of Huey Long, Charity had been housed in a handsome art deco–style building on the edge of the central business district. The staff, working with dozens of military personnel, had scrubbed clean the first three floors of the twenty-story hospital when the state agency that ran Charity ordered them to stop. We're concerned for your safety, the authorities said, but the doctors, nurses, and others on whose behalf the state was acting saw the move as nothing but a cynical play for a bigger FEMA payout. For years the state had sought to demolish Charity and replace it with a hospital that no longer had as its main purpose treatment of the city's uninsured. The state, several doctors charged, saw Katrina as a way to get the feds to pick up the bill.

At first those ordered to stop working on Charity defied an order they saw as irresponsible in a city with an acute shortage of hospital beds. They would be chased out several times before the state locked the building. Their makeshift crews—populated with medical professionals—had worn shorts and T-shirts while working on the building. But when the state invited television crews inside the shuttered facility to see the damage for themselves, they insisted that everybody sign a medical release form and wear protective suits. The magic number in post-Katrina New Orleans was 50 percent. FEMA would pay to tear down and rebuild a structure rather than simply repair it if the damage estimate exceeded half the replacement cost. A consultant for the state declared that fixing the facility would equal 65 percent of the replacement cost, but a FEMA representative, doubting the damage was anywhere that extensive, said

---

1. Bellevue Hospital in New York was founded that same year.

the agency would do its own assessment. In the meantime, this twenty-seven-hundred-bed hospital sat empty.

Public housing was proving another flash point in post-Katrina New Orleans. More than five thousand families were paying rent each month to the Housing Authority of New Orleans at the time of Katrina, and HANO, as everyone called the agency, had another two thousand apartments sitting vacant. Many of HANO's residents were older New Orleanians, but four in every ten residents worked. They were the working poor who changed bedpans, cleaned hotel rooms, and washed dishes. Reopening public housing as fast as possible seemed critical to reigniting the city's economy. But rebuilding the projects also meant inviting back a portion of the city's population living on public aid or disability.

Most public housing residents in New Orleans lived in complexes of low-rise, stolid brick buildings built in the 1940s and 1950s. Two of the city's four largest housing projects escaped Katrina with little damage. In this city desperate for affordable housing, at least a couple of thousand units could be made habitable with only cosmetic improvements. Yet that wasn't necessarily welcome news in a city where people were imagining much of New Orleans as a clean slate. "We finally cleaned up public housing in New Orleans," Richard Baker, a ten-term congressman from Baton Rouge, a Republican, was quoted as saying after Katrina. "We couldn't do it but God did." What a waste of a disaster, some argued, if the authorities simply allowed HANO residents to move back into their former homes.

PEOPLE CONTACTED BARBARA MAJOR to do something about public housing. They reached out to her for help countering the forces trying to shut down Charity. They called to talk about the schools or the fight over the placement of trailers. But Major's life then was her extended family and the epic fights she was waging with FEMA or an insurance company on behalf of one member or another of her clan.

She recalls feeling powerless at the time, not despite her exalted position as cochair of the Bring New Orleans Back Commission but because of it. She wanted to help black-owned businesses feeling locked out of the bidding for contracts, yet she couldn't get FEMA to return her own phone calls. "All I heard was pain," Major said. "I'd see people and I couldn't do anything.

THE "PIG." THAT'S WHAT the people who worked for the RTA called the former Piggly Wiggly grocery store in Baton Rouge that the agency leased following Katrina. The pig served as the RTA's temporary offices and its maintenance yard and a barracks for those who couldn't find housing in the area. This agency of thirteen hundred before the storm employed around three hundred as it struggled to rebuild post-Katrina.

One early task was tracking down the RTA buses that didn't drown. They'd sell for scrap the two hundred or so buses destroyed by the floodwaters, but another seventy buses had been parked on the high ground along the river. Those had been commandeered by people desperate to exit the city. Tracking them down fell to Jacques Robichaux, the agency's superintendent of bus maintenance. "That was a good portion of my life for months," Robichaux said. A few buses had been abandoned on the West Bank, but most they found scattered around the state. Two needed to be driven back from Houston. The agency would leave a pair upstate in Alexandria because town officials were asking the agency to pay what Robichaux thought were exorbitant towing and storage charges.

Initially, the RTA put its drivers to work running buses in Baton Rouge to help with overflow. It also set up a commuter line to New Orleans. By November, the agency was running several bus routes in New Orleans. Other modes of transportation were also expanding their service as more people moved back home. Whereas by the end of September the city's airport was handling thirty departing flights a day, that number doubled to sixty in November. Amtrak and Greyhound also started running more trains and buses to and from New Orleans.

The city was still under a bottled-water advisory, but in November the city's water agency declared water drinkable in every part of the city outside New Orleans East and the Lower Ninth Ward. Isolated patches of the city were still without running water, a circumstance that could prove disastrous in the event of a fire, but most of New Orleans was protected. Nearly half the toilets in the city were still not connected to the sewer system. Forty percent of the city was still without electricity.

Nearly 50 percent lacked natural gas for cooking or heat in a city where the nighttime temperatures were dipping below forty degrees.

Dan Packer and his team, under pressure from the City Council, developed a plan for Entergy to provide electricity to at least 80 percent of the city by year's end and gas service to that same proportion of its customers by mid-January. But those were just words on paper for a bankrupt subsidiary relying on its corporate bosses in Jackson, Mississippi, and volunteer crews from around the country. Entergy New Orleans was a utility with extraordinary expenses and only a small fraction of its pre-storm customer base paying for its services. Packer spent much of his time up in Washington, telling his woeful tale to anyone willing to meet with him, including Andrew Card, Bush's chief of staff. "The bottom line is that as a regulated monopoly, we're allowed to pass legitimate expenses along to customers," Packer said. "So either the government was going to help pay for a lot of the damage or ratepayers would."

In November, Bush announced that Donald Powell, who since 2001 had served as chairman of the FDIC, would replace Admiral Thad Allen as the federal recovery czar. The city also had a new best friend in Richard Baker, the Baton Rouge Republican overheard cracking that God fixed public housing in New Orleans the way no mortal could. His penance was a bill that proposed that the federal government pay 60 percent of the pre-Katrina value on any property abandoned by a homeowner or business choosing not to rebuild. The property would then be the city's to redevelop. The state's entire congressional delegation was behind what everyone was calling the Baker bill, as were Nagin and Blanco. Joe Canizaro also supported this legislation, which would provide the funding mechanism needed to rebuild New Orleans more sensibly.

"I think we all believed there would be more happening than is happening right now," Canizaro said in early December. Maybe Baker would break the logjam.

AFTER DENIAL COMES ANGER. The fall was also a time for recriminations and finger-pointing. Culprits were everywhere during the multiple hearings held by both the US Senate and the House looking into what went wrong in the days following Katrina. Depending on the day and who was talking, everything was Bush's fault, Nagin's, Blanco's, or that of the people who failed to get themselves out of harm's way. "Just baloney," Michael Brown had said of the White House's claim that they didn't realize a disaster was taking place in New Orleans until at least twenty-four hours after the levees broke. The Bush administration refused to make senior officials available to congressional investigators. The White House also held back a large portion of the Katrina-related documents that Congress had requested.

Across the river from New Orleans in Gretna, officials might have considered themselves lucky. In an era of twenty-four-hour news, their small burgh might have become another Howard Beach or South Central Los Angeles—a locale whose name invokes a racially charged incident that took place there—if not for a media distracted by so many other angles to the Katrina story. Yet even the relatively small amount of attention the story received sparked a defensiveness among town leaders. Two weeks after Katrina, the Gretna City Council unanimously approved a resolution supporting the "chief of police's decision to deny access to the city of Gretna." Signs started popping up on lawns around town: WE SUPPORT CHIEF LAWSON. People on the other side of the bridge, including some of those part of the RTA contingent, were talking to lawyers about a civil rights claim against the city. When the first of those suits were filed that November, Chief Lawson said, "It's being made into a racial issue by certain individuals, but that's not what it was all about."

It was a season for filing bold lawsuits. One local lawyer sued the Army Corps of Engineers, claiming fraud. The Corps had promised a levee system that could withstand a Category 3 storm, yet Katrina, a weak Category 3, if not a 2, by the time it hit New Orleans, caused the city's flood-protection system to collapse. John Cummings, a prominent trial attorney who was part of the big tobacco settlement years earlier, also sued the Corps. He didn't charge the Corps with incompetence or negligence but criminality. "If your supervisors are asleep—they simply don't supervise the installation of the sheet piling—that's incompetence or gross negligence," Cummings said. "But when they certify that the sheet piling is twenty-three feet and it's really seventeen feet, that's a crime." Others sued the Orleans levee board, which was responsible for maintaining the levees that the Corps had built. Suits would be filed as well over MR. GO.

Before the lawyers took aim at one another, the battle for the truth needed to be waged on the ground in New Orleans. On one side was the Corps, an operation with roots dating back to 1775 and a reputation to uphold. In the months after Katrina, spokespeople for the Corps insisted that the city's flood-protection system failed because it had not been built to withstand a storm as strong as Katrina. The levees had over-topped, they claimed, and the force of the water rushing over the walls had caused small sections to give way. On the other side were scientists such as Ivor van Heerden, deputy director of the LSU Hurricane Center, and among the first to suspect that the Corps was not being completely candid with the public.

For years, van Heerden had been outspoken in warning of the po-tential for catastrophic flooding following a bad hurricane. But Katrina had been a "decidedly mild hurricane," van Heerden said, at least from New Orleans's perspective. The levees should not have overtopped, ac-cording to the storm-surge models he and his colleagues had created. Their thesis was that the levees had collapsed due to faulty designs or problems in their construction, if not both. To figure out what happened, the state asked van Heerden, who taught in LSU's Civil & Environmen-tal Engineering Department, to assemble a group of colleagues. Team Louisiana, as they were called, looked through wrecked homes in search of battery-powered clocks and interviewed dozens of survivors to figure out what time the floodwaters hit a community. Others picked up shov-els to sift through the dirt and sometimes taste it, to see what clues the soil might offer. The more time van Heerden spent in deserted sections of New Orleans, the more he thought of all the lives lost and disrupted, and the angrier he grew.

"Call it a blame game if you must," van Heerden said, "but some of us were determined to find out exactly what had happened and to de-mand justice from the responsible parties."

14

LOOK AND LEAVE

Nearly two months after Katrina, forty thousand people were still sleeping shoulder to shoulder in emergency shelters around Louisiana. Kathleen Blanco's solution was an emergency order granting her the right to use state-owned lands to house evacuees, even if prohibited by local ordinance. Six hundred trailers were trucked to a small town on the edge of the Baton Rouge metro area. There, next to a juvenile prison, FEMA opened the first of a dozen-plus trailer parks around the state. FEMA opened similar camps in another sixteen states to shelter another thirty thousand evacuees, the majority of whom had been saved from New Orleans once the buses started rolling up to the Superdome or the Convention Center.

The largest number of evacuees went to Houston. Most of those ended up in either the Astrodome or the Reliant Center, where a professor named Caroline Heldman was horrified by what she found. Heldman, who taught political science at Occidental College in Los Angeles, had been so angered by images out of New Orleans in those first days after the flooding that she convinced the Pacifica radio station in Southern California to give her the press credentials she would need to get into New Orleans. En route, she stopped at the two in-door stadiums. There she found "fluorescent lights and loudspeaker announcements twenty-four hours a day, smells emanating from the bathroom, and guards walking patrols with M16s." That was in "stark contrast," Heldman said, to what she observed at the Qualcomm Sta-dium in San Diego (counselors, back massages, a bounty of fresh food) after a wildfire had made hundreds of people homeless several years earlier. Heldman, who is white, could walk freely through the two shelters, while a black colleague was "harassed" by soldiers, she said, though both wore the same press badge. People were free to hop a cab to the airport and fly anywhere they wanted if they had the money. But most of those who ended up in Houston were stuck wherever they had landed. Ninety-three percent of those in a Houston-area shelter, one poll found, were black. Three-quarters had kids with them.

Communities around the country showed great generosity toward the New Orleans diaspora, starting with the invitation to welcome peo-ple into their towns. Church groups organized clothing and coat drives, local businesses donated Pampers and toiletries and book bags for school-aged kids. One Houston school was so serious about its promise to teach the New Orleans evacuees that officials there checked in every day with the local shelters to make sure children were attending classes. Parents arrived without birth certificates and immunization records, but school officials told them to worry about that later. Churches held pot-lucks and campaigns to find spare rooms for those in need.

Yet the same television images that stirred up fears among officials in Gretna and Baton Rouge also impacted officials wherever New Or-leans evacuees showed up. At a high school in the Kansas City metro area, Dominique Townsend, a sweet-faced sixteen-year-old, black, was brought to the auditorium with all the other kids from New Orleans. There the authorities laid out a strict set of rules that had evacuee kids staying after school for infractions that didn't earn local kids the same punishment. "We were seen as the trouble children," Townsend said. They were even forbidden from sitting together in the cafeteria because, Townsend said, "we were known as the NOLA gang—whatever that meant." (NOLA—short for New Orleans, Louisiana—is a common way people refer to New Orleans.)

In time, the New Orleanians were the houseguests who overstayed their welcome. Just before Thanksgiving, a brawl between the locals and Katrina kids at one Houston high school was so big it made the newspaper. Similar melees broke out at high schools in Dallas and San Antonio. A white political science professor at Rice University in Houston overheard the black woman working the register at his local grocery store talk about "those people." He was baffled—until he realized she was referring to a group of evacuees from New Orleans.

Officials in Washington were also looking at the calendar. Three months into the disaster, the government was picking up the tab for the 150,000 or so storm victims still living in hotels around the country. The Bush administration decided that it had had enough in mid-November. That's when FEMA announced that people would be responsible for their own hotel bills on December 1. The agency paid contractors to slip warnings under the doors of evacuees and hired caseworkers for anyone needing help finding an apartment or other temporary housing. People would still be eligible for as much as $800 a month in rental assistance, a FEMA official announced, through the end of February. They just needed to be someplace other than a hotel.

A federal judge, a New Orleans native appointed to the bench by Bill Clinton, ruled that two weeks' notice wasn't enough warning. FEMA would announce several more final dates—December 15, January 7—but that only led to more legal wrangling. How could FEMA expect people to make long-term housing decisions, lawyers for the evacuees asked, when the city itself was still making up its mind about the future of their neighborhoods? Many clients wanted to move into a FEMA trailer on their property—except they still didn't have electricity or gas in their part of the city, and the long waiting lists suggested the agency wouldn't have a trailer if they did. The government managed to get almost everyone out of the hotels by the end of February, but that led to a new crisis as emergency shelters faced an influx of Katrina castoffs. They would need to be housed somewhere—a hotel, perhaps—until space could be found in a FEMA trailer park.

"I don't know if you understand the magnitude of this disaster," a FEMA spokesman told the *New York Times*. Nearly 1.5 million people registered for assistance in a disaster zone the White House was describing (somewhat hyperbolically) as roughly the size of Great Britain. Hundreds of thousands of people were also affected by Rita. Every household registering with FEMA for help received a minimum of $2,000, no questions asked. (Larger families could qualify for more.) FEMA picked up the tab for the buses and planes that shipped people around the country and spent another $3 billion on trailers. The government provided rental assistance to more than seven hundred thousand families after Katrina and Rita, at a cost of more than $4 billion. One item FEMA doesn't cover, however, is a return ticket home.

"As a practical matter, poor folks don't have the resources to go back to our city, just like they didn't have the resources to get out of our city," Joe Canizaro told the Associated Press. "So we won't get all those folks back. That's just a fact. It's not what I want, it's just a fact."

A MASTER PLAN BY the end of 2005 had been the mayor's mandate to his Bring New Orleans Back Commission in September. A plan in hand by the start of the new year was "a personal commitment we made to the president," Boysie Bollinger said in October. Yet by Thanksgiving even commissioners were admitting that they would miss their deadline. "Five weeks to get even a draft done? That's unrealistic," declared Tulane president Scott Cowen. The new deadline would be the president's State of the Union at the end of January.

The mealtime options were slim in small-town New Orleans. So when a subset of the commission—Canizaro, cochair Mel Lagarde, and a few others—would join Nagin at the Sheraton in a private room, they were doing so in plain view of the other commissioners, who tended to eat at the same second-floor restaurant before meetings. Alden McDonald never cared that he wasn't part of the in-crowd— "I have plenty to keep me busy," he said—but others did. "Just a few friends getting together with the mayor to talk," Joe Canizaro said. Countered Oliver Thomas, "No one goes over with us what they discuss at these lunch meetings. It would be nice if they did."

Canizaro's lament wasn't divisions within the commission but the lack of meaningful dialogue among its members. "I think we're at the point," he said in the second half of November, "where the commission has to ask whether or not it's going to be able to make the tough decisions we need to make." A case in point was the first meeting held after the Urban Land Institute presented the city with its recommendations. The commissioners spent more of their time excoriating *60 Minutes* for its piece the night before called "New Orleans Is Sinking" ("Can we or should we put New Orleans back together again?" correspondent Scott Pelley had asked at the top of the show) than talking about any of the ULI's recommendations.

Canizaro took a final shot at sparking a debate in mid-December. He reiterated his contention that he didn't think they could afford to rebuild all of New Orleans, but this time he cited findings of the ULI and also a Rand study that predicted that even three years after Katrina, nearly half the city's population would still be living outside the city. He offered a compromise: What if we let people rebuild anywhere they want and then reevaluate?

Alden McDonald spoke right after Canizaro. McDonald had remained relatively quiet whenever the commissioners met in public. "He's never a guy who says much in group settings," said Sally Forman, "but that only means people really listen when he does." McDonald began by giving his bona fides. He lived in a neighborhood that the experts were suggesting should be converted back to marshland. Most of his customers, too, lived in affected communities. Yet it would be cruel to encourage people to move back home "without first giving them all the facts," he said. The ULI had given a name to one fear—the jack-o'-lantern effect—but he had others. "We really need to ask what kind of community it will be if there aren't adequate services, if there aren't grocery stores and other things that people need to make a community worth living in," McDonald said.

Yet there the discussion ended. No one seconded Canizaro's motion, no one took up where McDonald had left off. Instead the commissioners declared this public meeting their last, then wished one another a good holiday season. It would fall on the committee chairs to work out the details of the plan, which is how a wealthy white Republican from the suburbs came to decide the future of New Orleans's low-lying neighborhoods.

FINDING WORKERS WAS DIFFICULT in a city still without most of its residents. The big debris-removal companies passed out flyers in central New Orleans promising $17 to $20 an hour plus benefits. Those willing to swing a sledgehammer gutting a home or business could earn nearly that much. Burger King was offering a $6,000 signing bonus at its New Orleans outlets, and Rally's, a local restaurant chain, nearly doubled its pay to $10 an hour for new employees. The city's hotels, claiming they were understaffed at a time virtually every room was booked for the foreseeable future, even won the right to import workers from overseas under a special government guest-worker program.

Boysie Bollinger, who ran one of the country's largest shipbuilders, was more aggressive than most in his search for workers. That September, Bollinger sent recruiters to FEMA camps across several states, yet still fell six hundred employees short of the number he needed to meet his orders. He blamed FEMA. What incentive did potential employees have, he wanted to know, when they were living on FEMA's dime? Bollinger even argued the point with George Bush. "I told the president, 'I think you're empowering people to stay where they are,'" Bollinger said. "He said he wasn't sure a two-thousand-dollar check meant someone was living it up."

Bollinger was a large man with a jowly face and gray hair he wore on the long side. He would dress up for commission meetings, sporting a blue blazer with an American flag pin, but invariably the bottom of his trousers would be up by his knees, showing off a pair of black alligator boots. "When I talk, people think I'm from New Jersey or Philadelphia," Bollinger said, "but I'm from the swamp." He was from Lafourche Parish, an hour south and west of New Orleans. Under Bollinger's edict, an employee of Bollinger Shipyards returned to work immediately or was given two weeks' severance and lost all health benefits at the end of the month. "We used termination as an incentive to get them back," Bollinger said.

But Bollinger seemed to be fighting a losing battle. The welder he paid $17 an hour could earn $25 an hour hanging Sheetrock. He needed to raise wages if he wanted to compete, but then there'd be no profit left, he claimed, in the deals he had already signed. Instead, Bollinger walked away from $700 million in contracts, though he had devoted part of the previous two years securing them. "I can make you a list three miles long of things the government is doing to hinder our attempts to get back and operating," he groused three months after Katrina.

LAKEVIEW GOT ITS POWER and other utilities before New Orleans East or most of the other low-lying neighborhoods. It was still October when Robert Lupo, who owned more commercial real estate in Lakeview than anyone else, hired a crew to clean out his properties along Harrison Avenue, the community's main business strip. "They brought their own food, their own water, plus showering and cooking gear," Lupo said.

New Orleans East wasn't completely dead that November, despite a lack of electricity. Sporadically a visitor would hear the beeping of a backhoe or see other pieces of heavy equipment at work. "Those are FEMA contractors," Alden McDonald explained, clearing away rubble. Every half dozen or so blocks, a group of workers, invariably all of them Latino, would be gutting a home. McDonald didn't know what he was going to do about his house. Neither did Cassandra Wall. But the longer a home sat untouched, the more it would deteriorate. Both were among those out in the East putting up the $10,000 or so it cost to clear out their ruined belongings and also the waterlogged Sheetrock that provided nourishment for the mold. "We wanted to keep our options open," McDonald said.

At least people out in the East and in Lakeview had options. Nagin's "look and leave" edict—the mayor's plan for staggering access to the city's worst-hit neighborhoods and therefore not overwhelming a fragile city—was still in effect. Even two months after Katrina, armed soldiers were still posted at the bridges leading into the Lower Ninth Ward. Not even those who could prove they lived there prior to the storm would be allowed past a checkpoint. Not until December 1 did the city lift the lockdown and grant residents of the Lower Ninth access to their homes.

A few residents managed to get past the barricades prior to the neighborhood's official opening. Greta Gladney, who runs a nonprofit in the Lower Ninth, hitched a ride with a journalist whose press pass allowed them in. Two main arteries bisect the Lower Ninth: Claiborne and St. Claude Avenues. The homes north of Claiborne were closest to the levee breach. These homes had been decimated, but not her mother's home, in the middle of the Lower Ninth, between Claiborne and St. Claude, nor most of the homes on the other side of St. Claude, closer to the river. Aside from that area north of Claiborne, the Lower Ninth looked like much of the rest of New Orleans. And also like St. Bernard Parish, whose predominantly white, working-class suburbs began just on the other side of Delery Street, less than ten blocks away from the home where Gladney grew up. There in St. Bernard, you could see the occasional house pushed off a foundation or a car leaning against a tree. Telephone poles and wires were dangling on either side of Delery. Yet its parish leader didn't bar residents from access to their homes once the waters receded.

"It was the people with means who got back to the city first, and they were the ones making the decisions," Gladney said. Not until May was drinking water turned back on. The electricity wasn't restored until June. "The Lower Ninth seemed last on everyone's list for everything," she said.

Nearly two thousand people showed up on the December day the city reopened the neighborhood. Among them was Willie Calhoun Jr., a fifty-five-year-old airport inspector and part-time minister who had lived in the Lower Ninth his whole life. His journey that day began with an armed National Guardsman checking his ID. A city official warned a group of them about the "extremely dangerous conditions," and the Red Cross passed out gloves, masks, water, and ice. Once on the other side of the bridge, Calhoun noticed that the FEMA contractors cleaning up other parts of New Orleans had spent almost no time on the Lower Ninth side of the Industrial Canal. "A wasted three months," Calhoun told himself.

For most, the visit confirmed the obvious: in a neighborhood of one-story shotguns and cottages that had taken on as much as twenty feet of water, there was little to salvage. People would find a bowl or a favorite piece of jewelry and call out. One woman found a framed picture of a son who had died a decade earlier. Yet despite the loss, Calhoun proclaimed the day joyous. "You saw neighbors you hadn't seen in the last three months," he said. "You saw people you had heard had died." He also saw, finally, progress. With the opening of the Lower Ninth, a Rubicon had been crossed. Insurance adjusters could now work up estimates. The FEMA crews could start clearing the streets. If nothing else, the authorities could at least remove the enormous steel barge that sat on top of a block of pulverized homes in the neighborhood. "I was still naive enough at that point to think the city really wanted to help us come back," Calhoun said.

A FEW WEEKS AFTER Katrina, Congress had approved a $62 billion emergency-relief package for the Gulf Coast. That would cover the cost of the early rescue efforts, including the deployment of thousands of troops to the area, and also the housing bills for all those hundreds of thousands of people made homeless by Katrina. In Mississippi, Governor Haley Barbour had declared forty-seven of the state's eighty-two counties disaster areas. Some of that $62 billion would be used to reimburse each for overtime and other storm-related costs. The same would happen in a large part of Louisiana. The bulk of the money would be used to help rebuild the roads, public buildings, and other essential infrastructure covered under rules established long before Katrina.

The question for Washington to answer was how much more money, if any, the region would receive to help with the rebuilding. Early on, Louisiana's two senators had put together an aid package for the region—and were mocked inside the Beltway. The $35 million they earmarked for a seafood marketing campaign provided cocktail-party fodder, as did the $25 million for a sugarcane research laboratory and the $8 million for the state's alligator farms. Their package included $40 billion for levee repairs and another $50 billion for unspecified projects the government would fund through a massive community-development grant. In all, the bill called on the government to commit to a combined $250 billion more in federal aid for the Gulf Coast recovery. "I think everybody realizes the Christmas tree was a little heavily ornamented," Boysie Bollinger said after the package's introduction.

Some in Congress were convinced the federal government was wasting taxpayer money rebuilding New Orleans. Others were disinclined to entrust so much money to a state where officials were known for enriching themselves and their friends. "Louisiana and New Orleans are the most corrupt governments in our country, and they always have been," Senator Larry Craig, a Republican from Idaho, told a home-state newspaper in December (that was eighteen months before the wider world would hear, after his arrest at the Minneapolis–St. Paul airport, about the "wide stance" he takes in a bathroom stall). As a preemptive measure, Blanco said, the state hired a pair of accounting firms to help watch for corruption. "We hired auditors to audit other auditors," Blanco said.

The approaching close to the congressional session added to the urgency felt by advocates for the Gulf Coast. The short attention span of the media was one worry, the roots people were putting down wherever they'd ended up another. "Forgotten Already" was the headline over the editorial the *Times-Picayune* ran on its front page in mid-November. A few days later, Bobby Jindal shared his frustrations in an interview with the *New York Times*. "Every day that passes, it will be a little harder to get things done," said Jindal, who had been elected to Congress from the New Orleans suburbs two years after losing to Blanco for governor. Even Haley Barbour, despite his place at the front of any line, voiced his displeasure. "We are at a point where our recovery and renewal efforts are stalled because of inaction in Washington, DC," Barbour told one of several congressional panels looking into the federal government's response to Katrina. Another Republican Party stalwart, Bob Livingston, told the *Los Angeles Times*, "Here we are in month four of a terrible, terrible tragedy, and other than hotel rooms and meals ready to eat and some reconstruction, we haven't gotten squat." The former Republican congressman turned high-priced lobbyist added, "I'm ready to start a revolution."

The Corps' early estimates put the price of a Category 5 storm protection system at $32 billion—eight times its annual budget. The Bush administration responded with $4 million for a study to put forward alternatives. That study would be due back to Congress by the end of 2007—more than two years later. The Baker bill, while popular among local officials, had critics on both the left and the right. On the left, people questioned a bill that proposed to provide 60 percent of the worth of a home when they saw the levee failures as 100 percent the federal government's fault. On the right, they wondered why the federal taxpayer should be expected to pick up *any* of the bill when the government already funded a flood-insurance program.

Congress recessed for the year without even considering the Baker bill. They would need to start over again in January. "We are about to lose New Orleans," the *New York Times* began an editorial that ran in the Sunday paper in mid-December. "Whether it's a conscious plan to let the city rot . . . or honest paralysis over difficult questions, the moment is upon us when a major American city will die. . . . If the rest of the nation has decided it is too expensive to give the people of New Orleans a chance at renewal, we have to tell them so. We must tell them we spent our rainy-day fund on a costly stalemate in Iraq, that we gave it away in tax cuts for wealthy families and shareholders. We must tell them America is too broke and too weak to rebuild one of its great cities."

15

A SMALLER, TALLER CITY

Joe Canizaro was exhausted. "I've been overwhelmed fully," he confided on New Year's Day 2006. He had Curtis, his house manager, and also Sue Ellen, but who was there to help him run his businesses while he was preoccupied figuring out how much of the city they should rebuild? His bank, called First Bank and Trust, demanded the most attention. It had outposts in Biloxi and Gulfport, two of the Gulf Coast's harder-hit towns, and it had losses on investments in New Orleans properties. Like Alden McDonald, Canizaro felt the pressures of the nervous regulators examining his books. "It's a lot right now," he confessed.

Fatigue put Canizaro in an expansive mood on this first day of the new year. He expressed disappointment in decisions that had already been made and also in decisions that had been put off. Every expert said the same thing: the city couldn't afford to rebuild every last neighborhood. He cited the Rand study showing no more than 60 percent of the city's population returning at the three-year mark: "It doesn't take a genius to figure if you're missing forty percent of your original population, then there's going to be shrinkage in the amount of land that's going to be needed."

Yet Canizaro said he was unwilling to pass a death sentence on any part of the city. The racial implications would be too great. "Unfortunately, a lot of poor African Americans had everything they own destroyed here," he said. "So we have to be careful about dictating what's going to happen, especially me as a white man." They would discourage people from moving back into areas that might well flood again, he said, but they wouldn't forbid anyone from rebuilding.

Canizaro had tried to elicit input from each of his fellow commissioners. Instead they seemed relieved that he, not they, would have to make the decision. "The commission really saw it as Joe's job to come up with a plan for the neighborhoods," Tulane's Scott Cowen said. Yet Canizaro wasn't going to reach a decision on his own. He and Ray Manning, the man chosen to serve as his cochair, had handpicked twenty-six people to serve on the commission's Urban Planning committee, and another fifty-plus people were serving on various subcommittees (Historic Preservation, Zoning, Housing). Canizaro had also opened his checkbook to buy the services of a well-regarded planning firm based in Philadelphia.

A realization came to Canizaro after the ULI left town. These outside experts were correct to categorize neighborhoods based on damage, but they had it upside down: people in the city's hardest-hit neighborhoods—the people who most needed help—should be the top priority. In the coming weeks, a plan took shape. Canizaro would recommend that the federal government give New Orleans money to hire teams of planners and other experts to help the residents of each flooded neighborhood decide whether to rebuild or relocate. "Let people see the pluses and minuses of moving back home," Canizaro said. "With these planning teams, we'll help people make an informed decision." They debated whether to provide four months or a year to convince a critical mass of a neighborhood's residents to move home. A buyout program along the lines of the Baker plan would be created to compensate communities who concluded they couldn't make it work. "What's important is we give people an opportunity to determine their own future," Canizaro said.

Canizaro felt anxious after laying out his plan in a phone conversation he had with Karl Rove between Christmas and New Year's. "Karl left me realizing we needed to do a better job of packaging and selling the plan," Canizaro said. Don't say they were hiring these experts to help residents figure out which parts of the city needed to be reverted to swampland, Rove suggested. Instead, say they were there to help increase the odds of a community's success for those residents who wanted to return. If nothing else, Canizaro's talk with Rove helped him realize details still had to be worked out. That Saturday they were holding the final meeting of the Urban Planning committee so Canizaro would be ready to share his plan with others at Mel Lagarde's house that Monday. On Wednesday, he would be presenting their recommendations to the public at a giant ballroom inside the Sheraton.

THE URBAN PLANNING COMMITTEE met Saturday in Canizaro's offices on the seventeenth floor of a brown marble tower on Poydras. The floors were a dark hardwood, the furniture antiques, the art on the wall expensive works dating back to the sixteenth and seventeenth centuries. Marble sculptures and priceless-looking urns were perched on pedestals along the hallways. Canizaro had asked some of his people to work that day to direct people to the big conference room in back, and to provide photocopying or other support.

A nearly all-male, all-white group gathered around a large conference table for the 1:00 p.m. meeting. Of the twenty or so people seated around the table, two were black and one was Indian-American. Curtis was there, dressed in a starched white shirt and black suit. He served people tea and coffee and other refreshments. Canizaro, short, with a square face, a strong jaw, and brown eyes, sat at the head of the table. He was dressed in a plaid sweater vest over a yellow dress shirt, chinos, and tasseled loafers.

Canizaro opened by telling everyone about his conversation with Rove. "The goal here is to accentuate the positive." He spoke in a clipped, authoritative manner that suggested a man accustomed to giving orders. The script they had worked out had Canizaro saying a few words of introduction at Wednesday's meeting and then turning the program over to John Beckman of Wallace Roberts & Todd, the Philadelphia-based planning firm Canizaro had enlisted. Beckman, who was sitting near

Canizaro at the front of the table, stood to talk. Beckman, thin, bespec-
tacled, white, with unkempt hair, had decades of planning experience
in New Orleans, including a hand in the city's successful creation of its
Warehouse District. Beckman began offering inspirational words about
the task with which they had all been burdened, but Canizaro, irritated,
cut him off: "Just get on with it." Later, Canizaro reminded his fellow
committee members that they all had a vote—except his vote counted a
hundred times more than theirs. It was funny the way he said it, but the
crack also left no doubt that they were just there to help the boss make
up his mind.

The group argued over words and images as Beckman walked them
through a PowerPoint presentation. They were recommending that the
city give every community four months to hammer out a plan. Canizaro
wanted to describe the process as "efficient," but someone suggested "equitable" as more "warm and fuzzy" and less "cold and calculating." Those
around the table generally agreed that the slide deck minimized the
once-in-a-lifetime opportunity the city had to remake its park system.
New Orleans had two spectacular signature parks in Audubon and City,
but otherwise precious little greenspace. Words were added: "Now is the
time many people want to sell property and so it's a win-win situation
for everyone."

Partway through Beckman's dry run, an image flashed on the
screen: an artist's rendition of the Lower Ninth Ward, showing the
kind of mixed-use developments (retail, housing, community space)
they hoped would pop up over the flooded parts of New Orleans. As
people around the table imagined it, parts of the Lower Ninth (and
every other flooded community) would revert to marshland. Meanwhile, the glimpse of the community shown looked like a kind of New
Urbanism pipe dream: two- and three-story, handsome brick buildings,
a new light-rail stop, and storefronts along a tree-lined boulevard dense
with happy shoppers. "Change it to 'the historic' Lower Ninth," someone suggested. Early on, Canizaro had decided that they would use the
Lower Ninth "to show that you can take one of the worst communities
and show how it has a brilliant future." In the end, though, the group
convinced him it would be wiser not to single out any neighborhood.

Beckman reached the end of his presentation, and Canizaro invited comments from people around the table. Pres Kabacoff was there, the developer whom Barbara Major mistrusted because he never mentioned how his altruistic projects would also make him money. Kabacoff had been all over the media talking about his idea for a "smaller, taller" city. Firms such as his would convert old factories into condominiums or hives for interesting businesses. Where they found empty lots or buildings that needed to be torn down, they would in-fill the commercial strips and other blighted spots with mixed-use developments and mixed-income developments that would let them take advantage of government programs. Kabacoff had dubbed his plan Operation Rebirth, but invariably he would bring up Paris when stating his goal of a New Orleans that offered visitors fifty to a hundred walkable blocks. "This working for you, Pres?" Canizaro asked several times during the afternoon. "You see anything here that gets in the way of your Paris thing?" Kabacoff, his gray hair in a small ponytail, would nod, indicating that all was good.

Another Canizaro favorite around the table was Reed Kroloff, the dean of Tulane's architecture school. Kroloff, who was white, had only been in New Orleans a year (and he would be gone eighteen months later when he moved to Michigan for a different posting). He spoke more frequently than anyone else except Canizaro and Beckman.

One question was how blunt they should be in expressing their belief that some communities, or at least large parts of some communities, shouldn't come back. "It depends on how much dancing around you want to do," Kroloff advised. Canizaro said he thought they needed to say that not every community would be coming back. Kroloff met him with a smile and said, "We all saw ULI give a logical, reasonable, well-thought-out presentation of a very logical, well-thought-out plan. And we then all watched them run into a buzz saw." Canizaro, they agreed, should say that there would be people "disappointed" at the outcome of the four-month planning process.

During the four months communities were supposed to be coming up with a plan, should they impose a temporary moratorium on any development there? The committee agreed that communities, rather than imposing a ban, should "discourage" homeowners from rebuilding in the hardest-hit areas. They imagined two kinds of communities in the flooded zone: those able to draw a critical mass of people and those that couldn't. But what was critical mass? Fifty percent of the people in a neighborhood giving a verbal commitment to rebuild? Seventy percent? "I'm one who likes to be definitive," Canizaro said. "But that really sets you up as a target." They would leave the phrase ambiguous. Another debate broke out over how much money they would request to fund the land bank the city would need to create in order to purchase properties in neighborhoods that decided to right-size themselves for the new New Orleans. "Twenty billion dollars?" someone asked. Canizaro declared that too big a number, but they never settled on a more palatable figure.

People were getting testy. Participants vied to be heard. More than three hours into the meeting, someone mentioned the renters: nearly seventy thousand rentals had been ruined by Katrina, but their plan did not provide any help for tenants. At that, one person threw up his arms; another ostentatiously rolled her eyes. A suggestion that the committee go on record as demanding that the Baker bill provide people with 100 percent compensation for damaged properties rather than 60 percent evoked a similar reaction.

Near 5:00 p.m., Reed Kroloff asked about building permits in the hardest-hit areas. It was one thing to discourage rather than forbid people from rebuilding during planning, but it seemed crazy to have the city sanction projects with permits. But Canizaro, who had several times mentioned the late hour, was out of time: "My wife's going to kill me if I don't get home." He told Curtis to get the car and be ready for him downstairs. He and Sue Ellen had dinner plans.

KROLOFF'S PERMIT QUESTION GNAWED at Canizaro all that night and through church the next morning. It was the first thing the sixty-four-year-old Canizaro mentioned after greeting an out-of-town reporter he had invited to lunch. Canizaro drove his late-model, silver Lexus to Andrea's, a favorite restaurant in Metairie. His wife sat with him in the front seat, the church pastor and the reporter in the back. "We issue permits, we're telling them it's okay to rebuild when we're still not sure," Canizaro said. The restaurant was only a few minutes away but he was already laying out the dilemma. He confessed he hadn't considered the question until Kroloff raised it—yet he couldn't stop thinking about it.

Lunch meant more unanswered questions. The federal government had yet to issue the flood-elevation maps that might require people to raise their homes. Would insurance carriers even issue policies in the flooded areas? What about the homeowners halfway through rebuilding when they learn their block is being reverted to open space? "It's amazing to me, the issues I hadn't thought of until now," he said.

THE FRONT-PAGE HEADLINE OF the *Times-Picayune* ensured a big crowd at the Sheraton that Wednesday: "FOUR MONTHS TO DE-CIDE." Several subheadlines followed. In red ink, the paper declared, "Nagin Panel Says Hardest-Hit Areas Must Prove Viability," and below that, in bold lettering, "Full Buyouts Proposed for Those Forced to Move." But people mostly remembered the large, four-color map of the city on the front page. An obscure graphic in the PowerPoint deck John Beckman had prepared ("I must have had two weeks of twenty-hour days," he said) used dotted black circles to show that communities lacking in parks would benefit from additional greenspace. The circles were "large to indicate that we have not identified properties," Beckman wrote. "Those will be determined with citizen involvement." But that fine print didn't make the newspaper. Instead, enormous green dots sat over New Orleans East, Gentilly, and the Lower Ninth Ward,[1] above a caption that read, "Approximate areas expected to become parks." More than one thousand people had jammed a giant Sheraton ballroom by the time the fire marshals declared that they would not let any more people inside. Members of the City Council held a press conference elsewhere in the hotel to denounce the proposal before it had even been introduced.

"This is a process," Nagin said in his introductory remarks. "This is a journey." The mayor, who, Canizaro said, had "signed off" on his plan at Mel Lagarde's house on Monday, spoke as if this moment were a mere stop along the way. Lagarde also said a few words, but the day belonged to Canizaro, who looked resplendent in a dark suit and red

---

1. But not Lakeview, given its proximity to City Park and other parklands there.

tie. "It's impossible to plan a city in three months, but we've tried," Canizaro said. He introduced Beckman, who asked people to imagine a New Orleans with a lot more greenspace and also light-rail lines criss-crossing it. The plan would remake commercial corridors and stressed the need for a stronger storm-protection system and called for coastal restoration. "New Orleans will be a sustainable, environmentally safe, socially equitable community with a vibrant economy," Beckman said. He reminded people that George Bush was scheduled to visit the city the next day. The president had asked New Orleans for a workable, realistic plan that he could fund. This plan, Beckman implied, was the city's shot at forcing Bush to make good on his promises.

Those in attendance, however, seemed only interested in what the Bring New Orleans Back Commission might be saying about their community. They were incensed mainly about Canizaro's call for a 120-day moratorium on all new city permits. All around the city people were tired of fighting FEMA and battling insurance adjusters. Now the city was proposing another roadblock to recovery. "Please let us build our own homes," pleaded a Lakeview homeowner named Charles Young. "Let us spend our insurance money, which we paid for on our own."

"This is a big, audacious plan put together by obviously brilliant people," said Freddy Yoder, the FEMA contractor on the board of the Lakeview Civic Association during his turn at the mike. "But you missed the boat. We don't need a rail system. We need housing."

Those were among the day's more measured comments. Harvey Bender, a laid-off city worker from New Orleans East, opened his re-marks saying, "I don't know you, Joe Canizaro, but I hate you." He then threatened to "suit up like I'm going to Iraq and fight this." Mtangulizi Sanyika, a professor of African World Studies at Dillard University, rep-resented a group called the African American Leadership Project. He accused the mayor of taking part in a "Katrina cleansing" that would let the city's moneyed interests steal African-American lands. Carolyn Parker, a resident of the Lower Ninth Ward, was more succinct. "Over my dead body," she told the commissioners. Another speaker decried a plan that would turn "black people's neighborhoods into white people's parks."

Canizaro defended his plan. He reminded people of how much of themselves they would be giving and how much of their hard-earned money they would be spending with no guarantee that their neighbors would return. "The city may not be able to provide services if you're stuck out there by yourselves," he said. But Canizaro had lost the room even before the lights were dimmed. "Telling people they can't rebuild for four months is tantamount to saying they can't ever come back," said former mayor Marc Morial when it was his turn at a microphone. "It's telling people who have lost almost everything that we're going to take the last vestige of what they own."

If the vast majority of those at the Sheraton that day thought the Bring New Orleans Back Commission had overstepped its mandate, some living in the high-ground neighborhoods felt that Canizaro had not gone nearly far enough. The reaction of John Kallenborn, the head of Louisiana operations for JPMorgan Chase, was typical. To him a four-month time-out while everyone talked more was nothing but a way of postponing the inevitable. Kallenborn, who had been on the mayor's short list for the commission (he was removed to make room for a black member), pointed to Scott Cowen, who as Tulane president had laid off more than two hundred faculty members and eliminated several academic departments. Cowen was getting grief from alumni, but he was also confronting an estimated $200 million in losses. The city, by contrast, Kallenborn said, was offering Canizaro's "crazy, halfway ideas that please no one."

Janet Howard, another Uptown fixture, agreed: "There are some very tough decisions that have to be made here, and no one relishes making them." Howard, a former corporate lawyer, had reinvented herself as a government policy expert. "But to say that people should invest their money and invest their energies and put all their hope into rebuilding, and then we'll reevaluate in a year, that's no plan at all."

LARGE CROWDS MILLED AROUND after the big meeting at the Sheraton. Canizaro would have been excused if he had escaped via a side door, but instead he headed into the audience. He was intent on finding Harvey Bender, the man who had gotten so personal when voicing his anger over the rebuilding plan. Bender had pointed an accusatory finger at Canizaro and bellowed, "You've been in the background scheming to take our land!" Early on, Canizaro had vowed to buy no real estate or take part in any new developments—to avoid the kind of charges Bender had just made. "I wanted to set the record straight," Canizaro said. "I wanted him to know I wasn't going to make a dime off any of this."

Bender was shocked when Canizaro asked for a minute of his time. Bender had attended some of the New Orleans East meetings that the Wall sisters had helped to put together in Baton Rouge. There, Canizaro was the bogeyman, the rich developer who had brought the ULI to town as a first step toward taking their land. A few days later, Bender was sitting on a silk couch in the corner of Canizaro's office. When Canizaro invited him to stop by, Bender asked if he could bring a few allies, but he ended up coming alone.

"He just wanted to hear my ideas for what we should do," Bender said. "My thing was that people had no idea what was going on. One day we're hearing we're rebuilding the whole city, the next people are talking about taking our homes. I just wanted to make sure everyone had the right to make up their own mind."

RAY NAGIN WAS NONCOMMITTAL. Talking to a gaggle of reporters as he left the Sheraton ballroom, he stressed that they were just at the proposal stage, but also added, "The realities are that we have limited resources to redevelop our city." The following day, Nagin met with the president. There were no alcohol-free beers or late-night cigars this time, only a brief tour through the parts of the city that had remained dry. "The contrast between when I was last here and today . . . is pretty dramatic," Bush said. "It's a heck of a place to bring your family."

Nagin seemed to endorse the Canizaro plan at a public hearing the following day when he said, "It's the way we're going to go, with some tweaks." Reporters assumed he meant dropping the idea of a temporary moratorium on permits. But then the mayor sat down with David White, the friend he had given a spot on the Bring New Orleans Back Commission. "I told him that from a planning standpoint, it probably made a lot of sense," White said. "But from a human standpoint, it made no sense at all." There were also the politics to consider. "A lot of people in the black community were looking at the first property they ever had in their family," White said. And with the mayor's race only a few months away, White counseled, "It sounded like the government was talking about taking that property away." One week after declaring his support for Canizaro's plan, Nagin announced that one of his "tweaks" would be his opposition to any proposal that limited people's choice to rebuild wherever they chose.

"I'm a property-rights person," Nagin said. "I have confidence that our citizens can decide intelligently for themselves where they want to rebuild." Anyone wanting a building permit, he said, was welcome to stop by City Hall to pick one up.

CANIZARO'S URBAN PLANNING REPORT had only been the first in a series of presentations the commission was unveiling that month. The education committee, headed by Scott Cowen, called for more autonomy for individual schools and greater accountability. The commission's government effectiveness committee endorsed the idea of consolidating the city's seven elected property assessors into a single office. Its economic-development committee stressed the need for the city to revive its port, by modernizing and pursuing new business. By then, though, no one seemed to be listening.

Despite the mayor's words, Canizaro was acting as if his plan had Nagin's full blessing. He announced that Ray Manning and Reed Kroloff would be heading up the neighborhood planning process that his committee had recommended. Neighborhoods would start meeting by February 20; by March 20 they would need to have a list of residents committed to returning. By May 20 the buyouts would begin. Kroloff and Manning identified a dozen teams of experts and even worked up a budget of between $6 million and $8 million. Apparently, a FEMA official speaking without authorization promised Canizaro and others that the agency was good for the money but then his replacement said that funding such an effort was forbidden under the law.

In February, the City Council decided to hire its own planning team. Their experts would help people rebuild rather than make up their minds. The council used $3 million in community development funds to hire the technical consultants needed to make their plan a reality. Meanwhile, the Louisiana Recovery Authority, unlike the Bring New Orleans Back Commission, had the statutory authority to approve or disapprove projects that the federal government would be funding through the state. Sean Reilly, a two-term state legislator who had made a fortune in his family's outdoor-advertising business, was the most outspoken of the LRA's members. "Someone has to be tough, to stand up and to tell the truth," Reilly said. "Every neighborhood in New Orleans will not be able to come back safe."

People were upset when two weeks after Canizaro's presentation, the president devoted only 160 words in his State of the Union speech to what some were calling the biggest disaster in US history and failed to mention New Orleans. But then, the mayor had promised Bush a blueprint for rebuilding by the end of December. Here it was the end of January and the federal government still didn't have a plan to act on.

Nagin meant it when he said he would not stand in the way of anyone wanting a building permit, no matter where in the city he or she lived. "People want permits to let them rebuild, let's give 'em permits," he told Greg Meffert, whose portfolio included the city's Department of Safety and Permits. Meffert shifted extra inspectors and other employees to the eighth-floor permits office. He reprogrammed the touch-screen kiosks the city had installed pre-Katrina and set them up in a large, open room at the end of a hallway. Roving "greeters" were assigned to help people in the fashion of airline agents working the check-in machines at airports. Others talked to people waiting on a line that on some days reached out the door to Poydras. "We'd literally see thousands of people in a week," Meffert said.

A homeowner had to do more than show up. For many the sticking point would be the number grade the city had already slapped on tens of thousands of homes across the flood zone. The grade had been determined in a fast and dirty process based on the elevation of the floodwaters in a community, the number of feet the first floor sat above the ground, and whether a home had a second floor. The scores had a ridiculous specificity—a piece of paper would declare a home 53.14 percent damaged—though these were at best a good guess. The expertise of the assessors was also questionable. To help it rate each house, the city had hired the Shaw Group, one of the big multinationals FEMA was using to oversee the cleanup (the federal government also used them to do construction in Iraq). The Shaw Group turned it over to subcontractors who, the *Times-Picayune* revealed, hired a pet groomer and a pizza deliveryman as inspectors.

Yet the number mattered. A number below 50 percent meant that, in the eyes of the government, you were renovating your house, not rebuilding it. Even if the federal government declared that homeowners needed to raise their homes to qualify for flood insurance, anyone with a number below 50 percent was grandfathered in. Meffert's problem was that his inspectors had saddled the majority of homeowners with a damage assessment above 50. The city would issue a permit to those with a score above 50 if they presented a plan for raising their home—which could cost tens of thousands of dollars, or as much as $100,000 if a home needed to be lifted above the cement slabs common especially in New Orleans East.[2] So Meffert created a quick appeals process that he programmed into the city's kiosks.

A new number below 50 percent wasn't automatic. Those with a damage assessment in the high 50s were treated differently from those clutching a paper showing a number in the low 50s to mid-50s. People had to put up some kind of argument to challenge the original assessment. Yet almost 90 percent of those asking for a number below 50 percent received one. By early February, the city was issuing as many as five hundred rehab permits a day.

The *Times-Picayune* had already published a long story on what was going on when the tale of the shrinking damage assessments made page one of the *New York Times*. Within forty-eight hours a quartet of unhappy FEMA officials stormed Greg Meffert's office, threatening him with legal action. "They're in my office yelling about how if I don't cease and desist, they're going to stop reimbursing homeowners and stop

---

2. Those with an assessment above 50 percent qualified for up to $30,000 in federal grants to underwrite the cost of raising a home.

reimbursing the city," Meffert said. But he worked for Nagin, not for FEMA, "and I had the mayor and others telling me, 'You must do this.'" The city's permits office would continue revising downward people's damage assessments.[3] "That's why Ray Nagin loved Greg," Sally Forman said. "He knew he could give something to Greg and Greg would make it happen."

Those committed to the long-term viability of the country's federal flood-insurance program were not amused. The US taxpayer pays for the heavily subsidized flood insurance program, and in return municipalities must enforce the government's guidelines. "If New Orleans is phonying the damage reports so as to allow inadequate construction," said a former flood-insurance director, "they ought to get thrown out of the program." Said another, "You can't destroy the flood program to achieve a short-term goal." But for Meffert, it underscored the extraordinary moment they were living through, when putting his thumb on the scale could have this profound an impact. "That was really the tipping point," Meffert said. "We were rebuilding the whole city no matter what anyone else decided."

SHORTLY AFTER THE SHERATON meeting, Nagin was in Washington testifying before Congress. The mayor used that moment in the national spotlight to plead for help. His city was broke, he said, and people needed trailers. More than twenty-one thousand names were on a waiting list, but five months after Katrina, FEMA had delivered only thirteen hundred trailers. Meanwhile, he watched as the federal government allowed its contractors to fritter away millions. His people did some calculations, he said. FEMA was paying $43 a cubic yard to haul away debris. But FEMA subcontracted to a subcontractor to a third subcontractor, who hired the people to do the work for $7 a cubic yard.

---

3. FEMA had its rigid ways, but Meffert was a computer geek before he was a top city official. "We took their formula and burned it into our kiosks," Meffert said. FEMA carried through on its threat of an audit, but the city had the documentation they needed under FEMA guidelines to modify a number. The city passed its inspection without any problem.

"I have been put in a position to fly back and forth between Baton Rouge and Washington, DC, to beg and grovel for money, and I don't appreciate it," Nagin said. "I implore you. I beg you. I'm getting on my knees, I'm puckering up. Help us. Help us today." He was back two weeks later to plead with the White House. He asked them for between $10 billion and $15 billion to help him rebuild New Orleans. You're asking for way too much money, they told him.

The news wasn't all bad. Before the end of 2005, Congress had approved $11.5 billion in block grants to help storm-ravaged areas, a measure the president signed. But Louisiana received barely half that money, though its people suffered three-quarters of the damage. The city's best hope was still the Baker bill. Let people complain that the government would be reimbursing at 60 percent of a property's pre-Katrina value, not 100 percent, but at least Baker's proposed Louisiana Recovery Corporation put the federal government on the hook for tens of billions of dollars. And it wasn't as if there were many viable alternatives in a Washington where Republicans controlled both the House and the Senate. Even Baker himself, a free-market conservative from the Baton Rouge suburbs, couldn't believe he was championing a measure that would make the federal government, at least temporarily, the largest landowner in New Orleans.

At first, the White House had flinched at this idea of a giant buyout bill with an open-ended price tag. In response, Baker added cost controls and, shortly into the new year, declared the odds better than even that it would pass. Yet the price tag turned out to be only one concern. The president had run on the idea of shrinking government, yet Baker's plan called for its expansion. It didn't sit well with some that those who'd bought flood insurance all those years would be treated the same as people who'd failed to do so. And then the government would be getting into the real estate business—a realm that Gulf Coast recovery czar Donald Powell thought better left to the free market. By the end of January, the Baker bill was obviously dead.

The governor was in Washington for the State of the Union address at the invitation of the White House. "I went hoping the president would share with us what his plan was for Louisiana," Blanco said. Instead she heard a few lines about all the country had already done for the people of the Gulf Coast before receiving a televised presidential kiss on the cheek afterward. "It's time to play hardball, as I believe that's the only game Washington understands," Blanco declared one week later in a speech before the state legislature. The next day, she threatened to block oil and gas leases worth hundreds of millions to the federal treasury unless the state received its "fair share" of the revenues.

The threat worked. It helped that the state and New Orleans had a good ally in Donald Powell. Powell, a working-class kid from Amarillo, Texas, listened more than he spoke in his first month as the region's liaison to the White House. He met with top decision makers, but he also put on jeans and boots and talked to people he met while walking different parts of the city. "I went with no preconceived thoughts," Powell said. "And I realized that while Mississippi was an act of God, Louisiana was an act of God and man." On the sly, Powell was also meeting with Sean Reilly of the Louisiana Recovery Authority. Together, the two of them had hatched a plan that would help make drowned-out Louisiana homeowners whole. Road Home, the governor eventually dubbed it. Under Road Home, every homeowner would receive up to $150,000 in compensation based on the pre-Katrina value of the home minus whatever insurance payments were received. (A person owning a $250,000 home who received $150,000 in insurance payments would, for example, receive a check for $100,000.)

One week after Blanco's oil-lease threat, Powell summoned Blanco and Nagin to Washington for a hastily arranged press conference. There he announced that the president would seek $4.2 billion in compensation for Louisiana homeowners—on top of the state's share of the $11.5 billion in block grants Congress had appropriated at the end of 2005. Blanco used the bulk of that money—$7.5 billion—to fund Road Home.

Twice Blanco had stood up to the president of the United States— and won. Despite pushback from the legislature's black caucus, she had acted decisively when she slashed nearly half a billion dollars from the state budget two months after Katrina; she had engineered a state take-over of New Orleans's failing schools. Yet the soft-spoken, sixty-two-year-old Blanco didn't demand the spotlight like a lot of politicians. She was who she was—a matronly looking grandmother and earnest public servant who would never act like the former mayor of New York after September 11. "I'm not a guy," she told the *New York Times'* James Dao that winter. "I can't be Rudy, whatever that is." Instead of praise for strong leadership, New Orleans talk-radio hosts mocked her as weepy and in over her head. Drivers applied DON'T BLAME ME, I VOTED FOR JIN-DAL bumper stickers to their cars.

When announcing the launch of Road Home in March, Blanco called it "our ticket to rebuild, recover, and resume our productive place in our nation's economy." The ads the state commissioned to advertise the program called it "Gov. Kathleen Blanco's Road Home." People around the governor imagined putting all those five- and six-figure checks in the hands of Louisiana voters. To their mind, Road Home would cinch her reelection, but Blanco herself was dubious: "I told my staff, I said, 'This sounds like a politician's dream, to hand out cash. Federal money.' But I told them, 'It's going to be miserable. Because there are people who are going to think it wasn't fairly done. No matter how fairly we structure it.'"

16

LIMBO

Christmas in 2005 for the McDonalds had been low-key. The children flew to Baton Rouge, rather than New Orleans, the family's home base for the foreseeable future. Christmas was more somber than in years past, but the holiday also took on larger meaning. They had all survived Katrina. "We had a lot to be thankful for," McDonald said. The kids joked that for once it was easy to pick out gifts for their parents, who pretty much needed everything.

The McDonalds tried not to think about all they had lost in the flooding, but with everyone taking snapshots, it was hard not to brood over the missing photographs and memorabilia. They'd stored most of their pictures upstairs, but their favorites were in scrapbooks on the ground floor, destroyed with everything else. McDonald had boxes of newspaper clippings and photos, along with other keepsakes. He kept the boxes in a nearby storage facility that also flooded.

They tried not to think about their house in New Orleans. McDonald's seat on the mayor's panel only made him more aware how uncertain the future was for communities such as his. Yet his insurance company was giving him until the middle of January to send them an itemized list of his house's contents. "They're asking me to write down everything I had in the house and how much I paid for it," McDonald said. That's how he spent his free time during the holiday break.

McDonald had agreed to serve on the Bring New Orleans Back Commission thinking that he would help prevent the city from devising a plan that treated the hardworking poor different from others. Yet he couldn't play hero when his fellow commissioners barely even mentioned the city's hardest-hit neighborhoods. Instead McDonald focused on smaller but critical issues such as the disconnect between the pre-Katrina price of a person's home and the post-Katrina cost to make it habitable. By McDonald's calculations, a modest, twelve-hundred-square-foot home in the Lower Ninth Ward was worth maybe $70,000 at the time of the storm. The same home in the Seventh Ward, where he grew up, might be worth $90,000. Yet the price tag for restoring either home would exceed $100,000. The spread in middle-class Gentilly was disturbing, too. There, a twenty-five-hundred-square-foot home worth maybe $200,000 before Katrina would cost roughly $250,000 to fix up. A lot of his neighbors in New Orleans East would be looking at the same problem. An estimated two-thirds of the damaged homes in New Orleans were valued at less than $125,000, but it would take a lot more than that for most to rebuild. "Some of us knew if we used pre-Katrina assessments for compensating people," McDonald said—as the governor was proposing to do under Road Home—"nobody in the black community was coming out anywhere near whole."

His neighbors may have resented members of the ULI as outsiders, but McDonald saw them as a talented team of housing experts and financial wizards who could help him think through his ideas. For most of the week the ULI was in town, McDonald described himself as "holed up in a hotel room with all these brilliant minds," wrestling over a plan that would let people rebuild regardless of what an assessor or an insurance company had said their home was worth before the storm. The blueprint they concocted after three days and nights sought to reshape New Orleans without needing to impose a ban on anyone.

Their plan included a land bank funded with federal dollars. This newly formed entity would take ownership of abandoned properties that people couldn't afford or didn't want to rebuild. The homeowners wanting to rebuild in, say, a more vulnerable section of the Lower Ninth could do so on their own using their insurance money—or they could choose a refurbished, like-size home through the land bank in a neighborhood the city wanted rebuilt. That would help guard against the jack-o'-lantern effect.

McDonald went further when he imagined the city focusing its resources on a community such as Pontchartrain Park, the first subdivision in the state of Louisiana to accept black homeowners when it opened in the 1950s. The residents of Pontchartrain Park tended to be older African Americans. Some couldn't imagine living anywhere else, while others couldn't fathom starting over. The Lower Ninth Ward also had an older population. What if New Orleans used redevelopment dollars, McDonald asked, to build a senior center in Pontchartrain Park? "Bring in an emergency health care center," he said. "A dialysis center. A walkable grocery store. You make it nice—a rec center, a movie theater—and come up with a transportation plan." Two things would happen, McDonald argued. The city would draw back residents of Pontchartrain Park who wanted to return. And officials would mollify some who felt the government was angling to seize their property.

McDonald's proposal was included in the Bring Back New Orleans Commission's final report. So, too, were ideas he contributed to its economic-development and education committees. "My hope at this point is that the leadership finally shows some leadership," McDonald said in February, one month after the commission's report had landed on Nagin's desk. McDonald might even have spent more time feeling frustrated in the coming months if he didn't have a bank to rebuild.

IF THE EARLY DAYS of Liberty's recovery had been about reconnecting with its customers, phase two, as McDonald took to calling it, was about taking stock. The bank's biggest vulnerability was its home-loan portfolio, so McDonald created a team to track down every last mortgage holder. Once their computer systems were operational again, they could see what insurance companies a homeowner used. They requested copies of the policies, which they would use to coach property owners on what they needed to say to their insurer. If the initial offer from an insurer was too low, someone with the bank would walk a loan customer through the appeals process. The bigger the settlement check for the homeowner, the less likely the bank would take a loss on a loan.

Reconciling the books proved painstaking as McDonald's finance people sought to account for each check lost during the storm. The physical cleanup was endless. Liberty hired an outside crew to gut and clean its water-damaged properties, but the thankless job of sifting through waterlogged file cabinets, folder by folder, looking for any paperwork that had survived the flooding, fell to bank employees wearing protective gear. Another enormous job had them itemizing every last item damaged in the flood for the bank's insurance company and accounting for storm-related expenses. McDonald or his people had been meeting with adjusters for months, he said in January, "but so far we haven't gotten a single check for a single roof on a single building."

Phase two was also about finding new business. Every day more longtime customers were closing accounts because they were living nowhere close to a Liberty ATM. McDonald anticipated the bank would be losing thousands more. McDonald initiated conversations with Walmart and other big-box retailers about in-store banking centers (he'd end up opening just two mini-branches in Walmarts) and pursued more business with large corporate depositors, such as Aetna and American Express, which were already Liberty customers. He also looked into the idea of opening strip-mall loan centers—storefronts that would make the kind of small-denomination loans Liberty specialized in earlier in its history. McDonald was thinking about Louisiana, but also Texas and Mississippi.

Mainly, though, McDonald focused on rebuilding his battered home-mortgage business, the biggest source of bank profits prior to Katrina. He hired someone to start spreading the word among mortgage brokers throughout the area that Liberty was offering 100 percent mortgage financing. His KIDs program—the CDs he sold at below-market interest rates—had brought in an extra $10 million in cash. That's the money he'd use to fund these no-down-payment home loans. In less than three months, Liberty's staff approved $10 million in home loans—a fraction of the $10 million a month they averaged prior to Katrina, but at least the bank was generating loan fees again and earning a higher interest rate on its money.

The Liberty mortgage team completed its assessment of its loan portfolio shortly after Christmas. An astonishing 98 percent of its home-loan customers carried flood insurance. Staffers cheered when the mortgage department announced that very few homeowners had allowed their flood insurance to lapse, but McDonald reminded them that only meant moving on to the next battle: "Now the question will be, did they have *enough* coverage?" The bank would also have to be patient, McDonald said, as he reminded everyone of the drawn-out battles they were all waging with their own insurance companies. The bank was buying new furniture and computers without being certain their insurance would reimburse them. They were spending tens of thousands more on the cleanup. Three times a week they were refilling the generators that kept the air circulating inside the bank's headquarters—at $150 a pop.

They had also gotten bad news from Washington. McDonald's friends in high places had tried but failed to include language that would have required the feds to rely at least in part on smaller community banks such as McDonald's when disbursing the billions in recovery funds that would slosh through the Gulf Coast. Liberty would be on its own in its search for new business, as would every other community bank across the region.

Yet McDonald was feeling optimistic. The new year saw McDonald back in a jacket and tie. The bounce had returned to his step as he worried less about survival and focused more on rebuilding. He opened a branch in Gentilly, a middle-class black neighborhood, and people were starting to make loan payments again now that the four-month moratorium the bank had granted to customers in flooded parts of the city had ended. Not everyone was making regular payments again, but most were, and even most of the delinquents had worked out a payment plan. It felt like the bank's earliest days: most people up-to-date on a loan, the rest wards of the bank with whom they needed to work one-on-one.

The best news of the new year was a call in early January from Russell Labbe telling McDonald the lights were again on at the bank's headquarters. Labbe had installed new circuit breakers in the building over the holidays and arranged for a city inspector to sign off on his work. Entergy was able to power them up only a few days later. "We were the only light out there for miles," Labbe said. The elevators weren't working (and wouldn't until after $350,000 in repairs), but at least they could turn off the generators. They were already working with BellSouth to restore the all-essential T1 line that would allow them to connect to the wider world with the new computer that had for months been sitting idle on the third floor.

ALONG THE REST OF the Gulf Coast, people stared at piles of sticks that had once been their house, or they were looking skyward to thank the force that had saved them. In a waterlogged New Orleans, everything was ambiguous, starting with the question of whether to rebuild. A flooded home meant endless conversations with insurance adjusters and no clear answers about how much money could be expected. People worried about what their neighbors might do. Would they walk away from the moldering eyesore that once was home? Every decision seemed to depend on at least ten unknowns. Were there schools? Did they still have a job? What might the federal government do about the levees? Would there be the medical facilities for the sick parent they were caring for? For themselves? Could they count on adequate fire and police protection?

Only 17 of New Orleans's 122 public schools opened that January. All were charter schools staffed with a mix of seasoned teachers and newcomers to both New Orleans and the profession. More than fifty private schools had reopened by the start of the year, along with a large portion of the city's network of Catholic schools. (Tulane and the University of New Orleans had reopened, and both Xavier and Southern University's New Orleans campus—two historically black colleges—were offering classes to any student able to get back to the city.)

Regular garbage pickup had resumed, but trucks came by once a week, not twice a week as before Katrina. Most of the refrigerators had been removed, but that only meant they were piled high in a landfill somewhere else in the city. The RTA was still running less than half its pre-Katrina routes, and even some of those were only partially restored. The green streetcars weren't running up St. Charles, and the RTA had limited railcars operating on a small section of Canal Street. The only line they had fully restored was Riverfront—a route used primarily to move tourists between the Quarter, the Aquarium, and the Convention Center. Before the storm the RTA had averaged around 125,000 daily riders, but that number was barely cracking 10,000 in January. "We needed more riders to pay for more drivers," explained Bill Deville, who had been named the RTA's "executive director for recovery" after the storm.

Cassandra Wall's sister Tangee, who had moved into her Warehouse District condo after Thanksgiving, started to work on her home by early March. She wasn't waiting on permission from the city or advice from the federal government. Her insurance company would pay what it would pay, and if that didn't prove enough, there might be a Road Home check. Her niece—Petie's oldest—was getting married that November. The ceremony would take place in an Uptown church and the reception would be at the Jackson Brewery in the Quarter, but Tangee was intent on hosting the wedding party at her home.

"You have to remember that we made a commitment before we left Baton Rouge that we were coming back," Petie said. "We didn't care how we were going to put it back. Even if it meant living in it half-built and spending whatever money we could save up to pay a guy to put up a wall, and then next month, saving a little more to pay him to put up another." To help make rebuilding feel like a cause, their group, Eastern New Orleans United and Whole, printed up black, white, and green lawn signs for people to put in front of their vacant homes: I AM COMING HOME! I WILL REBUILD!

Cassandra, however, wasn't ready. She was as angry as any of them at the way residents of New Orleans East had been treated. But to her that was a reason for them to stay in Baton Rouge rather than rush into the unknown. FEMA had still not issued the new flood maps that would tell residents and businesses how high they would need to rebuild after Katrina.[1] The agency had issued the new maps for Mississippi in November, but as January became February became March,

---

1. More specifically, the maps would indicate the minimum elevation of the first floor of any building to be eligible for the government's flood-insurance program.

New Orleans and the rest of southern Louisiana still waited. Cassandra feared if her family started working on their home, they'd learn they needed to spend another $100,000 they didn't have lifting it to qualify for flood insurance. They had remodeled shortly before Katrina. Maybe that was part of Cassandra's hesitation about coming back. On the Sunday before Katrina, they had pulled away from a freshly painted, peach-colored, two-story home with terra-cotta trim, surrounded by a white picket fence. It had then sat in six feet of fetid water in the September heat.

Cassandra had the FEMA identification number she would need whenever she needed something from that agency. She had her flood-zone number, which would be crucial once FEMA released its revised maps. And of course she had the claim numbers and the various phone numbers for her insurance carriers. Like many in New Orleans, she carried both a homeowner's and a flood policy, which meant working with two separate entities. The company that carried her flood insurance sent an adjuster to her house "in a timely fashion," she said, and two months later she and her husband had their check—$30,000, the maximum their policy paid out. She had the opposite experience with her homeowner's policy. Katrina had ripped off parts of her roof, which meant not just flood damage but extensive water damage on the second floor. She was frustrated by how long it had taken her insurer just to get someone to her house. That first adjuster lost the photos he had taken and then apparently his job. She would need to start over again with a second one, who offered her $30,000 on a $150,000 policy. That was the start of a fight that lasted nearly two years. (Ultimately, their policy paid closer to $100,000.)

Cassandra figured she made at least ten trips into New Orleans to meet with adjusters or others about the house. That was about all the glimpse of life in New Orleans East she needed. The traffic lights weren't working. There were no streetlights. The big Home Depot was open, as were a few car dealerships along the I-10 and a couple of fast-food places, with a few trucks serving Mexican food to the work crews. But that was about it. "What are you going back to?" she asked her sisters. In March, the couple bought a home in Baton Rouge not far from their hotel. Cassandra made up some flyers to advertise her tutoring service. Any more big decisions would be put off until the people in charge started making up their minds.

THE CITY WAS STILL in emergency mode and still producing weekly situation reports. The news wasn't always bad. By January, the city was claiming New Orleans was home to around 158,000 people—about one-third its pre-Katrina population. Government-issued trailers were starting to show up in the most damaged communities. But taken as a whole, the reports were a snapshot of a city still far from recovery. The city was now estimating that Katrina had created 50 million cubic yards of storm-related debris. As of early February, 6 million cubic yards had been removed—12 percent of the total. Countless cars still sat abandoned around the city.[2] Streets were still barricaded. That winter and through the spring they were still finding the occasional corpse.

The newspapers carried stories about a second wave of looters working abandoned parts of the city. They picked clean the second floor of Cassandra's home, a stash that included a fur coat she was kicking herself for not taking when she saw it there in October. The *Times-Picayune*'s Chris Rose told readers about a woman from the Ninth Ward who had for years done food prep at Antoine's: the crystal and china she had inherited from her mother had survived the flood but not the looters. "What kind of man picks over the bones of a destroyed life?" Rose asked.

The bad news seemed to come with each day's newspaper. Fixing the Superdome was essential in a football-mad city that also used the stadium to generate revenue. That was slated to cost $32 million.[3] The airlines were still operating less than half the flights as pre-Katrina. "Archdiocese Shutters Dozens of Churches," the front page of the *Times-Picayune* trumpeted in February. That included St. Augustine in

---

2. Another estimate put the garbage left behind by Katrina at 12 million tons—or seven times the volume produced when the Twin Towers fell.

3. Katrina's gusts, Jeff Duncan wrote in the *Times-Picayune*, "peeled the thick black rubber sheets from the Dome's exterior like an onion, dislodged three massive ducts, and punctured eight smaller holes in the surface."

Tremé, founded in 1841 and, the paper explained, "the mother parish of black Catholics in New Orleans." (The church would reopen after a pitched fight.) That same front page carried a story about rules so laxly enforced at a city-owned landfill that reopened after Katrina that a report concluded the city might be looking at a Superfund site in the middle of Gentilly. Only six months after Katrina, already two-thirds of the charitable donations given in the name of New Orleans had been spent.

The city was generating much more in sales tax—$5 million a month—than anyone had anticipated. But that still put it at less than half its pre-Katrina levels, representing tens of millions of dollars in lost revenues. The property tax bills hadn't even been sent, let alone collected on. Short of a bailout from somebody, the city was looking at a deficit of between $150 million and $200 million. "We've never seen anything like this, at least not in our lifetime," Roy Bahl, the dean of the Andrew Young School of Policy Studies at Georgia State University and an expert in public finance, said of New Orleans.

The big law and finance firms were the first to return to the city's office towers. Those employees who didn't live Uptown or on the West Bank moved in with relatives or took a hotel room. Next came larger companies that had the economic means to fix up a facility and also cover the extra costs of doing business in a disabled city. Chevron started moving its people back into New Orleans at the start of February, but only after purchasing an ambulance and hiring a paramedic in a city with an unreliable 911 system. Shell flew its thousand-person exploration and production unit back to the city later that month— but only after an extraordinary investment. Prior to Katrina, the US subsidiary of the Royal Dutch/Shell Group owned no residential properties, but it would spend $32 million on housing in the months afterward. "We bought condos," a Shell exec said. "We bought a lot of single-family homes. And we leased them out at cost to any Shell employee in need of housing."

Six in ten businesses operating in the central business district had reopened six months after Katrina, according to Don Hutchinson, the city's economic-development director. But even that figure was deceptively high. A lot of companies were moving back only some of their workforce. Dominion Resources, for instance, a large energy company, was leaving 40 percent of its people in Houston.

The view of the economy outside the central business district was dismal. The city had twenty-two thousand businesses within its borders before Katrina. Six months after Katrina, two thousand were open, Don Hutchinson said—less than one in ten. The one bright spot was the city's restaurants, yet by March only 29 percent of these had reopened. "The question isn't whether New Orleans is going to take a huge hit in terms of job loss," said Jay Lapeyre, a local business owner who had taken the reins of the Business Council from Jimmy Reiss. "The real question is where we'll have to rebuild from once we know where we've bottomed out."

NAGIN ASSEMBLED A COMMITTEE to advise him about Mardi Gras. They had plenty of reasons for canceling carnival that year. The city had no money, yet Mardi Gras meant paying for extra police protection and over-time for the sanitation crews. Most of the city's hotels were full with relief workers, contractors, and evacuees. Some worried about how it would look if CNN showed clips of people parading down St. Charles while the city's representatives were in Washington begging for billions. The death toll alone—eighteen hundred across the Gulf Coast, more than one thousand from New Orleans—might be motivation enough to cancel Mardi Gras.

Yet there was never any question the city would be holding its annual bacchanal, even if shortened by a few days. Mardi Gras was good for business, and it would be good for the psyche.[4] Nagin didn't waffle. Of course they would parade. The mayor never looked more take-charge

---

4. Nagin also thought it would be cost-free to the city given all the outside contractors making millions off the cleanup. The city hired a company to attract sponsors to underwrite some of the expense. Nagin hoped to raise $2 million, but only a single corporate sponsor stepped forward: Glad, which gave an unspecified six-figure donation along with a hundred thousand trash bags. Two days before the first parade, the City Council unanimously approved a bill to spend $2.7 million on police over-time and other city services without specifying the source of the money they were authorizing.

than on Mardi Gras Day—Fat Tuesday—sitting atop a white horse, dressed in the black beret and desert combat gear favored by Lieutenant General Russel Honoré, leading the Zulu parade down St. Charles Avenue in the morning sun.

THE LEADERSHIP RUNNING THE Lakeview Civic Improvement Association started talking immediately after the storm. Al Petrie, a Lakeview Civic board member, had fled to Houston, where he worked the phones in a borrowed office. "We had our first conference call five days after Katrina," Petrie said. In January, Petrie and others back in Lakeview started meeting every Friday morning at the Gulf Coast Bank branch in the neighborhood. The meetings were run by Martin Landrieu and open to anyone in Lakeview, but the people who showed up on the second floor every Friday tended to be those most active in Lakeview Civic, which dated back to 1924. Landrieu, a partner in a big downtown law firm, put himself in charge of zoning. Freddy Yoder, whom FEMA was paying to clean up Lakeview, took on infrastructure. Maybe they were meeting to prove their viability to the city, as Joe Canizaro had suggested they do, or maybe their gatherings were about devising their own recovery plans. Eventually, they created seventy-two subcommittees, including one that took on the task of mapping every broken streetlamp in the neighborhood, and another that investigated the mosquito problem caused by people's abandoned swimming pools.

A group from the Lower Ninth Ward met Uptown every Thursday evening at a Methodist church on Carrollton Avenue. They were from Holy Cross, the better-off corner of the Lower Ninth along the river, where the ground was higher and the homes generally nicer. Pam Dashiell, a single mom who did contract work for Shell, was president of the Holy Cross Neighborhood Association. As soon as her cell phone started working again after Katrina, Dashiell, who had endured several weeks perched in the St. Louis home of an acquaintance she hardly knew, was running up big bills trying to track down neighbors. "And when I wasn't calling, I was e-mailing and texting," she said. By mid-February, Dashiell and two others had tracked down three hundred of their neighbors—only a small fraction of those representing Holy Cross's fifty-five hundred residents.

The treasurer's report in February indicated their homeowners association had less than $1,000 in its accounts.

Yet Dashiell and her neighbors were well ahead of the rest of the Lower Ninth. No New Orleans neighborhood had as many of its residents dispersed around the country as the Lower Ninth[5] and its residents generally did not have the means to fly in for meetings. Another factor was that the people who ran the area's homeowners association were just as overwhelmed as everyone else. In mid-February, Charmaine Marchand, the area's state representative, created one. "No one else was organizing," Marchand said, "so I felt it fell upon me as the only elected official from the Lower Ninth to do something." So while other neighborhood organizations were counting heads and thinking about what they might say about their community to a planning body, those behind the newly minted Lower Ninth Ward Homeowners Association were writing bylaws and selecting officers.

Around eighty-five people showed up for their first meeting, held on a rainy Saturday afternoon near the end of February. This gathering, held on the second floor of the Holy Angels Academy in the Upper Ninth Ward—the parochial school Marchand had attended as a girl—was less about figuring out how to draw up a plan and more about the proper methods of mold remediation, the state of the levee system, and possible help from various governmental bodies, including FEMA, which had a representative in attendance. Rumors that the levees had been bombed came up a couple of times during a question-and-answer session, as did the charge that government negligence was responsible for their misery. "This wasn't a flood," bellowed one audience member, pointing a finger at the pleasant-looking FEMA woman with a perma-smile on her face. "A flood is an act of God. This was the government—the government!—doing a bad job of building levees and destroying our homes."

"We have to do more," Congressman Barney Frank, the Massachusetts liberal, told a group of storm evacuees who had traveled to Washington that February for yet another congressional hearing into Katrina.

---

5. That according to Muriel Lewis, director of the National Association of Katrina Evacuees.

"I hate to have to say this about my own government, but I believe what we are seeing with regard to New Orleans and the surrounding area is a policy frankly of ethnic cleansing by inaction."

MAYBE GREG MEFFERT HAD gotten a little ahead of himself. Touring the Lower Ninth in those first months after the storm could bring out the doomsayer in anyone. The cameras rolled as Meffert walked Scott Pelley of *60 Minutes* down a single street north of Claiborne Avenue, a few blocks from the levee breach. The camera lingered on one house sitting cockeyed and cracked on its foundation, and another that the floodwaters had split in two. Standing there in the street, Pelley asked Meffert how many houses he imagined they would have to demolish. "It could go up to fifty thousand homes," Meffert responded, nearly a third of the city's housing stock. That prompted Pelley to speculate that New Orleans was looking at what was "likely the largest demolition project in US history." It wasn't enough that all of New Orleans was worrying about the city's sending bulldozers to revert their street to swampland. Now they had to worry that the bulldozers were coming because some bureaucrat had deemed their home too far gone to save.

Just before the Christmas season, Meffert announced that the city had finished its block-by-block inspection of the flood zone. They had slapped just over fifty-five hundred homes, not fifty thousand, with the red tag that Meffert said meant a structure needed to be razed as a threat to public safety. The city would bulldoze the first set of twenty-five hundred homes over the next few weeks, Meffert said, while his people took a closer look at the remaining three thousand. The pronouncement opened a new chapter of court challenges, protests, and dueling press conferences. As in most every other hard decision in New Orleans following Katrina, individual rights were set against what the authorities thought was best for the wider community.

Meffert felt misunderstood through the entire ordeal. In his mind, he was the valiant public servant moving with deliberate speed to remove rubble that was not only hazardous but stood in the way of recovery. The city had the power to demolish a home without the owner's consent, he declared, if a structure posed an imminent threat. But the US

Constitution, the Supreme Court had long ago said, requires the government to give people "a meaningful opportunity to be heard" before seizure. The majority of houses in that first batch of twenty-five hundred were in the Lower Ninth, a part of the city that been open to residents for only a few weeks at the time of Meffert's announcement. Yet with little warning, the city was sending in bulldozers.

"In the Lower Nine, we understand and recognize that many of those properties will have to be demolished," said Tracie Washington, an attorney who represented several residents and advocacy groups bringing suit. Some only wanted a chance to pick through the remains in search of any small mementos that might have survived the storm. Others wanted time to see for themselves if it made more sense to start over than to rebuild.

A large protest formed outside City Hall two weeks after Christmas. Speaker after speaker denounced the mayor, including the City Council's Oliver Thomas, who threatened to stand in front of the bulldozers himself if they tried to knock down his family home without their consent. "If you're talking about my mama's house, I'm standing in front of it before you tear it down," said the hulking Thomas. "You got to be a bad dude to get through me."

The city avoided another protracted legal battle a few weeks into the new year by cutting a deal with those bringing suit. The city singled out over a hundred homes in the Lower Ninth that officials felt needed to be torn down immediately. Owners of these properties would have seven to ten days to challenge the city's decision. Others the city deemed in imminent danger of collapsing would have up to thirty days. "As a city, we have to move beyond playing victim, and we have to rebuild for everyone," Meffert said after the deal was announced. NO BULLDOZING signs started popping up not only on homes but also on trees and surviving segments of fencing around the Lower Ninth.

REBUILD AT YOUR OWN risk. That was Ray Nagin's advice on March 20 when he responded to the recommendations the Bring New Orleans Back Commission had presented to him two months earlier. Under the plan worked out by Canizaro and his committee, March 20 was to have been the deadline by which every neighborhood needed to have submitted the names of returning residents. Key components of the Canizaro blueprint were the panels of planners and other experts that would help communities as they wrestled with a plan. Those had yet to form. Still, Nagin said he expected reports from each of the flood-prone neighborhoods by June 30.

Nagin officially rejected Canizaro's suggestion that the city impose a temporary moratorium on work in parts of the city. That was no surprise with the election a month away. At the same time, he embraced the equally controversial suggestion made by the ULI that the city put off rebuilding the hardest-hit areas—what he dubbed "delayed recovery zones."

"If you go in those areas, God bless you," Nagin said when releasing what he called his "general guidelines" for rebuilding. "We'll try to provide you with support as best we can. But understand we're concentrating city resources in the areas that are in the immediate recovery zone." Barbara Major was among those speaking out against this idea of favoring healthier parts of New Orleans over those most devastated. Sure, planners had smart ideas for rebuilding the city more rationally, but they failed to understand a fact about neighborhoods such as the Lower Ninth Ward, Gentilly, and New Orleans East. "Black people only moved there because all the high ground had been taken," she said.

17

CHOCOLATE CITY

Louis Farrakhan, the Nation of Islam leader, was in New Orleans for the long Martin Luther King Jr. weekend to speak at what his organization was calling a Black Family Summit. Weeks earlier, Nagin had promised the local Baptist church where the event was to be held would have electricity, but at the last minute Farrakhan's people needed an alternative venue. Four months after Katrina, even the mayor didn't have the clout to turn on the lights in a church only minimally damaged by the storm.

The hotels in New Orleans were running at capacity that weekend. Evacuees were in town for an event sponsored by the city's big social aid and pleasure clubs, which have been fixtures of the city's black community dating back to Reconstruction. A group of them had joined together to put on a giant second-line—a New Orleans tradition where groups of musicians led revelers through the streets. They would be parading through Tremé that Sunday on King's birthday. Thousands had traveled home to New Orleans, at least for the night. "We're coming home!" the revelers started chanting. "We're back." Yet just as the musicians stopped playing, gunfire broke out. Three people were brought to the hospital for gunshot wounds.

Farrakhan and Nagin met later that night in the minister's suite at the Windsor Court. There, inside one of the city's pricier hotels, the two spoke about the shooting, but their main focus was the black diaspora—the hundreds of thousands of New Orleanians living elsewhere. This man whose words had proven so inspiring to Nagin a decade earlier implored the mayor to bring his people home. It is your obligation as an African-American mayor, Farrakhan counseled, to make sure New Orleans remains a black city. The two spoke for nearly three hours.

Nagin had a light schedule on the Monday holiday—just a morning ceremony at City Hall. There, Nagin would say a few words to honor Dr. King. Long ago his communications director had abandoned the idea that the mayor might deliver a speech if one of her people wrote it for him. "For Ray," Sally Forman said, "there was no greater sin than sounding scripted." He was an elected official more interested in "leaving a lasting impression," Forman said, "than presenting any memorable ideas." She had delivered a typed-out list of suggested bullet points to his office, but even then there was no telling if they would be used. His tendency to go off message had even become something of a public game between them ("Sally's going to need the smelling salts for this one," Nagin would say from the podium)—but the mayor had a more serious point to make. "Don't make me speak all English," Nagin snapped at Forman early in their relationship. "Don't make me look weak."

Mitch Landrieu, the lieutenant governor, was at City Hall that morning. Impossible to miss, he stood near the podium with a fussing baby in his arms. It had always been personal between Nagin and Landrieu, as the latter seemed bothered by the mayor's slights of his sister Mary. Just before Katrina, Nagin ran into Landrieu at an event. "Mitch got right up to Ray, yelling at him," Forman said. "I really thought it was going to end in a fistfight." A widespread rumor had Landrieu running for mayor against Nagin that April. Others around Nagin thought that his late-night meeting with Farrakhan explained the speech the mayor gave that day. Forman, however, believed it was the pending election that inspired her boss to make the "impromptu decision that he's not going to offer the same old same old with Mitch standing there."

Nagin, dressed in an open-collared, striped shirt, wore a black armband around one bicep. "I greet you all in the spirit of peace this

morning," Nagin began, addressing the majority-black audience. "I greet
you all in the spirit of love this morning, and more importantly, I greet
you all in the spirit of unity." People looked at one another, puzzled. This
was not a Ray Nagin any of them knew.

He could talk about what made King great, Nagin told the crowd, but
instead he wanted to tell them about his conversation that morning with
the slain civil rights leader. "I just wanted to know what would he think if
he looked down today. What would he think about Katrina?" The mayor
brought up Gretna in his imagined conversation ("I said, 'Mr. King, when
they were marching across the Mississippi River bridge . . . and they were
met at the parish line with attack dogs and machine guns firing shots
over their heads?'"). He brought up the suffering at the Superdome and
Convention Center and also the "knuckleheads [who] pull out some guns
and start firing into the crowd." With each incident, King expressed his
disappointment via Nagin. ("And Dr. King said, 'I wouldn't like that.'")

Nagin isn't one for long speeches. He mentioned black-on-black
crime and the decline of the African-American family and then got to
his point, echoing the theme of self-reliance that Farrakhan and his aco-
lytes had been preaching all weekend: it would fall on the black community to help itself. "God is mad at America," Nagin said. "He's sending
hurricane after hurricane after hurricane, and it's destroying and putting
stress on this country. Surely he's not approving of us being in Iraq under
false pretenses. But surely he's upset at black America also. We're not
taking care of ourselves. We're not taking care of our women. And we're
not taking care of our children when you have a community where seventy percent of its children are being born to one parent.

"We ask black people: It's time. It's time for us to come together. It's
time for us to rebuild a New Orleans, the one that should be a chocolate New Orleans. And I don't care what people are saying Uptown or
wherever they are. This city will be chocolate at the end of the day. . . ."
And then he added: "This city will be a majority African-American
city. It's the way God wants it to be. You can't have New Orleans no
other way; it wouldn't be New Orleans." After a smattering of applause
a self-conscious Nagin concluded, "So before I get into too much more
trouble, I'm just going to tell you, in my closing conversation with Dr.
King he said, 'I never worried about the bad people who were doing all

the violence during civil rights time.' He said, 'I worried about the good folks that didn't say anything or didn't do anything when they knew what they had to do.'"

SALLY FORMAN DIDN'T THINK it was a big deal when Nagin referred to New Orleans as a chocolate city. He had used the phrase before and nobody had ever cared. "I don't think Ray had any idea it would blow up like that," she said.

But Nagin's expensive campaign consultant, Jim Carvin, knew. Carvin had been on the winning side of six consecutive mayoral contests in New Orleans, including Nagin in 2002, but Nagin's speech left Carvin wondering about his chances at number seven. "It's always difficult when your candidate says something without discussing it with you," a droll Carvin says in the film *Race*, a documentary by Katherine Cecil about the 2006 New Orleans city election. "It was strictly shoot-from-the-hip Ray Nagin." Within hours of Nagin's speech, the cable news stations were carrying the story that the mayor of hurricane-ravaged New Orleans had just described Katrina as God's wrath. Soon the "chocolate New Orleans" line replaced the God theme. That line dominated the news for weeks. Within days, it seemed every tourist shop and street vendor in town was selling a T-shirt depicting Nagin as Willy Wonka and New Orleans as a chocolate factory. (One version: NOW WITH 50 PERCENT MORE NUTS!)

"It's part of our culture to talk about chocolate cities," Nagin told CNN the day after his speech. He mentioned the song "Chocolate City," George Clinton and Parliament's ode to Washington, DC. Washington was the country's first "chocolate city," Nagin explained, followed by Newark, Detroit, and New Orleans. Nagin would apologize for his comments—but only up to a point. "I crossed the line when I brought God into the discussion," he confessed to the *New Orleans Tribune*. "But I see no problem talking about New Orleans remaining diverse."

Uptown saw "chocolate city" as the end of Nagin. He was no longer the erratic mayor who maligned his own city by exaggerating the crimes that occurred after Katrina and then flipped, flopped, and stalled whenever he needed to make a decision. Now he was the buffoon. "Congress can finally stop accusing us of being corrupt," wrote Clancy DuBos, the chief political writer for the *Gambit*, the city's alternative weekly. "Nagin has finally given them a fresh argument: that we're stupid, incompetent, and led by a mindless racist."

Polls revealed a black New Orleans split over Nagin's speech. Eighty-two percent of the poll's respondents said they weren't offended by the "chocolate city" reference, though a majority agreed that he "could have said it better." Fifty-nine percent of blacks said they had a favorable view of Nagin (compared to 13 percent for Bush, 24 percent for FEMA, and 40 percent for Blanco). Warren Bell, a lifelong New Orleanian who had been the city's first black news anchor on local network TV, thought the whole event had been overblown. "New Orleanians refer to this as a chocolate city," Bell said. "Certainly the chocolate people did." Bell, who by that time was working in the president's office at Xavier, was no fan of Ray Nagin's, but he also viewed the mayor's reference, whether deliberate or not, as a brilliant political stroke: a way for the mayor to use his megaphone to signal to his African-American constituents scattered across the country that he supported their right to return. "The people for whom that was designed to appeal . . . are glad he said it," Bell said. "I think that endeared him to more black voters."

INCUMBENT MAYORS DON'T LOSE in New Orleans. Clancy DuBos, the political writer, searched back sixty years to find the last sitting New Orleans mayor denied a second term. But then, it had been a hundred years since a city had been devastated like New Orleans (San Francisco, 1906; Galveston, 1900). Six months earlier, Nagin was sitting on a $1.3 million campaign war chest and looking at what DuBos dismissed as "nuisance opposition." Post-Katrina, twenty-three people filed to run against Nagin. "A 20-Ring Political Circus," the *Washington Post* said of this election taking place at the end of April, eight months after the flood.

A real estate appraiser joined the race, as did a radio DJ, an aircraft mechanic, a paralegal, and two preachers. Manny "Chevrolet" Bruno, who ran against Nagin in 2002, was also a candidate. The motto of this unemployed actor working as a bookstore clerk was "A troubled man for troubled times." He proposed that the city legalize hashish and create a red-light district like Amsterdam's to pay for a state-of-the-art levee system. He suggested polygamy as a solution to the city's repopulation problem. Even one of Nagin's former chiefs of staff (his former *chief administration officer* in the local parlance) announced her candidacy.

Most of Nagin's twenty-one challengers were white. That was no surprise to Lance Hill, who described the 2006 mayor's race "as the white community's best opportunity in thirty years to take back political control of New Orleans." It wasn't just an academic from Tulane seeing it that way. "There's a lot of people in the black community," City Council president Oliver Thomas said, "saying that people in the white community are trying to pile on." Even evacuees around the country could see for themselves what was happening during an election covered by CNN, Fox, and MSNBC as if it were a national election. Chris Matthews would serve as co-moderator at the last big debate, broadcast nationally by MSNBC, before the election runoff.

Ron Forman, who had announced his candidacy a few months before election day, was the early favorite. He had the *Times-Picayune*'s endorsement. He also had the money, which he'd made sure to line up before entering the race. "I told them, 'Look, guys, I don't have the wealth,'" Forman said. "'If I'm going to step up, you have to step up with me.'" Three days later, he said, he had raised $2.5 million. Like in *Night of the Living Dead*, Forman joked, "people just keep showing up at my door each night, carrying stacks of checks, each one of them for five thousand dollars." Pre-Katrina, Boysie Bollinger donated $5,000 to Nagin's reelection campaign, but then various subsidiaries of his (Bollinger Gulf Repair, Bollinger Marine Fabricators) gave another $45,000 to Forman that winter. Jimmy Reiss and his spouse also gave Forman $10,000 between them, and Reiss served as a chief Forman fund-raiser. For Reiss his efforts served as penance for any role he had played in the creation of Ray Nagin. "Absolutely the wrong guy for the job at the moment," Reiss said. The plan to seize back control of City Hall seemed on track.

Then Mitch Landrieu entered the race.

IT HAD BEEN AN agonizing few months for Ron Forman, starting with the disintegration of his relationship with Nagin. "The core group of people I work and socialize with are more the wealthy, the business leaders, the philanthropic community," Forman said. "I was 'Ray's guy' to them." He had stopped defending Nagin around October, but it was one thing to let someone know you're disappointed in him and another to announce that you intend to take his job. He even sat down with Mitch Landrieu to try to convince him to enter the race. "But he tells me, 'I think I can do more good in Baton Rouge than New Orleans,'" Forman said. "And I believed him." Even after talking with Landrieu, Forman vacillated: "I told one person yes but then I'd tell someone else no."

Sally Forman informed her boss what was happening shortly after the Chocolate City speech: "I told the mayor, 'Unbeknownst to me, my husband has decided he's running against you.'" The resignation letter she released to the media stressed the respect she had for Nagin, but privately she confided to people that the end couldn't come soon enough. "Ray started to mistrust people around him, and some crazy things started to happen," she said. "He started fighting. There were lines being drawn."[1]

Ron Forman might have been the candidate of the Uptown blue bloods, but he wasn't one of them. His father was a welder, his mother a bookkeeper. He was a Jew in a community known to harbor anti-Semitism; worse, after earning an MBA at Tulane, he went to work for Mayor Moon Landrieu—a figure cursed up and down St. Charles Avenue, the liberal who handed the city over to the blacks. But after two years working for Moon Landrieu, Forman was put in charge of the city's zoo, a place so bad the *New York Times* had described it as a "ghetto for animals." He'd earn the business community's gratitude by transforming it into one of the city's crown jewels. The zoo, along with the aquarium, which had been born under Forman's tutelage (paid for by a tax on the city's homeowners), attracted more than 3 million visitors a year, and Forman was helping make everyone rich. A likable, large-featured man always quick with a quip, he was invited to join Rex and became a fixture at events wherever the privileged and the well-connected gathered. "If you were mayor or in the council, you were my friend," he said.

---

1. "I stayed low-key," Sally Forman said of her involvement in her husband's campaign. "Which was really weird. I was so active and here I was on the sidelines."

Forman pitied Nagin, whom he considered a friend: "We needed a Giuliani but that wasn't Ray. He had to live with that each day and it took its toll." It had once been a joke between Forman and Sally, the mayor's tendency to describe himself as "percolating" on a problem. But it was no longer funny. "I'm not trying to sound heroic, but someone had to pick up the flag that Ray had left lying on the ground," Forman said.

Running against Nagin felt awkward, but squaring off against Landrieu left Forman feeling "torn to pieces." Moon had been an early mentor; Moon's wife, Verna, chaired the zoo board. Forman had known Mitch since the younger Landrieu was a boy. His mother, Verna, would bring him to meetings and "he'd run around the boardroom, up on everything," Forman said. "He was wild." Forman was a fan of Mitch Landrieu the politician, who always knew he could count on a campaign contribution from Ron Forman. "This is someone I've been supportive of his whole career," Forman said.

Forman thought about dropping out. He even broached the topic with some of his backers. "But by that point, I had already spent three hundred thousand or four hundred thousand dollars of their money," he said. "I had made these commitments." He hoped his money and his message, bundled with the *Times-Picayune*'s endorsement, would secure him a spot in the runoff, against Nagin or Landrieu.

Forman proved a lousy candidate. He'd flash a smile and give people a pat on the back but never said anything. Privately, he agreed with those who said that a city built for almost 650,000 needed to shrink following Katrina, but when speaking in public, he avoided talking about the future of the city's flooded neighborhoods. "It became such a hot political subject that no one wanted to talk about it," he later confessed. When the subject of the future of the neighborhoods came up, he'd talk generically about the New Orleans he loved. "What makes us rich is our diversity," he would say. "Without diversity, we're the suburbs." It was critical that we give everyone a chance to come back home, he said, but offered no plan for doing so. He believed a lot of valuable ideas were hidden inside the Bring New Orleans Back Commission's report, but he left that unsaid as well.

Forman's campaign team broke the bad news to him a few weeks before election day. The election was a three-person race, as they had expected, but Forman was running third in a contest that would pit the top two vote getters against one another in a runoff. "The hard part," confessed Forman, "is when they tell you, 'You have little of the black vote, you have a lot of the white vote, you have a lot of the wealthy vote. You're being portrayed as the blue blood. And to change that, here are the ads we have about Mitch and Ray to bring down their numbers.'" He knew what the campaign professionals were asking him: How much did he want to be mayor?

THE PRESS WAS READY to crown Mitch Landrieu the winner even before election day. How could he lose? Landrieu was a well-known son of Louisiana politics with nearly twenty years in politics. He was the state's lieutenant governor. In a field of neophytes, Landrieu was a polished campaigner who had the media savvy to handle the extra burden of the *Washington Post*, the *New York Times*, CNN, and the hundreds of other out-of-town reporters who would be parachuting in to cover New Orleans's 2006 municipal elections. The racial politics also seemed to break Landrieu's way. He'd get his share of white votes and also do well in the black community. His voting record in the state legislature was that of an old-style liberal who cared about the downtrodden. More important was his father's reputation as the man who opened City Hall to blacks in New Orleans. "There's historically been a lot of carryover loyalty there," said Silas Lee, a local pollster and Xavier University professor.

Landrieu had grown up not in Uptown but Broadmoor, a mixed community in the western half of the city. "We were playing baseball against one another since the fourth grade," said Jacques Morial, the second-born son of the man who took Moon Landrieu's place as mayor and the younger brother of Nagin's predecessor.

Landrieu studied political science in college but also acting. He tried making it in theater before entering law school at Loyola University New Orleans. He was twenty-seven years old when voters sent him to Baton Rouge to occupy the same seat in the state legislature that both his father and older sister (whose place he took) had occupied. Landrieu was thirty-four the first time he ran for mayor in 1994, in an election he lost to Morial's brother Marc. Landrieu conceded that election by driving to the

Morial campaign party at around 1:30 a.m. to offer his congratulations face-to-face. In 2003, Louisiana elected him lieutenant governor.

Landrieu rushed to New Orleans after the flooding, the man of action venturing out on a skiff to help with the rescue. "It's important from my perspective for people to understand that leaders do what they're supposed to do," he said. (And if he had pictures of himself taken out on the water rescuing people, that's what politicians do.) His own home remained dry, but three of his eight siblings owned homes in Lakeview. All three moved temporarily to Monroe, Louisiana, four hours north, to stay with a sister living there. His parents' home in Broadmoor, the home in which they had all grown up, also flooded. His parents, too, would temporarily move to Monroe.

Mitch Landrieu turned forty-five two weeks before Katrina. He was trim with short-cropped gray hair and piercing blue eyes. His thick, butterscotch New Orleans accent seemed equal parts old South and movie tough guy. A disciplined politician, he demanded loyalty from a tight circle of advisers, yet he also exuded a warmth and a candor that set him off from other career politicians. Sitting for an interview with a reporter eleven days after the storm, Landrieu shared some ideas he had for reviving New Orleans. They included the creation of something akin to the Tennessee Valley Authority, if not a cabinet-level post to oversee the rebuilding of the ravaged Gulf Coast. But then Landrieu, self-aware and willing to make fun of himself, added that he was just making this stuff up. "Don't believe anything anyone is telling you," he said. "No one can really know what they're talking about yet. Just let things go in one ear and out another."

RAY NAGIN PHONED JOE CANIZARO to hit him up for a campaign contribution. Canizaro had been generous with Nagin in the past: Would he support him now in a tough reelection?

Canizaro responded curtly. He didn't mention how he'd put his relationship with the president on the line for New Orleans. He didn't bring up the hundreds of thousands of dollars he had spent underwriting the planning process. Instead he spoke about his efforts, and those of his fellow Bring New Orleans Back commissioners, and how they felt that their work had been for naught. "I said to him, 'Mr. Mayor, you've taken no leadership. You're not doing anything to implement any part of this plan we all worked so hard on.'" Later, Canizaro would imagine what else he could have told Nagin: how neighborhoods needed to better understand their topography, how there was money to relocate people for their own safety if only Nagin would give the commission's plan a chance. Instead Canizaro closed the conversation by declaring an end to their working relationship. "I just said, 'You and I are now finished.' I told him, 'I'm not going to help you anymore,' and that was the end."

Canizaro felt more sympathy than anger toward Nagin. Like Ron Forman, he believed he was looking at a man whose greatest crime was his inaction. "The mayor's answer is that people know best, and so anyone who wants a permit is free to build wherever they want," Canizaro said. On paper it might sound perfect: the citizens decide where to rebuild and the city responds accordingly. "You know the people who are going to suffer are those who can least afford it," Canizaro said.

At first Canizaro saw himself as a modern-day Haussmann (Paris) or Robert Moses (New York), the visionary who knocks down entire blocks of a city when he believes it's for the public good. But he was also a white man in a majority-black city. "This was a case where we could not play God," he said. "We would have created a revolution." Canizaro was comfortable where they had ended up by the time he presented his plan to Nagin: citizen councils in the flooded neighborhoods working with panels of local experts paid for by the government. Canizaro felt certain the president would make available the billions they would need to implement a plan that might have the authorities buying out thousands of homeowners.

Canizaro recognized that he had sided with the planners, the Ivy Leaguers, and other pointy-headed experts his ideological comrades loved to ridicule as thinking they knew better than everyone else. He was a friend of George Bush who believed in limited government. Nagin was a Democrat representing a majority-black city where Democrats outnumbered Republicans six to one. Yet Canizaro was disappointed government wasn't playing a more central role in the rebuilding. "You don't rebuild a city by letting everybody do as they please," Canizaro said. "That's why we have zoning laws. That's why we have rules around historic preservation." In the broken city of New Orleans, the black mayor adopted a free-market, almost libertarian approach, and the rich Republican developer could sound almost socialist, talking about government-funded citizen councils and the firm hand the city needed to play on behalf of the collective good.

PUBLIC HOUSING RESIDENTS WERE holding protests, demanding their right to return home, with more demonstrations over everything from bulldozers to Charity Hospital. FEMA was again in the news that March when it was revealed that ten thousand trailers it had stockpiled in Hope, Arkansas, were unusable in a floodplain, according to federal guidelines. Battles took place over the election itself. It was a wonder that television and the local newspapers had any room at all for their small bits of coverage of the candidates and the issues.

Only a militant few demanded that the electorate be confined to those residing in the city. Yet how does a municipality conduct a fair election with tens of thousands of registered voters scattered across the country? Nagin bought billboard space in Houston and traveled there as well, declaring, "It's a local election on a national stage." He also made campaign stops in Atlanta, Memphis, and Baton Rouge. Civil rights groups demanded that the authorities set up satellite voting facilities in any community home to a sizable number of evacuees. If the US government could help Iraqi expatriates scattered around the world vote in that country's elections, advocates said, they could do the same for Katrina evacuees.

Al Ater, Louisiana's secretary of state, proposed establishing voting sites out of state. The response was legislation to block Ater's office from setting up remote voting facilities even *inside* Louisiana. The bill never advanced, but it also ended any talk of out-of-state polling places. "It's almost so obvious that there's a concerted plan to make this a whiter city," said Stephen Bradberry, ACORN's lead organizer in New Orleans. "You don't want to believe it because it would be too disturbing." In the end, Ater set up satellite voting centers in ten locales around the state, including several in border towns nearer such places as Houston, Birmingham, and Memphis. He also set up a half dozen "supersites" in flooded parts of New Orleans such as New Orleans East and Lakeview (but not the Lower Ninth).

Using the change-of-address cards people sent to the post office, Ater sent voter information packets to as many evacuees as possible. That at least gave the addresses of the polling places and included the deadline for submitting an absentee ballot. But the documents, which included a section warning of the fines and potential jail time confronting anyone providing false information, no doubt scared some people from voting. Those living on public assistance, for instance, had been encouraged to obtain a local driver's license to qualify for any in-state help where they were living. Had they given away their right to vote by claiming an address outside the Orleans Parish limits? Voting absentee was a two-step process at a time most every evacuee no doubt felt overwhelmed. Interviews with evacuees after the election revealed that, despite Ater's best efforts, many believed they could vote only if they showed up in New Orleans on election day.

Three weeks before the election, a protest march was held at the foot of the bridge leading to Gretna. Jesse Jackson and Al Sharpton were there, as were Congresswoman Maxine Waters, Bill Cosby, and Bruce Gordon, the president of the NAACP. The signs ACORN handed out to the predominantly black crowd read IRAQ HAS FAIRER ELECTIONS. Both Nagin and Landrieu attended the rally, but only Nagin marched. Only Nagin was invited to share the stage with the other dignitaries.

The election was New Orleans's chance to have the public conversation that the Bring New Orleans Back Commission barely did. "We're debating whether property rights should trump everything or not," Nagin had imagined himself telling Martin Luther King. "We're debating how should we rebuild one of the greatest cultural cities the world has ever seen." Yet most of the candidates proved as reluctant to have those debates as Ron Forman. One candidate proposed that they move the University of New Orleans closer to the French Quarter because "kids like to study downtown." A former member of the City Council, a white Republican named Peggy Wilson, vowed to do everything in her power to ensure that the "pimps, drug dealers, crack addicts, and welfare queens" don't return to the city—and if people didn't get the point the first few times she brought it up at candidate forums, she ran ads making similar promises. Mitch Landrieu took a stance at the first debate: "To shrink the city's footprint is to shrink its destiny." Rob Couhig, a white Republican in the race, made the opposite argument: the city must shrink in size. But they were the exceptions in a race where the candidates instead promised to tear down all the big housing projects and vowed to block the building of a temporary FEMA trailer park in any community that opposed it.

Forman approved a thirty-second spot casting Landrieu as a free-spending liberal who saw higher taxes as the answer to every problem. But he proved himself too genteel to win at hardball politics. He nixed an ad casting Landrieu as soft on crime because as a state representative years ago, he had supported legislation giving judges the freedom to send first-time teen offenders to alternatives outside of prison. ("I *liked* that program," Forman said.) And he nixed another ad focused on a spike in violent crime in Nagin's first three years in office. "I knew these guys," Forman said. "I couldn't do it."

TEN DAYS BEFORE ELECTION day—and nearly eight months after Katrina—the federal government released its flood-elevation maps. Speculation in advance of the announcement anticipated a rule requiring homeowners to raise their homes seven or eight feet above the ground in low-lying areas. Others worried that they'd need to raise their homes by ten feet or more if they wanted to qualify for the federal government's flood-insurance program. Yet the federal recovery chief, Donald Powell, announced that homes and businesses in the most badly damaged parts of New Orleans would need to be raised between one and three feet.

The announcement caused more confusion than relief. The new flood-elevation maps freed tens of thousands of people from what the *Times-Picayune* called "rebuilding purgatory," but the wait struck many homeowners as pointless. They had gotten six feet or eight feet of water. Some had ten or more feet. What good would it do if a home flooded by eight feet of water in 2005 got five feet of water the next time? FEMA, said Sean Reilly, a member of the state's Louisiana Recovery Authority, had "simply abdicated" its authority.

The number, however, wasn't quite as random as it might have sounded. Ivor van Heerden at LSU's Hurricane Center said that if the levees hadn't failed—if they had merely been overtopped rather than breached—maybe three feet of water would have been in the streets.

MUNICIPAL ELECTIONS ARE HELD on Saturday in New Orleans. Turnout was high in Uptown and the sliver-by-the-river precincts, but not in large swatches of the Ninth Ward or Gentilly, where fewer than one in five people voted. The 2006 mayor's race was probably the most important in the city's history. Yet barely one-third of the electorate voted; twenty-five thousand fewer people cast a ballot in 2006 compared to 2002. Most of the missing voters were black.

Nagin took first with forty-two thousand and Landrieu took second with thirty-two thousand votes. Nagin fell short of 50 percent of the total vote, so a runoff would be held one month later. Forman took a distant third, yet his nineteen thousand votes exceeded the total received by the remaining twenty-one candidates. Forman drew few votes outside Uptown, the Garden District, or Lakeview. Landrieu, by contrast, picked up votes all over the city. Forman immediately endorsed Landrieu, surprising his wife. "He didn't even talk to Ray," she said of her husband.

Nagin didn't bother vying for his old supporters, most of whom had probably voted for Forman. The mayor captured 65 percent of the black vote in the first round of voting and just 7 percent of the white vote. Yet rather than reach out to whites in the runoff, he used the city's business elite to burnish his credentials in the black community. At a news conference held the day after his first-place finish, he mocked the likes of Jimmy Reiss, who said New Orleans needed to change or a lot of the people he knew would abandon the city. "Where are they going to find another New Orleans of 1840?" the mayor asked. "Businesspeople are predators. If the economic opportunities are here, they're going to stay." For good measure, he promised to mail a postcard to anyone claiming to give up on New Orleans. Or maybe he'd just say hello, he said, the next time one of them flew home on a private jet for Mardi Gras or a Friday lunch at Galatoire's.

Nagin's treatment by the white business establishment was a major reason the *Tribune*'s Beverly McKenna supported Nagin's reelection.

Nagin had been naive, she allowed. But she supported Nagin "with everything I had" in 2006 in no small part because of the way his former allies treated the mayor. "It was despicable what they did to him—so obvious and ugly and in your face. He was their candidate—until he wouldn't go along with their plans—so they just tossed him aside." Of course she'd stand beside the mayor after he stood up to his former allies. The Reverend Tom Watson, a black minister also in the 2006 mayor's race, during one debate blamed Nagin for the death of the thousand-plus New Orleanians during Katrina. Yet Watson, too, would endorse Nagin and even loan the campaign his church for a voter turnout rally on the eve of the runoff election. "Be Concerned," read the cover of the *Tribune*. "Be VERY Concerned. Get Angry. Get VERY Angry. Then Go Vote." The capitalized words appeared in red. Nagin might have shunned the likes of McKenna and Watson during his first term, but neither wanted whites to seize control of City Hall.

The occasional voter told a reporter that he or she was "voting vanilla." Others declared that they were voting chocolate. RE-ELECT OUR MAYOR read billboards the Nagin campaign leased in New Orleans and also Houston. So what if all the signs were in black parts of town? "This campaign is really not about me," Landrieu said on the stump. "I'm just a vessel. I'm just a symbol."

Landrieu ran as the unity candidate. "There's been a lot of racial tensions that have been pushed by the national media, but the truth is on the ground—and you're seeing it yourself—African Americans and whites really holding on to each other closely," Landrieu said at one rally. He held up a picture taken just after the storm of a black girl holding hands with a white woman in a wheelchair. "If the storm showed us anything, it indicated in a very clear way we're all in the same boat," Landrieu said.

Yet surprisingly Nagin proved the better candidate. He was his affable, assured self during a series of voter forums. Landrieu appeared stiff and scripted—the cautious politician believing the election was his to lose. Where Landrieu was short on specifics, Nagin spoke about the intricacies of the city's recovery efforts that had been his life for the past six months. The *Times-Picayune* endorsed Landrieu, but Robert Couhig, a white Republican who had taken fourth in the first round of voting with just over ten thousand votes, supported the mayor. To some,

Landrieu was still the liberal in the race and Nagin the more conservative, probusiness candidate. Television ads for Nagin stressed the lack of
scandal in City Hall—no small issue with all that money about to flow
through New Orleans.

Nagin attacked Landrieu at every opportunity. His foe was part of
the Landrieu "dynasty": the "Landrieu machine" would mean the return
of patronage and favoritism to City Hall. Nagin had since Katrina presented his opponent plenty of potential ammunition to wage a counter-
offensive. But the attacks never came. Pundits speculated that Landrieu
was being the good brother and making sure he didn't cause problems
for his sister the US senator when she ran for reelection in eighteen
months. Others argued he sought to protect his own reputation in the
black community, while a third group cast the Landrieu camp as confident they could win without resorting to a negative campaign. But
whatever the reason, Landrieu stuck to his unity theme. "WE'RE ALL
NEIGHBORS," read the full-page ad the Landrieu campaign bought in
the *New Orleans Tribune*.

Voter turnout in the runoff crept up two percentage points to 39
percent. The electorate was 57 percent black compared to the low 60s it
had been in recent elections. Nagin drew 83 percent of the black vote,
almost as high as the 86 percent share of the white vote he had won in
2002. Yet hostilities toward Landrieu and the Landrieu name within the
white community proved the difference. Nagin won 20 percent of the
white vote—triple his percent in the first round of voting. The mayor
won reelection by 5,000 votes out of 114,000 cast.

Nagin addressed the president at his victory party that night. "You
and I have probably been the most vilified politicians in the country,"
Nagin said. "But I want to thank you for moving that promise that you
made in Jackson Square forward." An appreciative George Bush phoned
Nagin the next day to offer his congratulations. The president was "pretty
excited," Nagin said at a press conference later that day, adding, "I think
the opportunity has presented itself for me to kind of go down in history
as the mayor that guided the city of New Orleans through an incredible
rebuild cycle." To those who were surprised by his reelection, he offered
that people "really don't get Ray Nagin." But that's all right, he added,
"Sometimes I don't get Ray Nagin."

18

THE MARDI GRAS WAY OF LIFE

The city held its first jury trial that June, more than nine months after the storm. The main holdup had been the flooding of the city's massive criminal justice complex in Mid-City. Defense attorneys and local prosecutors squared off in a pair of borrowed federal courtrooms, but that was reserved for procedural hearings, not trials. "It's like the final step," an Orleans Parish DA told the Associated Press on the first day since Katrina that a pool of prospective jurors gathered for a trial. The backlog of criminal cases stood at around five thousand.

The justice complex was still a long way from being fully operational, but the caseload seemed certain to swell. The National Guard left in February, and crime picked up again in New Orleans. The city was home to less than half its pre-Katrina population, and the New Orleans Police Department was back at around 80 percent strength, but officers still needed to patrol the same geographic area. Looting was rampant in more barren parts of the city, and FEMA trailers were everywhere. The city averaged six murders a month through the first three months of 2006, but those numbers doubled in April and May. In June, five teens were shot dead while driving a sport utility vehicle on the outskirts of the central business district. Three bodies were found inside the vehicle; the two others had been shot dead in the street while trying to escape. The mayor asked the governor to send a National Guard regiment of three hundred and Blanco complied, but not without a lecture about the need to impose a strict curfew on the city's juveniles. New Orleans police chief Warren Riley countered that the curfew was unenforceable when they had no place to lock up young offenders. The National Guard would remain in New Orleans another two years.

The Convention Center reopened that June in time to host the American Library Association. Mardi Gras had proven a boon for the city treasury, as had the New Orleans Jazz & Heritage Festival, which featured Dave Matthews, Jimmy Buffett, Paul Simon, Elvis Costello, and Bob Dylan. Yet Jazz Fest—officially now the New Orleans Jazz & Heritage Festival Presented by Shell—ended in early May. With the exception of the big summer R&B celebration *Essence* magazine had been holding in New Orleans since 1994, Jazz Fest represented the end of tourist season—and *Essence* had moved its big annual party to Houston that year. The city's hotel and restaurant owners were happy to see seventeen thousand librarians descend on New Orleans at a time of year when the temperatures typically topped ninety degrees, but the next big convention was the National Association of Realtors in November. Even the most optimistic forecasts predicted it would be two years before the city's convention business was restored.

June 1 marked the start of the new hurricane season. FEMA had a new director: the acting director the Bush administration had been working hard to replace. By one count, seven people turned down the FEMA directorship before the president made permanent the appointment of R. David Paulison. Paulison was best known as the FEMA official who, after September 11, urged all Americans to stock up on duct tape and plastic sheeting to guard against terrorist attacks.

The region's battered levee system had been more or less restored to its former state as the city braced itself for the new hurricane season. One million tons of Mississippi clay had been carted in to replace the silt that had washed away when the levees collapsed. Several giant steel gates were added at the mouth of each of the city's three biggest drainage canals. But $800 million later, New Orleans was safe so long as nothing stronger than a Category 2 hurricane hit the coast. The city, the *Times-Picayune's* Jed Horne declared, was "one storm away from extinction."

Adding to everyone's sense of doom were the news reports questioning the competence of the Army Corps of Engineers—the same Corps overseeing the levee repairs. Two independent forensic science teams had been investigating the cause of the flooding. One headed by a pair of Berkeley professors uncovered any number of mistakes at the hands of the Corps and the private contractors whose work they were responsible for monitoring. Sections of floodwall had been built on sand, clay, and marshland, which, one engineer offered, was like "putting bricks on Jell-O." In some cases, the contractors hired to do the work had not dug down deep enough. Dr. Raymond Seed, a professor of engineering at Berkeley and coauthor of the resulting report, would call the failure of the storm system "the worst engineering disaster in the world since Chernobyl." Team Louisiana was nearly as harsh. They concluded that if not for design flaws by the Corps, New Orleans would have experienced no more than a day of mild street flooding. Spokespeople for the Corps defended an agency that dates back to the Revolutionary War—until its own people released a six-thousand-page report confirming many of the outsiders' criticisms. "This is the first time that the Corps has had to stand up and say, 'We've had a catastrophic failure,'" said Lieutenant General Carl Strock, the commander of the Corps.

"Mad City," read the headline over a column by the *Times-Picayune's* Chris Rose. Chatting with his "fidgety glassy-eyed neighbors," he wrote, he found himself in line at a pharmacy speaking as if waiting for a table at one of the city's better restaurants: How's the Valium looking today? The Xanax didn't agree with you last week? I'm thinking of ordering the Paxil. "Everybody's got it, this thing, this affliction," Rose wrote. "This affinity for forgetfulness, absentmindedness, confusion, laughing in inappropriate circumstances, crying when the wrong song comes on the radio."

Yet ten months after Katrina, the local mental health system was still in near collapse. Suicides tripled in the months after Katrina. A fifty-three-year-old filmmaker took his own life as did an Uptown physician, who left behind a wife and children. Two parents with young children at the Academy of the Sacred Heart on St. Charles took their lives within a couple of weeks of each other. Brobson Lutz, a doctor whom *New Orleans* magazine labeled the "city surgeon general" a few years before Katrina, worried about the health of those who had moved back to New Orleans. Yet it wasn't airborne contagions or toxins in the soil that concerned this former public health director. "I have said from the beginning that the mental health concerns here are far greater than those we can expect from infectious diseases," Lutz told the *Times-Picayune*'s Chris Rose.

THE RTA HAD A little more than half its employees back when the agency started debating whether to resume limited bus service to Gentilly, to the Ninth Ward, and other parts of the city where small pockets of people had moved home. Barbara Major, named to the RTA board by Nagin in 2002, was among those arguing that the RTA had a central role to play in the repopulation of damaged parts of the city. "How can we expect these working-class communities to ever come back if we don't provide people with bus service?" asked Major.

RTA chairman Jimmy Reiss opposed offering bus service in places where there were so few people. With ridership down 75 percent ten months after Katrina, they didn't have the money. The agency was surviving only due to help from the federal government. "My job was to right-size the organization so its survival wasn't dependent on continued outside funding, which I knew would eventually be going away," Reiss said. "And she wants to run lines out to New Orleans East, where there was nobody." His priority, Reiss announced, was "running buses in the core because people need to catch a goddamn bus or streetcar to get to work."

At their monthly meeting, Reiss told his fellow board members that an outside consultant group had told him they needed to lay people off. Major responded with a speech about the teachers and city employees and others already fired. "The black middle class can't take another blow," she continued. A frustrated Reiss said they didn't have the money to run empty buses in deserted parts of the city. In response, Reiss said, "Barbara unleashed a racial diatribe at me publicly. So I called for us to go into executive session. She continued to rant and rave about racial issues. So I just walked out."

Major had already spoken to Nagin. "I'm getting rid of Jimmy Reiss," she told him. The mayor didn't defend his RTA chairman but instead asked, "Do you have the votes?" She did, she said. She quotes the mayor as telling her, "Then go for it, tiger." The part she left unsaid was that she was only doing what Nagin should have done months ago. "If he won't, I'll man up and do it," she joked with friends.

There was no showdown. Reiss called Nagin the day after he walked out of the executive session. The mayor didn't return his call so the next day he sent Nagin an e-mail. When that, too, went unanswered, Reiss resigned via a letter he sent to the *Times-Picayune*. "I basically gave up everything I was doing for five years to run the agency for the people who needed the transit, most of whom were poor and black," Reiss said. "I decided I wasn't going to take it anymore. So I quit."

"CONGRATULATIONS, YOU'RE ONE OF the first ten families in all of Lakeview!" a police officer told Connie Uddo. It was January 2006 and Uddo, her husband, Mark, and their two children had just moved back into their flooded home. The cop had seen lights on in the house and the next day knocked on the door. He was trying to make her feel good but his words caused her to cry. Nearly eight thousand homes in Lakeview, and they were one of the ten families crazy enough to move back.

"Everything smelled," Uddo said. "It was disgusting. I was miserable."

The Uddos had escaped to Houston ahead of Katrina. They stayed those first weeks after the storm in Kingwood, a suburb forty minutes north of the city. They lived with one of her husband's cousins until Uddo found them a borrowed home. They enrolled their kids in the local schools and found an apartment. Yet not a week after moving into their third temporary home, they'd moved into a fourth when Uddo's sister found them a place closer to home, in Mandeville, Louisiana, only thirty miles from New Orleans. The only catch was they needed to be out of the house by mid-December. That meant doubling up for a week or two with Uddo's sister's family so the kids could finish the semester. Just before Christmas, they moved Uptown into Uddo's mother-in-law's house—their sixth address in four months.

Back in New Orleans, Mark Uddo tried to convince his wife they were among the lucky ones. They owned a three-story home and rented out the bottom floor to a pair of tenants. They had taken on seven feet of water, but nothing reached the top two floors, where they lived. Their tenants were the ones who'd lost all their belongings. An electrician said that he could restore power in their house, and Country Day, the private school where Mark worked as a chef, was eager to get him back into the kitchen. Only a few minutes from their Lakeview home, Country Day was opening in time for January classes, as was Mount Carmel Academy, the private Catholic school their daughter attended. One of the city's top Catholic boys schools was in the next neighborhood over and had an opening. Just before Christmas, they held a family meeting to talk about moving home.

Mark was eager to get back to Lakeview. They would be close to his work and the kids' schools. And his back might stop aching. "I'm tired of sleeping on air mattresses," he declared. The kids said they were tired of living out of boxes. "We miss our home," both said. Uddo pointed out how depressing it would be to live there, but Stephanie, the fifteen-year-old, offered a rejoinder that left her mother unable to argue the point: "Mom, we're already depressed. We're going to be depressed here or depressed there, and I'd rather be depressed in my own bed in my own house." They'd move back to Lakeview soon after the start of the new year.

Those first months back home were harder than Uddo had imagined. Mark was understaffed in the kitchen and working long hours. One or the other of them would drop off the kids at school and then she'd be by herself. "I was in a kind of survival mode," she said. "A low-grade depression, just hanging on." One day while walking the dog she noticed there were no birds. That made her laugh: "Even the birds knew it was too early to come back," she told herself.

Uddo, who is white, is short and fit with hazel eyes and short, brown hair. Prior to Katrina, she taught tennis at City Park, a few minutes from their home. The flexible work schedule allowed her to stay involved in the lives of her children, yet she resented that she needed to work at all. "I was always telling my husband, 'You don't make enough,'" Uddo said. They'd go away on vacation—and Uddo would dwell on the second home they couldn't afford. "I had all this junk around money," Uddo said.

"Jealous of friends who had it. Scheming to get more." Now she lived in a home with a boarded-up first floor.

"There was no mail for a year," she said. "There was no newspaper delivery. There were no stores. There was nothing here. For the longest time, you'd have to go to a different part of the city just for a stick of butter." A twenty-foot sailboat rested in the yard next to hers with a note: "I'll come pick it up." A small motorboat sat for nine months on a train-trestle overpass near her house.

Uddo at least felt a sense of peace when she was inside the house. Everyone's bedroom was the same as it was before the storm. They were starting to reestablish routines. But around Easter, someone broke into Uddo's car. "That's when I wouldn't sleep," she said. Her part of the city had no streetlights, and she seemed to read or hear about another looting every day. "I felt like a sitting duck," she said.

She told Mark, "I can't do this, I'm afraid for the kids. I'm afraid for myself." While the rest of them were busy all day, she was walking the neighborhood, alone with her fears. "It felt unsafe, healthwise, all these moldy houses, all these toxins in the soil. I was concerned for what we were breathing," she said. She told her husband she wanted to sell the Lakeview home and move back to his mother's until they could formulate a new plan.

Mark could sympathize. "What we don't realize is how empty our tanks are," he told his wife. He gets up in the morning, he said, and it's like he's starting his day at empty. "We're physically and emotionally exhausted, and when you're that way, you just crumble at any small thing."

But he also appealed to his wife's practicality. He brought up the kids and how much happier they seemed now that they were back home. His job was intense, but he liked it, and it was only a few minutes from their home. "Do you want to drive from Uptown every day?" he asked her. That would add an hour or two of driving to their days. There would be the strains of once again living perched in someone else's home, and there were also the economic realities of walking away. Every bit of their net worth was invested in a home that seemed worthless unless they were living in it. Rather than give up on their Lakeview home, he hoped to rehab the first floor so they could fill it with tenants. The renters pre-Katrina covered two-thirds of the mortgage. "You need to find a purpose, Connie," he told his wife, "because this is our only option."

Not long after that conversation with her husband, Uddo spoke to a man who lived a few doors down from them, a doctor traveling regularly to the neighborhood to work on his house. She confessed how vulnerable she felt, and he suggested she host a neighborhood-watch meeting. "Who'll come, you and me?" she cracked, but organizing a meeting would feel as if she was at least trying. Maybe more people were camping on a second floor or sleeping in a car than she realized. She printed a flyer inviting people for gumbo and wine at the Uddos and walked her small patch of Lakeview, leaving one on the windshield of any car she came across. Thirty-five people showed up on a May evening in her desolate stretch of New Orleans to talk about crime in the community. That included the area's local police commander,[1] who came back the next day. "He tells me, 'Yours is the first organized meeting in Lakeview since the storm, I encourage you to keep going,'" she said. The commander suggested she meet Denise Thornton. Thornton lived next door in Lakewood, a pricey enclave of around four hundred homes that also flooded after Katrina.

Thornton, too, was back home despite her better instincts. Her husband, Doug Thornton, was responsible for reopening the Superdome by the start of the next football season. The Thorntons gutted their home a month after Katrina and had power before anyone else in their section of New Orleans. "My husband was connected and I used those connections," Thornton said. At first they lived upstairs, cooking on a portable stove in a makeshift kitchen, while a crew renovated the ground floor. By Valentine's Day, their two-story, brick house had been restored, and Thornton hung a banner declaring her home a beacon for the rest of the community. "I wanted a place where neighbors could come to get a drink of water, make a phone call, cool off in the air-conditioning, take a

---

1. Senator Mary Landrieu, who arrived with her brother Martin, was also there that night. "She gave me her cell phone number and told me, if I need anything, call her," Uddo said. Landrieu would phone Uddo throughout the recovery "just to see how I was doing and check in."

break from working on their house," she said. When she spotted a cable guy from Cox on a pole, she begged him to run a line to her house so she could offer visitors Internet access. By the mayoral runoff, she had put in new sod and prettied up her property with flower beds and saplings. "I figured anyone driving back to the city to vote is someone who is coming to see the neighborhood," she said, so she bought three hundred steaks and threw a block party. Mary Landrieu was one of her guests on that day in May 2006, as was Connie Uddo. "She came over looking all dirty and ugly," Thornton said of Uddo. "And very depressed."

Before the storm, Uddo had always steered cleared of politics. She rarely bothered to vote: "I'd be like, 'They're all corrupt anyway so why should I bother?' A very Mardi Gras mentality, I call it. Let's just have fun, let's look the other way if things get too serious." Yet she followed Thornton's lead and opened her home as an oasis for anyone needing a respite. Thornton had dubbed her home a Beacon of Hope, so they called Uddo's place a second Beacon and the first inside Lakeview. "I had air-conditioning," Uddo said. "I had a phone. I had a fax machine and Internet if people needed it."

Thornton had given Uddo a check for $1,000 to help get her started. Uddo used the money to buy shovels, chain saws, and other equipment they would need to start cleaning up the neighborhood. She went searching in City Park for what people called the Good News Camp, where she was told she'd find hundreds of out-of-towners who had come to New Orleans to help with the cleanup. "I'd ask them to send as many volunteers as they could, and they'd tell me, 'Okay, we'll give you thirty today,'" Uddo said. Her strategy was to attack one block at a time. "We'd clean yards, we'd clean the streets, we'd get rid of anything we came across." In time, she learned that the Corps was gathering each morning in a nearby grocery-store parking lot. "I'd tell them, 'Hey, I've got sixty volunteers today, we're working these three blocks, can you work behind me?' And they'd do it." After a few weeks, Uddo admitted, "The place was starting to look pretty good."

CONNIE UDDO SAW HERSELF as living in "the Mayberry of New Orleans" prior to the storm. Lots of people felt that way about pre-Katrina

Lakeview. The neighborhood had more of a small-town feel—a place apart from the rest of the city. A lot of that was geography. Lakeview was cut off from the rest of New Orleans by City Park on its eastern flank and also a pair of giant drainage canals that constituted its east and west borders. The lake constituted its northern border—or, more accurately, Robert E. Lee Boulevard and Lake Vista, the pricier community sandwiched between Lakeview and Lake Pontchartrain.

Some in Lakeview, a predominantly white province in a largely black city, dreamed of breaking off from New Orleans and creating their own municipality. The idea came up regularly at meetings of Lakeview Civic in the 1970s and 1980s. Peppi Bruneau, the area's state representative since 1976, was one of the lead secessionists. The plot to establish Lakeview as its own town peaked a decade before Katrina. "It was 1996, 1997, when crime was going up and there was no solution," said Freddy Yoder. "We thought we could do better as our own town with our own tax base." When then-mayor Marc Morial learned about what was going on, he told Yoder and his allies that he would fight them with everything he had or they could agree to a compromise: Morial's support for legislation that would allow Lakeview to create its own taxing district and charge homeowners an annual surcharge to supplement police protection in their neighborhood. By imposing a tax on themselves, Lakeview paid for extra police and reduced crime from around a thousand incidents a year to under two hundred. "Everyone was ready to make it into a racial thing, but the fact was we were fed up with not getting the services we were paying for," Yoder said.

The charge that Lakeview was a place hostile to blacks would be leveled again when Lakeview took on what locals called doubles—two-family homes that attracted renters. Martin Landrieu was the president of Lakeview Civic when the community demanded that the City Council impose a moratorium on new doubles. "We were just worried about Lakeview getting too crowded," Landrieu said, but he wasn't surprised that others suspected that racial fears were behind their actions. "I've sat in meetings in Lakeview and heard people in leadership say, 'We're not going to let the blacks in,'" Landrieu said. "I've heard people say some pretty racist things around here."

The city's "redheaded stepchild," Freddy Yoder said of Lakeview—the community that received nothing unless it demanded it. Lakeview's inferiority complex even spilled over regarding the Lower Ninth Ward. From the start, the Lower Ninth received outsize attention relative to its population and, many Lakeview residents would add, its importance. "It was always 'the Lower Ninth, the Lower Ninth, the Lower Ninth,'" said Robert Lupo, whose family had owned commercial property along Harrison Avenue in Lakeview dating back several generations. Al Petrie, who lost the home he had lived in since he was ten years old, said, "A lot of us were asking why we weren't getting the national attention like the Lower Ninth Ward."

Americans tend to tell a myth about disasters: everyone pulls together regardless of the race or social standing of their neighbor. Yet inside Lakeview there seemed little sense of camaraderie toward other parts of New Orleans also devastated by Katrina. Jeb Bruneau, then president of Lakeview Civic, would have poured resources into Gentilly, the community just on the other side of City Park from Lakeview. But New Orleans East and the Lower Ninth, he said, weren't worth salvaging. "In Gentilly, you had homeownership," Bruneau offered. "You had demographics—a mix of black with some whites. You could really make a difference there."

Freddy Yoder was also inclined to write off much of the eastern half of New Orleans: "I didn't have any problem with turning areas like the Lower Ninth Ward or New Orleans East into greenspace. That made sense to me." To him it wasn't about elevation or race or homeownership data. "At the time, I couldn't care about anyone else. I could only worry about my home and my community."

YODER CAME UP WITH the idea of block captains early on: deputize a person on every block to learn what their neighbors were thinking. Yoder, too, was behind the large map that showed up on an easel in the gym at St. Dominic, the giant church on Harrison and a favorite meeting place after the storm. Every green pin on the map represented another homeowner who was intent on moving home. Some, such as Yoder and Al Petrie, both of whom snapped up houses on the cheap from those who wanted out, needed multiple pins to represent their holdings.

"Make an offer, I'll take it, whatever it is," a neighbor had said to Yoder a few months after the storm. The man, Yoder said, owned a "big, beautiful house at the end of the block that was worth at least three-quarters of a million dollars." Yoder gave him $200,000 and spent another $150,000 fixing it up. That's how Yoder's daughter and her family ended up living on the corner in a $750,000 home that cost Yoder $350,000. Yoder also bought the house next door to his and more lots across the street.

The leadership of Lakeview Civic continued to meet every Friday in a conference room on the second floor of the Gulf Coast Bank branch. They mapped ruptured sidewalks and abandoned vehicles and downed utility poles in the neighborhood. And they continued to work on a neighborhood plan, though for whom and to what purpose wasn't clear. Their early efforts had been all about proving that enough of its people were moving back to merit a full share of city services. That's what it seemed the city needed for its flooded neighborhoods—at least until the City Council hired Lambert Advisory, a small, Miami-based planning firm that a few years earlier had advised the council on housing and economic-development issues. The council had hired Lambert to help what it called the "wet" neighborhoods. Under Lambert no community would have to prove viability. There'd be no need to study elevation maps to help people think through the potential for converting areas to greenspace. That summer, Lambert sponsored a three-day planning workshop for anyone living in the wet neighborhoods. There, they encouraged residents to think big. In Lakeview, they dreamed about creating their own zoning district. There'd be no more doubles, and they would make it more difficult for landlords to rebuild houses wrecked by the floodwaters.

"We were about ninety percent done with Lambert, and wouldn't you know, the process changed again," Landrieu said.

Maybe it was inevitable that a third party would step in to salvage the city's planning process. Blanco's Louisiana Recovery Authority—the LRA—needed a plan from the city before it would give New Orleans its share of the billions of federal dollars that would eventually reach the state. And New Orleans would potentially have competing plans or maybe no workable plan at all (the City Council had limited Lambert to the city's wet communities, and the LRA was demanding a city-wide plan). "This is a city that even before the storm had very little capacity," said Judith Rodin, president of the Rockefeller Foundation. "So when everything hit, the inability to recover quickly could have been predicted." Rodin, who had taken over Rockefeller only a few months before Katrina, knew New Orleans well through her husband, who had once served as dean of Tulane's law school. Ten days after the storm, Rodin announced a $3 million emergency housing grant to help New Orleans and told her people to be on the lookout for other ways they could help. That spring, the foundation wrote another check, this one for $3.5 million, and the United New Orleans Plan was born.

UNOP (pronounced "you-nop"), as everyone called it, would be a combination of both the Canizaro and Lambert plans. Communities would work with drainage experts and demographers to talk about the possibility of reverting land to greenspace. People in the flooded neighborhoods would have their chance to share their ideas for improving their communities—as they were encouraged to do by the Lambert planners. This time, though, the philanthropists (several other big foundations would join the UNOP effort) were vowing to include in the conversation the dispossessed who didn't have the money to participate in a process taking place solely in New Orleans. "We recognized the importance of ensuring that displaced residents had a seat at the table with everyone else," Rodin said.

People such as Martin Landrieu felt as if they were trapped in a real-life version of *Groundhog Day*, where they'd need to repeat the sequence until they got it exactly right. "This was a time when there'd be all these little restarts in every aspect of your life," Landrieu said. The insurance company would claim it never received the stack of receipts you sent a month earlier, or "it was the insurance company calling to tell you, 'Oh, yeah, your adjuster left, we need to assign you to a new person,' or it was calling the credit-card company for the third time because they still weren't sending to the right address. You'd keep having to have the same conversation over and over."

That summer, the team UNOP assigned to help the people of Lakeview develop a plan found Landrieu and the rest of them still meeting on Friday mornings in a borrowed conference room on the second floor of a flooded-out bank. "When UNOP came in and said, 'Okay, tell us the ten things you like most about your neighborhood and the ten things you like least,' I almost threw up," Landrieu said. Even if Rocke-feller was what the city needed, it's not what Landrieu and his counter-parts wanted. "At that point, we had been doing this for going on eight months," Landrieu said. "What I wanted to do is shoot them the bird and say, 'Fuck you.'" Instead they shared their concerns about doubles in Lakeview and the effect of rentals in their community. "Nearly two years of meetings," Landrieu said, "and I'm still not sure what they were about."

THE CROWD WAS SPARSE for a protest held that spring at an aban-doned senior center in the Lower Ninth Ward. Maybe seventy-five people showed up despite a rostrum of speakers that included the City Council president and a state legislator. "It's not easy but I try my best to make it back for events like these," said one participant, Ruston Henry, a second-generation pharmacist who served as president of the Lower Ninth Ward Economic Development Association. The storefront his father had opened north of Claiborne Avenue forty-five years earlier had been destroyed like most everything else in that part of the Lower Ninth. Henry was working in the pharmacy department of a Walmart outside Jackson, Mississippi. Before the rally started, he pointed across the street to a shuttered church and a boarded-up elementary school. An old, white Buick LeSabre sat under a crush of rubble. "I already feel like we're losing the area," he said. Some were advocating that the Lower Ninth be returned to swampland, but Henry worried about wealthy in-terests buying up large tracts of land to put up condos, casinos, or some-thing else that no one who lived there wanted. "We keep hearing about these developers coming around who want to take our land because they have all these dreams for our neighborhood," Henry said. "The Ameri-can Indians, I know how they feel now."

Charmaine Marchand spoke that day. So, too, did Cynthia Wil-lard-Lewis, who represented the Lower Ninth Ward (and a large stretch of New Orleans East) on the City Council. But the day's main draw was Oliver Thomas, who had just made headlines with a comment about New Orleans needing doers, not those who are "soap-opera watchers all day." He expected the criticism that rained down on him for his comment, he told the crowd, "because that's what happens whenever you talk about poor people being less dependent and taking care of themselves." He exhorted the crowd not to wait for government and led them in a chant, "Do it yourself." Yet months would pass before the first trailers were delivered to the Lower Ninth. By the time they started arriving that summer, Connie Uddo had been living in her home for more than six months. Denise Thornton had been home for nine.

In Lakeview, New Orleans East, and other more prosperous communities, people paid someone thousands of dollars to gut their homes or they did it themselves. For most in the Lower Ninth, hiring someone to do the work wasn't an option, yet how were they going to spend a few weeks in New Orleans to work on their home? They might be able to cover travel, but where would they stay in town for a few weeks? "None of us had money for hotels with the prices they were charging," said Charmaine Marchand. "We couldn't stay with family or friends because their houses were all destroyed." Despite red-tagged homes in Lakeview and other communities, only in the Lower Ninth Ward were activists standing in front of a bulldozer to stop the city from destroying a home without its owner's knowledge.

The same kinds of efforts taking place in Lakeview were also taking place in the Lower Ninth. Starting about six months after Katrina, a group of dazed residents started showing up at the Sanchez Community Center on Claiborne, not far from the levee breach. There in a dank, windowless room crawling with mold, they sat on rusty chairs in a part of town still without electricity. They knew that most of New Orleans, if not the entire world, felt their neighborhood should be left for dead, but they did what they could to help each other rebuild. They affixed a map of the Lower Ninth to poster board and had people write their name and number on a small piece of paper. Residents used a green pin if they intended to rebuild, yellow if they had not decided. People started bringing food. The wider world soon found them: Charmaine Marchand, organizers from other communities.

Legions of outsiders showed up to help in the Lower Ninth. Most of them were from a group called the Common Ground Relief Collective, founded shortly after the storm by Malik Rahim, a former Black Panther with a thick mane of gray dreadlocks. Rahim put volunteers to work cleaning out a church in the Upper Ninth, where they set up a base of operations. A nearby empty lot was transformed into a one-stop hurricane-relief center. A motto spray-painted on a sign read SOLIDARITY, NOT CHARITY. Common Ground volunteers handed out bleach to help people kill the mold and established a tool-lending library that included sledgehammers, crowbars, and respirators. They provided canned foods and later upgraded to hot meals. They gutted a nearby school and turned the classrooms into dormitories for volunteers by setting up twenty or so government-issued metal cots in each. In all, Common Ground volunteers gutted three thousand homes, businesses, and churches in the Ninth Ward. "The most glorious time of my life," Rahim said.

MALIK RAHIM WAS BORN Donald Guyton, a name he later rejected as a slave name. His mother washed floors at Charity Hospital, his father wasn't a presence in his life. He grew up in the black part of Gretna. One of his most vivid childhood memories, he said, was a battle over the right of black kids to swim in the city's sole public pool. The answer was to build a second one, "on top of the city dump and next to the garbage incinerators," Rahim said. He left before finishing high school and at seventeen enlisted in the army. "I started seeing the same thing in Vietnam I was seeing here," he said. "I refused to fight." He was discharged with no rank and found his way to a pipeline-construction site near New Orleans. "I asked about becoming a welder and I was told, 'We don't hire no niggers as welders.'"

Rahim was twenty-two years old when in 1970 he joined the New Orleans Black Panthers. The Panthers established a breakfast program in the Desire housing project in the Upper Ninth. They opened a clinic to test for sickle-cell, a genetic health scourge in the black community, among other efforts. But the local police perceived them as a threat and sent in a SWAT team to evict them, by force if necessary. After a brief standoff, the police asked for reinforcements, but by that time the project's residents had blocked the way. "People really appreciated what the Panthers were doing for the community—the breakfasts, the clinics," said Barbara Major, who was in high school then and living across from the Desire projects. Rahim was the Panther's defense minister—the second in command of his chapter. The police arrested him and several others for attempted murder. The charges were eventually dropped and Rahim took off for the West Coast.

In California, Rahim fell in with a group of activists seeking to take over a small, unincorporated town outside San Francisco and transform it into a black mecca. Nairobi, they would call it. They got as far as starting their own African-centered college before the idea fizzled. "I started doing things I'm not proud of," Rahim said. The low point was an armed-robbery conviction and a five-year sentence in a California prison. "I met an older inmate there, a dude who'd been down for more than twenty years, who convinced me that I was going to keep coming back unless I changed my ways." After serving his sentence, Rahim moved back to New Orleans, into the house his mother had bought in Algiers on the West Bank. He started an ex-offenders program and worked with Sister Helen Prejean, an outspoken critic of capital punishment and the author of *Dead Man Walking*. Rahim joined the Green Party and in 2002 ran for City Council on a platform that stressed a living wage, improved conditions in public housing, and the expansion of crime-prevention programs aimed at juveniles. He drew four thousand votes in a losing effort.

Rahim inherited the Algiers home when his mother died the year before Katrina. He chose to remain there through the storm not despite warnings of catastrophe but because of them. "How could I classify myself as a community leader if I leave when people might need help after the storm?" he said. He crossed the Crescent City Connection to help fish people out of the water on the other side of the bridge. Closer to home, Rahim needed his wits just to survive a harrowing few days living at the uneasy border between the blacks of Algiers and the whites of Algiers Point, a small enclave of well-preserved historic homes along the Mississippi. On the Wednesday after the storm, Rahim heard frantic knocking at his door. A neighbor, black, said he was scared for his life after fleeing, he said, a group of armed white men. Rahim didn't believe him until he rounded the corner and saw several men, rifles or guns in hand, walking the streets as if on patrol.

"I went straight to one of them that I knew, he was one of my neighbors," Rahim said, "and asked him, 'Man, what's going on? What you carrying all these guns for?' He tells me, 'We're protecting the neighborhood.' And this other guy walks over and says, 'You don't owe this nigger no explanation.'" Hearing a commotion, an older white woman opened her door, a moment that Rahim is convinced spared his life. The white men came looking for him a few hours later, Rahim said, but by that time he had picked up what he described as "reinforcements" and the men left. That week, Rahim said, he came across the bodies of several black men who had been shot, including one around the corner from his home.[2] A Danish filmmaker in Algiers working on a documentary he called *Welcome to New Orleans* interviewed a group of armed whites at a popular Algiers Point bar a week after Katrina. "It was like pheasant season in South Dakota—if it moved, you shot it!" one crowed.

Rahim still had family in Gretna—older relatives who might need his help had they been unable to evacuate ahead of the storm. But that meant getting past the checkpoints the police had set up at the Algiers-Gretna border. Every street was barricaded, Rahim said; because they didn't have enough police cruisers, they used fire engines and garbage trucks. "They had police on dirt bikes and in their cars, riding up and down, making sure no blacks were going over into Gretna," Rahim said. Ultimately he would gain entry using Rasmus Holm, the Danish filmmaker working on his documentary. "He opens his mouth, you know this dude isn't from anywhere near here," Rahim said. "But Rasmus says he's hired me to work on his house and they let us through."

While he was in California, Rahim had gotten to know Mary

---

2. Investigative reporter A. C. Thompson was among those stopping by Rahim's home to watch a tape he made after discovering the body around the corner. Thompson's terrific article, "Katrina's Hidden Race War," appearing in the *Nation* magazine three years after Katrina, suggested there was evidence of eleven shootings in Algiers after Katrina. "In each case the targets were African-American men, while the shooters, it appears, were all white."

Ratcliff, the editor of a small, black newspaper called the *San Francisco Bay View*. Three days after Katrina, Ratcliff called Rahim. She didn't figure she'd reach anyone living in the city's 504 area code, but Rahim answered. The words gushed out as Ratcliff typed. "This is criminal," he began. "Gangs of white vigilantes riding around in pickup trucks, all of them armed." He was angry that tens of thousands of people were still trapped in New Orleans. They had working water and sewer systems on his side of the river, Rahim said. The West Bank had remained dry. "Our parks and schools could easily hold forty thousand people, and they're not using any of it. People are dying." Rahim closed with an appeal for supplies, donations, and volunteers.

In 2005, there was no Twitter, and Facebook was still mainly a plaything of the college set. The term *social media* was only spoken inside the bubble of Silicon Valley. Mary Ratcliff included Rahim's address and phone number in the article she posted on *Bay View*'s website and in an e-mail she blasted to a wide circle of contacts. Within the week, Rahim was a guest on *Democracy Now!*—a popular left-leaning news program carried by hundreds of cable stations around the country. "The volunteers started coming," Rahim said, "and I kept finding them things to do." People claimed any bit of floor space they could find to put down a sleeping bag in the three-bedroom home Rahim had inherited from his mother. Dozens camped outside—in his backyard, on the front lawn, and on his front and back porches. "I had seventy people scattered around the property," he said, "and just about every one of them white." Another forty stayed in the donated tents they set up next door. Ultimately, somewhere around twenty-five thousand volunteers arrived to help in the two years Rahim was running Common Ground—or thirty thousand if you include those who came after he was pushed out of the organization he had formed.

Several of the first volunteers to show up at Rahim's door were community-health people with a van filled with medical supplies. Rahim set them up in the abandoned storefront mosque down the street. They spray-painted FIRST AID on the door, and ten days after Katrina, they were helping diabetics requiring insulin, victims needing a wound dressed, and the like. Eventually, the clinic found a more permanent home in a corner storefront painted blue and pink. "The little clinic that could," the

New York Times declared two years after Katrina—an oasis in a "shattered health care system."[3]

Other volunteer efforts popped up in the months after Katrina. The Peoples Hurricane Relief Fund was founded by a group of black locals. They were fighting the demolitions in the Ninth Ward, as well as organizing protests to demand that public housing be reopened. ACORN was a presence in the Lower Ninth, and many people were coming to New Orleans as part of a church group or some other civic affiliation. Reportedly, more than ten thousand college kids came to help gut homes and businesses that spring break. Becky Zaheri, a lifelong New Orleanian and stay-at-home mom prior to the storm, created Katrina Krewe, which drew hundreds of volunteers twice a week to a trash-strewn neighborhood. Habitat for Humanity made a multimillion-dollar commitment to work on housing for displaced musicians. The big, established charities such as the Salvation Army and the Red Cross came under criticism in the weeks after Katrina. The Red Cross's white, older volunteers, residents claimed, largely ignored the black community. Though the agency drew around 60 percent of the $3.6 billion people donated to the hurricane-relief effort in the first six months after the storm, it was accused of doing far less than half the work of tending to storm victims.

Yet no group matched Common Ground and the breadth of services it offered. People were concerned about the poisons the floodwaters left behind, so Common Ground started a toxins-testing service and gave away red worms and plants that help leach harmful chemicals from the soil. The group created a pest-control unit and launched a pirate radio station dubbed Radio Algiers ("reporting from the West Bank of occupied New Orleans"). They established a free legal clinic and a women's shelter. The exploitation of immigrant workers became a concern so the collective recruited lawyers for those brave enough to file a complaint. In the Lower Ninth, a Rahim lieutenant declared, their goal was nothing short of at least one restored home on every block to thwart developers looking for undeveloped tracts of land.

---

3. In 2007, the Common Ground Health Clinic broke with the rest of the collective and thrived as a free-standing institution.

The Common Ground workers were easy to identify in post-Katrina New Orleans: swarms of whites, sometimes dressed in masks and gloves if not moon suits, gutting a home in a mostly black neighborhood. An inordinate number of these volunteers had dreadlocked beards, face piercings, and/or tattoos. The core group helping Rahim run the collective were leftist activists, at least a few of whom described themselves as "revolutionaries."

Rahim was initially worried how his flocks of white volunteers would be received inside the black community, but they were embraced wherever they showed up. "I wouldn't've believed it if I didn't see it myself," Rahim said. He mentioned a young white man he called Jimmy Mac who lived with him for several months. Somehow, Jimmy had gotten his hands on a Penske truck, which he would drive to Mississippi every day. He'd fill it with food and medical supplies and drive back to New Orleans. "He's doing all this at his own expense," Rahim said. "No one's paying his gas, we're not paying the charges on the truck. We'd just give him a list of places around town that needed supplies, and he'd go into the African-American communities and pass out whatever he managed to pick up." Those places included the Fischer housing projects on the West Bank, which had remained dry. "Fischer is one of the toughest places in town," Rahim said. "But no one would think of touching Jimmy Mac. He'd go through and it was like he walked on water."

Common Ground didn't limit itself to the Ninth Ward. Ultimately, the collective had people working in nineteen parishes around Louisiana. They'd set up outposts, too, along the Gulf Coast in Mississippi and Alabama. Bruce Springsteen donated $100,000 to the cause and Dave Chappelle $150,000. Michael Moore gave $120,000 and paid Rahim's cell phone bill.

"My own version is that New Orleans was on the verge of a race war back then," Rahim said. "What stopped it was the fact that we had young white kids that came down and did what nobody else would do." That was the miracle of Katrina for Rahim: that so many white outsiders saw New Orleans as if it were also their problem. "If I was them, I would've said, 'Fuck them. They got their black mayor. They got their black City Council. Let them work their own selves out of this mess.'"

19

DARKNESS REVEALED

The East had few street signs, but Liberty's headquarters were still easy enough to find: a wounded, six-story glass box missing several windows in a part of town dominated by subdivisions and off-ramp detritus. The hard part was finding a way inside. The front doors were padlocked. One year after Katrina, the only way into the building was the heavy metal door that Russell Labbe had used when there was still ten feet of water.

Inside, even rooms devoid of furniture and carpet still reeked, even months after the storm. The building had three elevators, but they still didn't work. Every day Alden McDonald, sixty-two years old, and his staff walked five flights of stairs to reach the bank's executive suite.

It had not been easy since Labbe had phoned McDonald at the start of 2006 to tell him the lights were back on. McDonald loved the idea of his lit-up glass tower as a beacon drawing people back to the East, but that also meant doing without phone and Internet while waiting for BellSouth to finish replacing trunk lines and switching stations destroyed by flooding. "We basically need to rebuild the entire telecommunications infrastructure in the eastern half of the city," BellSouth's director of operations said. Not until the second half of March could

McDonald reestablish phone service and the Internet connection that would finally allow him, more than seven months after it had arrived, to connect the bank's new mainframe computer to the global banking system. Sometime that spring they lost power in the building for a couple of weeks. The salt water had corroded the bank's underground wiring. "It was horrible," the seventy-year-old Labbe said. "I'd start early in the morning and work till night, breaking concrete to get at wires. It made me old." A generator on-site allowed them to at least keep the lights on and computers running.

Liberty had almost no neighbors at the one-year anniversary of Katrina. The power was still shut off intermittently and garbage pickup was erratic. Lunchtime was depressing: you'd brown-bag it, buy from a truck, settle for fast food, or drive fifteen minutes to Tremé for a table at Dooky Chase's. The bank still had important mail sent to the Southern branch because delivery in Baton Rouge was more reliable. Before the storm the bank had thirty-five thousand customers, but was now down to fewer than twenty-five thousand and maybe as few as twenty thousand.[1] "I have to get an exact count on that," McDonald told a visitor that summer, before his voice trailed off. Liberty didn't require the 150 employees it had on the payroll prior to Katrina, but it needed more than the 90 it had in August 2006. That kept expenses low, bolstering profits, but it also made it harder to generate new business. McDonald wanted to open a fifth branch in New Orleans, but the bank was having trouble finding the tellers, branch assistants, and loan officers needed.

There was good news to report at the one-year anniversary of Katrina. As expected, 2005 proved the most abysmal year in the bank's history. But McDonald was shocked that their losses weren't bigger. Pre-Katrina, the bank had been on pace to make around $3 million, but a few weeks after the storm, McDonald was anticipating year-end losses of $10 million or more. Yet Liberty ended up losing a more modest $3.4 million in 2005. The real surprise was 2006. Liberty reported

---

1. By comparison, at Dryades, another black-owned bank in New Orleans, two-thirds of its roughly three thousand pre-Katrina customers had shut their accounts by August 2006.

$2 million in earnings in the first half of a year that would prove its most profitable ever.

"Liberty seems to have done a remarkable job in a trying situation, certainly better than I ever thought possible," said William Cunningham, CEO of Creative Investment Research, which monitors the financial health of minority-owned financial institutions. "But my concern is with the health of the bank two years, three years out, especially with so many questions around the rebuilding." McDonald harbored the same worries. He only had to consider his own subdivision. Of 150 families, he knew maybe 10 taking steps to rebuild. He counted himself and Rhesa among the undecided. His best guess was that maybe half the East was returning.

Liberty still had no branches in the East, but McDonald opened what the bank dubbed a "recovery center." There, a homeowner could arrange financing to finish rebuilding—and also grab one of the Liberty I'M COMING BACK! lawn signs sprouting around the East. McDonald dialed down the risk by declaring that Liberty would no longer write no-down-payment mortgages, but that also meant the bank would be writing fewer loans. He started talking more about the possibility of doing business in Texas and other places where large concentrations of New Orleans evacuees had relocated. "I've got to go to where my customers are," he said.

THE CITY COUNCIL ENDORSED the UNOP process that Rockefeller and the other foundations were funding. So, too, did the mayor. That July, a citywide meeting was held for anyone wanting to learn more about UNOP. As if people weren't confused enough, Paul Lambert—the planner who had been hired by the City Council—took out a full-page ad in the *Times-Picayune* imploring people not to waste their time talking to anyone from UNOP.

Lambert's team continued to hold planning sessions around the city. They were in New Orleans East in mid-August, where they wowed a few hundred people showing up at the St. Maria Goretti Church. They showed sketches of the neighborhood populated by people enjoying the new jogging and biking paths that could be built and spoke of the "world-class health care" they could enjoy. They imagined sound barriers along the interstate, and parks where there had been low-rent apartment buildings because, as one facilitator said, "it's up to the community to decide where we put the greenspace." What he and his cohorts failed to tell the standing-room-only crowd, though, is that they were fulfilling a contract that had not been voided just because the City Council had decided to throw in with a different set of planners.

Kathleen Blanco had given everyone hope that February when she announced Road Home—the multibillion pot of money to help flooded homeowners whose insurance companies had left them short. A few weeks later, the *Times-Picayune* published the Web address for applying for Road Home along with a telephone number. From that point on, virtually every article written about the lethargic pace of the New Orleans recovery mentioned Road Home and included an obligatory paragraph about the billions in federal housing aid that would be flowing into New Orleans. But first HUD needed to endorse the state's plan, and not until June 2006 would the president authorize the money. When in August, six months after first announcing the program, Blanco was on Poydras to announce the opening of the city's first Road Home office, she blamed delays on "government speed." The reporters descending on New Orleans around the time of the one-year anniversary were still stressing the potential of Road Home—optimistically imagining the billions in housing dollars that would hit the city that fall.

At least a program was in place to help homeowners. Renters, though they constituted a majority in New Orleans, would be on their own. Rents had spiked 39 percent in the twelve months after Katrina— another hurdle for those of modest means anxious to get home. Most public housing units remained off-limits, and the city's landlords didn't seem nearly as susceptible to the pioneer spirit galvanizing homeowners around the city. In communities thick with rental units such as Central City and the Seventh Ward, entire blocks sat untouched, rotting in the heat twelve months after Katrina, making them that much harder to restore. "You drive around and you pretty much see nothing going on. It's depressing," said Henry Jones, who was living in a trailer in the East while he and his wife fixed up their home. An estimated sixty-eight thousand rental units were destroyed or heavily damaged by Katrina.

The state was offering no-interest loans to anyone willing to fix up or build rentals in New Orleans—except those taking the money were permitted to charge market-rate rents. That would do little to help low- and moderate-income residents who wanted to move back to New Orleans.[2] Those tenants looking for a below-market-rate unit signed up for federally subsidized Section 8 housing and hoped that one day their phone would ring. Early on, Alden McDonald had suggested using federal vouchers to foster homeownership and bring families home. Let a person qualifying for a Section 8 voucher (basically, anyone earning under $10 an hour) pair up with a sibling or a parent or a grown-up child to purchase a two-family home. Then ease the rules so that the Section 8 recipient could use his or her monthly voucher to help cover the mortgage. But like everything else born under the rubric of the Bring New Orleans Back Commission, it was ignored.

"I'll confess to being frustrated," said Norman Francis, whom Blanco had put in charge of the Louisiana Recovery Authority. "Without a plan, I don't see how we bring our low- and moderate-income renters back."

TO HER SURPRISE, CASSANDRA WALL began working on her old house. Eventually, they'd be moving home or selling the place; either way, she figured, it couldn't hurt to fix it up. Shortly after she started work, though, she discovered the home had been broken into. "They stole every last copper pipe out of there," she said.

Cassandra was still making regular trips to New Orleans. She visited her mother, who was sick with cancer, and made the long drive when her sisters tried to revive their tradition of Sunday-night dinners. But she also felt the pull of her new life in Baton Rouge. She had found work teaching composition at a local community college and was making progress reviving her tutoring business. Her husband was having a

---

2. Eighteen months after Katrina, Road Home announced a program to replenish the area's rental stock by helping small landlords—those owning five units or fewer—repair flooded units. But property owners first needed to make repairs that could reach into the hundreds of thousands of dollars and rent out a unit before they could be reimbursed. The goal was the restoration of eighteen thousand units, not the four thousand the state actually financed.

hard time dealing with a job that meant a demotion in responsibility, and Katrina was taking a toll on Brandon. He was doing well in school, but he was looking at another school year in Baton Rouge, rather than eighth grade back in New Orleans with his friends. "You're fighting here, you're fighting there," Cassandra told her sisters. "You realize you can't fight everyone and everywhere at once." That was her way of informing them that work on her old house would cease until further notice.

Tangee was the first of Cassandra's sisters to move back into her home. She burned through most of her savings, but she was intent on showing the world that the East was coming back. "Our community paid our taxes," she declared at around the one-year anniversary, with her home around 80 percent rebuilt. "We pumped money into the economy. We deserve the right to return like any other part of New Orleans." On Saturdays, she ventured farther east to a meeting in the Village de L'Est, a Vietnamese community coming back faster than other subdivisions in the area. "A group of us decided to get behind this push for everyone in the East to pull together, rather than it being a subdivision-by-subdivision thing," Tangee said. Father Vien The Nguyen hosted the weekly meetings. Petie showed up at these meetings when she could, as did Robyn.

Petie was making progress on her place but at a slower pace than Tangee—room by room, Petie said, "if not one wall at a time." Whenever she had the money, Petie would head to Lowe's, where day laborers, almost all of them Latino, lined up each day looking for work. "You go saying you're looking for people to hang Sheetrock and offer one hundred dollars a day," she said. "And then if they do a good job, you pay them more and keep them going to the next thing." One year after Katrina, she figured her home was about 40 percent rebuilt.

Robyn was back in New Orleans, but she hadn't done any work on her home. She was busy at work and didn't feel like competing for contractors, plumbers, and electricians. "It was crazy, the prices people were asking," Robyn said. "I took my time because I could afford to." Once the lease expired on the condo she had rented in the Warehouse District, she moved back to her mother's home in Broadmoor. Cassandra's sister Contesse was still in Baton Rouge. Contesse had gutted her home to preserve her investment, she said, but that was it. "I'm not making up my mind," she announced, "until the people in charge make up theirs."

Tensions formed between the sisters. That was obvious one year after Katrina when the five of them gathered at a crowded Barnes & Noble café in Metairie to talk about the recovery. That week the *Times-Picayune* had run a page-one story declaring that without a major upgrade to the levee system, New Orleans East, sandwiched between Lake Borgne and Lake Pontchartrain, with MR. GO acting as an accelerant, would remain vulnerable. The article reinforced for Tangee the desire to fight for the East, but for Cassandra it was another reason to wait until people in Washington had a chance to work things out.

"I'm not coming back until I know we have Category 5 protection," Cassandra said.

"We need a massive protest in Washington to make sure that happens," Tangee responded. "It's our constitutional right to have our government protect us."

The five of them agreed that life would not be easy for anyone choosing to rebuild. The question was what responsibility they had as de facto spokespeople for the area. "Only the strong will survive," Petie declared.

"Then why are you encouraging everyone in the East to rebuild?" said Contesse, who made no effort to hide her irritation. She was single and self-employed. She sometimes struggled to make her bills. Even if she had wanted to start rebuilding, she didn't have the savings to float a six-figure repair bill while waiting on insurance companies and any help the state might provide through Road Home.

"If a community doesn't come back," Petie said, "people will condense. They'll move to an area that's coming back." She sounded like Joe Canizaro, suggesting that people pour everything they had into returning—and if it didn't work out, our apology for having put you through all that trouble.

"It's dangerous to encourage people to move back someplace where there are no hospitals," Contesse snapped. "You don't encourage people to come back when there are no schools or adequate day care." Pre-storm, Contesse taught an average of thirty students at her seminars on intellectual property. Could she even draw a class of ten if she moved back to New Orleans right now? "I love my community like everyone else, but it's not fair what you're asking of people," Contesse said.

"This is where we chose to live," Tangee said. "This is where *all* of us chose to live."

Seeking a safer subject, they talked of the good things going on in the East. Tangee told them about Rodney's Snowball opening on Lake Forest Boulevard and a Super Cajun, which at least meant decent takeout. "And who's eating there?" Cassandra asked. Driving around earlier that day, she had seen maybe three trailers in her subdivision of seventy-five homes. Contesse had also been shocked by how little activity she saw when she visited her neighborhood on a Saturday. "A few people repairing roofs," Contesse said. "A few trailers but few people actually living—"

"I'm *living* out there," Tangee interjected. "There's a lot more activity than she's saying."

"Excuse me. Excuse me. I'm there two or three times a week," Contesse said. "I've lived there since 1988, I know what my neighbors are thinking." Contesse brought up the displeasure she felt toward Tangee as one of those working to block the rebuilding of the apartment buildings along the interstate. "That's discrimination," Contesse charged. "You can't say the homeowners deserve the right to return but not the people in the apartments."

"I don't want to hear any more of this gloom-and-doom talk!" Tangee exclaimed. The media and the politicians were bad enough, but her sisters had joined the naysayers. "We need to give people hope, not tell them everything that might be wrong," Tangee said. The day before, she had been at the big New Orleans East neighborhood meeting organized by planners working with Lambert. "They put forward a wonderful plan." Tangee told them about the better class of retailer they would draw to the area and also the higher-caliber restaurants. "And that's not a fight I'm willing to run from."

Several sisters chimed in at once, but Contesse kept talking until the others were silent. She reminded them of her community involvement over the years and caused snickers when she claimed, not for the first time, that the idea for Eastern New Orleans United and Whole was hers, not Tangee and Robyn's. ("With Contesse, it's always me, me, me,"

Petie later said.) "I've always been very outspoken," Contesse said. "I've always been politically active. But I'm being practical."

Normally, Tangee plays peacemaker, but she was one of the main combatants. Robyn stepped into the breach: "No one is saying the East is coming back tomorrow. No one is saying the East is coming back next year. But I think we can all agree the East will be back in five years. And I for one am going to do my part to see that it comes back as someplace we'd all want to live."

"And what do you do during those five years?" Contesse asked.

Robyn: "I live in my house."

Petie: "You live in your house and be happy you're home and you stop complaining."

One of the sisters growled in a playful way to suggest a catfight, prompting a burst of giggles. Contesse, however, was not in a laughing mood. Her voice louder, her tone stentorian, she said, "You're still talking individuals. I'm talking community. I'm talking about looking at the greater good."

RAY NAGIN SLIPPED BACK into his Katrina wear with the media in town in anticipation of the one-year anniversary. The mayor donned a red, short-sleeved polo for a tour of the Lower Ninth for *60 Minutes*. Nagin was probably aiming to play the role of the leader who has everything under control, but even he seemed shocked by the lack of progress there. The Lower Ninth in August 2006 looked as bad as it had when *60 Minutes* was there in October 2005.

Nagin started Ray-Raying about the bulldozers and property rights and the delays these fights were causing, but the reporter assigned the story, CBS's Byron Pitts, cut him off. Pitts pointed to the flood-damaged cars lining the road and a splintered home with only a small corner of its roof still intact—objects that could have been cleared months earlier without a complaint. A defensive Nagin tried to appear nonchalant, but his words would echo for days on cable and elsewhere: "That's all right. You guys in New York can't get a hole in the ground fixed and it's five years later." "New Orleans Mayor Takes a Swipe at NYC," read a CBS press release that guaranteed Nagin's inelegant words would overshadow talk of New Orleans twelve months after the storm. "I meant no disrespect for anyone," Nagin explained on that week's *Meet the Press*. But he would refuse to apologize, earning the mayor a stern lecture from Tim Russert about what the country owed those who lost family members on that hallowed ground.

Closer to home, Nagin pontificated on the future of some of New Orleans's neighborhoods in a sit-down with the *Times-Picayune*'s Gordon Russell for a big anniversary piece they would be running in the Sunday paper. "New Orleans East is showing some signs [of recovery], but it's vast, it's going to hit the wall," Nagin said. "There's just such a big footprint, I don't think they're going to get the clustering they need. So I think you're going to have little pockets in the East." He was more pessimistic about the Lower Ninth: "I've been saying this publicly, and people are starting to hear it: low-lying areas of New Orleans East and the Lower Ninth Ward, stay away from." Nagin singled out the area north of Claiborne Avenue by the levee breach: "We can't touch that." At a press conference that same week, he offered this advice to the citizens of New Orleans: "You can't wait on government. You have to figure out a way to partner with your neighbors." Then, sounding more fortune cookie than mayor, he added, "The road to recovery is long and arduous."

Nagin was traveling a lot—too much according to some. There was even a rumor that the mayor had moved to Dallas, where his wife was still living a year after Katrina. No one could begrudge the mayor his flights to Washington, but he also made fund-raising trips to Baton Rouge, Philadelphia, and New York, according to a website called wheresnagin .com. A local radio talk-show host took to referring to the mayor as "Ray Nay-gone." A new *Onion*-like publication, the *New Orleans Levee*, ran a Ray Nagin version of *Where's Waldo?*

Nagin post-Katrina was a man without allies and with few friends. The first three years of his tenure had been marked by breakfast meetings at Le Pavillon with the likes of Joe Canizaro and dinners with representatives of the business elite at Clancy's, where tuxedo-clad waiters served the Uptown royals their shrimp rémoulade and crawfish étouffée. Forget Ron Forman—the "so-called friend who ran against me," as Nagin put it on the campaign trail. The two saw one another around town, but Forman described their encounters as civil but brief. "He was always cool

Ray: 'Hey, man, how you doing?' A high five, maybe a hug," Forman said. There'd be no contact between Nagin and Jimmy Reiss, and it was over with Nagin's former friends from the Business Council.

It didn't need to end between the mayor and Bill Hines, who had helped run the mayor's 2002 transition team. The managing partner at the city's largest law firm, Hines was an old-fashioned Rockefeller Republican who pushed a pro-business agenda but was otherwise liberal on most issues. He was a generous philanthropist who could be counted on to support any effort that had as its goal helping the less fortunate. Voluble and fun-loving, intent on eating each day the best New Orleans had to offer, Hines was in the business of getting along with everyone. He would see former mayor Marc Morial at a Hornets game—at least when the city had a professional basketball team (the Hornets would play their home games in Oklahoma City for two seasons after Katrina)[3]—and give him a hug hello, scandalizing his Uptown friends. Hines and his wife had gone out with Nagin and Seletha during the first term, but any semblance of a friendship ended after Hines threw his support to Mitch Landrieu. Despite Hines's efforts, he and Nagin were now just nodding acquaintances. "I think Ray lumped me in with the rest of the white business community and that was that," Hines said.

David White had stuck by Nagin. "Probably Ray Nagin's only real friend," Ron Forman said. Yet White was also shy, and his relationship with the high-profile Nagin put him closer to the spotlight. Money was also a complicating factor. "I didn't really get involved in city politics in Ray's second term," White said.

The rest of Nagin's inner circle was also disintegrating. Greg Meffert resigned that summer. The two hadn't known one another before Nagin offered him a top job in his administration, but within several years they were vacationing together with their wives and kids. They were in Hawaii in 2004 and Jamaica a couple of months after Katrina. "We were daredevils, action junkies, whatever you want to call it; that's why we got closer than anybody else," Meffert said. "Otherwise, there was very

---

3. The team would change its name to the Pelicans a few years after moving back to New Orleans.

little I have in common with the dude." Meffert had never made it a secret that the $150,000 a year he was earning as a top mayoral aide was nothing compared to what he could command in the private sector. In a farewell press release, Nagin described Meffert as "instrumental in our recovery and revitalization."

Nagin hired a white woman named Donna Addkison to retool his executive team after Meffert left. Addkison had been the deputy chief of staff to a Mississippi governor. Nagin charged her with running about half the city bureaucracy. She would be gone after a year. About the only top person left from Nagin's pre-Katrina days was Brenda Hatfield, the old friend he had brought in to serve as his chief of staff after his first two picks washed out.

"I don't know if Ray ever recovered from the hurricane," said Ron Forman. "He seemed a real lonely figure in his second term without anyone to really talk to."

RAY NAGIN CLAIMED NEW ORLEANS had a population of roughly 250,000 at the one-year anniversary—a little over half of its pre-Katrina population. Entergy, however, claimed they were delivering power to only eighty thousand customers that summer, including trailers—barely 40 percent of its pre-storm load. The post office estimated that New Orleans was a city of 171,000—37 percent of its population before Katrina.

Most every part of the city had electricity, gas, and sewer service. Drinkable water was available everywhere but the Lower Ninth and small pockets around the city. Yet not until November 2006 could Nagin announce that every part of New Orleans had working sewers, drinkable water, phones, and power. Even then, he couldn't make any promises. The water system was a sieve: because of thousands of cracks in the lines, the city was pumping 130 million gallons to deliver 50 million gallons of drinking water to customers, the *Times-Picayune*'s Michelle Krupa found, at a cost of $200,000 a day. But at least residents could count on water when they turned on the faucet. The city's gas and electric company, Entergy, was in bankruptcy and claiming $680 million in storm losses. The Bush administration had already rejected its request for a taxpayer bailout, and the utility was threatening a 25 percent rate increase without state aid from Baton Rouge. Twenty-one months after Katrina, Louisiana would give the company $172 million in aid through its community development block grant program. Meanwhile, blackouts were frequent in a jury-rigged power system sensitive to overloads and even the weather.

The city had made progress. A baler had crushed three hundred thousand ruined refrigerators into one-ton, rectangular-shaped cubes and sold them for scrap. The Corps and its contractors had begun to remove the tens of thousands of abandoned cars littering the city's streets. Yet even as the Corps did its job, the trash continued to pile up as more people cleaned out their homes. The Corps shipped in giant shredders for the ruined Sheetrock, soaked furniture, and the other detritus the city was kicking to the curb. That helped reduce the volume, but the garbage still needed to end up somewhere. In February, with the city's landfills filling up, Nagin issued a temporary six-month permit allowing for a dump site along the border of the Bayou Sauvage National Wildlife Refuge, on the eastern edge of New Orleans East. That led to another battle. The proposed dump was down the road from the Village de L'Est, whose residents blockaded the road until Nagin agreed he wouldn't extend the temporary permit. That left the city scrambling to find alternatives.

People around the city were getting sick from mold. The "Katrina cough," locals called it—a dry, persistent hack brought on by mold spores and other irritants in the air. To John Biguenet, a local playwright who had more than four feet of water in his home, people who had endured a year of Katrina couldn't fully enjoy a movie or a favorite TV show. "People lost their ability to let go and allow themselves to fully inhabit another character," Biguenet said. On Sundays, Biguenet and his neighbors would gather at what some called the Pretend Café. They'd brew their coffee at home, take a folding chair and the paper, and head for Fair Grinds Coffeehouse, though the popular Mid-City café was still closed. During these weekly gripe sessions, Biguenet usually carped about his insurance company and the frustrations of starting over again with a new claims adjuster. He remembered six or seven adjusters, but his wife swears they went through nine in twelve months. "We were like traumatized war victims," Biguenet said. "You don't realize how strange things are when you're in the middle of it."

Four of the city's seven general hospitals were still closed, including Charity. A survey taken several months before the anniversary found that 77 percent of the city's primary-care physicians were still not back. Eighty-nine percent of its psychiatrists were still missing. "There is no hospital at all in the city for psychiatric patients," Loyola law professor Bill Quigley wrote on *CounterPunch* at the one-year anniversary. The metro area had 450 psych beds before the storm. It now had 80.

In June, the federal government had announced its intention to demolish the city's four largest housing projects—the Big Four, as they were known. That represented nearly five thousand apartments and well over half the city's public housing units. Under the HUD plan, private developers would build mixed-income complexes in place of all four. "In its rush to demolish the apartment complexes—and replace them with the kind of generic, mixed-income suburban community so favored by Washington bureaucrats—the agency demonstrates great insensitivity to both the displaced tenants and the urban fabric of the city," wrote *New York Times* architecture critic Nicolai Ouroussoff. Residents and their supporters established a tent city outside the city's largest housing projects and shouted down the federal housing officials who arrived to explain their plan. Protesters broke into one of the Big Four to help a man move back into his old apartment, and then, after he was booted by an armed SWAT team, several residents broke into another. Lawsuits were filed on behalf of residents and a small demonstration held outside Nagin's home. Among those speaking out against the demolition plan was Tulane's Lance Hill, who told the *New York Times'* Susan Saulny, "The people who've been planning the recovery process never wanted poor people to return to the city in the first place." But Hill and the protesters would find few allies among elected officials, black or white. They were noticeably silent on the issue. "The city has nothing to do with this," Nagin said. Only around one thousand of the housing authority's units had been reopened since Katrina.

The Great Experiment, as some would eventually call the transformation of the city's public schools, was another issue dividing the city. Where before Katrina the city was home to only a few charter schools, soon New Orleans would become the first school district in the country with a majority of its students enrolled in a charter school. Two dozen charters opened in anticipation of the new school year. No one knew what to expect in this overwhelmingly poor school district. Prior to the storm, three in every four public school students qualified for a subsidized lunch. By Katrina, only 4 percent of the kids attending the public schools were white.

For some, anything would be an improvement over what they had pre-Katrina. The dropout rate at some high schools had been as high as 70 percent, and the city's math and reading-proficiency scores were consistently among the worst in the state. A "dysfunctional catastrophe," one unhappy white parent said of the pre-storm schools, under the "control of a corrupt district office." He was inclined to celebrate more power in the hands of parents, where he thought it belonged, but others stressed that a duly elected school board—a majority-black body—had been stripped of its authority. Others displeased with the state's custodianship pointed to bad experiences in other places, where the charters accepted only children willing to obey their rules or rejected those with learning disabilities and other students who might drag down test scores. The parents of those kids would need to fend for themselves.

BROKEN STOPLIGHTS STILL DANGLED in parts of the central business district. Stores even in the center of town remained shuttered a year after Katrina. To reach the city's economic-development office one entered through a side door, as the revolving doors out front were still boarded up.

Shell was back, but Chevron announced it was moving its offices to higher ground in the suburbs. Traffic at the port was almost back to normal, but the city's manufacturing base post-Katrina was almost non-existent. One survey found that twelve months after the storm, two in every three businesses were still closed. Shops catering to tourists complained that they were doing maybe half their pre-storm business. One local economist predicted that 40 percent of the city's businesses would end up a casualty of Katrina.

The few big-box retailers knew they could do a brisk business even in sparsely populated parts of town—basically Home Depot and Lowe's—but the big national and regional chains were slow to reopen. At first that surprised Richard Campanella, a geographer at Tulane who has written extensively about New Orleans and its history, but it came to make sense. The small mom-and-pops had everything invested in one store. "They have no choice but to do whatever they can to come back," Campanella said.

After September 11, the state and federal governments had set aside $500 million to help small businesses in New York. That figure would be $38 million for small businesses in Louisiana hit by either Katrina or Rita. Sitting in Memphis, Anthony Patton was technically still president of EBONetworks. Running a ten-person firm he touted as the South's "premier African-American marketing company," he had earned a spot on the Bring New Orleans Back Commission. Yet one year after Katrina, he had no clients and no employees. "All the African-American businesses are gone," Patton said.

The optimists thought about the billions in government money that would soon be washing through New Orleans. They imagined "an arts-infused mecca for youthful risk-takers, a boomtown where entrepreneurs can repair to cool French Quarter bars in ancient buildings after a hard day of deal making," wrote the *Times'* Adam Nossiter, who lived in New Orleans at the time. The pessimists worried that New Orleans was on its way to becoming the country's next Detroit—a city of abandoned neighborhoods. Others fretted that the new New Orleans would become a hollowed-out, Disneyfied version of itself. The city's aristocracy would still put on carnival each year, and the city's main attractions would remain its food and music. But in this vision, about all that would be left of New Orleans would be the tourists and the people getting rich off them, along with the low-paid housekeepers, waiters, busboys, and bartenders to keep everything going.

Houston was home to more evacuees than anywhere else. That first spring after Katrina, the city polled those who had availed themselves of a free housing program set up to get people out of the Astrodome and other shelters. Nine months after Katrina, only one in seven of them had a job. Most were either people over fifty-five or single mothers. "Over ninety percent of the people here are either suicidal or hopeless," a dispossessed thirty-four-year-old named Alphonso Thomas said of his fellow evacuees.

"Time has long since passed for the able-bodied people from

Louisiana to either find a job, return to somewhere in Louisiana, or become Houstonians," a Houston congressman named John Culberson, a
Republican, said of the "deadbeat" New Orleanians who had invaded his
city. Those stranded in Houston were blamed for an increase in crime (a
claim later refuted by studies). Where once displaced New Orleanians
were slapping a THANKS HOUSTON bumper sticker on a car, many now felt
as though they had worn out their welcome.

NAGIN FIRST IMAGINED FIREWORKS. He suggested a "comedy night"
as well for the evening of August 29. Ultimately, the city chose a more
solemn set of events to commemorate the one-year anniversary of Katrina. At a prayer breakfast that morning, Nagin rang a large silver bell
at 9:38 a.m., which is believed to be the time of the catastrophic Seventeenth Street breach. Later that morning, Nagin joined the president,
who was in town and speaking at a new charter school. Bush declared
August 29, 2006, a National Day of Remembrance and reiterated the
pledge he had made at his Jackson Square speech to do whatever it took
to rebuild New Orleans. His motorcade then crossed the bridge in the
Lower Ninth Ward, where the president visited the home of R&B leg-
end Fats Domino, who had been airlifted from there several days after
Katrina.

No one knew exactly how many people had died in Katrina. They
never would after the State of Louisiana, in 2006, defunded the project
it had set up to identify unidentified bodies and calculate how many
bodies might have washed out to sea. Some bodies were still buried in
plain sight, such as the body that had been discovered in the rubble just
before the anniversary. One year after Katrina, the best the authorities
could do was to declare that at least eighteen hundred people across the
Gulf Coast had died in the storm. More than eleven hundred of them
were from New Orleans.

KATRINA OFFERED PLENTY OF ammunition to Democrats seeking
to discredit a sitting president with Republican majorities in both the
House and the Senate. "We know the storm was a tragedy, but a bigger

tragedy is how the federal government responded," Harry Reid, then the Senate minority leader, declared in August, a little more than two months before the 2006 midterm elections. That summer it seemed half the Bush cabinet was on the Gulf Coast to announce new initiatives. "I take full responsibility for the federal government's response," Bush declared around the first anniversary. Yet it was too late for a president saddled by both Katrina and Iraq. Democrats gained thirty-one seats in the House that November—enough to make Nancy Pelosi that body's first female Speaker. Harry Reid would take over as majority leader after the Democrats picked up six seats in the Senate.

The city of Gretna returned to the news that summer. The state attorney general, Charles Foti Jr., completed his investigation into the blockade. Foti was a local, a white man who had recently been elected AG after thirty years as the Orleans Parish criminal sheriff. Rather than take a stance, Foti had his people deliver a report on the case to a long list of law enforcement officials, including the FBI, the local US attorney, and US attorney general Alberto Gonzales. Others were free to venture into the racial politics of Gretna should they choose.

In August, Orleans Parish's district attorney, Eddie Jordan, who was black, announced he had formed a grand jury to investigate the incident at Gretna. Another five civil suits were filed against the city, including a class action suit prepared on behalf of the RTA workers. "We saved our city," said Gretna police chief Arthur Lawson. "We put officers on the streets. We didn't allow joyriders or people to come into the city who didn't reside in the city. We set up perimeters. Our plan worked." Now the judicial branch would decide whether, in protecting Gretna's streets, rights had been trampled.

THAT SUMMER, LAKEVIEW CIVIC held a rebuilding workshop in the gym at St. Dom's. Connie Uddo stood to talk about Beacon of Hope. Afterward, a priest named Will Hood introduced himself and asked her to take a walk with him.

He was new to Lakeview, Hood confessed, a navy chaplain recently returned from duty in Iraq. He had been hired as the rector of St. Paul, an Episcopal church in Lakeview, with the understanding that he would probably shut down the church and its school. The parishioners he met, however, didn't seem ready to give up. Each more or less greeted him the same way: Thank God you're here, what can we do to help? He convinced the bishop to let him try to save St. Paul, he told Uddo, and had even secured funding from the diocese to help him rebuild the neighborhood.

Hood and Uddo were a few blocks from the church when the priest pointed to an empty building. He'd already spoken to the landlord, he said. The place would be ready and available within four weeks. He wanted to use the space to create a recovery command center. "But I can't do it and rebuild a church and school," he said. Did Uddo want the job?

Uddo first asked whether it made a difference that she was Catholic. Her second question was why her. Hood told her he had driven through her neighborhood and been impressed. "I can tell you're combat-ready," he told her. One month later, on the August 29 anniversary date, Uddo opened the doors to St. Paul's Homecoming Center. Uddo figured she'd be there a year, maybe two, and then go back to teaching tennis.

20

ROAD HOME

Professional football returned to New Orleans in the fall of 2006. The city had been excited about a team that ended the 2004 season with four consecutive wins, but after the storm hit, fans suffered through a dismal year. The Saints lost thirteen of their sixteen games playing "home" games in Baton Rouge, San Antonio, and even New Jersey, where the end zones of the Meadowlands were spray-painted the Saints colors and the hometown Giants wore their road uniforms.

The league did what it could to give the state, which owns the Superdome, the time needed to ready the stadium. The Saints played their preseason home games in Shreveport and Jackson, Mississippi, and their first two regular-season games were on the road. Under a new head coach, Sean Payton, and led by a new quarterback, Drew Brees, the Saints won the first two games of the season, raising expectations for the first professional football game to be played in New Orleans in twenty-two months.

The Superdome, a vast upside-down dish that seats seventy

thousand, was sold-out. U2 and Green Day played a mini-three-song set[1] before the game began, and former president George H. W. Bush was there for the coin toss. Four plays into the game, a Saints reserve named Steve Gleason blocked a punt and a backup cornerback named Curtis Deloatch recovered the ball in the end zone for a touchdown. "It was like an explosion," Deloatch said. "It was like I just gave New Orleans a brand-new city." The Saints beat their division rival the Atlanta Falcons, 23–3, in a stadium Coach Sean Payton declared the loudest he had ever heard. That year the team notched only its second play-off win in franchise history and would miss out on its first Super Bowl appearance after losing to Chicago in the NFC championship game.

MARTIN LANDRIEU AND HIS team had submitted their plan for Lakeview to the city. So, too, did Charmaine Marchand in the Lower Ninth and others around the city. New Orleans, however, was still a long way from submitting a written plan to the Louisiana Recovery Authority to free up the billions in recovery dollars that New Orleans was due. The city still hadn't heard from those who hadn't managed to make it home yet—and Carey Shea, the Rockefeller Foundation's point person in New Orleans, was determined that they have their say before a plan was submitted.

Shea, from New York, moved to New Orleans over the July 4 weekend 2006. Talking to people involved in the planning that summer, she concluded that Nagin had made a key tactical mistake when he gave the job of rebuilding to the Bring New Orleans Back Commission. Ordinary New Orleanians needed to feel as though they had been included in the decision making. Instead they were asked to wait patiently while a group of CEOs and other elites determined their future. Shea also came

---

1. The bands played a modified version of "The Saints Are Coming," a song by the Skids. A recording of the song was sold to raise money for Music Rising, a charity cofounded by U2 guitarist The Edge and aimed at replacing instruments destroyed by Katrina.

to believe the city had brought in the Urban Land Institute prematurely. At that point the city needed group therapy, not a bunch of outsiders telling them they needed to give up on their homes.

"What the plan was missing was community buy-in," Shea said. "So I went to the other foundations that had been watching a little bit from a distance and shared my concern that voices weren't being heard from what everyone was calling then 'the diaspora.'" A foundation created by George H. W. Bush and Bill Clinton—the Bush-Clinton Katrina Fund—chipped in $1 million. The Annie E. Casey Foundation, the State of Louisiana, and other organizations contributed millions more.

They would need all that money and more for what Shea had in mind. A woman she knew had attended a September 11–related event at the Javits Center in New York that had been organized by a group called AmericaSpeaks. Shea's friend had been impressed by the diversity of the crowd that had arrived at the Javits Center that day and wowed by the technical capabilities of a group that issued every participant an electronic pad for instant voting. "They're like a production company in the business of putting on these ginormous meetings," Shea said of AmericaSpeaks. "It's very therapeutic. The person running the thing cries. There's praying, there's music." But maybe most important, "they're really good at creating consensus around broad issues." Shea hired AmericaSpeaks for what they were calling a Community Congress—the big event held in New Orleans in October 2006 to give ordinary citizens a chance to talk about the city's future.

Shea was impressed as she watched AmericaSpeaks prepare in the months before the Community Congress. Their people put together a list of FEMA trailer camps in southern Louisiana and sent people to visit each one. They arranged for vans and buses to shuttle those needing transportation. They also contacted people in Houston, Atlanta, and other cities to spread the word.

But the Community Congress would prove a disappointment. They had expected 1,000 people but only 350 showed and half of them were staff. Three-quarters of those in attendance were white, and nearly half had an annual household income above $75,000—hardly the dispossessed population organizers were hoping to hear from. Just their luck,

NPR reporter Martin Kaste was in town for a piece on the city with
no plan and captured the disappointment. "We're like lemmings going
off a cliff," one participant told Kaste for a report that aired on NPR a
week later.

VIOLENCE WAS STILL A constant in a city that had enough problems
without people killing one another. An Iraq war veteran living in the
French Quarter killed and mutilated his girlfriend and then threw himself off a nearby hotel roof. On Halloween, a gunman walked into a
Quarter nightclub and shot five people. Drug-related murders were on
the rise and domestic violence spiked, driving up the number of women
living on the street. "People don't realize this isn't a normal community
yet," New Orleans police chief Warren Riley told *USA Today*. Was it any
wonder that a University of New Orleans political scientist found that
32 percent of returnees were considering leaving?

Chief Riley and his top people were still working out of trailers.
New Orleans still had no working crime lab. FEMA had filed the requi-
site damage-assessment reports for the city's police headquarters and its
damaged precinct houses, but that was only the start of a long, drawn-
out process. When the money might be pried from the federal treasury
so work could begin on essential government buildings was one of many
unknowns inside City Hall. A beleaguered police department was also
contending with scandal. Six days after Katrina, the police, responding
to a call for help on the Danziger Bridge, a small stretch of high ground
between Gentilly and New Orleans East, killed two people and shot
four others, though civilian witnesses claimed all of the victims were
unarmed. So, too, did other officers. One victim was a mentally disabled
man shot in the back while trying to run. Seven officers were indicted on
charges ranging from obstruction of justice to murder.[2]

---

2. A jury would find four of the seven officers guilty of using a weapon in the commission of a violent crime. One, a sergeant named Kenneth Bowen, was also convicted
   of stomping on Ronald Madison, a forty-year-old disabled man. A second sergeant
   was found guilty of aiding in an attempted cover-up of the crime. The convictions

The year 2006 ended grimly with the murder of a drummer from the popular Hot 8 Brass Band. (The shooter killed the wrong person.) The new year wasn't a week old and already the city had recorded eight murders. In a city where the typical murder victim was a young black man living in a high-crime area, the body count included a young Uptown woman found shot dead in her bed and a prominent local filmmaker killed during a home invasion in the Marigny district. Her husband, a doctor, was also shot, while their two-year-old son survived. "Killings Bring the City to Its Bloodied Knees," cried the *Times-Picayune* on its front page the next day. A crowd of around five thousand showed up at City Hall for an anticrime rally and hurled angry words at both the mayor and Chief Riley. The killings, however, continued. Pre-Katrina, the police would record around a thousand violent crimes each quarter. Fewer than half the city's population had returned, but there would be more than thirteen hundred violent crimes reported in the first three months of 2007.

"Surge in Homeless Hits New Orleans," read a *Christian Science Monitor* headline that March. Whereas the city had around six thousand homeless people before Katrina, now an estimated twelve thousand people were sleeping in cars, abandoned motels, or under highway overpasses. Most of the city's emergency shelters were still closed, while meanwhile a new population was demanding the attention of people such as Martha Kegel, the Stanford Law grad who ran a local advocacy group for the homeless: "people in their late eighties," Kegel said, "who never in their lives expected to be homeless."

The housing policies adopted by some of New Orleans's suburban neighbors didn't help a city in dire need of more affordable units. St. Bernard Parish, the white-flight suburb just south and east of New Orleans, passed what its sponsor called a "blood-relative ordinance." In a parish where whites owned 93 percent of the housing stock, the new law

---

were vacated in 2013 on charges of "grotesque prosecutorial misconduct" after a top lawyer in the US Attorney's office was caught posting inflammatory online comments before and during the trial. A new trial was ordered.

dictated that landlords could rent only to family members.[3] The parish would pass another law barring the redevelopment of any property with more than four units. The main target of this second ordinance seemed to be the Village Square, a sprawling, hundred-building complex occupied mainly by low-income African-American renters. Officials in Jefferson Parish blocked construction of a two-hundred-unit residential facility for the elderly, and at least one city there placed a moratorium on multifamily units.

Insurance companies were a constant topic of conversation in wounded New Orleans. Those who had splurged on a comprehensive homeowner's policy learned that *comprehensive* didn't include floods. Homeowner's insurance generally covered wind damage, but even a hole in the roof through which rain had fallen might not be enough proof that a house had been damaged by more than floodwaters. People believed that the insurance companies offered a fraction of what they owed and then waited to see who had the will to fight for more.[4] The Louisiana Department of Insurance was receiving twenty thousand calls a month. Nearly five thousand people had leveled a formal complaint in 2006. Sixty-six hundred insurance-related lawsuits had been filed in federal district court in New Orleans by the first half of 2007.

Alden McDonald had no argument over his personal insurance coverage. He had received the maximum $250,000 from his flood insurance carrier plus another $75,000 or so to cover his home's contents, but he had no roof damage and didn't expect any more money under his homeowner's policy. But his brother Byron needed to sue his carrier

---

3. A federal judge found that the ordinance violated federal antidiscrimination laws. The parish was forced to pay fines and court costs exceeding $1.8 million.

4. "Delay, deny, defend"—that's how a Rutgers professor named Jay M. Feinman described the insurance industry's strategy in a book by that title published several years after Katrina. The strategy, Feinman reported, had been laid out in a Power-Point presentation that came to light during a lawsuit against Allstate. When a policyholder files a claim, the aggressive insurance company makes a low offer, a McKinsey & Co. consultant explained: let people fight if they think they deserve more.

before he received anything near what he felt was a fair settlement. Flood insurance had paid the full $250,000 on the two-story, $350,000, brick home Byron owned in Gentilly. But the Hanover Insurance Group offered him close to nothing under a $200,000 homeowner's policy despite the hole in his roof after the wind tore off a ventilator. Hanover claimed Byron owed *them* money given the $1,500 check they mistakenly believed they sent to Byron and his wife to cover their temporary living expenses. A month before they were scheduled to go to trial, Hanover settled for an amount Byron cannot reveal given a binding nondisclosure agreement.

Insurance-industry spokespeople pointed out that carriers had collectively paid out a record $11 billion to homeowners in Louisiana after Katrina. But the $49 billion in profits insurance firms pocketed that year was also an all-time insurance-industry high. The state officials behind the Road Home program were among those convinced insurers were short-changing people. By their calculations, homeowners were paid on average $5,700 less than they were owed—no small matter for a program created to make up the difference between what a property was worth and the actual insurance payment a homeowner received. State officials figured that would add another $900 million to the cost of making people whole under Road Home.

WARD "MACK" MCCLENDON FELT numb that first year after Katrina— asleep, he said, even with his eyes open, "hoping I'd wake up from a bad dream, except it only kept getting worse." McClendon had planned on riding out the storm at his daughter's home in Atlanta, but the traffic was so bad he stayed that Sunday night at a no-name motel in Opelika, Alabama. His daughter was about to give birth to her first child, but he heard about the levee breaches and returned to New Orleans rather than continue on to Atlanta, less than two hours away. "I'm telling you, I wasn't in my right mind then," McClendon said. Back in New Orleans, he paid way too much to hole up in a fleabag motel while waiting the two months it would take him even to see his house in the Lower Ninth Ward.

McClendon lived one block from Flood Street in a city where the

Army Corps of Engineers had its main offices on Leake Avenue. "That should've told me something right there," McClendon said. "But like my mama was always telling me, I wasn't always so good at listening." He was a squat, dark-skinned black man with Popeye forearms and a fireplug physique. His voice, proper and refined, suggested a thespian past, but his education stopped after high school when he took a job laying cable for the phone company. McClendon was twenty-nine years old when he fell from a ladder and fractured several discs in his back. Permanent disability would pay him two-thirds of his salary for life. He spent most of the next decade bouncing around the country, but returned to the Lower Ninth just before his fortieth birthday. "I realized I needed three things in life," McClendon said. "Good food. Good people. Good music. And no place I looked at offered as good a combination as New Orleans."

McClendon ran his own small salvage yard in the years leading up to Katrina. Mostly he spent his time restoring antique cars. He'd buy junkers for a few hundred dollars, if not the price of a tow, and then haunt the antique-car shows in search of parts. "You can make ten times the money you put into them," McClendon said. "But you drive 'em and think about how much work you put into it and you don't want to ever let them go." He was up to fourteen cars at the time of Katrina. The floodwaters destroyed all of them. None of them were insured.

The house he owned on Caffin Avenue in the Lower Ninth proved a bigger blow. It wasn't much to look at from the street: a narrow, two-story place with a plain exterior. But McClendon knew he was looking at his dream home the first time he stepped inside. The old house had wood floors, high ceilings, crown moldings, and a pair of tiled fireplaces. With four bedrooms upstairs, it was a lot more house than a single divorcé needed, but he had eight kids, and though all of them were grown, he liked that he could offer them a sanctuary if they ever needed it. He paid $72,000 for this handsome old home only a couple of blocks from the Mississippi. He redid the floors downstairs and restored all the wood molding and baseboards. He installed new cabinets in the kitchen and spent weeks working on the old, wooden banister leading up to the second floor. In July 2005—one month before Katrina—he rounded up several friends to help him move furniture. He had finished work on the first level and was moving everything downstairs to start work on the second.

"Had I reversed it," McClendon said, "I would have saved just about everything." Instead five feet of floodwater sat in his home in the weeks after Katrina and he lost everything but a duffel bag of clothes. He had survived, unlike hundreds of his neighbors. But sitting alone in his lousy hotel room, he said, "I really felt like there was a personal vendetta against me."

McClendon put his name on the waiting list for a FEMA trailer. He jumped when after about six months the agency offered him a trailer in Slidell, more than thirty miles from his home. The first anniversary of Katrina came and passed before FEMA delivered a trailer to his property on Caffin. Home was now a three-hundred-square foot, white rectangle with water that never quite got hot enough, but he was back in the Lower Ninth, gutting his home. It felt like forward motion.

Still, sifting through the remains of his life, he couldn't help but feel sorry for himself. "What's it like to lose everything overnight?" he asked. "I can tell you." In a culture in which our possessions can define us, he continued, he had nothing. Only later, sitting in his bare office in a strange-shaped, multicolored building he dubbed the Lower 9th Ward Village Community Center, lighting up yet another Kool as executive director of the refuge he had created, could McClendon declare, "Katrina is the best thing to ever happen to me."

PEOPLE WORKING WITH COMMON GROUND, the volunteer group that Malik Rahim founded in the days after Katrina, posted hand-painted street signs around the community. That way at least they knew where they were when driving around the Lower Ninth. Confrontations over the city's aggressive demolition plans were now being fought in the courts rather than on people's front lawns. The Episcopals staked an important flag in the community around a year after Katrina when they sanctioned the Lower Ninth's first house of worship. The Church of All Souls first met in a parishioner's garage but soon moved into a building that had been used by a big discount drugstore chain. St. Walgreens, people called it, or the Walgreens church.

Brad Pitt started showing up in the Lower Ninth after Katrina. The star had first fallen in love with New Orleans while there in 1994 to work on *Interview with the Vampire: The Vampire Chronicles.* "Everything was sexy and sultry," he said. "I'd ride my bike all over the place, amazed by the architecture. I'd return to New Orleans every chance I could." He was in Calgary shooting a new Jesse James movie when Katrina hit, but a few weeks later he was in New York, attending the first Clinton Global Initiative. That proved all the inspiration this self-described "architecture junkie" needed. Pitt reached out to William McDonough, a leading voice in the sustainability movement, and teamed up with the group Global Green USA, which had already started doing work in the Lower Ninth. "There is a real opportunity here to lead the nation in a direction it needs to be going, and that is building efficiently," Pitt said at a press conference eleven months after Katrina. He put up $200,000 to fund an international design competition in search of architects that would help build environmentally friendly, storm-safe homes in the Lower Ninth.

The Dr. Martin Luther King Jr. Elementary School sat derelict on Claiborne Avenue, a half dozen blocks from the levee breach. The school had been deluged with so much water that dead fish were found on the second floor. King lost ten students in the flooding and twenty of its parents. A family of four lived a few blocks from the school, two honors students and parents active in the PTA. All four perished that day.

King Elementary was relatively new in the Lower Ninth—barely a decade old at the time of Katrina—yet it was beloved by parents. Even as 96 percent of its students qualified for a subsidized or free lunch, its kids scored well on standardized tests. A big reason for their success was Doris Hicks, a commanding black woman who had grown up in the neighborhood. Hicks had been the principal of King since the day it opened its doors.

Hicks was in Dallas after the storm. Her staff was scattered everywhere. They had been fired en masse after Katrina, but less than two months after the flood, a group of them started to meet. Hicks flew to New Orleans from Dallas once a month. A third-grade teacher named James Mack drove from Cincinnati. As a group, they were generally hostile to charter schools; before the storm, Hicks herself had declared them "the demise of public education." But their priority was reopening their school, and the new state-created Recovery School District made plain they looked more favorably on those claiming the charter banner. So the

Dr. Martin Luther King Jr. Charter School for Science and Technology was born. Hicks signed up 95 percent of her old staff and put Hilda Young in charge of the board of directors they formed. With more than thirty years with the Orleans Parish school district, Young had worked both as a principal and in the district's central office. Her job was to secure them the state certification they would need before they could open their doors. "The only school approved for a charter at the time without the help of an outside management group or nonprofit organization," wrote *Education Week*'s Lesli Maxwell. King received its certification in March 2006.

They had a building: their old elementary school on Claiborne. The question was what shape it was in. Not trusting the new Recovery School District to tell them, Hicks called someone she knew at the Washington Group, an engineering firm in Denver that did work in New Orleans and had established a relationship with King Elementary. "They send in a team of people, and a week and a half later, I have this detailed report," Hicks said. The building needed a lot of work, but the firm declared it structurally sound and worth saving. It didn't matter. The people who ran the Recovery School District deemed the building a hazard and ordered it razed. "Their attitude was 'The mayor is going to greenspace the neighborhood anyway,'" Hilda Young said. "That's when we realized they didn't want us to open." If they were going to save their school, they were going to have to do it themselves.

Two policemen were standing in front of the school on a March morning seven months after Katrina. That's how Hicks knew someone had tipped the district office off about their plans. A padlock was also on the school door. But Hicks, who stood more than six feet tall, wasn't backing down. She had her engineer's report and the support of Marlin Gusman, the parish's sheriff. Besides, she had lined up around 250 volunteers, most of them from Common Ground, and they had a job to do. "We just cut those big padlocks off all the doors," Hicks said. "And everybody got to work." The police would kick them out several times during the four days it took to gut the school, but the cleanup crews would simply wait an hour or two before sneaking back so they could continue their work.

The parents of nearly a thousand kids signed up to attend King in the fall of 2006. The old building on Claiborne wouldn't be ready for the new school year, but the district promised them a middle school in the Upper Ninth that had been shuttered even before the storm. The building would be ready by mid-August, district officials promised, which is when Hicks wanted to start classes. Closer to the date, the district told Hicks they would need to wait until September 7. Even then Hicks found a school with moldy walls and peeling paint. "The rodents were probably saying, 'You moving into our school?'" Hicks said. "They were running around like they owned the place."

King held its first day of classes on the school's front steps. "We broke kids into sections: kindergarten, first graders," Hicks said. "Teachers had lessons, gave homework. Hot breakfast every day, hot lunch. I wanted the world to see. We're ready to educate our children of color. But we seemed to be the only ones who cared about really doing that." A few days later, the district found them an alternative building—an elementary school Uptown that had suffered only modest roof damage, but in a majority-white neighborhood.

"We were very grateful," Hicks said. "We put letters in the mailboxes of all our neighbors, introducing ourselves and saying thank you for your hospitality. Everyone was very, very nice." The best news from her perspective was that the district now had ample reason to find King a more permanent home in what one school official delicately called a "more demographically suitable neighborhood." Education officials operating out of Baton Rouge put King on the priority list it shared with the Corps. Hicks and her people wouldn't spend even a full year Uptown before the district delivered them the keys to the old place on Claiborne, now painted yellow with purple trim. It looked even better than it did before the storm.

A FEW MONTHS AFTER she started working with Will Hood, Connie Uddo asked him to compare Lakeview to Iraq. She wanted to hear about people worse off than they were. Hood laughed and said there was no comparison. "You look so much worse," he said.

"Worse?" a startled Uddo asked.

"Connie, Iraq is a few bombed-out buildings. When we blow up a bridge in Iraq, we fix it. And guess what? I can skype from Iraq. Here you can't even get a freakin' phone line." That night she shared her exchange with Hood with her husband. She had conjured up the worst war zone her mind could imagine, but Mark told her of course Lakeview looked more battered than Fallujah or Tikrit. "I remember feeling sick to my stomach," she said. Nothing had changed, but she now felt overwhelmed.

Uddo already had the phone numbers for several tree cutters from her months running a Beacon of Hope out of her home. She knew whom to contact to haul away a flooded car. The challenge was gathering more numbers. "It's like a scavenger hunt after a disaster," Uddo said. "How do I get that tree off my roof? What do I do with my car? How do you make sure the mold doesn't come back? I hear there are all these volunteers, but where do I find them?" The advantage of the recovery center she was running was that she'd only need to answer each of those questions once. "We called ourselves the second responders," she said.

Uddo proved resourceful. People complained that living in a FEMA trailer or perched on a second floor meant they had no way to wash their clothes. So Uddo used a small part of her budget to create a laundry room in a double-wide in the church parking lot. She set up computers for visitors to use and made sure they had enough shovels, wheelbarrows, and other tools for both volunteers and homeowners needing to borrow them. She also came up with a solution to contractor fraud. "You had people coming into town, slapping a magnet [sign] on their car, and saying, 'Hi, I'm a contractor, give me thirty thousand dollars and I'll get started on your house,' and that's the last you'd hear from them." So Uddo started a version of Angie's List: plumbers, electricians, carpenters, and others who were bonded, certified, and endorsed by neighbors. Volunteers who wanted to help Lakeview called, but not if it meant sleeping on the ground in the Good News Camp. So Father Hood found her around twenty-five army cots, and they converted the upstairs of St. Paul's Homecoming Center into volunteer housing.

Uddo had plenty of help. Another five Beacons had opened across Lakeview. There was also Lakeview Civic and Freddy Yoder's army of block captains. "We counted everything," Yoder said. "Sunken streets. Recessed curbs. Manholes, catch basins, you name it. If there was any damage to the infrastructure of the community, we documented it." They'd meet every Thursday to plot the damage on grid maps of

Lakeview and prepare reports that Yoder would pass along to the city's Public Works Department.

Uddo also had the help of a woman everyone called Miss Rita—Rita Legrand. Legrand, seventy, and her husband, seventy-five, had moved back to Lakeview a few months after the Uddos, in April 2006. She helped Freddy Yoder organize the precinct-captain system and eventually took over Lakeview Civic's Blight committee. It was her job to police her fellow homeowners and go after those not taking care of their property.

The City Council had given communities a powerful tool when it passed, eight months after the storm, the Good Neighbor Plan. Under Good Neighbor, homeowners who had not gutted their home by the one-year anniversary of Katrina were technically in violation of the law. The bill was championed by Lakeview's representative on the City Council. "It's Good Neighbor that we used to pressure people into making a decision," Legrand said. Let other communities fret over the rights of the displaced and worry that their neighbors needed more time to repair a home. "I'd really push people," Legrand said. "I'd tell 'em, 'Fix it up or sell it, you have to make up your mind.'" And if they still failed to act, she'd invoke Good Neighbor. "We started going to City Hall and pushing to have hearings," Legrand said. "I'm very good at aggravating people when I have to."[5]

NEW ORLEANS SEEMED STALLED as 2006 turned into 2007. On the eighth floor of City Hall, where once the clerks were issuing four hundred residential building permits a day, now they were averaging maybe fifty. The determined pioneers who had either the money or the grit had moved home, but everyone else seemed to be in Baton Rouge or Houston or with relatives in Cincinnati or Phoenix. A second family moved back to Uddo's street a year after Katrina. But six months later, they were

---

5. The Nagin administration would quietly end its Good Neighbor program a year after it went into effect, citing a shortage of inspectors. At that point, there was a backlog of seventeen thousand citizen complaints that the city had yet to review.

still the only two families on their block. "You brought me here to help Lakeview rebuild," Uddo groused to Father Hood. "But instead I'm still spending all my time cleaning up."

Uddo used trees to lift people's spirits and perhaps her own. She knew little about landscaping so she turned to Al Petrie, who headed Lakeview Civic's beautification committee. Petrie used his connections in the oil and gas business to raise $75,000 to start a tree fund. Teams of volunteers did the planting, including around a dozen West Point cadets who spent their spring break in New Orleans. Crews started digging on upper Canal Street, planting live oaks, slash pines, bald cypress, and other trees. "People would honk their horn, they'd raise their fists out the window," Uddo said. "People would stop their car, get out, and cry. It meant a lot."

Meanwhile, Uddo and everyone else in flooded New Orleans struggled with the Road Home application process. "It took a master's degree to figure out the forms," Uddo said. She eventually convinced Road Home to send a counselor to her center once a week. "Every week we'd have a line out the door," she said. The better she got to know the Road Home representative, the more dispirited she would feel. "Policies are inconsistent," the woman confided in Uddo. "Every day something changes—and then you have some employees saying one thing and some saying something else."

People who had once struck Uddo as eager to move home were giving up. Even some of those who were back home seemed to be losing their nerve. "They'd tell me it was their neighbors that made them love Lakeview," Uddo said, "but now the only neighbors they have are the rats and possums and raccoons living in the blighted houses all around them."

THE ROAD HOME PROGRAM, as conceived, was simple. Road Home would make up the difference, up to $150,000, between the pre-storm worth of a home and the insurance payments people received. There were caveats. A homeowner who'd lived in a flood zone but failed to carry flood insurance was penalized. Those choosing to walk away from a property were sent a smaller check than those who committed to rebuilding. But for those rebuilding, the math was easy. If a couple received $220,000 in insurance payments for a home an assessor appraised at $300,000 prior to Katrina, they would receive a Road Home check for $80,000.

Blanco insisted that Rita victims be included in Road Home. "I'm governor," she said. "Am I going to say to people hit by Rita, 'You were in the wrong storm, sorry'?" She also decided to hire an outside firm to administer the program. "There was this constant chatter, this repetition that Louisiana is corrupt," Blanco said. She wouldn't give Washington more excuses for holding up the state's money. In June 2006, the state hired ICF International to decide how much each homeowner would get.[6]

The price tag for ICF's services was a staggering $900 million. That was more revenue than the company had booked in the previous four years combined. This consulting firm that boasted of the work it did for the federal government and global oil companies was based a thousand miles away in Virginia, explaining a travel budget of $19 million. A month before securing the Road Home deal, ICF filed to go public. So on top of everything else, the executives put in charge of what was being billed as the largest housing-recovery program in the country's history were distracted by an impending IPO. By summer 2006, more than 80,000 people had submitted a Road Home claim. By year's end, 123,000 had applied.

Every Road Home applicant was photographed and fingerprinted. ICF blamed the policy on the antifraud guidelines established by the LRA. Nagin brayed that the company was treating people like criminals. A state senator from Baton Rouge named Cleo Fields facetiously suggested that the company should take a DNA swab from every homeowner. The fingerprints were only an early safeguard in a process that Daniel Rothschild, a researcher with the Mercatus Center, a conservative policy group at George Mason University, found had fifty-seven steps, until ICF trimmed it to a forty-three-step process. ICF would demand documents that a drowned-out homeowner wouldn't reasonably be expected to have.

6. ICF was founded in 1969 as the Inner City Fund, a venture-capital firm whose mission was to finance inner-city businesses.

Everyone seemed to know someone who'd submitted a thick packet of supporting materials only to be told that ICF couldn't find it.

In November 2006, Cassandra Wall and a couple of her sisters took part in a protest in Baton Rouge to demand the state do better. Fifteen months after Katrina and six months after the company had taken charge of Road Home, ICF had disbursed all of $700,000 to eighteen homeowners. Blanco exacted a promise from ICF to inform at least ten thousand homeowners by month's end of the dollar amount they would be receiving. ICF did—and then sent out thousands of follow-up letters apologizing for informing an applicant of the wrong grant amount. "Road Home or Road Block?" the *New Orleans Tribune* asked on its cover that month.

In December, the legislature held hearings looking into Road Home. Only a paltry eighty-four homeowners had received a check. Legislators expressed their frustrations over a program that, from the outside, didn't seem complex. Verify that people are whom they claim to be and that they in fact owned the property they were claiming. Check with the assessor's office to see what a house was worth prior to the storm or use some of the hundreds of millions of dollars the state was paying the company to hire its own appraisers. The insurance payments could be confirmed by checking industry records. Both the House and Senate passed resolutions directing the governor to fire ICF International. The vote in the House was 97–1.

No one was more frustrated by Road Home than Charmaine Marchand, who for three days camped out on the capitol lawn to draw attention to her grievances. She lamented all the money the state could have saved—and the locals that could have been put to work—if the state had run the program out of its community development program. "Instead, ICF is flying its out-of-town people to Louisiana, racking up bills," Marchand said—and also boasting about all the money it would be making off Road Home in the documents it filed to go public. Blanco convinced Marchand to take down her tent by inviting her and other New Orleans legislators to the governor's mansion for a meeting with Michael Byrne, the former Homeland Security official ICF had put in charge of Road Home. "I share the frustrations of our people and the legislature, but common sense must prevail," Blanco said. "This isn't a time to start from scratch, which would make people wait even longer." Byrne vowed that they'd soon be sending out five hundred checks a day. Again ICF fell well short of its promises.

In February, California congresswoman Maxine Waters brought her Housing subcommittee to New Orleans for a hearing on Road Home. "I'm on the phone every day pushing for solutions," Blanco testified. At least the governor could reach someone with ICF. Others testified about their difficulties even reaching anyone connected with Road Home. A recorded message greeted callers with a promise to return any message within forty-eight hours—except Michael Byrne confessed that winter that ICF hadn't hired enough people to follow up on that promise.

Blanco was up for reelection that fall—November 2007. Smelling blood, Bobby Jindal declared his candidacy that January, setting up a rematch of their 2003 race. Two months later, Blanco gathered her staff together to tell them she wouldn't be running for reelection. "I am choosing to do what I believe to be best for the state," the governor declared in a televised address. She had already raised $3 million in campaign funds but polls showed her with only 35 percent of the vote in a head-to-head race with Jindal. "This may be the first time in history that a non-term-limited governor decided to step down rather than seek reelection," declared Pearson Cross, a political science professor at the University of Louisiana–Lafayette. The only comparison Cross could conjure up was LBJ's decision to drop out of the 1968 presidential race because of Vietnam.

In May, Mary Landrieu invited Connie Uddo to Washington to talk about Road Home at the Senate's ad hoc subcommittee on Disaster Recovery. Only 10 percent of the Road Home applicants had received a check but a top Blanco aide announced that Road Home was on pace to run out of money long before every eligible homeowner received a payment. I'm exhibit A of the problem confronting New Orleans twenty-one months after Katrina, Uddo told the senators. "I'm the cheerleader who keeps telling people to hang in there," she said. Yet even the captain of the pom-pom club confessed that she was wrestling with despair.

AT LEAST ONE SET of government functionaries were on the job: the bureaucrats in City Hall overseeing the list of condemned properties.

In July 2007, the city published so many thirty-day notices on homes deemed a "serious, imminent and continuing threat to the public health, safety, and welfare" that the list filled twenty-five pages in the *Times-Picayune*. "We don't want to demolish anything if the owner is taking action," a city attorney explained. "But the onus is on the property owner." Feeling frustrated by the constant delays, FEMA officials had told the city that the agency wouldn't pay the demolition costs for any home after August 29, 2007—the two-year anniversary of Katrina. Bulldozing a home and carting away the debris could cost anywhere between $6,000 and $10,000. City officials were determined to knock down as many as they could before the federal government's deadline.

The city kept one list. FEMA kept another: for the demolition crews it kept under contract. Getting your home off one didn't necessarily get it off both. IdaBelle Joshua was a seventy-nine-year-old, disabled widow temporarily living 150 miles from the two-story brick home she owned in the Lower Ninth Ward. Joshua had spent more than $5,000 gutting and cleaning her place. She even stopped by City Hall in early July, where two employees, she said, assured her that her house was safe. Yet two days later, a nephew phoned Joshua with bad news. He had stopped by to mow the lawn. The house was gone.

The *Wall Street Journal* told Joshua's story in a page-one article by Rick Brooks. The reporter seemed to have little trouble finding people shocked to learn their property was on a demolition list. A man named Michael DeZura told Brooks about a building he was fixing up. It would have been reduced to rubble, DeZura said, if a friend hadn't called him in Houston to let him know a city crew was disconnecting the utilities. Mary Harrison had already put a new roof on her home and had people working on the wiring and the plumbing when she heard from a neighbor that a demolition order had been slapped on her door. She spoke to people at City Hall and then phoned FEMA, but no one could help her. "They can't find me on the list to take me off," she said.

21

"YOU'LL SEE CRANES IN THE SKY"

He had no written contract. There was no job description. He didn't even have an official title, only that generic moniker the media gives anyone in a job like the one he was taking. Ed Blakely was the "recovery czar" no matter what it might say on any org chart.

The airport terminal looked like a morgue and smelled like one, too. That at least was Blakely's perception on that winter day in 2007 when he landed there to start his new job. The ride into town was "nauseating," he said. Again it was the stench. Eighteen months after Katrina, was it possible dead animals were still rotting in the streets? Sitting in the passenger seat of a city-issued SUV dispatched to pick him up, he saw piles of garbage everywhere. Abandoned autos were stacked in piles and tucked under overpasses. Passing City Hall, he noticed a neon sign with several burned-out letters: C TY H L. He shook his head and asked himself what it meant that he would be working somewhere people didn't have the good sense to kill the sign's switch until it was fixed.

The next day—Blakely's first on the job—began at Le Pavillon, where Nagin had reserved a corner table for them. Donning the red power tie that his wife had picked out for him, Blakely expected to talk strategy. At the least Blakely hoped they could settle on a job title. Instead Nagin brought along an aide and the three of them worked on a press release to announce Blakely's hiring. Their next stop was a City Hall press conference, where reporters pounded Blakely with questions about the recovery. Back in the mayor's office, Blakely called it a "rough and irritating start." Nagin told him to get used to it—and then "giggled uncontrollably," Blakely said, "like a schoolboy telling a dirty joke."

"No one offered to help me or show me around," Blakely complained. He found a vacant room with a desk and phone and claimed it. There was no invitation to lunch and none to dinner. That night, Blakely, who had lived most of his life in California, walked St. Charles Avenue in search of something to eat. Supper that night was a can of beans and a packet of rice. So much for southern hospitality, he thought to himself. Earlier that day, standing in front of the press gaggle and feeling "suddenly flushed and combative," he blurted out that the city would have a plan of action by year's end. Before going to bed on his first night as recovery czar, Blakely started on a list of questions. Atop the paper he wrote, "Who is responsible for this recovery?" Then he added a second question to his list: "What is the recovery plan?"

BLAKELY SEEMED THE IDEAL choice when Nagin decided he needed a recovery czar. Blakely is black—no small issue in a racialized fight. And he had the credentials. He had chaired the Department of City and Regional Planning at the University of California at Berkeley until taking over as dean of the management and urban-policy graduate program at the New School in New York. He had helped Oakland recover after the Loma Prieta earthquake in 1989 and had been appointed vice chair of the committee created to rebuild downtown Manhattan after September 11. Some criticized Nagin for failing to conduct a formal search before hiring Blakely, but even those lobbing that complaint allowed that it would have led to his office door.

Blakely described himself as reluctant to take the job. At sixty-eight, he had only recently taken a position at the University of Sydney, where he was teaching urban planning and running a planning research center. He and his wife were happy there, and he enjoyed the extra money he was earning as a consultant operating in a new corner of the globe. His wife told him he could take the job with two conditions. One was that he commit to a single year with an option for a second, subject to her approval. The other was that he keep his permanent visa, which required him to spend at least part of the year in Australia.

True to his word, Blakely made a ten-day visit to Australia within a few weeks of his start date. The media pounced, and he promised to stick around until his job was done, no matter how long it took. Within two months of arriving in New Orleans, Blakely had already broken one of his vows to his wife.

Blakely had imagined himself playing the role of a true recovery czar: the only person whose voice counted if the topic was rebuilding. Counterparts elsewhere in the bureaucracy had a different view. When he met with Louisiana officials, he demanded more control over New Orleans's share of federal money that passed through the state. They told him no but promised to work with him. More disheartening for Blakely were his meetings with the New Orleans Redevelopment Authority, or NORA, the body responsible for blighted or abandoned properties in the city. It would be up to *him* how they invested precious redevelopment dollars, Blakely announced the first time he sat down with NORA. Those with NORA countered that they had already chosen shovel-ready projects to finance, but Blakely held his ground. "There were perhaps five or six people" in the world capable of overseeing their recovery, he told them, and they were looking at one of them. Let him decide what they would fund, or he was flying home to Sydney.

The wise planner first expresses his love for a city before talking about everything that needs fixing. Blakely instead expressed contempt. In that first trip back to Australia he said of New Orleans, "We have an economy entirely made up of T-shirts. That is our major import and export." He described New Orleans as "a third-world country" in an interview with the *New York Times*, an "insular" place with battling racial factions that were "a bit like the Shiites and Sunnis." "It's a culture of domination rather than participation," he told the *Times'* Adam Nossiter. "So whatever group gets something, they try to dominate the whole turf." He had ideas for drawing newcomers to New Orleans, but he worried, he said, what they would think of the locals. "Who are these buffoons?" he imagined them asking.

Everyone seemed to have Ed Blakely stories. Sally Forman met him at a dinner party, where she introduced herself as the mayor's former communications director. "I know who you are," he told her. "You used to work for the *Times-Picayune*." Sally Forman had never worked at the *Times-Picayune* but Blakely was insistent. "I didn't know what to say so I just walked away," she said. Paul Beaulieu met Blakely when the recovery czar gave a talk to a group of black journalists. Blakely was talking about various neighborhoods but not Beaulieu's, so he asked about New Orleans East. "He acts all insulted, like how dare I question him," Beaulieu said. "I thought he was an arrogant little shit."

Yet New Orleans was starved for leadership. The Rockefeller Foundation's Carey Shea saw Blakely speak at a big citywide meeting not long after he had started in his new job. "He gives this incredibly ego-laden speech, saying, 'I'm your quarterback and I'm going to lead you and I'm going to be the one to save New Orleans,'" she said. "And I remember the person next to me saying, 'My God, we finally have a mayor.'

"For some the attitude toward Ed was, finally someone is in charge. It might have been Alexander Haig, but at least it was someone."

SHEA HAD HER OWN problems—making sure that UNOP's next big plenary session, Community Congress–II, was a success. Satellite centers were set up in schools and other facilities in Baton Rouge, Atlanta, Houston, and Dallas. Letters were sent to 120,000 displaced New Orleanians, who were promised transportation, child care, and food. Breakfast and lunch would include vegan options. Spanish translators were hired, as were Vietnamese. They would try reaching football fans by hosting a party in Atlanta for anyone wanting to watch the Saints play the Falcons. Admission was a promise to show up at the local satellite center the next weekend.

The price tag for Community Congress–II was steep at $2.4 million, but Shea saw it as money well spent. About a thousand people showed up at the New Orleans Convention Center on a sunny Saturday sixteen months after Katrina. Another fifteen hundred were linked to New Orleans via giant television screens. ("Say hello, Houston!") Half the participants had an annual household income under $40,000, and 63 percent were black. AmericaSpeaks's instant voting system showed that 45 percent of the people supported a policy that let homeowners in the low-lying neighborhoods do as they saw fit, but 42 percent said they "strongly supported" an arrangement that would let people swap lots and rebuild in clusters. Fifty-nine percent of the people also agreed that for the city to come back, there needed to be a strategy for helping renters back to the city.

There would be more meetings. A Community Congress–III drew 450 people to the Convention Center and another 800 people at the satellite sites. "We will codify all your hard work into the law of the land," the mayor assured participants. Another speaker laid out a program he called Elevate New Orleans, which would help neighbors cluster on higher ground. A consensus was forming around a few core ideas, UNOP's Troy Henry assured everyone. Henry was a local consultant, black, hired to coordinate the findings of the 150-plus professionals enlisted to figure out everything from hospital-bed ratios to flood patterns. People favored a plan that treated every neighborhood the same, Henry said. A majority also believed the authorities needed to do a lot more to bring people home.

UNOP had created layers of sector captains, district leaders, and community-support people. Some among them thought it would be destructive to bring up issues such as flood risks and repopulation rates at the big community meetings. Others thought it would be irresponsible not to. They agreed to mention these touchy issues at the big plenary sessions but not center discussion around them. An artful compromise was reached by those writing the UNOP plan: "Every citizen . . . has the right to return to New Orleans," but people also have "a right to return to a safer, smarter, stronger city."

Yet even submission of a final plan in February 2007 didn't end the planning process. Four months passed before the City Planning Committee gave its approval of a 510-page report UNOP had labeled a *Citywide Strategic Recovery and Rebuilding Plan*. Another month passed before the City Council gave its endorsement. Not until June 2007—nearly two years after Katrina—could the city deliver the plan Washington and

Baton Rouge demanded before they would liberate some of the recovery dollars the city so desperately needed.

ONLY JOE CANIZARO SAID yes when a lawyer named Jeff Thomas offered his services free to members of the Bring New Orleans Back Commission. Thomas couldn't blame the others for ignoring him. He was a former biology teacher from Pennsylvania who had spent a few years in Washington, DC, working for a government watchdog group. He'd only arrived in New Orleans in 1998, to start Tulane Law. At the time of Katrina, he was an associate at a small firm whose only credential was a desire to better understand the arcane rules governing a disaster. "Right away I got up to speed on the Stafford Act and HUD enabling legislation," Thomas said.

Thomas also read what he could about communities that had endured a major disaster. Everyone seemed to be banking on political influence, but Thomas concluded that it would make little difference who might be friends with the president. The bureaucracy had its fixed way of doing things, and so more important than Joe Canizaro or Boysie Bollinger were people able to master the language and arcane procedures of the relevant federal agencies. Thomas wrote a white paper on the need for a city recovery office staffed with people who understood the nuances of administrative law, but it was roundly ignored until Blakely offered him a job in City Hall. He would be part of the small team charged with taking the city's recovery plan and, as he put it, "fitting it into a framework that would make people in Washington happy."

UNOP was putting the final touches on its report at around the time Thomas started working for the city. He saw utility in a plan that set out a basic vision for New Orleans. The intense citizen involvement would give anything they produced legitimacy in the eyes of the bureaucracy. But he shook his head as he paged through plans that struck him as more a wish list than a strategic rebuilding plan. Whether it was UNOP's plan or Lambert's or the vestiges of what Canizaro had proposed, in each case the assumption seemed to be that the city would have unlimited funds to rebuild. "No one had had that basic conversation about how money would be an issue and they needed to set priorities," he said.

For Thomas and others working in Blakely's office, the job would mainly be about managing expectations. The Bush administration was claiming the federal government had already committed more than $100 billion to the Gulf Coast, but that included the $16 billion in claims the national flood insurance program would pay to policyholders and also the tens of billions spent on the rescue and temporary housing. New Orleans was in line to receive billions in FEMA "public assistance dollars," but that money could only be spent fixing public assets (a library, a fire station, a sewer line) damaged by the storm.[1] Only around a few hundred million dollars would be made available to the city to spend as it wanted. This was community disaster money from HUD, the coveted "flex money" that allows a community to think outside the constricting silos created by bureaucrats. All those plans to reimagine streetscapes, build parks, attract greengrocers to food deserts, and otherwise transform wrecked neighborhoods would need to be funded primarily through this one pot of money.

Introducing a dose of realism into the process was the aim of the press conference Blakely, less than three months into the job, held at the end of March. He wouldn't and couldn't try to fix the entire city at once, Blakely said. Instead he identified seventeen commercial corridors around New Orleans—"nodes"—that would be his focus, at least in this first phase of his tenure. Some would be in the most damaged parts of the city, but others would be in parts of New Orleans that had taken on no water because, he said, small improvements there could leverage greater investment in the city. The Lower Ninth and New Orleans East

---

1. FEMA had proven more flexible in recent years over the spending of its public assistance dollars. If, say, a municipality wanted to merge two firehouses into one, FEMA was open to letting locals do that, but those discussions, Thomas said, should have started a few months after Katrina. "By the time we all got there, a list of hundreds of public assets were already in process to be funded for rebuilding," Thomas said. "It wasn't impossible to reverse course on any single project, but doing so would be time-consuming and further delay the money when people were already fed up with waiting. We were playing catch-up from the moment we arrived."

were in line for $145 million of redevelopment money. Lakeview would receive a commensurate share. "It's not big, and I hope you guys put that message in the paper," Blakely said. He warned that theirs might be a fifteen-year recovery.

The "first decisive plan from City Hall," the *Times-Picayune* declared on its front page. Members of the City Council quoted on the subject said that they were pleased. It was an impressive early effort from a man who had made so poor a first impression—at least until reporters started peppering him with questions ("Mr. Blakely, what would you tell people who've already invested their life savings in a community not included on your list?") During the question-and-answer phase he blurted out, "You'll see cranes in the sky by September." That promise led the news that night, not the modesty of his plan. "It was a totally unrealistic promise," Thomas said, but also about the only thing people would remember of Blakely's plans in the coming months.

THE SUBJECT COULDN'T HAVE been more obtuse when Senator Barack Obama addressed a mostly black audience at Hampton University, a historically black college in Virginia. In June 2007, four months after Obama announced he was running for president and nearly two years after Katrina, Obama brought up a provision of the Stafford Act that requires locales to match 10 percent of federal disaster money.

"Now here's the thing," Obama said. "When 9/11 happened in New York City, they waived the Stafford Act—said, 'This is too serious a problem. We can't expect New York City to rebuild on its own. Forget that dollar you got to put in. Here's ten dollars.' And that was the right thing to do.

"When Hurricane Andrew struck in Florida, people said, 'Look at this devastation. We don't expect you to come up with your own money. Here's the money to rebuild. We're not going to wait for you to scratch it together—because you're part of the American family.'"

Katrina was different, though. Despite pleas from local officials, the Bush administration had been reluctant to do the same with Katrina money. "What's happening down in New Orleans?" Obama continued. "There the feds were asking, 'Where's your dollar? Where's your

Stafford Act money?' Makes no sense. Tells me that somehow, the people down in New Orleans, they don't care about as much.'"[2] Obama
would be accused by conservative commentators of "whipping up race
hatred and fear."

WHEN INSIDERS SPOKE ABOUT the city's next mayor, one name came up
more than others: Oliver Thomas. Even George Bush could be counted
as a Thomas admirer. That, at least, is the way Karl Rove told it in his
memoir. The president attended a meeting of local leaders in March
2007, where he spoke with Thomas. "Afterward, Bush remarked it was
good that at least one New Orleans official had his head on straight and
his focus right," Rove said.

The same storm that shrank so many elected officials had the opposite effect on Thomas. The storm enlarged him. This son of the Lower
Ninth had slept in his fourth-floor office in City Hall the night of Katrina. He then spent much of the next week out on the boats, pulling
people out of the water. At night he camped out on the second floor
of his flooded home. A constant presence in those early months after
Katrina, a baseball cap on his head and a smile usually on his face, this
large man with a soft voice and appetite for people called to mind Bill
Clinton. His public persona was the everyman who seemed as adept at
charming the aging Uptown doyenne ("You're getting younger and more
beautiful every day") as reaching young toughs in the hood. Around a
year after Katrina, he held a press conference calling on the housing
authority to fix up its buildings rather than tear them down, but then
added that they should limit the tenants to people willing to work. "If
your legs don't hurt, you can walk somewhere," he said. "If your arms
don't hurt, you can pick something up." He consistently polled above
40 percent with whites and double that with blacks.

Then, a couple of weeks before Katrina's second anniversary, a

---

2. The 10 percent match would be waived that same year under the new Democrat-
   controlled Congress, which passed legislation wiping away the obligation; the president then signed it into law.

contrite Thomas appeared on television, apologizing for taking nearly $20,000 in bribes.

People wanted to believe the best of Thomas. His home had flooded after Katrina, he was the tireless advocate in an all-consuming job that paid $40,000 a year. Yet the truth was far more prosaic. He struggled with a gambling problem, and several years before Katrina he had taken payoffs from a black businessman worried he would lose his parking contracts with the city after Ray Nagin took office. Thomas saved his constituents the expense and the bitter taste of a drawn-out legal process by pleading guilty and relinquishing his seat after thirteen years on the council. "I cannot begin to describe the anguish I feel for disappointing you," Thomas said through tears after entering his guilty plea in a federal courtroom. "You trusted me, and I have placed that trust in question. You have every right to be angry and suspicious. I am deeply sorry." The judge sentenced him to thirty-seven months in prison.

THE CITY COMMEMORATED THE second anniversary of Katrina much as it did the first. Nagin rang a bell at precisely 9:38 a.m., and again he welcomed the president to New Orleans. For the second year in a row, Bush visited a newly christened charter school—this time Doris Hicks's school in the Lower Ninth. The night before, the president dined at Dooky Chase's, a favorite for the city's black political class. For once Bush would be in New Orleans and not be on the defensive. The president had signed legislation authorizing the Corps to spend another $7 billion improving the levee system. He was about to sign a second bill that would free up another $3 billion for Road Home, bringing its price tag to $10.5 billion.

New Orleans had more good news that summer. The US census estimated that 288,000 people were living in New Orleans two years after Katrina—up significantly compared to 170,000 twelve months earlier. About half the Road Home applicants had received a check from the government, and the city's sales tax revenues were approaching pre-Katrina levels. But as always, any number of reminders remained that the city was still far from recovery. New Orleans still had two-thirds fewer hospital beds and corresponding long waits at the hospitals in the surrounding parishes. "I've been telling people, 'Don't bring your parents back if they are sick,'" said a Mid-City doctor who'd moved his practice to the suburbs. The city had two-thirds fewer day-care centers. Even the population numbers were deceptive given all the planners, relief workers, and other do-gooders temporarily calling the city home. About 200,000 of the city's pre-Katrina population of 455,000 were still living someplace other than New Orleans.

Roughly forty-five thousand families made homeless by Katrina or Rita were still living someplace courtesy of the American taxpayer. Most had found an apartment, but thirteen thousand families were still living in a FEMA camp. The one in Convent, Louisiana (population seven hundred), was called Sugar Hill, a mobile-home park "wedged amid the refineries and cane fields," according to the *New York Times'* Shaila Dewan, who traveled there for an article about the dispossessed published two years after the storm.

At Sugar Hill, Dewan found Cindy Cole. Pre-storm, Cole had been paying $275 in the Lower Ninth for a two-bedroom house next to her mother's and across the street from her aunt's. Two years after the storm, Cole and her three small kids were living somewhere with no playground and a grocery store that was miles away. Her aunt was also staying there and looked after her kids when she got a job at a Jack in the Box, but neither woman owned a car. After Cole lost her ride to work, she had to quit. Her hometown of New Orleans was desperate for cheap labor, but Cole had no savings and therefore had no way of escaping Sugar Hill. "We in storage," said Cole's aunt, Ann Picard, of their bleak life stranded an hour west of New Orleans.

22

EIGHT FEET ACROSS

Police in New Orleans were quitting at a rate of seventeen per month in 2007. The turnover rate in the DA's office hovered at around 30 percent a year. In Louisiana, the law dictated that a prosecutor secure an indictment within sixty days of a felony arrest or that person walked. Before Katrina, the DA might lose two hundred suspects a year that way. After Katrina, the DA's budget had been slashed 20 percent and that number reached one thousand.

Relations had never been good between the police and Eddie Jordan, New Orleans's first black district attorney. But when his office indicted seven policemen in the Danziger Bridge case, hostilities between the police and the top prosecutors broke out into the open. Claiming his office could not track down a key witness, Jordan released a suspect in the shooting that had left five teens dead. A few days later, the police held a press conference to present the witness that the DA's office claimed couldn't be found.

Jordan resigned as DA in the fall 2007, early in his second term, not because of his office's abysmal conviction rate or the stresses of the job. Long before Katrina, in 2003, Jordan had boldly taken over the DA's office after the twenty-nine-year reign of Harry Connick Sr. (yes, father of *that* Harry Connick). Jordan was the US Attorney who took down former Louisiana governor Ed Edwards on racketeering charges and busted a criminal gang thought to be responsible for dozens of murders. Within a few weeks of taking office, he fired forty-three holdovers from Connick's office, all but one of them white, as the city would learn after the fired attorneys filed a race-discrimination suit. A jury found in their favor and Jordan's office was facing a fine in excess of $3 million. Jordan appealed the ruling, lost, and resigned two months later, in October 2007.

Bobby Jindal was elected governor that fall. What might have been a close race before Katrina was distorted by a missing sixty thousand black voters in New Orleans—more than Blanco's margin of victory in 2003. Bigger names on the Democratic side such as John Breaux, the former congressman, bowed out of the race rather than take on a thirty-six-year-old wunderkind. Jindal's only misstep on a path that had him aiming for the White House seemed the personal essay he wrote as a young associate with McKinsey & Company and debating between acceptances to Harvard Medical School and Yale Law. The piece, published in a small religious journal called the *New Oxford Review*, detailed the high school crush that caused him to convert to Catholicism and the exorcism he said he witnessed in college.

"Very, very conservative," a political consultant who did work for Jindal said of his former client. "And very, very ambitious." He could have added tireless, which is what many Louisianans seemed to care about most a couple of years after Katrina. Jindal won with 54 percent of the vote, making him the country's first Indian-American governor. Celebrations were reported in Jindal's ancestral home back in India, but not in New Orleans. Still a long way from recovery, the city was looking at four years and probably eight of a governor slashing state funding to fulfill a promise to cut taxes.

That fall saw the revival of the city's black radio station, WBOK. The station had been another casualty of Katrina until a wealthy benefactor hired longtime journalist Paul Beaulieu as his general manager and revived it. Signs posted around town read THE WBOK IS BACK AND TALKING BLACK! The station's first day on the air was less than two weeks after Jindal's victory and a few days after Jordan's resignation. Already

Beaulieu (pronounced Bool-yay), who hosted the afternoon drive-time slot, was talking about what he called "the big takeaway." Beaulieu, with a voice that sounded as if he gargled with concrete, spoke of the peaceful coexistence that had lasted between black and white for years. Of the city's business elite, he told listeners, "Their attitude was 'We've got ours, we run downtown and the hotels and the restaurants.' They were happy to let us have our political piece." But no longer. "What I see happening here is an attempted takeover."

There was no shortage of topics to fill the air. "The rebuilding effort has the potential to sustain hundreds of local, black-owned firms for decades to come, some experts predict," the *Tribune* had written a few months after the storm. Yet two years after Katrina, only a small fraction of disaster dollars seemed to be ending up in the hands of black-owned firms.[1] Road Home was another regular topic. In Lakeview, people were upset over the long wait for a Road Home check. But in other parts of the city, they were angered as well by how the numbers were calculated. People in New Orleans East, Gentilly, and the Lower Ninth would also have to wait, but then the check they received was likely to leave them well short of the cost of rebuilding. The residents of older, lower-income black communities faced another hurdle with the Road Home bureaucracy. Some were living in a home passed down from a grandparent or a favorite aunt. Often no legal trail existed to prove someone owned a home, just his or her word and land records that had washed away with the storm. Road Home had been designed for a middle-class population, not people on the economic fringe.

In the pages of the *Tribune*, Beverly McKenna decried what she called the "built-in bias" of a Road Home program that put more money in the hands of a couple from Lakeview than New Orleans East. "Barriers erected to make it harder for people to get back," McKenna said.

---

1. Congress and the Bush administration eased affirmative action rules immediately after Katrina, ostensibly to speed up the recovery. As a result, only around 1.5 percent of the earliest recovery contracts went to a minority-owned business, the Government Accountability Office found, or less than a third of the 5 percent normally required.

"People willing to preserve your music and your culture but it's the rest of you they don't want." Shortly after Eddie Jordan stepped down, McKenna put a to-do list on the cover of the *Tribune*. A fat red check mark was next to "Get rid of D.A. Eddie Jordan." Check marks were next to other items ("Take over public schools"), but empty boxes next to another seven. "Toss out notion of one White and one Black Council At-Large seat," one of the undone items read. "Demolish public housing," read another. She would put the same list on the cover six months later, this time with several more items checked off.

FIVE OF THE CITY'S seven council seats were filled through district elections. The most prized seats were the two at-large seats, chosen through a citywide election. The top vote getter in the at-large contest serves as council president. Theoretically, in a majority black city, both at-large slots could be filled by an African American. But in a compromise reached years earlier, one had been designated the unofficial black at-large seat and the other the unofficial white one.

Oliver Thomas filled the so-called black at-large seat at the time of Katrina. A woman named Jackie Clarkson was the white at-large council member. When Nagin first proposed setting up FEMA trailer sites around the city, Clarkson had led the council opposition against the plan. In the spring of 2006, in the same election that saw Nagin defeat Landrieu, Clarkson lost her seat to Arnie Fielkow, who is also white. Fielkow had worked for the New Orleans Saints but had been fired shortly after Katrina because he wouldn't quietly support an owner contemplating moving the team to another city. Fielkow bested Thomas's vote total that election and took over as council president. In that same election, a local white lawyer named Stacy Head ousted a black incumbent in a majority-black district that hadn't had a Caucasian representative in more than thirty years.[2]

---

2. The incumbent, Renée Gill Pratt, was later sentenced to four years in federal prison for siphoning off hundreds of thousands of dollars earmarked for charitable and educational programs.

The special election to replace a sentenced Thomas was held that November. "As long as it was a black majority, it was, 'Let's share power, there'll be one black at-large seat, one white,'" Beverly McKenna said. One of the two Cynthias, Cynthia Willard-Lewis, who represented the Lower Ninth and parts of New Orleans East, announced that she was running for the open seat. So did Jackie Clarkson, who saw in Thomas's resignation a chance to rejoin the council. Black voter turnout was about half what it had been in the 2006 election. Clarkson defeated Willard-Lewis by fewer than three thousand votes. For the first time in more than twenty years, the city now had a majority-white City Council.

The public housing fight ended shortly after the Willard-Lewis defeat. Protesters descended on City Hall just before Christmas 2007 to watch the City Council weigh in on the federal government's decision to tear down the Big Four projects and replace them with mixed-income housing. (Nagin had already signed off on the deal.) When the seats in the council chamber filled, the police barred more people from getting inside. Demonstrators tried pushing through an iron gate, and the police responded with pepper spray and Tasers. Inside the chambers, scuffles broke out between police and some of the more aggressive protesters, with more clashes in the hallway. More than a dozen people were arrested.

Inside the chambers, the council unanimously voted to raze all four developments. After the vote, Stacy Head blew kisses to angry protesters still milling about the chamber. "A mistake," Head later admitted.

WHAT WERE FEDERAL BUREAUCRATS to do when they needed to house so many people all at once? The majority of the 145,000 emergency units FEMA ordered just after Katrina weren't the larger mobile homes they would normally use after a disaster but less sturdy structures the agency called travel trailers. "Quality suffered dramatically because of the drive and pressure to put these trailers out," Terry Sloan, a floor supervisor with one FEMA-selected manufacturer, Gulf Stream Coach, told CBS News nearly two years after Katrina. Cheaper wood products were used in these no-frills metal boxes, the ventilation was poor, and the floors and the cabinets were treated with formaldehyde, which let off toxic fumes in hot, humid conditions. Formaldehyde is a known carcinogen that aggravates respiratory ailments, and some studies have linked it to leukemia.

Open the windows, FEMA recommended to those living in one of its travel trailers. At that point, there were more than twenty thousand FEMA trailers in New Orleans. Use the air-conditioning. FEMA assured people that the trailers posed no serious health risk—at least until February 2008, when the agency announced that tests showed trailers in the Gulf Coast emitting as much as five times the formaldehyde levels that the Centers for Disease Control deemed safe. Two and a half years after Katrina, FEMA declared the units unsuitable as long-term housing. The agency swapped in replacement units and spent $10 million a month on storage and maintenance until the bosses in Washington could decide what to do with the tainted trailers.

BY 2007, BRAD PITT was spending a lot of time in the Lower Ninth. He and Angelina Jolie had bought a home in the Quarter at the start of the year, paying $3.5 million for a six-bedroom, five-bath property that included a private courtyard and a separate, two-story guesthouse. Then Pitt went about the hard work of winning community support for the houses he had in mind. The famous actor was there in a church rec room when people gathered to talk about the community's future, sitting in a wobbly metal chair and drinking the same bad coffee as everyone else. Locals were happy to embrace Pitt—as long as he ceded to their demand that he build not in the Holy Cross community, as originally planned, but in that part of the Lower Ninth closest to the levee breach, where there were few houses still standing. "People there were so worried about condos or casinos or Donald Trump coming in even though it wasn't clear that Donald Trump or anyone else wanted them, they scared away developers," said the head of a nonprofit that looked at constructing houses in the Lower Ninth. "Brad Pitt was pretty much the only person who could do anything significant there. He was so rich and so good looking and determined that they weren't able to drive him away."

At that year's Clinton Global Initiative in New York City, Pitt announced his intention to build at least 150 storm-safe, environmentally correct homes in the hardest-hit portion of the Lower Ninth Ward.

Pitt wrote a check for $5 million to an organization he called Make It Right, as did Steve Bing, a film producer who had reportedly inherited $600 million from a grandfather who had made his fortune in real estate. Pitt asked his well-heeled audience to match the $10 million that he and Bing had committed.

Pitt filled in some of the details a few days later in an interview with the *Times-Picayune*. He estimated that each home would cost between $100,000 and $174,000 but the typical buyer wouldn't pay anywhere near that amount. Anyone owning a home in the Lower Ninth at the time of Katrina was eligible for a Make It Right home. They only needed to turn over any insurance or Road Home money they received and no person would pay more than 30 percent of his or her monthly income on the mortgage. The houses would all be built north of Claiborne in the few blocks closest to the levee breach, which had a lot more empty cement slabs than intact houses. Over the coming weeks, Pitt would borrow from the artist Christo to give people a more visual sense of what he had in mind. Anyone crossing over the Claiborne bridge into the Lower Ninth near the end of 2007 saw clusters of hot-pink homes. "Not real houses," wrote the MTV reporter who flew to New Orleans to interview Pitt, "but something akin to life-size Monopoly houses, which serve as placeholders." Pitt went on the *Today* show to talk about his plans, as well as *Entertainment Tonight* and *Larry King Live*. King several times gave viewers the URL for Make It Right.

"We're trying to send people to the website . . . to get families into homes by the end of summer," Pitt told King. "We need America to come together like they did directly after the storm and help the families here meet that financing gap to build properly, to build safely. . . . We're asking for foundations, for community groups, church groups."

LEN RIGGIO, THE CHAIRMAN of Barnes & Noble, also wanted to help rebuild homes in New Orleans. He, too, wanted to create energy-efficient homes elevated above the floodplain. He and his wife, Louise, wrote a $20 million check from their family foundation to create what they called Project Home Again.

Riggio hired Carey Shea, the Rockefeller Foundation's eyes and ears in the UNOP process, as executive director of Home Again. Like Pitt, Riggio, who lived in New York and Palm Beach, figured he would focus his efforts on the Lower Ninth Ward. Shea convinced him to build someplace else. Investing in the Lower Ninth was like focusing on the South Bronx in the 1970s and 1980s, she told him; the need there was great, but that was true of other parts of the city as well. In February 2008, Riggio held a press conference in Gentilly, the working-class black neighborhood where he promised to rebuild 120 homes. A resident would be handed the keys to a fully furnished rehabbed home in exchange for the deed to their flooded house. The home was theirs free and clear as long as they lived there at least five years. Lucky Gentilly residents were chosen through a lottery. In the coming months, Riggio would receive a fraction of the press attention as Pitt, but then, he was the public face of a bookstore chain, not a movie star, and he chose to help a less mediagenic community.

SEPTEMBER 2007 CAME AND went with no cranes in the sky. What Blakely produced instead was a more detailed list of the projects his office would champion. At a press event that month, Blakely was still focused mainly on the seventeen targeted "recovery zones." He unveiled 167 smaller projects in the targeted areas that his team had culled from UNOP and the other planning efforts.[3] They included after-school centers and health clinics and also the reopening of Methodist Hospital in New Orleans East and the restoration of the Pontchartrain Park golf course in Gentilly. FEMA had identified more than eight hundred public assets—police stations, various properties owned by the RTA, badly damaged streets—that it promised to restore to their pre-Katrina condition, but three dozen of those on Blakely's list were in need of more than a simple repair. Blakely also announced several larger projects, including a new biomedical hospital complex that business leaders hoped would

---

3. "He used the plan to get the money—and then crapped all of our work and decided to create his own," said Troy Henry, a local black businessman who was central to the writing of the UNOP report. "He tells people, 'Congratulations if you live in one of these seventeen recovery zones but if not, good luck because you're on your own.'"

establish the New Orleans area as a center of biomed research. The challenge would be to find the money to pay for it all.

A few months after Katrina, the federal government announced low-interest loans for businesses willing to build in the Gulf Coast region. These Gulf Opportunity Zone Bonds could possibly be used to help fund at least a few of Blakely's proposed projects. But most everything the city had in mind would need to be funded with HUD "flex money" distributed by the state. "HUD basically tells the state, 'Here's the money, here are our rules, and by the way, we'll audit everything to make sure you do it right,'" said Jeff Thomas in Blakely's office. The state set aside $1.1 billion in flex money for the parishes suffering damage from Katrina or Rita. New Orleans's share would be just over $400 million—not nearly enough to cover even this more modest assortment of city improvements.

Funding even a single project would prove an endurance test. That much became clear to Blakely and his staff after they submitted to Baton Rouge their list of projects they wanted funded. A month later, a consultant working for the state sent them a flow chart laying out the steps required to secure HUD money. It measured eight feet across. "It took us six months just to get two feet," Thomas said. Battles within City Hall also needed to be waged. "We were just this little group of thinkers in the corner coming up with nifty ideas," Thomas said. "Everything we did had to be blessed by these other departments."

The biomedical center proved the most controversial item on Blakely's list. Maybe building a hospital complex on the edge of downtown would establish New Orleans as a center of biomedical research, maybe it wouldn't, but if Blakely's plan was successful, it would mean the city would no longer have a public hospital. This "anchor for the city's economic recovery," as Blakely sold it to Nagin, was slated to cost more than $1 billion to build. For Blakely's idea to work, the city would need the money the state would be receiving to rebuild or replace Charity Hospital. They would need, too, money the federal government planned to spend refurbishing the city's VA hospital, which was badly damaged in the storm. Federal officials were on board with a proposal that had them building a hospital on the same site as the state's so long as the city found a suitable property. State officials also signed off on the deal. Callers to WBOK had been urging the mayor to demand that the state refurbish

Charity. Instead the city was plotting a new facility that guaranteed that the old hospital would never reopen.

The disenchantment of the activist set deepened as the plan took shape. Blakely ceded control of parts of the project to the state because the state had stronger eminent domain authority than the city. The site the city chose to build the twin hospitals was a neighborhood just east of downtown that had suffered only mild flooding and was coming back a lot faster than most. Many homeowners there had restored their homes or were doing so when the city unveiled its plans. The city needed sixty-seven acres to build the two hospitals, which meant tearing down or moving 250 homes, 150 of which had been deemed "historically significant" by the National Trust for Historic Preservation. Several blocks heading east-west were permanently closed off to traffic, as were several blocks going north-south. When the Department of Veterans Affairs threatened to pull out of the deal and build outside the city, Blakely promised them $75 million in HUD disaster money to offset their construction costs—one-fifth of the city's precious flex dollars. The price spiraled from $1.2 billion to nearly $2 billion, by which time the naysayers had renamed the project the Tajmahospital.

WHERE WAS NAGIN? THE *Tribune*'s Janet Stanton even ran a joke column asking that question. Was the mayor suffering post-traumatic stress disorder? "Was he bored with the job?" Stanton asked. "Ready to throw in the towel? Mortally wounded during battle by those he considered friends?" Talking to people around Nagin, she tried to suss out what might be going on, but "even the mayor's most ardent supporters dropped their eyes and shrugged."

Nagin's greatest attribute was that he looked the part of mayor. Even in the early months after Katrina, Nagin seemed to glide through the city, flashing a smile for the cameras, reassuring people. Yet now Blakely was the front man everyone saw on television and quoted in the news. One of the few glimpses of Nagin midway through his second term was that of a mayor angry at the media. He threatened to "coldcock" the news director of the local CBS affiliate over the station's demand that the mayor produce a copy of his work schedule. By the start of 2008—with more than two years left in his term—he was granting few interviews to local media.

But Nagin didn't entirely disappear. In February, the mayor and Chief Riley were together for a photo op showing off $1 million in guns and other equipment the city had secured to fight against soaring crime. Joking around, Nagin picked up one of the assault rifles and aimed it at his chief. The next day, the mayor's press office sent out an angry release arguing that Nagin had merely been lowering the gun when a *Times-Picayune* photographer snapped the shot appearing in that morning's newspaper. That May, Nagin mentioned a homeless encampment near City Hall during a welcome speech he delivered at the Convention Center. The real solution to homelessness in the city, he joked, would be "some bus tickets . . . one way." Another time he suggested that a murder rate that was tops in the nation wasn't all bad because it "helps keep the New Orleans brand out there."

Ed Blakely said he felt as though he were working inside a "cocoon"— and a tense, unpleasant one at that. "Black people have a hard time taking instruction from white people," Blakely said. "It's really bad. I've never encountered anything like this."

RAY NAGIN'S POLICE GUARD sat outside a private dining room at Antoine's in the French Quarter. Two years into the mayor's second term, he had asked his old ally, Bill Hines, to meet him for dinner. Occasionally, a waiter would need to enter the room, but otherwise, it was just Hines and the mayor in a room that would more comfortably seat twenty. "It was almost like we were getting together as old friends to clear the air about this thing that happened between us," Hines said. "He got off his chest how the white business community deserted him and how that made him feel."

The two spoke for something like two hours. "I could say he was almost Richard Nixon–like, in a bunker, sharing all these resentments," Hines said. The two shook hands at the end of what Hines described as a "very strange dinner" and would never speak again.

NAGIN AT LEAST HAD his family. Seletha and Tianna, his daughter, were still in Dallas, as best anyone could tell, but his sons were in New

Orleans. Eight months before Katrina, Jeremy and Jarin had founded Stone Age, a home-improvement company focused on granite and marble kitchen-countertop installations. Nagin had put up the seed money and figured he'd be a passive investor. But that was before Katrina turned a modestly interesting idea into a potentially lucrative one. Half the city needed new countertops—and Stone Age's strategy was to establish itself as the go-to countertop installer for one of the big-box retailers in town.

"Like any father," Nagin said, "I wanted to help my sons." And also help himself. His parents, Nagin's son Jeremy said, "have invested a significant amount of our family net worth and taken on major debt to put this company in position for growth."

Stacy Head, the newly elected member of the council, gave Nagin a chance to make himself invaluable to Home Depot. At the end of 2006, the company announced its intentions to build a new store in Central City in Head's district. Home Depot would bring two hundred jobs to a desolate part of town, but it needed the city's permission to block off several streets. Eager to please her new constituents, Head proposed a "community benefits agreement": the store could have its zoning changes in exchange for a $12.50-an-hour minimum wage and a promise to hire from the neighborhood, among other concessions.

Ray Nagin phoned Home Depot CEO Frank Blake. "I got a voice mail from Mayor Nagin saying that he understands we have a problem with a neighborhood group and asking whether we need his assistance," a baffled Blake wrote to Kent Knutson, the company's chief lobbyist. "Do you know what this is about?"

"Most likely, it's about Nagin's son's desire to be a vendor," Knutson wrote back, "and install kitchens/countertops for us using a company that he and his dad own together." Knutson labeled Nagin and also the community group Head was working with "shake-down artists." The difference, though, Knutson added, was that "Nagin wanted work for Stone Age" while "the community groups wanted higher wages and money for projects."

Nagin sent e-mails to other Home Depot executives, promising to help them any way he could. When the City Council held a hearing on Head's plan, the mayor sent his economic-development director to testify. We're elated Home Depot wants to move into Central City, she said, and oppose the idea of a binding community-benefits agreement. Under the terms the city reached with the company, there was no binding agreement, just a promise by Home Depot to consider qualified low-income applicants from the area. A month later, Home Depot chose Stone Age as the exclusive granite installer for several Home Depot locations.

Nagin negotiated Stone Age's rates on behalf of his sons. He met with Home Depot officials at the Stone Age storefront and signed e-mails he sent to executives there "C. Ray Nagin, mayor." Cane Womack, the Home Depot manager in charge of service contracts for the Gulf Coast region, didn't know what to say when Nagin asked him to direct ten to twenty jobs a week to his sons. In Womack's view, Stone Age was a young company not ready for that workload. But he complied, the Home Depot manager said, because if "you tell the mayor no, it could cause some problems for you."

A year into their arrangement, Nagin complained to Womack that Stone Age wasn't getting enough jobs to justify the money they had spent on the special equipment Home Depot required them to purchase for certification. Despite some complaints about Stone Age's work, Womack tried to placate the mayor. "Given the political nature of this relationship," Womack wrote in an e-mail to a fellow manager, "I think it's better to move forward."[4] When in March of 2008, the *Times-Picayune*'s Gordon Russell broke the story of Stone Age's relationship with Home Depot, he quoted several competitors in the granite business who felt they had been unfairly passed over in favor of a small, untested firm.

At Cox, Nagin had made around $400,000 a year. As mayor, his salary was $131,000. David White started sending Nagin money in the middle of the the mayor's first term. At first it was $3,000 a month but soon $7,500 "to make ends meet with his family," White said. But the checks stopped shortly before Nagin's reelection. Nagin was working harder than ever before in his life, yet he wasn't making nearly enough to cover the costs of two households. Even on those rare occasions when Seletha and Tianna were in town, it's not as if he could even enjoy a quiet meal out with his family. "People would literally sit down at the table

---

4. Citing poor service, Home Depot severed its ties to Stone Age in 2008. The company went out of business the following year.

with us and ask me questions about city business or about a problem they were having," Nagin said. "I would have to take notes."

The citizens of New Orleans paid for Nagin's 2006 Valentine's Day dinner with his family at the Grill Room inside the Windsor Court: $225. They bought the mayor dinner the night he turned fifty ($250) and picked up the $175 tab when the Nagins celebrated their twenty-fourth anniversary at Stella in the French Quarter. A Mother's Day celebration at Morton's in 2008 cost the taxpayers nearly $500. So what if some of the meals—$252 at Crescent City Steaks, $229 at Ye Olde College Inn, $290 at the Sun Ray Grill—fell on a Saturday or Sunday night? "Just another day as mayor of the City of New Orleans," Nagin explained.

BILL CLINTON WORE COWBOY boots, brown slacks, and a tucked-in, red polo shirt. Brad Pitt wore a gray newsboy cap, jeans, and a white dress shirt with the tails out. In March 2008, the Clinton Global Initiative hosted six hundred college kids at Tulane for a three-day discussion. On their last day in the city, students visited the Lower Ninth Ward to turn their words into action. Holding shovels, rakes, and other tools, they aimed to clean up that corner of the community where Make It Right wanted to put up a house. The two high-watt celebrities showed up for a groundbreaking ceremony, where Pitt proclaimed, "We hope to see a huge change here in the next six months."

JOHN MCCAIN HAD VOTED against a 2005 bill that would have granted a year's worth of unemployment benefits to anyone losing a job because of Katrina. He also joined a group of Republican senators opposed to a $28 billion hurricane-relief measure that the Bush administration supported. Yet in April 2008, the Republican Party's presumptive nominee needed to distance himself from the Bush administration. His campaign launched a "forgotten places" tour in April 2008 that included stops in Youngstown, Ohio, and Appalachia and ended in the Lower Ninth Ward. "I want to assure the people of the Ninth Ward, the people of New Orleans, the people of this country: never again, never again will a disaster of this nature be handled in the terrible and disgraceful way this was handled," McCain said. Asked whether he thought the Lower Ninth should be rebuilt, the candidate paused for several seconds and then confessed that he had no answer: "We need to go back to have a conversation about what to do: rebuild it, tear it down, you know, whatever it is."

New Orleans saw a lot of both McCain and Obama in 2008. Both supported paying for a flood-protection system that could withstand a Category 5 hurricane. Both spoke of the need to restore the coastal wetlands. Yet New Orleans always seemed more Obama's home turf, the perfect venue for contrasting his approach with that of conservatives. In a speech he gave at Tulane, candidate Obama mentioned the twenty-five-thousand-plus families still living in trailers or a FEMA-subsidized apartment and also all the schools and hospitals and fire stations that remained shuttered.

"We have to understand that Katrina may have battered the levees, but it also exposed silent storms that have ravaged parts of this city and our country for far too long," Obama said. "The storms of poverty, joblessness, inequality, and injustice: those are the storms that swirled before Katrina hit." He told the audience about an evacuee he had met when he visited Houston after the storm. "We had nothing before the hurricane," she told the future president. "Now we've got less than nothing."

HEAVY RAINS IN THE spring of 2008 caused severe flooding along the upper Mississippi River Valley. For Rush Limbaugh, the images out of places such as Cedar Rapids, Iowa, where the water ran ten feet high in the streets, called to mind New Orleans a few years earlier. The contrast between the two events, he told his listeners, was stark.

"I see people working together," Limbaugh said of the Midwest floods. "I see people trying to save their property. I don't see a bunch of people running around waving guns at helicopters, I don't see a bunch of people running shooting cops. I don't see a bunch of people raping people on the street. I don't see a bunch of people . . . whining and moaning—where's FEMA? Where's Bush? I see the heartland of America. When I look at Iowa and when I look at Illinois, I see the backbone of America."

23

FATIGUE

In the summer of 2008, Father Hood called Connie Uddo into the rectory office. The city was approaching the third anniversary of Katrina, and he needed to tell her he was leaving. "My work here is done," he said. He had been assigned to a naval base in Africa. He asked Uddo what she wanted to do.

By mid-2008, 80 percent of those qualifying for a Road Home payment had received a check. The average payout of just under $60,000 per household was less than what many had expected, but enough so that Lakeview was noisy with the whine of table saws and pounding hammers. Every Wednesday night that summer, Uddo's organization sponsored a community barbecue at an empty Knights of Columbus hall that volunteers were refurbishing. The church sprang for live music, her husband cooked, and for $5 people ate unlimited food and drink (first responders and kids were free). The Starbucks on Harrison opened in June 2007. Parlay's bar was back in business, as was the local deli and the Gulf Coast bank. "It was starting to feel like a community again," Uddo said.

Plenty was still left to worry about. More people talked about moving back than hired a contractor. Some were what Lakeview Civic's Al Petrie labeled "turncoats"—people choosing to sell rather than rebuild. As much as people wanted to forget about the Urban Land Institute, the phrase it popularized, the jack-o'-lantern effect, had taken root. Road Home allowed people the option of selling their property to the state, which fed anxieties about outsiders building in Lakeview. Martin Landrieu and others came up with a program called the Lot Next Door, a citywide initiative that gave neighbors first dibs on any parcel adjacent to their own. "We were scared to death with what the city was going to do with these properties," Petrie said. Zoning in Lakeview barred the building of multifamily units, but Petrie's fear, and that of others, was that NORA, the agency responsible for abandoned properties in the city, would sell bundled lots to outside developers. "The last thing we wanted was tract housing that would undermine everything we were working so hard to achieve," Petrie said.

Uddo was tempted to quit despite the work still to be done. Let Lakeview Civic wage war with the bureaucracy. Hood told her she was probably suffering from post-traumatic stress disorder. She agreed but confessed, "I know if I'm taking care of other people, I don't have to look at myself." Maybe it was time to focus on herself. "I really wanted to say, 'Let's have a normal life again,'" Uddo said. But the experience of running the recovery center had made it hard to walk away. When your job is putting shattered lives back together, she asked herself, how do you go back to teaching tennis?

The next time Uddo saw Hood, she asked him to take a ride with her through Gentilly. Her son attended school there, and every day she saw the contrast between Lakeview and its neighbor just on the other side of City Park. Driving through the area, Hood said out loud what she had already told herself: Gentilly looks the way Lakeview did two years ago.

"Don't you think if they had a hub of recovery, they'd be further along?" she asked him.

"What are you thinking?"

"I'm thinking it'd be a shame to just walk away. I'm thinking I've learned so much that I'm a disaster-recovery manager now."

"Are you up for it?"

"I feel like I can do a lot of good in Gentilly." Hood spoke with the diocese, which proved willing to keep funding St. Paul's Homecoming Center even as it shifted its focus to Gentilly. The question was whether people there wanted the help—and if it might be too late.

IT WAS A HARD couple of years for the McDonalds, Rhesa especially. "It was a whole new world in Baton Rouge," Rhesa said. "Finding our way around. Finding places we liked to go. And then my father got sick." Revius Ortique, eighty-one years old when Katrina hit, had always been a commanding figure in her life. He was now suffering from a mysterious autoimmune disorder that no doctor could diagnose. "We got to know the Baton Rouge health system quite well," Rhesa said. He wasn't so sick that he needed to be hospitalized, but that meant it fell on Rhesa and her mother to care for him. A husband working in New Orleans all week added to the stress.

The first time Rhesa saw their old house in the Lake Forest Estates subdivision was in the spring of 2006. One visit was all she needed to make up her mind. "She told me she didn't want go back. Ever," McDonald said. The home sat untouched while husband and wife talked over their options. The green dot over the East had been replaced by a giant question mark. Many of their friends and neighbors had given up on the community, if not New Orleans. "We truly didn't know what we were going to do," Rhesa said. Complicating their decision was Rhesa's commitment to caring for her parents. For everyone's sake, they would need to find a home with two master bedrooms.

Rhesa thought about remaining in Baton Rouge. "My mom and I started to like it there," she said. "We thought, 'There's some very nice areas there, we might as well stay.'" Her father was the one who insisted they move back to New Orleans. A friend came up with the solution when she suggested they consider the Park Island house where Rhesa's parents had lived since 1989. Park Island offered them waterfront property on the Bayou St. John, yet in Gentilly and therefore closer to town than New Orleans East. Why not use their insurance settlement to turn Park Island into the home they were looking for? An architect drew up plans that added a second bedroom suite downstairs without any structural changes, and the decision was made: the McDonalds would move to Park Island, across the street from the Nagins.

McDonald arranged for the construction on the front end of the project. Rhesa handled most everything else. "I'm driving back and forth from Baton Rouge constantly," Rhesa said. The renovations would take more than two years—too long for Revius Ortique. He suffered a stroke in June 2008 and died several days later, at age eighty-four. Five months later, in November of that year, more than three years after Katrina, the McDonalds moved back to New Orleans. The RV that had been Alden McDonald's temporary home in New Orleans all those months he donated to a local religious order that worked with wayward youth.

A FAVORITE STORY RHESA tells about her husband dates back to a time before children and the big house in Lake Forest Estates. On vacation in the Bahamas, they had been looking forward to a romantic dinner but were disappointed to find a long line of people ahead of them. She next spots her husband, the bank president, a serving tray in hand, busing tables. A horrified Rhesa, the princess who grew up with her own private bathroom, almost shrieked, "What are you *doing?*" Matter-of-factly, McDonald told her, "They're shorthanded. And I figured if we're ever going to get a table, I need to help out."

Friends and peers who knew him well offered the same clichés about McDonald. He was a doer. If anyone could save Liberty, they said, it was Alden McDonald. By 2008, he was making a believer of people in the wider world. *Fortune* magazine included McDonald on its "Portraits of Power" list. Sheila Bair, the chairwoman of the FDIC, named him to a task force she created to find alternatives to check cashers, payday lenders, and other fringe financial institutions feasting on the working poor. In the pages of the *American Banker*, he was the "high-energy CEO" who had pulled off a miracle. Liberty booked $3.6 million in profits in 2007—nearly twice what it earned in 2004, the last full year before Katrina. "I wasn't sure Liberty was going to make it, but within a couple of years, we're more profitable than ever," said board chairman Norman Francis. "That was Alden's crowning glory."

Pre-Katrina, Liberty had eight branches in New Orleans. Three years later it would still have just five. Fewer people in the eastern half of New Orleans meant fewer customers, but McDonald found new business. He hired specialists who would allow him to take advantage of federal programs that gave big tax breaks on investments in low- and moderate-income communities. Liberty bought a mortgage company in Baton Rouge and another in Houston and purchased land in Jackson to build a third branch there. At the start of 2008, McDonald bought a three-branch, black-owned bank in Kansas City. It hadn't been long ago that skeptical regulators seemed convinced Liberty would need to find a larger suitor to survive. Yet those same regulators came to him in 2008 as a potential buyer for the troubled Douglass Bank in Kansas City. There would be more feelers from regulators in 2008 as subprime loans took down the global economy, causing more bank failures.

The subprime crisis was largely a nonevent for Liberty. A large share of its business was home loans to people of modest means. Many had a below-average credit score. But unlike many banks then, McDonald had subprime customers but never made subprime loans. Liberty instead focused on financial education and worked with customers to improve their credit.

New Orleans, not Liberty, would suffer after the subprime melt-down caused a global freeze in the lending markets. FEMA and HUD money would still reach the city, but not private investment. All those plans to build or rebuild hotels, condos, and other commercial projects would be stymied in a market where safe projects struggled for money, let alone speculative projects in a partially rebuilt city with an uncertain future.

THE FINAL MONTHS OF 2006 had been good ones for Cassandra Wall and her sisters. Their mother was again living in the family home, where they celebrated Christmas as a family. "It really felt like it had before the storm," Cassandra said. She had even found a program in Baton Rouge called InCourage, which provided free counseling to Katrina survivors. She took advantage of ten sessions as did her son, Brandon. She got more involved with the local church.

"I thank heaven I had some semblance of a support system in place," Cassandra said. Because as bad as 2005 had been, she said, "2007 would be worse."

Cancer took her mother's life on Valentine's Day. She was seventy-four years old. The diagnosis predated Katrina, but Cassandra and her sisters believe the storm accelerated her demise. She had had a horrible experience dealing with her homeowner's insurance and ended up part of a class action lawsuit that hundreds of New Orleanians filed against a local company. "She was fighting this battle for her health and then the storm came along," Cassandra said. "And now she's fighting not only the cancer, but she's fighting to get back home and she's fighting this insurance company. And with all of us fighting battles of our own, we weren't there to help her like we were before the storm." Daisy Wall's death meant they no longer had a family matriarch. "She really was the one holding us together," Cassandra said.

Cassandra and her husband divorced that year. Plenty of their fissures predated Katrina, but Cassandra blamed the storm. She resented that she felt alone whenever she was contending with the insurance company or Road Home or even the cleanup of the house. "Mentally, I felt he subtracted himself from all that," she said. She also felt the storm hit her husband harder than it did others. "Post-traumatic stress disorder" was her amateur diagnosis of her husband. To the extent he spoke about what he might be going through, he talked about the photos of his long-deceased parents lost in the storm. "I really think that pushed him over the edge," Cassandra said.

"We could all see it happening," Tangee said. "There wasn't a big insurance payment there. He was really missing his old job. Katrina put a real strain on their relationship." Eventually, Cassandra and her husband received a Road Home check for $105,000. The lawyers would need to figure out how they would split it up.

Postdivorce, Cassandra worried more about her son than herself. Brandon was just starting high school at the time of the divorce.

"Brandon's a real child of the storm," Cassandra said. "He also lost his home. He lost his community. He was separated from all of his friends. And he lost his father in the sense that they've had little contact."

MACK MCCLENDON TOOK PERVERSE pride in telling people he ended up in a formaldehyde trailer. It further underscores his having lived the full Katrina nightmare. He spent much of the second year after Katrina working all day in the muck and mold of his ruined house and then breathed formaldehyde all night. He never developed respiratory ailments, but many of his neighbors had a noticeable Katrina hack. Eventually, the federal government told him he needed to leave the trailer so they could cart it away. He would pick up the tab, not the government, for the bargain hotel in the central business district that was his home for the two months it took him to find a two-bedroom place in the Lower Ninth for $850 a month. Now that McClendon was no longer sleeping on his property, his home proved an easy target. He counted five times that people broke in. Thieves stole his copper. They took his tools. They even pulled out some of the new wiring that he had paid an electrician to install.

"It seemed the harder I worked at rebuilding, the further behind I got," he said.

McClendon felt largely alone living on an empty street without neighbors. Before the storm, he had his eight kids, seven of whom lived in New Orleans. Now they were living in Atlanta, Houston, and Lafayette. Only one had moved home. McClendon loved being a grandfather, but the ones with children all told him the same story. "I said to one of my daughters, 'When are you going to bring my babies home?'" McClendon said. "And she said, 'If I bring them home, I don't love them.'" Not knowing what his daughter meant, she explained, "When your grandkids were in New Orleans, they were hyperactive. They talked about giving them drugs. In Houston they're on the principal's honor roll." He told her he'd visit as soon as he could.

McClendon waited for the Road Home money he hoped would allow him to continue working on his home. Occasionally he'd visit one of the preservation-society warehouses that opened after Katrina, on the lookout for old doors and other components he would need to rebuild. Otherwise he seemed to obsess over a place a few blocks from his house. The strange-looking building had a curved, corrugated-tin roof and resembled an airplane hangar. It had been built as a food-science laboratory when much of the area was covered with sugarcane. Over the years, it had housed a boat-propeller maker, a beauty school, and an auto repair shop. A church had taken over the building a few months before Katrina, but McClendon wasn't sure anyone had even bothered to look inside to assess the damage.

"I used to go over there and stare at it," McClendon said. In his fantasies, he owned the building and used it to work on and store his cars. The large holes Katrina had punched in its roof suggested that he might be able to afford a property that would have been well out of his price range before the area flooded. At City Hall, he looked up the name of the owner, who was happy to show him the property. "It looked like half the Lower Nine had floated inside," McClendon said—and smiled to himself. "The worse it looked, the better the price I knew I'd be getting," he said. He put down only a few thousand dollars for a ten-thousand-square-foot building he bought for $180,000.

McClendon can't quite explain what happened next. He was not ten steps inside the building, he said, when a thought stopped him. The space would serve as a perfect home for a community center. "I went in there wondering where I was going to set up my little shop, but I'm thinking of kids playing basketball. I'm thinking cooking classes, choir practice. All the things our community needed," McClendon said.

McClendon tried pushing the thought away. "I really just wanted to get back to tinkering on my antique cars." That's what he would have done only a few years earlier. "Before Katrina, I wasn't really paying attention. Even if I could feel something wasn't right, I would say to myself, 'It's not my business.'" Yet if not him, then who?

Others were working to save the Lower Ninth. Common Ground was still active in the area and there was also the Lower Ninth Ward Neighborhood Empowerment Network Association, which everyone called NENA. NENA was formed around a year after Katrina by Patricia

Jones, an accountant who had bought a home in the Lower Ninth with her husband two years before Katrina. Jones had drawn the notice of a long list of funders, including Capital One, the Ford Foundation, and the United Way, and NENA was helping a long list of Lower Ninth residents work out a rebuilding plan. But a dozen-plus organizations were aiming to do the same thing, and people resented the perception that her funding made Jones a first among equals. "Patricia has to get over herself," a friend of McClendon's complained. "She has air-conditioning. That's why we meet there." Other fissures included old divisions between Holy Cross and the rest of the Lower Ninth. Some in Holy Cross, near where McClendon lived, seemed intent on setting themselves off from everyone else at a time McClendon thought everyone needed to work together.

Any number of other irritants were also prodding at McClendon, urging him to get more involved. The disaster-tour buses, for instance. He was relieved that a couple of years after the storm, people still came to gawk. "The worst thing to happen to the Lower Ninth," McClendon said, "would be if everyone just forgot about us." But then he learned the tour operators were charging $35 to $65 a head. "None of that money was coming back to the community." The City Council passed an ordinance banning tour buses from crossing the Industrial Canal, but that meant McClendon and others complained instead about a government that passes a new rule and then fails to enforce it.

McClendon attended a community meeting. He wasn't sure what his goal was that first time he rose to speak. He began by declaring the Lower Ninth was doomed if there wasn't a place for residents—children, the elderly, everyone around the room—to come together. He mentioned the building he had just bought and the possibility of converting it into a neighborhood center. "The idea was to ask if people even thought it was a good idea and hope they say no," McClendon said. "And of course everyone says yes."

McClendon had arrived with an escape plan. If this place is to be a *community* center, he told people, the community needs to help me fix it up. He gave people the address and said he'd be there working on the building all weekend if anyone wanted to help him. "I figured people were too busy with their own stuff to show up for anything. But wouldn't you know, the whole community shows up."

PATRICIA JONES AT NENA had been going nonstop. An organization that started to help people seeking their fair share of Road Home money had morphed into a center for people struggling to rebuild without enough money. Every person who walked in the door was a potential full-time project. An architect advised people on structural issues, and others helped residents navigate the permit process. NENA even got into home building. Yet as the city approached the third anniversary of Katrina, Jones and her family were among those living in a home that needed work. Much of the first level was still without flooring. A cinder block served as the front stoop. An exhausted Jones needed to slow down, and take care of her own. In time, she would step away completely from NENA.

Malik Rahim, too, needed to pull away. People thought Rahim stopped coming around the Lower Ninth because he was running for Congress in 2008 as the Green Party candidate. The truth, however, was that the Lower Ninth Ward felt to him like defeat. "I think of all the work we did, and I look at it and it makes me feel ill," Rahim said. He blames Ray Nagin more than anyone else for letting down the Lower Ninth. "You can't say it was because of racism, because we had a black mayor," Rahim said. "Every time I go back there, I always remember that. And it always takes me *days* to get over it." In 2009, the sixty-two-year-old Rahim became bedridden for weeks at a time with high blood pressure and respiratory problems. He blamed all those months working in moldy rooms but also the Lower Ninth Ward.

Initially, Mack McClendon imagined that he was re-creating the rec center of his youth. But speaking to his neighbors and others, he realized that a more pressing need was a kind of free hostel for volunteers wanting to rebuild the Ninth Ward. McClendon found dozens of surplus cots. He secured several restaurant stoves and a pair of industrial-size refrigerators, along with microwaves, toaster ovens, and army blankets. Rice in coarse, bulky burlap bags; eight-pound cans of tomatoes; oversize jars of Jif; blocks of cheese—McClendon took whatever was offered. He stored lawn mowers, weed whackers, rakes, and sledgehammers in a shed in the back. The Lower 9th Ward Village Community Center, McClendon called his creation: a hub that could house seventy people at a time and as many as one hundred during spring break and summer.

"I never did anything to spread the word," McClendon said. "People just found me." Religious-based groups stayed at the Village. So, too, did college-based organizations and groups of high school students. Thousands of out-of-towners stayed at the Village in 2008, and McClendon hosted even more people the next year. "I was very angry after Katrina," he confessed. "I felt the government didn't care and I also felt that people didn't care. But I found out I was hugely wrong, at least about the people part. People care. They care a lot. They just don't know what to do to help."

FROM HIS NEW PERCH, McClendon saw the darker side of human nature as well—disaster as an opportunity to profit off misery. A constant of life in the Lower Ninth then were stories about neighbors ripped off by a contractor. Invariably, the victim was an older homeowner who was still stuck someplace far from New Orleans. "Most of these people never had more than five thousand dollars at one time in their life, but you give them eighty thousand dollars and say, 'Now go rebuild your house,'" McClendon said. "They don't know from unscrupulous contractors." A neighbor stuck in Houston would find a contractor promising to do the job at a price she could afford. She'd tell a friend, who called the same man hoping for the same deal. "In a lot of cases, they just took the money and ran," McClendon said. More common, though, was the contractor who started a job but vanished long before completing it.

It wasn't just the elderly, as McClendon learned. He thought he could trust the man he gave the $30,000 he received from Road Home. "They were supposed to fix my roof, put up walls, other things," McClendon said, "but they didn't do any of the things they promised to do." He could complain to the authorities, but why? "They'd get a slap on the wrist if anyone could even find them, and I'd still be out my thirty thousand dollars."

RAY NAGIN WAS FED up. Here he had a delegation from Congress visiting the city, and on TV, Lee Zurik, the same reporter who had been hounding him about his schedule, was accusing the city of wasting precious dollars through a city agency called NOAH.[1] The *Times-Picayune* had jumped on the story, as had the ever-ambitious Stacy Head. "The gotcha mode, it's got to stop," Nagin demanded at a news conference that summer. Nagin singled out Zurik, whom he called "reckless" for basing his reporting on "amateur investigations."The mayor didn't mention her by name, but he was talking about Karen Gadbois.

Gadbois was indeed an amateur, but that made it even more remarkable what she had dug up. Gadbois was a textile artist and an art dealer, not a muckraker, and a newcomer who had moved to New Orleans a few years before Katrina. Her passion wasn't the local food or music but the city's brightly painted bungalows, Victorian shotguns, and Creole cottages with crumbling cornices and sagging roofs. On the city's demolition list were historic homes in her neighborhood that to her eye had suffered minimal structural damage. She created the website Squandered Heritage, which documented her search for answers. Gadbois focused on NOAH because that seemed the one agency that might be able to help. NOAH housed a $3.6 million city program created to gut, clean, and board up the storm-damaged homes of people too poor or too old to take care of the job themselves. Surely officials at NOAH would appreciate the importance of saving some of these structures.

Sifting through the public records, Gadbois noticed that houses NOAH claimed to have gutted were on the city's bulldoze list. Driving the city in her green Honda Element, she visited hundreds of properties that NOAH claimed to have cleaned up. Only a small portion had been touched. Zurik at WWL-TV and the *Times-Picayune* discovered that NOAH claimed to have gutted homes cleaned out by a church group.

---

1. More formally, the New Orleans Affordable Homeownership Corporation.

"Completely untrue," the mayor said of the charges Gadbois, Zurik, and others were leveling at NOAH—and then the FBI raided NOAH's offices. When three weeks later Nagin appeared before the City Council, he said, "The record keeping we're finding, with NOAH, is not that good."[2]

NAGIN WAS IN AN irritable mood on the morning of the third anniversary of Katrina. A small crowd gathered at a cemetery several miles from City Hall where the bodies of unknown flood victims were buried. There, with the television cameras rolling, Nagin lashed out at those attacking him. People talk about loving New Orleans, he said, but "you go to a blog, or you read something, it's divisive, it's hateful, it's mean-spirited. My question to you is, how can you love New Orleans if you don't love all of us?"

The National Guard was still patrolling New Orleans three years after Katrina. The visitors bureau could accurately claim that violent crime dropped in 2008, but that's only because so many murders and armed robberies occurred in 2007. Nine people were shot during the 2008 Mardi Gras, five of them during an argument between two teens outside the big Holiday Inn where the National Guard operated a command post. More than one-third of the city's homes were still vacant. The last of the FEMA group trailer sites closed in May, but that meant thousands were again living in hotel rooms subsidized by the federal government.

The demographics of the city were changing as Jimmy Reiss and some of his wealthy Uptown friends had hoped. Data from the Social Security Administration showed it was sending out half the number of retirement checks as it did pre-Katrina and making only 40 percent as many disability payments. State figures showed a 50 percent drop in

---

2. Ultimately, five people pled guilty to charges connected to the NOAH probe: four contractors who confessed to taking pay for work they didn't do and Stacey Jackson, the woman Nagin had put in charge of the program. Jackson, who confessed to taking kickbacks, was sentenced to five years in jail.

the number of kids in New Orleans covered by Medicaid. Public school enrollment was still barely half of what it was pre-Katrina. Public transportation ridership was down three-quarters.

Nagin ordered a mandatory evacuation the day after the third anniversary. Hurricane Gustav was bearing down on New Orleans, and the National Hurricane Center was warning that it had Category 5 potential. "The mother of all storms," Nagin declared, potentially larger and more dangerous than Katrina. This time the city made plenty of buses and trains available to those needing help getting out of town. All but ten thousand people left the city ahead of the storm. Gustav ended up a Category 2 storm that veered shortly before reaching New Orleans. The media cast Nagin as Chicken Little. "Next Time, We Won't Leave," read the headline over a *Times-Picayune* column.

The year 2009 proved worse for Nagin than even 2008. A lien was filed against the town house in Dallas. The couple were apparently so far behind in paying their dues that the homeowners association was threatening to auction off the property to collect the $1,500 they owed. In May, the *Times-Picayune* revealed that a city contractor, not Greg Meffert, had paid to send Nagin and his family to Jamaica after Katrina—five first-class tickets costing more than $6,000. That same firm, NetMethods, paid the tab on a trip Nagin's family took to Hawaii (prior to Katrina) and also leased a private jet to fly Nagin to Chicago for a Saints play-off game against the Bears. Meffert, who accompanied Nagin on all three trips, had brought NetMethods into City Hall to install free Wi-Fi around town as a way of closing the digital divide between black and white. That never happened, but Meffert charged more than $130,000 on a NetMethods American Express card in his last eighteen months on the city payroll. That fall Meffert was indicted on more than forty felony counts.

Nagin's team continued to dwindle. Not even Blakely stuck around. Despite his vow to stay until his job was done, one year before the end of Nagin's term, he declared that the city was well into its recovery and patted himself on the back. "The fastest recovery that anyone has ever seen," he said in his farewell press conference. Six months after moving back to Australia, he told an interviewer that while he believed a little bit of racism was in everyone, "it's deeper, more viral, more visible, and more entrenched in New Orleans than any place I've ever seen." This time he focused on what he observed in white New Orleanians: "There's blood in the water, and they can recapture the political apparatus and kind of put their foot back on black people's throats."

Before the storm, Nagin drew consistent approval numbers in the 70 to 80 percent range. A poll taken a few months before Nagin left office, in mid-2010, showed him with an approval rating of 24 percent. "My family can't wait until I'm out of office," Nagin told CNN. "My wife has a countdown in her head that she can recite for you anytime you ask." The station then cut to Seletha: "Seventy-six days, six hours, thirty minutes, and maybe five seconds." Presumably, her husband's time in the spotlight would soon be over.

24

VANILLA CITY

The Lower Ninth Ward's Pam Dashiell knew she could sound strident when correcting people who referred to the *natural disaster* that had destroyed much of New Orleans. The city, Dashiell insisted, had been the victim of a *man-made disaster*. If not for the catastrophic collapse of the city's *man-made* flood-protection system, the media would have been reporting on some roof damage in New Orleans and a modest amount of water in the streets before returning to the ruined Gulf Coast. Blaming *nature* for the flooding of four-fifths of New Orleans, Dashiell and others argued, was to absolve the federal government of responsibility for the city's near death.

Various lawyers had made that same argument in class action suits filed on behalf of homeowners against the federal government. The shock came when a federal judge added his voice to those making the man-made argument. Four years after Katrina, in November 2009, Judge Stanwood Duval Jr. ruled in favor of a group of homeowners who had brought suit against the Army Corps of Engineers. The US government was largely to blame for the flooding of New Orleans, Duval wrote, and must therefore compensate homeowners and businesses that suffered due to its negligence.

Duval's ruling had limits. It wouldn't benefit anyone living in New Orleans East, for instance, or Lakeview. That's because the suit pertained only to the Army Corps of Engineers' failure to maintain MR. GO, not the shortcomings of the city's levees. Duval left no doubt that, if he could, he would have ruled against the government in the numerous class action lawsuits brought over defects in the flood-protection system. "Many of the levees protecting New Orleans and the surrounding area were tragically flawed," Duval wrote, and the Corps was "not free, nor should it be, from posterity's judgment concerning its failure." The law, however, granted the government immunity, even if a plaintiff could prove that the levee system was poorly designed or badly built. Yet in Duval's reading, that immunity did not apply to a man-made shipping channel such as MR. GO, nor did it protect government from its responsibilities as a steward of its projects.

"Once the Corps exercised its discretion to create a navigational channel, it was obligated to make sure that channel did not destroy the environment surrounding it, thereby creating a hazard to life and property," Duval wrote. As early as 1988, he found, the Corps knew that "all of the engineering blunders that it had made now put the parish of St. Bernard at risk." They knew, too, from the multiple reports submitted by one of its own consultants, a geologist, that MR. GO was hastening the disappearance of the wetlands and causing erosion along the levee banks. Yet the government failed to heed its own consultant's warnings or take any of the remedial steps he and others recommended.

"The Corps' lassitude and failure to fulfill its duties resulted in a catastrophic loss of human life and property in unprecedented proportions," Duval wrote. He found that MR. GO wasn't the main reason New Orleans East was covered in water, as lawyers for the group of homeowners bringing the case claimed, but saw it as a primary culprit in the flooding of St. Bernard Parish and the adjacent Lower Ninth Ward.

"My head is spinning," Dashiell told the *New York Times*' Campbell Robertson after Duval's ruling. "Maybe things are really breaking for the people."

FOOTBALL GAVE NEW ORLEANIANS another reason to cheer in the fall of 2009. The Saints won their first few games of the season and then the next several, causing people to believe that maybe this Saints team was good enough to make the Super Bowl. They kept winning until they were 13 and 0, and people were talking not just about the Saints winning their first Super Bowl, but the possibility that they would register only the second perfect season in NFL history. Waitresses working even white-tablecloth restaurants dressed in black-and-gold jerseys, as did musicians performing in local clubs. The Saints' Super Bowl run caused people to band together in happy delirium rather than split apart in their suffering post-Katrina.

The team faltered near the end of the regular season but kept winning in the play-offs to earn its first trip to a Super Bowl. Churches canceled evening mass on Super Bowl Sunday; schools canceled class the next day. A game pitting the Saints against Peyton Manning and the Indianapolis Colts set the Nielsen record for the most viewed telecast in broadcast history, drawing five hundred thousand more people than the 105 million Americans who tuned in for the final episode of *M*A*S*H*. The Saints won the game by two touchdowns. That night, New Orleans taught other cities how to celebrate a championship.

The only downside in the Saints' improbable run was the timing: the election to choose a new mayor was scheduled for the day before the Super Bowl. The municipal elections were already taking place barely five weeks after the holidays and in the midst of carnival season. Who would govern New Orleans for the next four years was critical, but the football coverage ensured that one could turn on the television and forget there was even an election.

The Saints' good fortune was also Mitch Landrieu's, the front-runner in the race. Landrieu, the state's lieutenant governor, had told people he wasn't a candidate. He had even called a press conference in the summer to declare himself uninterested in making a run for mayor in 2010. But then a few days before the filing deadline, he announced that he had had a change of heart. "I will do everything I can to make sure that I bring the people of this city together," he said, "to heal the racial divide that has kept us apart for so long." The black front-runner, a longtime state legislator named Ed Murray, dropped out a few weeks later. He was confident he would force Landrieu into a runoff, he said, but to win he would need "to make an emotional appeal based on race and that wasn't something I wanted to do."

There would be no runoff this time. Landrieu may have been running in a city divided between black and white, but he was also the only candidate on the ballot who had ever held elected office. After eight years of Ray Nagin, New Orleanians seemed in no mood to hand the reins to another neophyte. Landrieu trounced all comers in the white community and won a majority among black voters—at least among the 28 percent of black registered voters who cast a ballot. Landrieu captured two of every three votes and beat the second-place finisher by more than 50 percentage points. When he assumed office in May 2010, several months shy of the fifth anniversary of Katrina, he was the city's first white mayor since his father left office in 1978.

THE SAINTS LEFT THE city giddy. And Landrieu's victory—or at least the end of Ray Nagin's tenure—left many New Orleanians feeling hopeful about politics. But a few weeks before Landrieu's inauguration, an explosion on an oil platform just off the Louisiana coast killed eleven workers, and the rupture released 200 million gallons of oil into the Gulf of Mexico.

The BP oil spill lasted eighty-seven days, stirring up anxieties across the country but especially in southern Louisiana. Fears about tainted oysters depressed restaurant sales. Tourists had another reason to avoid the city, and hundreds lost their jobs as the spill forced many businesses to shut down. Even the infamous formaldehyde trailers returned for a cameo as the cleanup contractors sought the cheapest option for housing their work crews. "I don't think the reservoir had been filled yet, and now you're hit again," the Reverend Vien The Nguyen, a leading voice in the East, told the New York Times. "You can run on fumes, but after a while they run out."

FOR EIGHT YEARS, THE city had had a mayor whose first rule seemed to be that no one would ever see him sweat. Mitch Landrieu, by contrast, would slip off his suit jacket to ensure you spotted the saddlebags of perspiration under his arms. "The mayor is a very persistent and impatient person," said Jeff Hebert, the young phenom Landrieu put in charge of blight removal in the city. "His attitude is, 'A lot of this stuff sat here for going on five years, there's no more excuses, we've got to get it done.'" Within a hundred days of taking office, the mayor released a list of a hundred projects; all of them, he promised, would be completed by the end of his first term. James Carville, who lived Uptown with his wife, Mary Matalin, was advising Landrieu. Carville saw a gubernatorial run in Landrieu's future, but only if they could tout him as the man who saved New Orleans.

Ideology also separated Landrieu from his predecessor. Nagin had been the political moderate whose press secretary combated rumors that he had once been a Republican. Landrieu, by contrast, was a more traditional liberal who spoke often of his Jesuit upbringing and the duty he felt to help those in need. "I know Mitch pretty well," said Bill Hines, the political lawyer. "I'm certain had he been elected in 2006, he would've fought tearing down public housing and he would have resisted the move to charter schools." Another big difference between Landrieu and his predecessor was that whereas Nagin had been a loner without allies, Landrieu, brother to a sitting US senator, had long-standing relationships with powerful people in Baton Rouge and Washington.

Governing wouldn't be easy in a city where power had shifted so dramatically from black to white. The same election that crowned Landrieu as the first white mayor in thirty-two years also created a 5–2 white supermajority on the City Council. The parish again had a white district attorney, and all but a half dozen of the city's schools were being run by a majority-white board in Baton Rouge. A few months before the mayor's race, DC had sent David Gilmore to take over the Housing Authority of New Orleans. Gilmore arrived with a reputation as a talented turnaround specialist, but he was also a white man running a housing authority whose tenants were nearly all black. He was also answerable to pretty much no one but himself: he was the sole commissioner serving on the one-person board of directors to which he reported.

Landrieu had grown up at the dinner table of the man who had done as much as anyone else to integrate City Hall. Mitch Landrieu's politics were more or less those of the legislature's black caucus, and his relationships with African-American elected officials from New Orleans were strong. In many ways he acted as a savvy politician aware that he would preside over a divided city where resentments ran high. He bought billboards around town that read ONE TEAM. ONE FIGHT. ONE VOICE. ONE CITY. That was the theme of his inaugural address and would be the guiding principle, he declared, of his tenure. Two days after he took office, Landrieu sent a letter to Attorney General Eric Holder, asking for the help of the Justice Department's Civil Rights Division in overhauling a police department sometimes viewed by black New Orleanians as an occupying force—and other times as an indifferent one. "Nothing short of a complete transformation is necessary," the new mayor wrote.

At first, Landrieu seemed similarly sensitive to the black community's concerns in his choice of a new police chief. With his inauguration more than two months off, Landrieu named a multiracial task force of nearly two dozen to help him scour the country in search of top candidates. To chair the committee the mayor-elect named two well-regarded figures in the black community. Yet members complained that the mayor's transition team declined to share with them the criteria they were using to sort through potential candidates or even the names of applicants. Danatus King, president of the local chapter of the NAACP, stepped down, saying he wanted to avoid being used as "window dressing." Two more members of the task force resigned, and a fourth was removed the day after she made her frustrations public. The day after sending his letter to Eric Holder, Landrieu announced his choice: Ronal Serpas, a white man who had spent the previous six years running the Nashville police department after twenty-one years with NOPD.

"A sham process produced a sham choice," declared John Slade, who cohosted WBOK's *Showtime in the Afternoon* with Paul Beaulieu. Slade was the younger of the two and also more sarcastic and funnier. Beaulieu was the cantankerous, gravelly voiced uncle who cracks up the kids at the Thanksgiving table with his irreverent commentary. At least we'll have plenty to talk about in the coming years, Beaulieu and Slade agreed shortly after Serpas's appointment.

THREE MONTHS INTO HIS tenure, Landrieu ventured to the Household of Faith church in New Orleans East. The mayor was inaugurating what he called "budgeting for outcomes"—a gathering in each of the city's five council districts to give citizens input on the budget. "We're doing the first of these meetings in New Orleans East," the mayor began on a muggy night in August 2010, "to honor the frustration and anxiety and uncertainty that exist in the East about whether you're a real part of the city of New Orleans."

In time, the routine would become familiar to New Orleanians. If it was the summer, the mayor and dozens of City Hall employees would be visiting your part of the city. Attendance was mandatory for department heads and other top staff, including police and fire. Any person living in that district was allowed two minutes at the microphone. The mayor, sitting at a table, scribbled on a legal pad; after the last person had spoken, the mayor would address people's questions and concerns, one by one. At one of these forums, Landrieu, an average-size man with close-cropped hair and a doughy face, was the thespian skilled at communicating empathy to a large audience. "It's amazing to watch," said Connie Uddo. His eyebrows would gather into a small peak above watery-blue eyes. He'd bite his lower lip, he'd shake his head slowly, as a citizen of his city shared his or her tale of woe. A frown would take over his face. He'd address every constituent by first name and asked department heads to stand and account for themselves. "Mitch is so good at letting people know he really heard them and really cares," Uddo said.

That first meeting at the Household of Faith church lasted three hours. Dozens spoke, all voicing similar grievances and pleas. They were angry about the slow pace of the recovery and scared about the future of the East. They were fed up with the overgrown, empty lots. Where were the inspectors to enforce the rules for maintaining a property? The East still had few stores. The closest emergency room was twenty minutes away. The residents felt like easy targets in a city awash in crime. "We need your help, Mr. Mayor!" one woman told him that night.

Landrieu finally stood to speak at nearly 11:00 p.m. "A lot of you talk about blight, but I wanna talk about race for a second," Landrieu began. He could order his people to crack down on the scofflaws who failed to take care of their properties. He would sign demolition orders if that's what was required. "But if I start taking people's houses who aren't back from Houston and Atlanta—our brothers and sisters—then people on CNN are gonna run up on me and say, 'Why are you trying to stop people from coming home? Why don't you want the brothers and sisters to come, lil' Mr. Mitch, looking the way you do?'"

There was no mistaking the sentiment expressed inside the Household of Faith church that night: people wanted him to do something about the blight. But the mayor had a point to make: "We've erred on the side of people who haven't returned. What I hear you saying is it's time to err on the side of those who've moved back. Is that it?" The crowd roared yes. Again, Landrieu brought up race: "I promise you, as soon as I lay it down, somebody's gonna come down here, and there's gonna be a march, and somebody's gonna try to turn it into something it's not."

"We got your back!" a woman yelled out. The audience broke into applause.

YET PLENTY IN THE black community were dubious that Landrieu had their back. Prior to Katrina, Waste Management, a publicly traded multinational, handled most of the garbage pickup in New Orleans. But Katrina caused the city to fall so far behind in its payments to Waste Management that the company declined even to submit a bid when its contract came up for renewal. Under Nagin, the multimillion-dollar garbage pickup contracts ended up with a pair of local, black-owned firms. The *Tribune*'s Beverly McKenna considered it one of Nagin's most significant accomplishments. So, too, did WBOK's Paul Beaulieu. The economic revival of the black community, both argued, required a healthy black business sector—and if both firms proved loyal WBOK and *Tribune* advertisers, that only underscored their point about black businesses being an essential part of the ecosystem. "They gave jobs to people who otherwise would have a hard time finding them," Beaulieu said. "Ex-cons trying to clean themselves up, people who might not have graduated from school, jumping on and off trucks, making good money, providing for a family."

Stacy Head, the white city councilwoman, was the first to cast suspicions on the no-bid deal the Nagin administration had cut with the two firms. Satisfaction with garbage pickup had increased since the switch, but the city was also paying more, Head showed, than their counterparts in neighboring Jefferson Parish. Those defending the two companies pointed out that hauling garbage in a crumbling city with narrow streets costs more than in the suburbs, but that nuance disappeared in the media coverage. Landrieu, who had inherited a budget shortfall of nearly $100 million, sided with Head. Renegotiate your rates, Landrieu insisted, or he would explore the legality of voiding the contracts.

Who could argue with the $5 million a year the mayor saved the city after the two firms renegotiated? But these two homegrown firms were two success stories in a community feeling shortchanged even as billions in recovery dollars were flowing through the city. Said John Slade, Beaulieu's WBOK cohost, "This mayor's attitude is, 'We're going to take everything from black hands. We'll let them have crumbs.'"

CHARITY HOSPITAL WOULD NEVER reopen as a health care facility. In 2010, a federal arbitrator decided in the state's favor in its dispute with FEMA over the damage to Charity. FEMA officials thought they were being generous when they set aside $125 million to reimburse Louisiana for a facility they believed had suffered only minimal structural damage, but the arbitrator ordered the agency to pay nearly four times that amount. That $475 million check from the feds would allow the state to start construction on its hospital at the ambitious new biomedical center the city had decided to build at the edge of downtown—a project Landrieu supported. For nearly three hundred years, New Orleans had been home to a public hospital whose primary mission was caring for those without health insurance. The uninsured would be treated at a new state hospital that would, once built, be less reliant on public dollars and serve both private and indigent patients.

In 2010, a federal judge would rule against those feeling their rights had been trampled when the authorities prevented pedestrians from escaping New Orleans over the bridge into Gretna. The authorities in Gretna may have proven bad neighbors when they locked their doors in the midst of a crisis, said US district court judge Mary Ann Vial Lemmon, but restricting pedestrian traffic into their city "is not an unreasonable restraint of liberty." Five class action lawsuits had been filed against

the Gretna police and other law enforcement agencies. All of them were
tossed out of court before a trial. A grand jury had also declined to indict
any of those behind the decision.

Those living in the Lower Ninth Ward and St. Bernard Parish also
received bad news. An appeals court overturned Judge Duval's decision that
the government needed to compensate homeowners and businesses there
because of the Corps' neglect of MR. GO. A three-judge panel agreed with
Duval that MR. GO "greatly aggravated the storm's effects on the city," but
ruled the law "completely insulates the government from liability."[1]

ACCORDING TO THE 2010 census, 343,829 people lived in New
Orleans—29 percent less than before the storm. Some 24,000 fewer
whites resided in the city and 119,000 fewer blacks. Whereas before
Katrina the city was more than two-thirds African-American, it was
now less than 60 percent black. The census also showed a modest
bump in the number of Latinos living in New Orleans.

Fewer children were living in New Orleans five years after
Katrina—44 percent fewer, according to the census. Overall, Lakeview
was missing one-third of its people and New Orleans East more than
40 percent. The official population of the Lower Ninth Ward was down
more than 80 percent. One in every four residential properties across
New Orleans was categorized as blighted or vacant—fifty-four thousand addresses across the city. The city was certain to lose seats in the
state legislature after new legislative districts were drawn in 2011.

Education persisted as an issue dividing the city. Nearly two-
thirds of the city's public school students were now attending a charter
school—a higher proportion than anywhere else in the country. Those
seeing charters as the solution to the abysmal pre-Katrina performance
of the Orleans Parish schools could point to rising test scores, just as

---

1. The hopes of people in the Lower Ninth and St. Bernard Parish would be revived
    when, in May 2015, another federal judge, ruling in a second MR. GO case, or-
    dered the US government to compensate homeowners and businesses for at least
    some of their flood losses.

skeptics stressed that most schools were still posting failing grades. The editorial boards at the *New York Times* and *Washington Post* were impressed with the progress being made, as were the liberal thinkers at the Brookings Institution, which hailed the early successes and dubbed New Orleans "one of the boldest public school experiments under way in the country." Yet more than a few parents longed for the traditional neighborhood-based system, whatever its flaws, when the alternative was now lotteries held to fill spots at popular schools and children attending schools on the opposite side of town.

Barbara Major was among those charging that the charters were cherry-picking the system's better students to keep their scores up and leaving slower learners and their parents to fend for themselves. The Southern Poverty Law Center sued the state and Orleans Parish schools for shortchanging the education of forty-five hundred special-needs students.[2] Teach For America, which was supplying the local schools with fresh college graduates, almost all of them white, was another flash point. Depending on whom you asked, the Teach For America kids were recent college grads whose youthful exuberance enlivened the classroom or clueless interlopers set loose inside the schools after a five-week summer-training program.

The demand for affordable housing in New Orleans continued to outstrip supply. Around the United States, an alarmingly high 40 percent of all renters spent more than 35 percent of their income on housing. In New Orleans five years after Katrina, that number topped 60 percent. More than three thousand names were on the waiting list for public housing in New Orleans, and another twenty-nine thousand people were still hoping for a federal housing voucher that would cap the amount they paid for housing at roughly 30 percent of their income. Further limiting people's options was a public transportation system that had 60 percent fewer riders than it did pre-Katrina and therefore couldn't afford to offer the same service as before the storm. Meanwhile, thousands lived in their ruined homes because they couldn't afford to live anyplace else.

---

2. The suit was settled at the end of 2014 when the authorities agreed to many of the policy changes that parents and their advocates were demanding.

New Orleans had a decent mental health care system prior to Katrina. But Charity Hospital was closed and Governor Bobby Jindal in 2009 cut off funding for the adolescent mental health facility the state operated in New Orleans. The city had endured a terrible trauma yet lost dozens of psychiatric beds along with hundreds of mental health professionals. Five years after Katrina, the suicide rate in New Orleans was still at least twice as high as it was before the storm.

Not all the news was bad as the city approached the fifth anniversary of Katrina. Civic engagement was higher than ever in the Big Easy, a locale historically short on activism even in the face of a dysfunctional government and monumental social problems. "I must've gone to three hundred meetings in the first two years after Katrina," said Lakeview's Miss Rita—Rita Legrand. Before Katrina, she never attended any. A notoriously weak public defender's office was transformed post-storm into a well-functioning one. Charity Hospital wouldn't be reopening, but a spate of community-based clinics had opened around the city, providing the poor better access to preventive care and other health services. Arts organizations were generally strong in an environment where foundation money was available to groups working to preserve the city's culture.

Legions of young college grads resettled in New Orleans after Katrina. Some were idealists who had shown up to help rebuild the city after Katrina and never left (the YURPs, they were called: young urban rebuilding professionals); others were hipsters and artists and self-described "gutter punks" who saw in New Orleans a cheap way to live in a city with a vibrant music scene, great food, and a unique culture. Locals complained about the high rent, but outsiders saw a bargain when it was stacked up against prices in Brooklyn or the San Francisco Bay Area. Others saw financial opportunity in a town enjoying a kind of mega-stimulus program, fueled by billions in recovery dollars, while most of the rest of the United States was slogging through a recession. "For the first time in decades," the *Times-Picayune* reported, "New Orleans is attracting waves of young professionals." Entrepreneurs were creating new businesses at a pace greatly outstripping pre-Katrina numbers. Even wages were up in New Orleans, as was median family income. Just as Jimmy Reiss and his allies had hoped when dead bodies were still in the streets, while the city's poorest residents were still having a hard time returning, the city would be more prosperous.

THE FIFTH ANNIVERSARY OF Katrina fell on a Sunday. A light, steady rain fell all day. There was the customary tolling of bells and prayer services, and also a large demonstration occurred in the Lower Ninth Ward, where more than a thousand people showed up to protest the lack of progress in their neighborhood. Maxine Waters, a high-profile congresswoman from Los Angeles, black, took aim at "low-down, dirty insurance companies," Road Home, and also the charter-schools experiment. "We want our public schools back," Waters said to loud applause.

Barack Obama came to town for the fifth anniversary. He had been heckled the first time he had visited New Orleans as president ("We're working as hard as we can," a defensive Obama had said). This time he arrived intent on proving his commitment to the city. A few days before Air Force One touched down in New Orleans, the administration had announced a $1.8 billion school construction grant—a lump sum that parish officials could spend as they chose, without needing FEMA to sign off each time they decided to rebuild a school. On a stage at Xavier University, a historically black college that had been rebuilt since the storm, Obama reiterated a pledge he had made as a candidate to restore the coastal wetlands and declared that the area's new flood-protection system—what he called "the largest civil works project in American history"—would be ready by the next hurricane season. "My administration is going to stand with you, and fight alongside you, until the job is done, until New Orleans is all the way back," the president said.

Mitch Landrieu spoke that night at the refurbished Mahalia Jackson Theater in Tremé. He reminded people of the ways New Orleanians had come together after Katrina: "Young black boys pushing an old white man in a rusted wheelchair to find water," he said. "An old white woman holding the hand of a crying black girl who had lost her mother." That, he said, should be their template. "To become the city of our dreams, we must follow a righteous path guided by the lessons learned from Katrina. Love thy neighbor, our diversity is our strength, never give up." His next lines he would repeat throughout his mayoralty: "We are not rebuilding the city we were. We are creating the city we want to become."

25

BLIGHT

Alden McDonald's grim survey of New Orleans East began in a large boardroom down the hall from his office. Five years after Katrina, on the sixth floor of his bank's headquarters, the flood seemed as if it had happened twelve months earlier. The east-facing windows looked out onto a stretch of emptiness that had once been a giant mall. Where once there had been stores, now there was just asphalt and weeds. Read Boulevard—the next exit up the highway—loomed in the middle distance. McDonald pointed out a tan building around the same height as his: the vacant "thodist" hospital (the first two letters in the sign METHODIST had fallen off). The hospice next door was boarded up, as was a black office tower once filled with doctors and other professionals.

The windows on the north side of this glass box more or less at the East's epicenter offered an equally bleak picture. A pair of large, empty parcels on the other side of the I-10, the former sites of a Walmart and a Sam's, were now just giant wounds on the landscape. The three-story office building next to McDonald's was shuttered, as was the shattered green-glass rectangle on the other side of that. McDonald pointed out several more office buildings: "Empty, empty, empty." Before Katrina, more than a dozen office buildings were in that part of the city. "I'm still the only one open in the East," he said, yet he still had plenty of vacancies. Five years after Katrina, his building sat half-empty.

McDonald continued his tour of the battered East behind the wheel of a black Lexus sedan. Near his office were a trio of strip malls. "All of them one hundred percent occupied pre-Katrina," he said—all three now vacant. Nearby an abandoned nursing home and a two-story, brick rehab center were covered in graffiti. The next exit off the interstate and the one after that offered more of the same: stretches of boarded-up strip malls and destroyed businesses. A Days Inn had reopened along the highway and also a Comfort Suites, but he pointed out two other motels that had slashed their prices and reopened as flophouses for transients. There were several car dealerships and gas stations, a few places to grab food, but not much else.

"We have no jobs out here," McDonald said. "We have no commercial business to speak of."

McDonald occasionally left a main artery to dip into a subdivision. Lake Forest Estates—McDonald's old neighborhood—was faring better than most. So, too, was Spring Lake, which benefited from an active neighborhood group. Yet both were littered with ruined homes on every street. Less fortunate communities weren't even one-third back. "It's like the ULI had warned us—the jack-o'-lantern effect," McDonald said. Prior to Katrina, New Orleans East was home to four Catholic churches. Five years later, only one had reopened.

McDonald the banker had identified patterns in the repopulation of the East. The first people to move home were invariably those who only recently had taken out a mortgage. They owned so little equity in their homes that it was likely the bank would end up with all their insurance and Road Home money. "They had to rebuild or they'd be walking away from their down payment," he said. He watched others use Katrina to pick up a house they could never have afforded before the storm. "You have a whole new class of people who are moving in," McDonald said. "People who got big insurance checks, money from Road Home, seeing an opportunity to move up." He might have done the same if he were in their position, but it all changed the feel of the community. "Neighbors aren't connected like they were before,"

McDonald said. "Where in the past someone might know ten people on their block, now they know four."

Eating in New Orleans East still meant fast food, a food truck, or a temporary perch in one of a few open take-out places, so McDonald headed west toward the center of town. As lunch approached, McDonald took a detour first through the Seventh Ward, where he had grown up, and then Gentilly, where Liberty was focusing a lot of its post-Katrina efforts. If anything, the Seventh Ward was starker than New Orleans East, with more shuttered businesses and wrecked homes still sporting the National Guard's conspicuous Katrina tattoo. Forty percent of its residents were still missing, according to the 2010 census.

McDonald's mood brightened once he passed into Gentilly. He showed off the half-wrecked building he had bought under a government program created to encourage investment in blighted neighborhoods. He planned to turn it into a professional building. He had bought a wrecked mini-mall nearby under the same program. "At least there's life back here," he said.

Those were modest investments compared to the $20 million loan fund the bank had created to help those who still didn't have enough money to rebuild fully after insurance and Road Home. (Liberty set aside another $20 million for a similar loan fund for homeowners in the Lower Ninth.) Called the Gentilly Homeowner Initiative, the program began with a survey of the community's needs. That's how McDonald learned of a working couple with three children squeezed into the two rooms they had had the money to rehab. They needed around $80,000 to finish the rest of the house, but both worked service-industry jobs and didn't make enough to justify a loan half that size. McDonald's people would need to play a role closer to that of case manager than loan officer. "We partnered up with nonprofits able to give them free labor so they'd only have to buy supplies," McDonald said. Sometimes that meant working with Connie Uddo's organization. "We're trying to find creative, nontraditional ways to help people."

Lunch was at Dooky Chase's, a favorite of the black professional class (George W. Bush and Barack Obama have both eaten there). Over Leah Chase's signature fried chicken and sweet-potato salad, McDonald talked about his life since the storm. He and Rhesa couldn't be happier in their home along Bayou St. John. It was as if they had found a little bit of Uptown in a hidden part of Gentilly: a two-story, white clapboard house with a closed-in porch. But that brought into relief the disparity between his life and that of so many of his neighbors. For Rhesa's sixtieth birthday that year, he had spilled a few thousand dollars on a blowout party at Bullet's, a popular local club, and bought her a new Lexus SC 430 sports car. Yet a preoccupation during his driving tour of battered New Orleans were those of modest means trying to get by in a city where the price of everything from rent to property taxes to insurance had gone up.

The bank was thriving even as the eastern half of New Orleans struggled. McDonald was the focus of a long, flattering profile in the pages of *American Banker*—his second in two years. This time the magazine's focus was McDonald's plan to transform Liberty into the country's premier community-development bank. As McDonald explained, a wealth of government programs offered tax credits and similar incentives to any entrepreneur funding projects in a moribund community. That would be the focus of a failed bank Liberty had just bought in Detroit and also the one it had acquired in Kansas City a couple of years earlier. That would become a greater part of Liberty's focus in New Orleans as well.

Liberty was operating twenty-four branches in six states, but McDonald told *American Banker* he felt they weren't running anywhere near their potential capacity. He was convinced that bad subprime loans meant too many banks were still struggling to survive—and he was intent on ensuring Liberty remained hunter rather than prey. That was one advantage of having lived through Katrina: "I know distressed loans better than anyone else."

PEOPLE NOTICED THE BRAD PITT homes. They were strange but beautiful, designed by Frank Gehry, Thom Mayne, and other internationally acclaimed architects—brightly colored works of art erected in the barren moonscape of the Lower Ninth Ward north of Claiborne. One house looked as if it had been artfully sawed in half; a second seemed as if it were several homes fused into a single structure. Another resembled a steel shipping container, except with a front door and a wedge-shaped roof. Some stood atop stilts, and one the color of a berry-flavored drink was built on hidden pontoons so it could float if there was another flood. "They're the ugliest houses I've ever seen," declared Henry Irvin Jr., who cut so high a profile in the Lower Ninth post-Katrina that even Mitch Landrieu once referred to him as the area's true mayor.

The cost rather than appearances offended Alden McDonald. Pitt had predicted that each Make It Right home would cost between $100,000 and $174,000 to build, but apparently that estimate was calculated before his people priced the formaldehyde-free wood, termite-resistant lumber, fiber-cement siding, and custom-built cabinets they used. Each home was platinum LEED-certified and featured solar panels and a stylish metal roof. The average home ended up costing $270,000—or considerably more than that if factoring in the cost of a full-time executive director, counselors, a PR person, and other staff. Then it worked out to closer to $500,000 per house. McDonald appreciated that the utility bills for one of Pitt's Make It Right homes were a fraction of what a resident would pay in a traditional home—a huge savings in the warm months. But the banker within couldn't square the idea of spending a few hundred thousand dollars to build a home that would be worth half that amount on the open market. "He had the money to put a lot more people into homes," McDonald said.

Yet McDonald had also sat on an airplane next to the manager of a fast-food restaurant who'd shown him pictures of the Brad Pitt home she had chosen as if she were sharing photos of a newborn grandbaby. He'd witnessed the magic of the Make It Right homes as had Thom Pepper, who had taken over as Common Ground's executive director after the group's founder, Malik Rahim, could no longer bear to come around. The BellSouth man had initially told Pepper that the company would never restore phone service north of Claiborne. No one from the city would ever commit to a date for new streetlights or even permanent street signs. Then the media arrived trailing Pitt and occasionally a former president. "Make It Right forced the city to start addressing infrastructure issues," Pepper said.

Mack McClendon thought the Make It Right homes were "weird." He resented that so few locals worked on its construction crews. But McClendon was convinced that if not for Pitt, that corner of the Lower Ninth would have been snapped up by developers intent on building big—condos, a hotel, maybe even a casino. "I'm afraid to think about what would have happened if Make It Right didn't build these houses when they did," McClendon said.

"As far as I'm concerned, the hero of the Ninth Ward is Brad Pitt," Malik Rahim said. Added the former Blank Panther, "We tried and we couldn't do nothing. We couldn't save it. But Brad Pitt—an actor, this white dude—did."

YET PITT ONLY BUILT on a few streets closest to the levee. Another twenty or so blocks were between the Make It Right homes and the St. Bernard Parish line. Most of the homes in this part of the Lower Ninth had been bulldozed. Even five years after Katrina, entire blocks remained uninhabited. Henry Irvin Jr., the area's unofficial mayor, never doubted he would rebuild. He had bought a home in the Lower Ninth in 1964, and he would be back in his one-story, redbrick home north of Claiborne in 2009. A caved-in home sat two lots over, and a Baptist church was down the street, but otherwise he was by himself. "You can buy junk food here and you can get alcohol," said Jenga Mwendo, who moved back into her refurbished Lower Ninth home in 2008. "You can go to church, you can fill up with gas, you can get your car fixed. That's pretty much it. You have to cross the bridge for everything else." For a time, Common Ground was able to operate a health clinic, but funding dried up and it closed shortly after the fifth anniversary. With no health clinics, Mack McClendon asked, was it any surprise that maybe 5 percent of the community's older homeowners were back?

The Lower Ninth was home to five public schools prior to Katrina. In 2010, the neighborhood still had just the King charter school that Doris Hicks and her people had opened. The area still had no high school, so King's board voted to truck in trailers to add the ninth through twelfth grades. "We couldn't even get money from the district to pay for the modulars," said Hilda Young, the school's board president.

The Lower Ninth lost more of its earliest leaders. Charmaine Marchand announced in 2011 that she would not run for reelection due to family obligations. Her father was suffering from advanced dementia; her mother, too, was sick. She also had financial pressures as a single mother earning less than $50,000 a year as a state legislator. She was a lawyer and needed to make more money. Another early pioneer, Patricia Jones, who had founded the Lower Ninth Ward Neighborhood Empowerment Network Association, or NENA, also disengaged from her community work to spend more time tending to family and work.

Pam Dashiell stepped down as head of the Holy Cross Neighborhood Association to cofound the Center for Sustainable Engagement and Development, an environmental group focused on the Lower Ninth. Dashiell's group made reclamation of the Bayou Bienvenue—the once-thriving wetlands that was now stumps in a stagnant swamp—a priority and also addressed the toxins she believed had contaminated the area's soil. "I don't think anybody understands the effects of climate change and global warming better than the people of the Lower Ninth Ward," Dashiell told the *Gambit*.

Dashiell would prove the Lower Ninth's saddest loss when she died at her desk in December 2009. She was sixty-one years old. "A guiding force in the rebuilding efforts," Brad Pitt said of this woman he described as a "dear friend." Her funeral was held at All Souls—the Walgreens church. Among those eulogizing Dashiell was Bill Waiters, a supervisor at a nearby Domino sugar plant. Waiters, who had taken over as the head of Holy Cross after Dashiell, had been two weeks from moving back into the Victorian home he owned near the Industrial Canal when a faulty heater in the bathroom caused the house to burn down. The fire happened on the same day he learned Dashiell had died.

THE CHURCH GROUPS AND college students and shaggy-haired idealists kept finding the Lower 9th Ward Village, and Mack McClendon kept feeding them and providing them with a place to sleep. The volunteers attacked the overgrown lots that threatened to swallow parts of the Lower Ninth whole and took part in "buildathons" organized to help a homeowner who didn't have the money to hire a crew. McClendon sent teams to neighbors who had turned to him for help and housed volunteers who came to work on the Bayou Bienvenue for Pam Dashiell's group. By the five-year mark, McClendon had hosted more than ten thousand volunteers.

McClendon knew he should have been working on his own home, but who had the time—or the money, for that matter? He had thought donations and T-shirt sales would prove enough to cover the costs of running the center, but he was always dipping into his savings—to pay an overdue electric bill, to pick up the grocery tab when the center was running low on donated supplies. He could no longer afford the apartment he was renting, so his friends and volunteers helped him create a mini-loft inside the center. The light fixtures were bare bulbs dangling from exposed wires in a pair of rooms that totaled maybe 250 square feet. The furnishings were castoffs, as was the stained carpeting. His bedroom was a small dresser and a futon on the floor. "I went from a four-bedroom house with a living room, dining room, and den," McClendon said, "to living in a little closet that had me sleeping on the floor."

Originally, McClendon thought he was creating a community center for a neighborhood in desperate need of one. He had the outside painted an array of bright colors: green, red, purple, blue. Above the door, someone had painted WHERE IS YOUR NEIGHBOR? along with a giant, multicolored map of the United States. Each dot—in Maine, Montana, Arizona, Washington, Wisconsin—represented another displaced resident of the Lower Ninth. Most impressive was a handsome mosaic next to the front door that spelled out LOWER NINTH WARD VILLAGE, along with a we-are-the-world logo that had a pair of black arms embracing people of all races.

Inside were a warren of offices and a giant, high-ceilinged room where the volunteers slept. The "media room" was filled with donated computers, and a "homework lab" was outfitted with tables and chairs. A shed in back was filled with footballs, soccer balls, and bikes. A third room served as a lending library, stocked with donated books and tools. A couple of used desks were in the room McClendon claimed as his office, but most of the space was taken up by beat-up tables, mismatched chairs, and worn-out couches. Here McClendon hosted organizing meetings to talk about everything from the Village to the neighborhood's future.

Slowly, the Village made the transition from makeshift hostel to gathering place. McClendon set up basketball hoops behind the building and built a stage for a weekly Open Mic Night. Four years after the flood, McClendon started hosting what he called town hall meetings on the fourth Saturday of every month. That proved essential to a community that felt ignored and in need of public meeting space. The gatherings started promptly at 11:00 a.m. and rarely lasted more than an hour. Speakers could talk for no more than five minutes and needed to stick to the agenda.

"We wanted to minimize venting," McClendon said. "The idea was that we had business to take care of and didn't have time to waste."

While McClendon's firm hand as a moderator impressed his fellow activists ("Mack ran the best meetings," said Common Ground's Thom Pepper), his cooking skills were what guaranteed a crowd. "When we wanted to really turn people out, I'd do one of my seafood boils," McClendon said, though in his mouth it sounded like a seafood *burl*. A stalwart few dozen were regulars at these monthly meetings that typically focused on a single topic: the lack of streetlights, say, or the government's failure to take care of abandoned properties under its jurisdiction. "But if I told people I was burling seafood, I could pretty much guarantee standing room only," McClendon said. The real business seemed to happen in the hours before the crowds arrived when McClendon, standing in front of a humongous, restaurant-size silver pot, a spoon in hand, would talk strategy and plot with others to save their community. On those days McClendon—who prior to Katrina barely made time to vote—seemed to be at the center of whatever was happening in the Lower Ninth.

CONNIE UDDO KNEW IT would be hard starting over in a new neighborhood given her race, her outsider status, and also the size and complexity of Gentilly. Its pre-Katrina population was roughly four times that of Lakeview and had a daunting twenty-two neighborhood associations. Money, too, separated Gentilly from Lakeview. Gentilly had small pockets of affluence, such as Park Island on the Bayou St. John, where Ray Nagin and Alden McDonald lived, but the average home there sold for around $150,000. "You don't see contractors out here," a retired mechanic named Albert Felton, seventy-six, told a reporter who found him working by himself on his Gentilly home a couple of years after Katina. "We can't afford them." Uddo opened St. Paul's Homecoming Center at the start of 2009 in a Gentilly house that volunteers had refurbished.

Uddo was cautious her first few months in Gentilly. She met with the president of each neighborhood association. She complimented them all on the job each was doing and stressed that she was there to help, not tell them what to do. Each association head shared with Uddo more or less the same set of stories. People wanted to return but didn't have the money to rebuild. A lot had started to rebuild but ran out of money long before they could finish, often because they had been ripped off. "I feel like ninety percent of the homes I work on in Gentilly involve some kind of contractor fraud," Uddo said.

Road Home was another culprit. In her testimony before a Senate subcommittee in May 2007, Uddo spoke about the program as thwarted by bureaucratic incompetence. In Gentilly, she recognized the more basic flaw in Road Home. Sheetrock cost the same whether you lived west of City Park in Lakeview or east in Gentilly. So, too, did an electrician and a roofer. Yet Road Home decreed that the same three-bedroom, two-bath arts-and-crafts home was worth $100,000 less in Gentilly than in Lakeview. It still cost around $200,000 in post-Katrina New Orleans to rehab a two-thousand-square-foot house even if insurance and Road Home only added up to $140,000.[1]

Gentilly was three-quarters black, but several years after the storm, no one seemed to care that Uddo was a white woman from Lakeview. "By that point, if you were saying, 'I can help,' it didn't make a difference what race you may be," Uddo said. She gave each resident she met the same small speech. She talked about her success in Lakeview but

---

1. A federal judge announced in August 2010, two weeks before the fifth anniversary of Katrina, that he was likely to rule in favor of a claim by housing advocates that Road Home discriminated against African Americans. He also ordered the state to stop using pre-storm market values to calculate any future Road Home grants. But Louisiana had by then sent out checks to nearly 128,000 homeowners, and less than $200 million in disaster aid remained. Housing advocates settled the case when the federal government agreed to set aside an extra $500 million to help low-income homeowners. "We felt it was better to get money now to help people rather than dragging this out with years more of fighting," said James Perry, the executive director of the Greater New Orleans Fair Housing Action Center, one of the groups bringing the Road Home suit.

stressed that she wasn't a miracle worker. "All I can promise you is that I'll do my best," she would tell someone walking into her group's offices. "I'll look for funds to buy the materials you need to work on your house. I'll look for volunteers to help you. I can't tell you how long it'll take, but I'm not leaving you."

That last point impressed Cathey Randolph, who had worked as a case worker at Uddo's Lakeview center. "So many people came around promising this and promising that, and then they'd just disappear," said Randolph, who is black. "Connie stayed."

Uddo's role as a second responder evolved. Whereas in Lakeview her job had been more about the community, in Gentilly she focused on individuals. A lot of the job now was finding outfits willing to donate supplies and volunteers able to do specific work. When the kitchen and bath manufacturers were in town for a meeting at the Convention Center, that proved a perfect opportunity to help the Davis family, who for years after Katrina were still preparing their meals on a hot plate and a microwave in an upstairs bedroom. A volunteer group gave the Davises a new kitchen, along with two other families that had turned to Uddo's group for help.

"I saw a lot of people getting to the ten-yard line and running out of money," she said. "They'd be living in homes where the floors were buckling from flood damage. Or they had managed to redo the whole downstairs except they had no walls." Uddo was confident she could always find people willing to hang Sheetrock or install a floor. She started pitching to funders a program she called Home Stretch, to provide the money for the supplies people would need. "The idea was with free labor, you could 'stretch' a five-thousand-dollar or ten-thousand-dollar supply bill into a completed project," said Uddo, who raised $220,000 for the program from the Greater New Orleans Foundation.

Uddo had hired Cathey Randolph to concentrate on homeowners who were a lot more than a working bathroom or a paint job away from moving back home. That included people such as Sylvia and Anthony Blanchard, an older couple still living in a FEMA trailer when, three years after Katrina, they contacted Uddo's group.

The Blanchards had already started work on the modest, two-bedroom house they owned in Gentilly when Road Home informed them they had failed to submit proper proof of ownership and would be receiving no money from the state. The Blanchards hadn't used a traditional lender but had instead bought their home from the seller through a bond-for-deed arrangement. Their records had been destroyed by the flood, but Sylvia Blanchard, who had put in twenty years as a court clerk before her retirement shortly before Katrina, copied records at City Hall that showed that they were paying taxes on the property. She made copies of other records documenting their ownership and submitted an affidavit from the previous owner. When Road Home responded with a second rejection letter, the couple drove to Baton Rouge to talk with someone in the governor's office. No one there would help them.

"I fought for my country!" Anthony Blanchard yelled after they were turned away. He was a Vietnam vet with three Purple Hearts who had retired from the post office shortly before Katrina. "I was shot at. And what does my country do for me? They kick me in the head." Security escorted the couple out. On the day the couple received a letter from Road Home telling them that their appeal had been denied, Anthony suffered a massive stroke.

The couple had burned through their savings. Each received a pension, but they needed that money to cover their monthly expenses. Then Uddo and her organization showed up. It took two years, but in June 2010, Sylvia and Anthony could finally move into their home. Six months later, Anthony Blanchard was dead at seventy years old. "It wasn't Hurricane Katrina that killed him," his wife said. "It was the recovery."

26

THE SORE WINNER

It was an extraordinary gesture by a man new to politics. Troy Henry's concession speech after taking second in the 2010 mayoral race would have sufficed. "Mitch is going to be a fantastic mayor," Henry told his supporters, gathered at the Chateau Bourbon in the French Quarter. "I'm going to support him in any way he needs." Then, Henry walked to Mitch Landrieu's victory party to congratulate the mayor-elect in person. Landrieu called Henry to the stage and the two embraced. Landrieu next lifted Henry's arm and asked the crowd to give his worthy challenger a round of applause.

This moment of black-white unity was captured by the television cameras. Henry thought Landrieu meant it when he whispered in Henry's ear during their embrace that he looked forward to working with Henry over the coming months. "I guess you can say I'm very naive," Henry said. "He's been very vindictive."

Never mind the city contracts with Henry's consulting firm that were terminated after Landrieu took office. More disheartening was when the mayor obstructed a pair of projects Henry was working on with his childhood friend, the actor Wendell Pierce.[1] After Katrina, Pierce and Henry created the Pontchartrain Park Community Development Corp. to help restore their neighborhood, which Pierce dubbed the "black Mayberry." Together they also started Sterling Farms to bring quality grocery stores to parts of the city where they were scarce.

Their efforts in Pontchartrain Park ran into trouble when Henry and Pierce partnered with an out-of-town developer who failed to deliver on his promises. They had raised millions of dollars, though, and eventually moved ahead with a plan to build geothermal, solar-paneled homes in Pontchartrain Park—despite a lack of support from City Hall. "The last thing Mitch wanted to do," one former Landrieu appointee said, "is work with Troy on Pontchartrain Park. Mitch hates Troy's guts."

Both Henry and Pierce believe the mayor also stood in the way of a Sterling Farms store slated for the Lower Ninth Ward. "Once the city learned me and Wendell were the developers, our financial backers withdrew their support," Henry said. That was in 2011, six years after the storm.

"The mayor, I learned, is a sore winner," Henry said. Jacques Morial, who had known Landrieu since they were boys, used that same phrase to describe his old friend. "Mitch could be a great mayor," Morial said. "People expected the charming, consensus-building type they knew in Baton Rouge. But he's not governing as mayor that way. He doesn't look for consensus." Instead, Morial said, you're a loyal member of the mayor's team or you're part of the problem—in a city Landrieu stressed needed to speak with a single voice. "Frankly," Morial said, "I see this version of Mitch as a bully."

CEDRIC GRANT WAS LANDRIEU'S choice for making sure more cranes were in the sky. Grant, a genial black man who had filled top posts under both former mayor Marc Morial and Kathleen Blanco, inherited Ed Blakely's six-hundred-item wish list and turned it into the one hundred Katrina-related construction projects that Landrieu promised would be completed by the end of his term. Grant stood out as one of Landrieu's

---

1. Pierce is an actor best known for his roles in *The Wire* and *Tremé*.

more impressive hires—the man able to apply defibrillator paddles to a recovery that was flatlining. A little more than halfway through the mayor's term, Grant was so confident that he would deliver on the first hundred ideas by election day that he added another two hundred to the list, including around seventy-five road-repair projects.

Jeff Hebert, the young black man Landrieu put in charge of blight, also proved a smart pick. Charged with returning ten thousand blighted properties to the tax rolls by the end of Landrieu's term in 2014, Hebert implemented what he called BlightStat, based on the CitiStat crime-tracking system first championed by Baltimore mayor Martin O'Malley. "We did calculations on everything from how many inspections we needed in a month to reach our goals to the number of judgments we needed," Hebert said. He gave iPad-like tablets to the city's inspectors and created an easy-to-use Web page where residents could file complaints and monitor progress on individual properties. Blight vigilantes such as Rita Legrand in Lakeview appreciated a system that sent out an automatic notice after an inspector visited a site and alerts that let you know when a hearing was scheduled.

Landrieu was the beneficiary of some good timing. He had an ally in the White House in Barack Obama and benefited from the return (prior to his taking office) of the city's investment-grade bond rating, which allowed New Orleans to borrow at a more favorable interest rate. Cedric Grant also appreciated the work his predecessors had done moving projects to the other side of the state's eight-foot flow chart. Projects that would become signature Landrieu initiatives—the city money set aside to help draw grocery stores to so-called food deserts, a Soft Second Program to help those $20,000 or $40,000 short of the money they needed to rebuild—were ideas born in Ed Blakely's shop.

After the ineffectual Nagin, however, Landrieu's aggressiveness was impressive. That was most obvious in his administration's pursuit of FEMA dollars long after federal officials figured they had closed the books on New Orleans. Inside FEMA, they might have thought they had completed their block-by-block assessment of the damage to the city's streets, sidewalks, and buried pipes. To Landrieu and his people, that represented only phase one of an ongoing process. Convinced that the city's infrastructure was more damaged than FEMA was acknowledging,

Grant and his people insisted they open the streets. The city documented every underground leak it found and submitted detailed reports noting the impact of post-storm debris removal on streets, down to the weight of the trucks and the routes each took. Eight years after Katrina, Grant said, someone on his staff was meeting with FEMA at least once a week. Every two weeks, Grant himself sat down with someone from FEMA, and the mayor met monthly with the agency's regional director. Under Landrieu, Grant claimed, the city wrested an additional $600 million in repair money from FEMA. Sewerage and Water picked up an extra $400 million–plus.

Landrieu was candid about the hard choices he and the city faced. A pair of expensive federal court orders required the city to improve the parish jail and its police department. A state court in 2013 ordered the Landrieu administration to pay $17.5 million to cover its 2012 obligation to the firefighters' pension fund. He had tried but failed to convince Baton Rouge to let him raise the taxes on hotel stays and cigarettes sold within the city limits. Even with all that additional FEMA money, the city faced the same problems as other municipalities around the country. Those overseeing the city's libraries were crying out for more money as were those responsible for the city's parks. That was the challenge of running a US city in the twenty-first century, Landrieu explained to people, especially an older one with a near-infinite list of needs. "Money I spend on street repairs or because a federal judge orders me to," he said, "means money I can't spend on police or fire or safety and permits or recreation."

Yet the other Landrieu was petulant and thin-skinned, obsessive about the smallest details. Gordon Russell, who was city editor of the *Times-Picayune* through the first couple of years of the Landrieu administration, was always hearing from one of Landrieu's people about his unhappiness with something in the paper that day. "It'd always be about the smallest stuff," Russell said. A single paragraph buried deep in a news story, a throwaway item in a reporter's notebook column. "I'd be almost embarrassed for him," Russell said. "I'm thinking, 'Let it go, man. You're king of the world around here. Why do you care?'"

The experiences of people such as Troy Henry started spreading through political circles. Landrieu denied any retribution was behind his dealings with Henry, but others told a similar story. A children's advocate claimed that after complaining about the city's parks department, the city blackballed her nonprofit. A local legislator opposed a Landrieu plan to slash the number of judges in Orleans Parish, and the mayor and his people tried to have the man removed as chairman of a local development district. A local lawyer outspoken in her opposition to a new Tulane football stadium saw an end to her contract handling zoning cases for the city.

Tyler Bridges, a reporter for *The Lens*, an online investigative site focused on New Orleans, collected these and other stories in an article running under the headline "'Enemy for Life': Mayor Mitch Landrieu Accused of Steamrolling Those Who Disagree with Him." Confronted with the stories Bridges had collected from the thirty-plus people he had interviewed, Landrieu said, "The record of accomplishment speaks much more loudly than the noise of those people who have been told no." A more memorable defense, though, came in an e-mail sent around by a political consultant and Landrieu supporter named Cheron Brylski: "There are assholes and then there are PRODUCTIVE assholes. And in politics, the productive ones are often what you need when you have some place to go and no easy road to get there."

A MILESTONE WAS REACHED in early 2012 when the last of the FEMA trailers were removed from New Orleans. The homes of some people around town were still not finished, but city officials said it was time to rid the neighborhoods of these "eyesores." Code enforcement inspectors handed out tickets, threats were made, hearings held, and appeals lost. "Another page has turned in New Orleans's post-Katrina history," Mitch Landrieu said when FEMA finally declared his a trailer-free city.

Pages were not only turned but eliminated when that spring *Times-Picayune* publisher Ashton Phelps Jr. announced the newspaper would move to a three-day-a-week publishing schedule (Sunday, Wednesday, Friday).[2] Seven years after Katrina, New Orleans would

---

2. Shortly after Phelps's announcement, the *Advocate* in Baton Rouge announced that it would publish a daily New Orleans edition and then poached many of the *Times-Picayune*'s best people.

rank as the largest US city without a daily newspaper. "I'm glad,"WBOK talk jock John Slade said on the air. "That means the landed Confederate gentry's megaphone has shrunk."

The positive news included a $14.5 billion flood-protection system as impressive as it was expensive. The new pumping station the Army Corps of Engineers had built just south of the city was the planet's largest; a two-mile steel wall was built on the city's eastern edge to protect New Orleans East, the Lower Ninth Ward, and St. Bernard Parish from storm surges. The Corps had built or rebuilt several hundred miles of levees and floodwalls since 2005, along with seventy-three pumping stations and a series of massive gates to seal off waterways ahead of a storm. MR. GO was sealed closed. The naysayers said the Corps had designed its system to withstand a hundred-year storm—that is, a storm that has a 1 percent chance of happening in a given year—not a five-hundred-year storm as some had advocated. Still, what the Corps had built for New Orleans, declared Mark Schleifstein, the *Times-Picayune*'s longtime hurricane and environmental reporter, was a "far cry from the flawed structures that failed during Hurricane Katrina." He also declared it "the best flood control system of any coastal community in the United States."

Government, after pressure from community groups around the city, was doing a better job of maintaining properties under its control, though at a steep cost. The state was spending millions a year cutting the grass and maintaining the insurance on homes that had ended up in the Louisiana land trust because their owners had opted to give up their property under the Road Home program. The city launched a Nuisance Lot Maintenance program with work crews trying to combat the underbrush in those patches of the city where the vegetation was threatening to take over.

A TEACHER NAMED GWENDOLYN RIDGLEY received welcome news a couple of months before the seventh anniversary of Katrina. Ridgley, who had been trapped in her attic for two days after Katrina, had worked for the Orleans Parish schools for thirty-two years when, along with seven thousand of her fellow employees, she was fired by the school district. In June 2012, a state judge ruled in favor of Ridgley in the class action lawsuit she and other teachers had filed. The district didn't follow its own rules before terminating its employees, the judge ruled, and then compounded its mistake by failing to give tenured preference as new schools opened after the storm. The judge awarded Ridgley $480,000 in back pay and damages, a decision that meant the schools faced a possible $1.5 billion judgment.[3]

The Super Bowl was held at the Superdome—now officially the Mercedes-Benz Superdome—at the start of 2013. New Orleans had hosted nine of the first thirty-six Super Bowls, but this was its first since Katrina. Mitch Landrieu seemed intent on showing off his city. Banners were hung throughout the central business district while crews spent a month giving the airport a makeover. A new streetcar line connecting the stadium to the French Quarter and other tourist spots was inaugurated days before the game. They even prettied up the Lower Ninth with palm trees along St. Claude and Claiborne Avenues. "Now, isn't that ridiculous?" asked school principal Doris Hicks. Her school was still teaching some students in trailers, and blight was everywhere. "And here the city is spending all these millions of dollars for the Super Bowl while people around the city want to know when the city might have the money to fix the streets or fix a sidewalk?"

RAY NAGIN CONTINUED TO make the occasional cameo. He released a memoir, *Katrina's Secrets: Storms after the Storm*, about those few weeks he was the best-known mayor in America. "It was towards the end of my final term as mayor that I started to get significant encouragement to document what really happened after Hurricane Katrina," he wrote in the opening pages. Apparently, though, none of those doing the encouraging were in the book business as Nagin needed to pay to

---

3. A five-judge panel would unanimously uphold the lower court's ruling, but news accounts made clear that this victory would be hollow. The appellate court slashed the damages due the former employees, but even this $750 million or so in back pay was greater than the district's annual budget. In November 2014, the Louisiana Supreme Court ruled against the teachers, who vowed to appeal the ruling to the US Supreme Court.

self-publish his work. He was invited on the *Today* show to promote it and also *The Daily Show*, where Jon Stewart asked him what he'd been up to since leaving office. "I'm doing disaster consulting," Nagin began. Stewart laughed, thinking the former mayor was making a joke, and then launched into his own shtick: "I do disaster recovery. I sell hair-care products."

Nagin had been out of office for nearly two years when the news broke that he was the target of a federal investigation. A grand jury, the *Times-Picayune*'s David Hammer reported in February 2012, was looking at whether the former mayor accepted bribes and favors from people doing business with the city. By then, Greg Meffert had cut a deal with the US Attorney's office and was telling prosecutors everything he knew. So, too, were several city vendors facing federal indictment. Meffert claimed his former boss knew that a city contractor was paying the bill for the trips to Hawaii and Jamaica that he, Meffert, arranged on behalf of Nagin and his family. (Meffert also claimed this same city contractor paid for $1,500 in landscaping work at the mayor's house after Katrina.) In a more damning line of inquiry, federal investigators were asking if Nagin arranged for the president of a home-restoration company to secure tens of millions in city contracts in exchange for help with the countertop-installation business Nagin and his sons had founded.

The former mayor would again be in the news when he and his wife sold their Park Island home. The Nagins initially asked $729,000 for a place they had bought for $345,000 in 1998, but ultimately lowered the asking price to $525,000. The house sold for $485,000 in July 2012. Seven years after Katrina, the public face of New Orleans to much of the world lived in a two-bedroom town house in a Dallas suburb. There, five hundred miles from New Orleans, the former mayor learned the news, in January 2013, seven-plus years after the storm, that the federal government was indicting him on twenty-one counts of public corruption, including fraud, bribery, and tax evasion.

SUPERSTORM SANDY ALSO PUT New Orleans back in the national news in October 2012, seven years after Katrina. Sandy caused 160 deaths compared to the 1,800-plus who died because of Hurricane Katrina. Dubbed a *superstorm* because its winds were below hurricane strength when it hit the Northeast, the extreme weather in a heavily populated section of the country still caused an estimated $65 billion in damages. That compared to the $135 billion attached to Katrina. Eighty percent of New Orleans had flooded compared to relatively small stretches of New York or New Jersey, yet that didn't stop Senate majority leader Harry Reid (frustrated that the House Republicans were blocking a $60 billion emergency-aid package he had proposed) from taking the Senate floor to declare that Katrina was "nothing in comparison to what happened to the people in New York and New Jersey."

Connie and Mark Uddo were among those traveling to the East Coast to help. "We flew up with Mitch [Landrieu]," Connie Uddo said. She spoke with people in Toms River, New Jersey, to prepare them for the work ahead and offered to help any way she could. Mark cooked for seven hundred in the Rockaways in New York. "People on the East Coast have no idea what they're in for," said Cassandra Wall after the storm.

DON'T CALL HIM A white mayor. That's what Mitch Landrieu told an interviewer. And don't describe New Orleans as a majority-black city. "New Orleans has never been a white city or black city," Landrieu explained. "It's a melting pot. The people of the city have received me that way, and we are making this a place for everyone."

Plenty of people in the black community looked favorably on Landrieu. He at least tried to project himself as the mayor of all New Orleans, and his work ethic was admirable. Black New Orleans disproportionately benefited from every extra dollar the mayor and his team wrested from FEMA, and blight reduction—a top priority for this mayor—was a far more severe problem in the city's black communities than in its white ones. The mayor endorsed an outspoken black woman, Cynthia Willard-Lewis, over an outspoken white woman, Stacy Head, in their run for the always-contentious at-large seat (Head won by 281 votes) and angered supporters in Lakeview when he announced the city was spending $45 million on road repairs in the Lower Ninth Ward and only $14 million in their neighborhood. The streets in Lakeview were bad but not nearly as treacherous to drive as those of the Lower Ninth. But the relative state of the roadways wasn't the point to people in Lakeview.

"I took the mayor to task in a public forum," said Robert Lupo, who owned multiple commercial properties in Lakeview. "I told him, 'Here we're back and dealing with streets so bad that people are getting flat tires, but instead of investing in us, you're putting all this money into a part of the city the marketplace has rejected.'"

Yet Landrieu was a white elected official in a majority-black city, even if he rejected those labels, and some would always have a hard time seeing beyond his skin color. During the 2010 election, Troy Henry had asked if maybe it was "unhealthy" for a majority-black city to be run largely by white officials, and more than a few people in New Orleans were inclined to believe it. Landrieu won friends in black New Orleans when he sided with Willard-Lewis over Head, and then lost them a couple of years later when he endorsed a conservative white woman over a black woman, a former district court judge, in a majority-black district. At a high-profile ceremony, Landrieu signed a consent decree with the Justice Department that committed the city to overhauling its dysfunctional police department—but then he claimed it would cost too much and asked a federal judge to release New Orleans from the agreement. Aside from the president himself, no member of the Obama administration was more often criticized on Fox News and in the conservative media than Attorney General Eric Holder. Yet the Democratic mayor of New Orleans gave them their talking points for a couple of days when he labeled Holder's Justice Department "a kind of rogue agency."

Beverly McKenna, the publisher of the *Tribune*, confessed that she felt exhausted by the promises made by white politicians. "I had kind of had it by the time Mitch was elected," she said. Twenty-five years earlier, her husband had been voted onto the school board. There, he met fierce resistance whenever he agitated for blacks to be included among the architects, construction firms, and suppliers used by district officials. It was like nothing had changed, she said. Landrieu, she said, had done "almost nothing" to help along other minority-run companies vying for the city of New Orleans's business.[4] "He might cast himself as this liberal champion," McKenna said of Landrieu, "but once in office, people show who they really are."

Barbara Major, the former cochair of the Bring New Orleans Back Commission, was also frustrated by Landrieu. "You have all this money coming into the city," Major said. "A hospital being built. Schools. Roads. These other projects. But you look at the crews working on these projects, and they don't look like New Orleans." A vibrant black community needed a healthy business sector, yet she didn't see that as a priority to Landrieu. "Here's this mayor known for cracking heads and throwing tantrums when his people don't give him what he wants," Major said. In 2010, the City Council passed an ordinance that said that at least half of all recovery dollars should end up in the hands of locally owned businesses and 35 percent needed to go to "socially and economically disadvantaged business." Yet the Collaborative, a local group that Major and others created to help minority- and women-owned enterprises secure more government contracts, estimated that established, white-owned businesses still accounted for more than 95 percent of the contracts let by the city.

No issue seemed to rile up WBOK's John Slade as did Landrieu's pick for police chief, Ronal Serpas. On *Showtime in the Afternoon*, he would review the chief's résumé. Left the NOPD in 2001 after a reprimand for deceptive bookkeeping practices (to buy tactical equipment for the department's Special Operations unit). Hundreds of misdemeanor sex assaults had been reclassified as more serious sexual crimes after he stepped down as Nashville's police chief, and some complained that the New Orleans police were doing the same under

---

4. The Landrieu administration boasted that between 2012 and 2014, DBEs—disadvantaged business enterprises—received $100 million in city contracts, but 80 percent of that total went to the two garbage-collection firms engaged under Nagin, and the rest included a mix of women-owned firms and others qualifying as DBEs.

his tenure—downgrading rapes to assaults.[5] The city's homicide rate was still one of the worst in the nation, and so many cops were quitting that in 2012—two years into Serpas's tenure—the police union paid for a survey to isolate the problem. The answer in part was a lack of faith in Serpas, whom some in the City Hall press corps had dubbed Chief Wiggum from *The Simpsons*. Only 12 percent of the force, the survey found, agreed with the statement that Serpas's policies "made the NOPD a more effective crime prevention and public safety organization." By the end of Landrieu's term, the city would be some 400 cops short of its goal of 1,575 officers.

Slade was mugged on Good Friday 2013—the first time in his life that he was a crime victim. The assault left him shaken but also proved fodder for his show. He blamed the mugging on school reform and also used the crime to flip on its head the white fears invariably stirred up when someone black takes over as mayor. "Thirty-two years of black mayors and I've never been touched," he would say. Yet with a white mayor in office, he'd ask, how can I ever feel safe?

---

5. In November 2014, the city's inspector general charged the department's special victims unit with failing to investigate hundreds of sex-crime complaints, dismissing them as misdemeanors not worth their time.

27

RETURN TO SPLENDOR

"Everything is coming up roses!" exclaimed real estate developer Pres Kabacoff. It was eight years after Katrina and Kabacoff was holding forth on the hidden blessings of New Orleans's near-death experience. The sixty-eight-year-old Kabacoff, sitting in a dark wicker chair in his resplendent offices on Gravier Street in the central business district, reminisced about the New Orleans of his youth, when the Crescent City's 630,000 people ranked it as the largest in the South. School integration, white flight, an oil bust, crime—from the 1960s onward, the metropolis he loved was on a "continuous downward path."

"It took a Katrina to finally turn things around," he said.

For nearly a decade, Kabacoff had been peddling an ambitious plan to reshape the historic center of New Orleans. It was about building on your assets, he told anyone willing to listen. The French Quarter and the Marigny were thriving, but what about the Bywater, a riverfront neighborhood sitting between the Marigny and the Lower Ninth Ward? Or Tremé, which bordered the French Quarter and stood out as another old New Orleans neighborhood in desperate need of redevelopment. Two new hospitals were going up in lower Mid-City, another neglected black community. The hospital complex "lookcd likc a little bit of Houston in the middle of New Orleans," said columnist Stephanie Grace (first of the *Times-Picayune*, then the *Advocate*). But the new jobs would mean a boost in the median income and more retail, especially with the demolition of Iberville, one of the Big Four public housing projects. "We could use a little gentrification in this town," Kabacoff said.

Nagin had nodded his head and done nothing whenever Kabacoff talked about his ideas, but the Landrieu transition team invited him to cochair its housing task force. That experience prompted him to lay out his vision in a long essay. "A Return to Splendor," he called his magnum opus—and, not for the first time, was criticized by some within the black community. "People can be very touchy about race around here," he offered.

Kabacoff felt he had done his penance long before Katrina. In the 1990s, his bête noire was Barbara Major. The two clashed over his proposal to tear down a sizable housing project occupying prime real estate in the lower Garden District near the river. His plan had him displacing hundreds of residents to build a mixed-income development he had dubbed the River Garden Apartments. "My penalty was to go to one of her 'enduring racism' seminars," he said. "I brought my entire team and we all sang 'Kumbaya.'" He was pleased to report that, post-Katrina, there wasn't the same pressure on developers to kowtow to the locals. The Big Four were being demolished in stages, so vestiges were still standing, yet any residual anger was directed at the City Council and federal government, not the private developers like himself who were profiting from the decision. Each of the Big Four was being replaced by faux town houses that called to mind nothing so much as Rivcr Gardcn. Kabacoff was a partner in the makeover of the giant Iberville project, but largely his firm was focused on housing conversion projects in the historic riverfront neighborhoods. "There's a lot of juice flowing through New Orleans after Katrina," Kabacoff said, and he was intent on using any available pot of federal money to see through a vision he had been touting for the past decade. "The good news for New Orleans is that peoplc likc mc, pcople with capacity, we stepped up," he said. "We didn't give up on New Orleans."

Kabacoff preferred to see himself as a visionary and ponytailed iconoclast rather than one of the city's wealthier developers. His girlfriend, Sallie Ann Glassman, described herself as a voodoo priestess, an artist, and a social-justice activist. "Exotic," the *Times-Picayune* said of the two-story home the couple built in Bywater and filled with art. They purchased a vacant furniture store nearby and renamed it the Healing Center. They painted the facade orange and leased space to an organic restaurant, an art gallery, a co-op grocery, and a yoga studio. Artists and young people moved into Bywater. Restaurants opened along with cafés, clubs, and other businesses catering to the community's newest residents. A neighborhood that had been slowly gentrifying prior to Katrina now felt enough like parts of Brooklyn that some were calling Bywater "the Williamsburg of the South."

How could he not feel optimistic? Kabacoff asked. Sitting in an office filled with African and Asian art and wearing Native American jewelry, he spoke of the hospital complex and its potential to remake what he had long viewed as a forlorn edge of downtown. Neglected landmarks such as the Saenger and Mahalia Jackson Theaters had been refurbished, and the storm had galvanized support in Baton Rouge around long-sought reforms such as the merger of the area's levee boards and a consolidation of the city's seven assessor offices. A revamped education system had everyone he knew feeling hopeful about the parish schools for the first time in at least a generation. Creativity and energy were transforming Bywater and also Tremé and Mid-City, another older part of town going through similar changes. "The city has never looked better," Kabacoff declared.

He was not alone in that view. "New Orleans is such a better place than it was pre-Katrina," Bill Hines, the lawyer once so close to Nagin, declared several years into Landrieu's tenure. Over dinner at a favorite Uptown white-tablecloth restaurant, he, too, spoke of the strides made by the city's underperforming schools and the demolition of the projects. His law firm had doubled in size since the storm, and his happy ending—new furniture in a refurbished home—seemed an apt metaphor for New Orleans. A decaying city that had been crumbling for decades was enjoying a massive makeover courtesy of FEMA and HUD. Tourists were spending at record levels, and the city's convention business was strong. "New Orleans is a very hot property," Hines said. As proof he mentioned a recent news story putting Louisiana ahead of New York and second only to California in film productions. "I'm seeing before my eyes the rebirth of New Orleans."

Hines would get no argument from Michael Hecht, white, the CEO of Greater New Orleans, Inc., an economic-development nonprofit. On the twenty-third floor of Canal Place, in an office overlooking the Mississippi, Hecht expressed concern for a "fragile black middle class" (Hines shared the same worry). But eight years after Katrina, Hecht, a post-Katrina transplant, declared the city to be in the midst of an economic renaissance. Where pre-storm New Orleans was a town growing increasingly reliant on tourism, he said, the city had invested in a giant biomedical center that promised a shift toward better-paying jobs. The tech scene that he and others had helped midwife had prompted the *Atlantic* to declare New Orleans a "start-up city." *Forbes* listed New Orleans second in its 2011 "Best Cities for Jobs" feature, and the next year *Travel + Leisure* ranked New Orleans first in its annual list of "America's top cities." The latest census figures showed that the city was attracting another four-thousand-plus people each year, most of them presumably the smart, young artsy types the editors of *Forbes* had in mind when they declared New Orleans "Number One Brain Magnet in the US." New Orleans, Hecht declared, "is one of the great comeback stories of all time."

Even Ted Quant, an ally of Lance Hill's who cofounded the Twomey Center for Peace Through Justice at Loyola University, saw great improvements in the city that had been his home since 1970. Quant, who is black, occasionally visited Pres Kabacoff's Healing Center. "There's live music, a grocery store with great produce, a theater," Quant said. "What's there not to like about a place like that?" Personally, he had no complaints. He had money in the bank and found plenty of places to go when he and his wife wanted to enjoy a night out on the town. He counted himself among those dubious that the charter-school experiment would save the next generation of students, but his kids were already grown. His primary worry was for all those people working minimum-wage jobs who could no longer afford the rent. "The city does look good," Quant said. "But for whom?"

VIOLENT CRIME OCCURRED AT twice the national rate eight years after Katrina, even though New Orleans was a smaller, whiter city. New Orleans was also a less affordable city, the Greater New Orleans

Community Data Center reported shortly before the eighth anniversary of Katrina. Despite the economic renaissance, more than half the
city's renters were still spending at least a third of their pretax income
on housing, and the employment among working-aged black men had
ticked up a mere two points, from 46 percent to 48 percent. The average education level among both blacks and whites had increased post-
Katrina, yet the city's poverty rate was 29 percent in 1999 and still 29
percent when in 2013 the Data Center released its "New Orleans Index
at Eight." The Bloomberg wire service found that inequality was greater
in New Orleans than any other US city except Atlanta. The disparity
between rich and poor in New Orleans put the city on par with Zambia.

The remaking of public housing in New Orleans was near complete
eight years after Katrina. It represented another audacious experiment
watched by researchers around the country. Only one-third of the units
overseen by the Housing Authority of New Orleans would house low-
income residents. Another third had been set aside for moderate-income
locals, which, after lobbying by Kabacoff and others, was increased from
60 percent of the area median income to 120 percent, or $71,000 for a
family of four. The last third were reserved for market-rate rentals. Financing proved difficult after the collapse of the global credit markets
in 2008, but Goldman Sachs, Warren Buffett, and hedge-fund manager Julian Robertson were among those funding this privatized "public"
housing. The federal government chipped in an additional $18 million
in FEMA dollars to pay the construction costs. Millions more in precious community development funds were also used.

New Orleans, which had fourteen thousand public housing units
in the 1990s, now had fewer than three thousand low-income apartments. The federal overseer the Obama administration sent to run the
Housing Authority of New Orleans was issuing more rental vouchers
than in the past, but participation by landlords in the Section 8 program
had dropped steeply post-Katrina. At the eight-year mark, the city had
thirteen thousand people on its voucher waiting list and another three
thousand families waiting for traditional public housing.

The RTA was still running only half the number of bus lines as
before Katrina. Those who couldn't afford a car in a city in which one
in every three people earned under $20,000 a year faced much longer

waits for the buses that did run. Before Katrina, a bus on the Galvez line, which connects the Upper and Lower Ninth Wards to the rest of the city, ran every seven minutes during peak ridership hours, said Mitchell L. Guidry Jr., the RTA's director of planning. Eight years after Katrina, a bus ran every forty minutes. The city's streetcar lines also suffered from tight funding. Where once twenty cars ran on St. Charles during the commute hours, now there were eight. The typical wait was now fifteen minutes rather than five.

Nearly 80 percent of the city's public school students were attending a charter school eight years after Katrina. Articles reported on the New Orleans schools miracle, and counter-articles exposed such claims as a myth. In 2013, Oprah Winfrey's production company debuted *Blackboard Wars*, a series about a failing New Orleans school and the high-profile charter champion determined to prove his method can work in any environment. Less than a year later, abysmal test scores and falling enrollments caused the school to shut its doors.

"This is a tough thing to say, but let me be really honest," Arne Duncan, US education secretary, offered around the fifth anniversary of Katrina. "I think the best thing that happened to the education system in New Orleans was Hurricane Katrina." Parent advocate Karran Harper Royal was among those offended by the remark and also baffled by it. Royal was a black woman who had for twenty years been fighting for better schools in New Orleans. More recently, she had started answering the complaint line for a group she was a part of called the Education Equity Roundtable. Some days she was receiving two or three calls from unhappy parents looking for the group's help.

"If I had to choose, I'd vote to go back to the old system," Royal said. "People needed stability after Katrina, but instead we got a system where schools are constantly opening and closing and you can never be sure where your child is going next year. There was a lot of dysfunction in the old days, but at least your children attended community schools. At least you knew the people and knew they cared."

NEW ORLEANS COULD BOAST of its beautiful new flood-protection system, but the gift came with a price tag. The Corps was transferring responsibility for the levees in stages, and state and local officials were scrambling to find money to staff the pumping stations and pay for basic maintenance. That included the cost of occasionally raising the earthen levees to account for rising water levels and a sinking landscape. The levee boards had the authority to raise funds through property taxes, but any increase first had to be approved by a majority of voters in districts that covered several parishes.

The state's receding coastline was another worry. The federal government had spent multiple billions on a storm system with a built-in obsolescence if the wetlands continued to disappear. Between 1932 and 2010, according to the Data Center, the New Orleans region lost 948 square miles of coastal wetlands—nearly one-third of the marshland that served as a natural defense against storm surge. After Katrina, a new Coastal Protection and Restoration Authority was formed. Eventually, the legislature approved a $50 billion, fifty-year coastal restoration master plan. State and federal dollars would be used to fund the hundred-plus projects the state's master plan identified to help Louisiana recover and protect its coastal lands. But even including fines related to the BP oil spill, the state had raised less than $3 billion by early 2015.

One of the regional flood-protection districts saw an obvious way to fund some of the work: make the people who helped cause the problem pay to help fix it. The Southeast Louisiana Flood Protection Authority–East, or Slfpa-E, voted unanimously to file suit against nearly a hundred oil and gas companies. Their industry carved up the southeastern Louisiana marshes, the suit argued, accelerating the loss of the wetlands and making New Orleans more prone to flooding. So why shouldn't the gas and oil interests pay to help correct the problem? "This protective buffer took six thousand years to form," wrote John M. Barry, the author and historian who served as the board's vice chair. "Yet . . . it has been brought to the brink of destruction in a lifetime."

28

"GET OVER IT"

Alden McDonald saw virtue in a city thrumming with young energy—Brooklyn on the bayou. He and Rhesa even signed up for 504 (named after the New Orleans area code), a new program in which volunteers hosted dinners for newcomers wanting to feel more rooted in their adopted city. The McDonalds would feed a dozen or so people at a time in the hopes of teaching them something about New Orleans and maybe even inspiring them to get more involved in their community. "We could use all the help we could get," McDonald said.

McDonald was as big a cheerleader for the makeover of public housing in New Orleans as Pres Kabacoff or Bill Hines. The tours he offered interested out-of-towners now included Columbia Parc, the new development near his home, built in place of the old St. Bernard complex. "It's one of the bright spots to come out of this thing," McDonald said. The first shock was physical: twenty or so blocks of dreary brick tenements had been replaced by rows of brightly painted town houses, complete with wrought-iron balconies, along with the occasional low-rise Creole cottage mixed in. Columbia Parc could accept only around one-third of St. Bernard's former residents, but McDonald focused on families

fortunate enough to secure a replacement unit. Each apartment was outfitted with a washer-dryer. Granite countertops were standard, as were
stainless-steel appliances and faux-hardwood floors. An early-learning
center, a computer room, a swimming pool, a health club, and a movie
theater were on-site. "This was a case of an agency taking the opportunity to build things the right way," McDonald said.

Yet McDonald was not nearly as beamish about New Orleans's future
as his peers in the white community. He also brought visitors to Pontchartrain Park, only a couple of minutes from Columbia Parc. There, in
this subdivision central to the rise of the black middle class in New Orleans, refurbished ranch homes abutted houses that seemed untouched
since the storm. Eight years after Katrina, McDonald said, maybe 60 percent of the homes in Pontchartrain Park were habitable. Other parts of
Gentilly—areas only a few blocks from his own home—were filled with
moldy houses crumbling from neglect. "See all those vacant lots?" He
pointed to an empty-looking street. "They were occupied pre-Katrina."
Driving around the nearby Seventh Ward proved equally disheartening.
"There's still so much to be done." McDonald worried about a lack of
urgency given all those who had declared victory over Katrina.

New Orleans East was faring better than Pontchartrain Park or
the Seventh Ward. Estimates put the population at between 80 and 85
percent of its pre-Katrina numbers. A supermarket had finally opened
six years after Katrina. A second opened a year or two later. Stores and
eateries were leasing space in the strip malls, at least those located along
the main roads. A beautiful new library had opened a few blocks from
Liberty's office. Schools were under construction around the East. Cassandra Wall's sister Tangee, who had remained politically active, saw the
revitalization of Joe W. Brown Memorial Park as critical. Rather than
use FEMA dollars to simply restore this 163-acre park, the Landrieu
administration sought partners in Nike, Allstate, and the Brees Dream
Foundation to make it better. The park was now home to a regula-
tion-size football field, a state-of-the-art track, tennis courts, an indoor
pool, and a rec facility that hosted after-school programs aimed at teens.
The city was also creating miles of walking and jogging trails in the area.
Seven and a half years after Katrina, at the start of 2013, construction
began on a new hospital at the site of the old Methodist facility.

Yet eight years after Katrina, New Orleans East hardly seemed a synecdoche for the "higher and better" New Orleans that George Bush was imagining in his Jackson Square speech two weeks after the storm. Locals were happy to see construction start on a new hospital. But where once the East had two hospitals, a single 80-bed facility was replacing a 181-bed institution. The new hospital would have no maternity ward. People were happy to have a couple of supermarkets, but the East had six prior to Katrina. An occupied storefront seemed better than an empty one, but now so many were filled by pawnbrokers, check cashers, and dollar-discount stores. "From the highway, we take on the look of a poor community when nothing could be further from the truth," said Sylvia Scineaux-Richard, president of the East New Orleans Neighborhood Advisory Commission (ENONAC).

Fewer low-rent complexes were along the I-10 than before the storm. Some had been converted to luxury apartments, and even those still filled with Section 8 tenants were upgraded to comply with new zoning rules championed by ENONAC (minimum square footage, a washer-dryer in each unit, a three-story height limit). Yet abandoned apartment buildings were still visible from the highway, as were the restaurants and big-box retailers that still hadn't reopened. Walmart was returning to the East, but not the giant mall next to Liberty Bank or the movie theater in which McDonald had invested. Commercial strips a few blocks off the highway were still in shambles. Commercial properties in the worst shape—those whose owners failed to do basic maintenance such as mow the lawn or board up broken windows—were singled out by Tangee Wall and her allies during one of their "blight rallies." Their targets included a hospice, a nursing home, and a pair of churches. "You'll hear people say, 'I thought this place would have been better a loooooonggg time ago,'" Wall said. "They're giving up, leaving their home to the mortgage company and starting over somewhere else."

Some subdivisions in the East had few empty homes. But others still had fewer than 80 percent of their pre-Katrina population eight years after the storm. Cheap Chinese restaurants and seafood shacks and the big fast-food chains were well represented, but nice restaurants and decent stores were lacking. The Eastover golf course was still closed. McDonald estimated that one-third of his friends had not returned to New Orleans. "I still have family members stuck in Houston. Some cousins," McDonald said. "They're terribly homesick. But people had to make choices." They found a better job, according to McDonald, or they were reluctant to move home when their kids were doing well in school. "A very different population lives here now."

Liberty Bank continued to expand, moving into the Chicago market at the start of 2013 when it bought a failing black-owned bank there. Soon, McDonald was wrestling a new, enviable worry: slowing down the pace of growth so that the bank, which now operated branches in seven states, didn't cross the $1 billion threshold. If it did, it would have to submit to more rigorous regulatory exams. "I'm too old for that," McDonald said. After more than forty years at the helm of Liberty, McDonald had been on the job longer than any other sitting black bank president. Approaching seventy years old, he took to calling himself "the grandfather of black banking."

McDonald looked at the Uptown elite differently after Katrina. He had let his membership in the Business Council lapse, he said, "because I did not approve of their behavior after Katrina." Many peers whom he considered friends before the storm he now held at a distance. He would rejoin the Business Council seven years after Katrina—only once he was convinced that the organization was interested in promoting diversity.

"Ninety percent of what they were pushing for in Dallas they got," he said—and the remaining 10 percent seemed still in play. In 2011, a downtown business group hung banners along the streets reading WELCOME TO YOUR BLANK CANVAS—presumably referring to places at least some people considered home. Communities such as Bywater and Tremé were now out of reach to many with deep roots there, forcing people to find cheaper housing outside the city. The tradition of second-line parades— the brass-band-led celebrations that take place in the city's black neighborhoods—continued, but not without controversy. Events that before Katrina attracted a mostly black crowd of maybe a couple of hundred were drawing a mostly white audience of fifteen hundred. The worry among some black New Orleanians was that transplants were so eager to embrace the local culture that they threatened to suffocate it. Ill feelings were compounded when the newcomers drawn to Tremé by its rich history then called the cops to enforce a long-ignored city ordinance that prohibits the playing of live music on the streets after 8:00 p.m.

McDonald felt especially frustrated with the town's hotel and restaurant owners. His father, a waiter for fifty-two years, was very much on his mind whenever industry people asked him for a meeting. For many hotel chains, they told McDonald, their New Orleans property was the most profitable in their portfolio. Restaurants were able to charge more for food and drink without any drop-off in business. The future only looked bright for a tourism economy that they declared more profitable than ever.

"Then tell your people to give the workers a raise!" McDonald countered. "I'll tell them, 'You correct this or you're going to end up with a population so poor they're not going to be able to even afford the rent here.'" The homeowner who paid $600 a year in property tax before the storm was now looking at an annual bill of nearly $2,000. Flood insurance rates had increased threefold. Homeowner policies had gone up by around the same amount. People's water bills are slated to more than double by 2020 to pay for much-needed repairs to an ailing water and sewer system. "What that means is the poor will stay poor and the middle class can never get ahead," McDonald said. Liberty was thriving, but not those McDonald and others had wanted to help when they started the bank in 1972.

"GET OVER IT." THAT'S what Jimmy Reiss wanted to tell people still bringing up Dallas eight years after Katrina.

Sitting in the ground-floor café of a Poydras high-rise, Reiss spoke of the twenty years he had spent "working my ass off and getting only shit. Racially, they were against something a white man tried to do even if it was for the good of everybody." He read from a one-page stat sheet he had brought with him that showed New Orleans circa 2005 to be a high-crime city with too many unemployed black men, lousy schools, and a crumbling infrastructure. His only crime after Katrina, he said, was that he had proclaimed the obvious: New Orleans had too many poor people.

EIGHT YEARS AFTER KATRINA, Cassandra Wall gathered with her family at her sister Petie's home in New Orleans East. Cassandra's niece—Petie's oldest—had just given birth. Petie had invited everyone over to celebrate.

Cassandra couldn't have been happier for her niece and her husband. But as invariably happened when Cassandra was in New Orleans, she felt relieved her visit would be short. "I'll go and be glad I went, but I feel out of place," Cassandra said. "Being there, I feel the disconnect. I feel the loss."

Thanksgivings and Christmas dinners were still held in New Orleans. The five of them made the effort to get together around Mardi Gras and for other celebrations, and also for the occasional dinner because it had been too long since they had seen one another. "I'd still describe ourselves as close," Cassandra said. "We still love each other. It's just different." They agreed to avoid certain topics, and tensions would flare when invariably they ended up talking about them anyway.

"Cassandra changed a lot," Petie said. "It's not just geography. Her opinions about New Orleans changed and that's been hurtful. Because this is home."

Cassandra had thought it was inevitable that eventually she would end up back in New Orleans. The house in Baton Rouge, she always thought, was about giving Brandon stability while he went to school. Surely New Orleans would be ready by the time he finished high school. But occasionally she'd drive through the old neighborhood, and all she could see were the homes that were still unoccupied and the same FOR SALE signs from the last time she'd visited. Brandon graduated in 2011 and matriculated at Xavier. Her son was living back in New Orleans, yet, two years later, she was still in Baton Rouge.

"I live here but I don't consider Baton Rouge my permanent home," she said. "I feel disconnected from both places. It's a bad feeling."

Her sisters didn't want to believe she had given up on New Orleans. "We've all done our share of traveling, overseas, all over the US," cousin Robyn said. "We've all talked about it, how we've never found a place that compares to New Orleans." Tangee, Petie, and Robyn were working hard to make New Orleans East what it once was—and felt the sting every time they heard Cassandra say, "The home I know doesn't exist anymore." Even Contesse—prickly, contrarian Contesse—chose New Orleans when she moved back into the old house they'd inherited in Central City.

"Well, I happen to love traditions and customs, they're important to me," Robyn had said at one of their gatherings. She figured if Cassandra felt she had the right to vent her opinions about the place where they lived, they had the right to offer a counterview. Petie nodded her head in agreement. This time Cassandra remained silent despite the implied criticism that she didn't care about the things that made New Orleans unique. Cassandra was tired of their disappointment, and they tired of what Petie described as "her constant negativity about the place I happen to live."

"All this divisiveness," Petie said, "started when the two of them"—Cassandra and Contesse—"didn't want to come home."

"You go through a traumatic event like this," Tangee said, "and it's never going to be the same."

From the perspective of her sisters, maybe Cassandra's greatest transgression was that she came to this realization before the others. "A tragedy happened and destroyed what we had," Cassandra said. "You just have to move forward and build something new because—and there's no way around it—it's gone and never coming back."

MARTIN LANDRIEU—SON OF a politician, brother of the incumbent mayor—was too much of a diplomat to declare the new Lakeview a vast upgrade over the old one. "I can't use the word *better* given the circumstances," he said. But eight years after Katrina, he marveled over Lakeview's makeover. For years, he was part of a group working to draw a younger demographic to a neighborhood that, pre-storm, was dominated by older, smaller homes. "We didn't have the closet space young families wanted, we didn't have the amenities." Katrina corrected that. Modest-size ranch homes were torn down and replaced by sturdy two- and three-story places. Homes that survived the bulldozer had undergone six-figure rehabs that meant all-new kitchens, bathrooms, and open floor plans in vogue.

"The kind of change that would have taken us thirty or forty years," Landrieu said, "took seven or eight."

The *Times-Picayune* ran a feature in 2011 about this community that "stands out for the economic rebirth it is experiencing even as a national recession has stymied growth." Six years after Katrina, it seemed a retail outlet would have a hard time even finding an empty storefront. "Commercial space is getting to its saturation point," a dry cleaner told the paper. Where Alden McDonald and others were constantly in touch with big-name retailers in the hopes of drawing them to the eastern half of the city, Robert Lupo, Lakeview's top commercial landlord, was swatting them away. "I can't tell you how many calls I get from the national chains," Lupo said. But he had to tell them he had no vacancies. "All of my businesses are happy," he said. "People here have all this disposable income." Lakeview had fewer homes and more double lots after Katrina, but by 2013 it had more people because of all the families that had moved there.

"The big fights in Lakeview right now are people building multi-million-dollar mansions," Freddy Yoder said. "Housing prices are going up astronomically."

The range of restaurants struck Cassandra Wall when one day she drove down Harrison Avenue, Lakeview's main commercial strip. She saw more upscale eateries in a few blocks than in all of New Orleans East. Driving the side streets made her more depressed. "Compare Lakeview to the East," Cassandra said. "It makes no sense." Two middle-class, professional-class communities, yet one was thriving, and the other was a place she couldn't live. "You tell me the difference between the two communities," she requested, then supplied the answer. "Race. Of course."

Jeb Bruneau, the president of Lakeview Civic at the time of Katrina, spoke of the grit among his neighbors when asked why Lakeview and not New Orleans East. "We didn't wait for government but decided to do for ourselves," Bruneau said. Connie Uddo, despite the racial bias she recognized in the Road Home program, agreed: "People want to say people here had more money. But rich or poor, black or white, if you were wiped out, you were wiped out. The difference is we got organized faster. We realized early on that government wasn't going to be there, so we didn't wait."

Martin Landrieu wasn't sure what the explanation was, but Jeff Hebert, the man his brother the mayor had put in charge of blight, said he's puzzled over the question of Lakeview versus New Orleans East for years. Lakeview was on the right side of nationwide trends (the revival of communities closer to the core city, the community feel of its commercial strip), Hebert pointed out, while New Orleans East was on the wrong side (suburban sprawl, strip malls, office parks off the interstate). The compact size of Lakeview compared to New Orleans East was another advantage.

Yet none of those, Hebert said, offered anywhere close to an adequate explanation for what he saw going on in the two neighborhoods. "I look at the data out in the East. The high homeownership. The income numbers. The high levels of disposable income. And the answer I keep coming back to is race."

CONNIE UDDO WAS STILL working in Gentilly eight years after the storm. She thought about shutting down her organization, but she reminded herself of how much happier she was after Katrina than she was before. "I kind of like this Connie Uddo a lot more than the other one," she said.

Uddo was now running two nonprofits: the Homecoming Center in Gentilly and also a group called Hike for KaTREEna. The latter had been founded when a lifelong New Orleanian named Monique Pilié quit her job at Federal Express six months after Katrina and pledged to plant a tree for every mile of the Appalachian Trail that she walked. Uddo, who had started working with Pilié around a year after Katrina, agreed to take over after Pilié moved from the area. Under Uddo, the group planted its twenty-five thousandth tree in Jackson Square in mid-2014.

Money was a constant worry. The Episcopal Diocese of Louisiana shut down its office of disaster recovery around the fifth anniversary of Katrina, so from 2011 on, Uddo has been on her own. Her survival has come largely courtesy of a wealthy benefactor whose parents had attended St. Paul, the church in Lakeview where the Homecoming Center started. Contributions came as well from Drew Brees's foundation, and she got a $40,000 check when she was featured in a New Orleans–based episode of ABC's *Secret Millionaire*. But even these "gifts from my angels," as Uddo described them, wouldn't prove enough.

"You talk to potential funders and it's like, 'We've moved on,'" Uddo said. "But come to Gentilly, go to the Lower Ninth Ward or New Orleans East, and you'll see we haven't recovered."

AT LEAST MACK MCCLENDON had the Lower 9th Ward Village. That provided some solace when, a few weeks before the eighth anniversary of Katrina, McClendon received a legal notice telling him he had lost his home through foreclosure. "I could be mad at myself for letting it happen, but I'm not," he said. He knew if not for the Village, he would have moved back into his home on Caffin Avenue. "But once you know what you're born to do, you get up every day and do it." He had met with members of the Congressional Black Caucus who had stopped by the Village on a fact-finding tour of New Orleans. He had given a place to stay to groups representing more than a hundred colleges and ultimately housed somewhere around twenty thousand people. How could he have any regrets?

"My mom always used to say, 'You've got to find your purpose in life.' And I always thought, What's she talking about? Now I know. As much as I loved that house, it was still just a thing." To keep things in perspective, he thought of his daughter's death around seven years after Katrina. A bad fall when she was in her third trimester sent her to the hospital. The baby lived, but the doctors couldn't stop his daughter's cranial bleeding. "She was my baby girl, just twenty-one years old," he said.

Around the time of his daughter's death, McClendon put his monthly town hall meetings on indefinite hold. "I stopped because it's one thing to agree on what the problems are, but what's the point when nothing changed?" To get to a Village meeting, residents would drive the same rutted, fractured roads pocked by crater-size hollows that made the word *pothole* seem inadequate. They'd pass the skeletal remains of the businesses still shut down years after Katrina and the jungles of weeds growing where homes used to be.

McClendon had mixed feelings about Mitch Landrieu. The mayor at least showed that he cared about the community in ways that his predecessor had never bothered. "The Lower Ninth Ward," the mayor had vowed at a groundbreaking for the high school the community was finally getting, "is going to become the symbol for how America can find her greatness again." Yet McClendon was also cynical about the money the city spent on the BREATHE LIFE. BREATHE LOWER NINE. banners that lined a dozen blocks of St. Claude and Claiborne, the two main commercial strips in the Lower Ninth. "You'll see Landrieu when you've got the cameras around," McClendon said. Landrieu was there when FEMA broke ground on a new community center on Claiborne (approved the year before he took office), and he was there holding a ceremonial shovel when they broke ground on a new FEMA-funded fire station one block away.

Before Katrina, McClendon figured that maybe ten nonprofits were operating in the Lower Ninth Ward, "and I guarantee you they didn't have a million-dollar budget between them." After Katrina, he counted fifty-three. "At least three or four of these post-Katrina nonprofits went through a million dollars." He had raised all of a couple of hundred thousand dollars over the years, yet managed to house and feed tens of thousands of volunteers.

"Something went wrong when so many millions were spent and a lot of my community still looks like it did three months after Katrina." It seemed to McClendon that enough money had been spent "to build this community four times over."

McClendon never took foundation money, unlike so many others in the Lower Ninth. "I'm the type who would have driven a funder crazy," McClendon said. "If I had the money in hand and saw someone in need, I wouldn't care what that money was designated for, I'd help that person." Instead McClendon made a different kind of mistake when in 2012—seven years after Katrina and nearly five years after he first opened his doors—he agreed to turn the back portion of his center into a skateboard park with money from a local rapper named Lil Wayne, the philanthropic arm of the soda maker Mountain Dew, and Make It Right. McClendon was savvy enough to get his funders to cover the cost of his liability insurance, but the contract he signed meant he was responsible when a building inspector told him the building's electrical system needed a major overhaul to bring it up to code. Seven and a half years after Katrina, the doors to the center were locked.

McClendon used Facebook and YouTube to appeal for donations. "I'm amazed and humbled by the number of people who wanted this place open as bad as me," he said when several months later he was able to reopen. Yet several months after that, he was begging for money again on an East Coast fund-raising trip that had him visiting seven states in six days. He spoke at a church in Atlanta and a synagogue in the Bronx, and visited several colleges, but raised barely $10,000. His next step was a Kickstarter campaign that would fall more than $40,000 short of the $75,000 he had been seeking. "I've spent my life savings to get to this point," he said. "I just don't have any more to give."

The occasional splashy effort to help the Lower Ninth was still made. In 2013, the year the Super Bowl returned to New Orleans, a group of large homebuilders and the NFL Players Association announced Touchdown for Homes with the idea of building dozens of homes at a barren edge of the Lower Ninth. They paid for three and stopped when they were able to sell only one to a qualified buyer. The streets were in terrible shape, the listing agent told a *Times-Picayune* reporter one year after the Super Bowl. The adjoining lots were choked with weeds, and there were no stores and no public transportation. "It shouldn't be like that eight years after the storm," she said.

Brad Pitt and Make It Right were still building homes in their small sliver of the Lower Ninth Ward. Fund-raising was an issue for many Katrina-inspired organizations, but not Make It Right. The group raised $5 million at the 2012 New Orleans fund-raiser Ellen DeGeneres hosted. A year later, Chris Rock was the MC and Bruno Mars was the featured entertainment. The organization raised another $4 million. The problem was scale. The Lower Ninth had eight thousand homes before Katrina. Eight years later, Make It Right had built ninety homes, and a group called Lowernine.org had done maybe seventy. Common Ground had done ten.

Nearly a decade after Katrina, it was still possible to drive several blocks in the Lower Ninth without seeing a single occupied home. Data from the US Postal Service showed that of the mailing addresses in the Lower Ninth before Katrina, only 32 percent were now occupied. At that rate of reoccupation, it wouldn't be until around 2040 that the area recovered its population.

Epilogue

Ray Nagin was thicker around the middle. Gray flecked his mustache. A spell of gout had given him a pronounced limp. In January 2014, nearly four years after he had left office, Nagin was again in New Orleans, to stand trial in a federal courtroom. New Orleans, now a few years shy of its three hundredth birthday, had long been known as a city on the take. Yet Ray Nagin the reformer—the outsider who vowed to clean up City Hall—was the first mayor in its history to be indicted on crimes committed while in office.

There might even have been a time when New Orleans would have relished the idea of Nagin on the witness stand, explaining his lackadaisical manner or his inability to act more decisively when so many were looking to City Hall for leadership. But the charges against him, while serious, wouldn't force him to explain his failings as mayor. Instead, this man about whom people had said at least he was honest was defending himself against claims that he used his position as mayor to enrich himself.

Federal prosecutors had assembled a strong case—so seemingly airtight that the legal experts trotted out by the media all seemed to assume the former mayor would accept the lighter sentence the government was offering him in exchange for a guilty plea. One by one, others indicted by the US Attorney's office in New Orleans had agreed to testify against the mayor in return for leniency. Those included not only Greg Meffert, the former chief technology officer and close Nagin confidant who had pled guilty to taking more than $600,000 in kickbacks,[1] but also several executives who had done business with the city. One, Rodney Williams, the owner of Three Fold Consultants, claimed his firm had had no success securing city business until he and his partners invested $60,000 in Stone Age, the countertop-installation business Nagin owned with his two sons. After that, they secured nearly two dozen city contracts worth $3 million. Williams pled guilty to bribery in 2012. Frank Fradella, the former CEO of Home Solutions of America, told a similar story. Eager to capitalize on the billions in recovery dollars being spent in New Orleans, Fradella, who'd pled guilty to bribery charges in 2013, invested $50,000 in Stone Age, sent the company two truckloads of free granite, and picked up the tab for the private plane that flew Nagin, Meffert, and others to a Saints play-off game in Chicago in 2007. Home Solutions of America received $4 million in contracts for post-Katrina repair work.[2]

If found guilty, Nagin was looking at the possibility of twenty or more years in jail, but the former mayor denied he had done anything wrong. "I really think he believed he could Ray-Ray his way out of a jail sentence," Ron Forman said.

The morning Nagin was slated to testify, he arrived at court looking carefree, carrying a take-out cup of coffee. He joked with people he knew in the hallway and winked at others. Inside the courtroom, his lawyer walked him through his story, and Nagin, looking relaxed, spoke to the jury. On the witness stand, he was again the affable elected official boasting of all he had done to help the citizens of New Orleans in a crisis. He assured the jury that the safeguards he had put in place meant that not even he, as the city's chief executive, could show favoritism to any contractor. He made jokes and maintained his breezy attitude even after the prosecutor began his cross-examination. Nagin's lawyer complained that Assistant US Attorney Matthew Coman was crowding his client,

---

1. Meffert was sentenced to thirty months in prison.

2. Both Williams and Fradella received a one-year prison sentence.

but Nagin said he didn't mind. He invited his adversary to get as close as he'd like. "I can deal with it," the former mayor said. "We're friends."

Nagin's facade began to crack his second day on the witness stand. The mayor's smile grew thin as Coman walked Nagin through the trove of text messages, e-mails, and other incriminating documents the government had unearthed. The more Nagin denied Coman's accusations that he had sold his office for personal gain, the testier he grew. "Come on, man," Nagin snapped, "you're a very seasoned attorney. Let's do this right." The former mayor refused to agree to basic facts, questioning even his signature at the bottom of a letter. He blamed others—his secretary, his accountant, a city attorney—for documents that cast him in an unflattering light. Katrina was his excuse for personal flights that had been purchased with a city credit card (who had time for accurate record keeping in the midst of a crisis?) and his explanation for why he wouldn't know that a city contractor had picked up the cost of a private jet. He was working twenty hours a day to rebuild his broken city, he said. So what if sometimes he had the city pay for a meal with his family? "You have no idea what it was like," an exhausted Nagin told Coman.

The jury convicted Nagin on twenty of the twenty-one counts brought by the government. Six months later, Judge Ginger Berrigan sentenced the former mayor to ten years in prison. Prosecutors had been pushing for a stiffer punishment, but Berrigan, a former defense attorney appointed to the bench by Bill Clinton, cited Nagin's age (fifty-eight) when announcing her sentence, along with the irreparable harm he had done to his own reputation, and the unlikelihood he would ever again be in a position to violate the public trust. The Nagins had lost their Dallas town house through a foreclosure sale and were living on food stamps, according to a letter Seletha Nagin had written to Judge Berrigan prior to her husband's sentencing. Despite their pleas of poverty, Berrigan ordered the former mayor to pay more than $500,000 in fines. Nagin would appeal his conviction, said his high-priced defense attorney, who then filed paperwork removing himself from the case. "The defendant in this matter is indigent," he wrote, and therefore eligible for representation by the federal public defender's office.

Nagin, defiant to the end, refused to apologize for violating the public trust. Instead he tied his prosecution to his outspokenness in the days and weeks after his city had flooded. "Some of the stances that I took after Katrina didn't sit well with some very powerful people," Nagin told a local television reporter the day of his sentencing. "So now I'm paying the price for that." In September 2014, Nagin began serving his sentence in a federal prison in Texarkana, Texas.

MITCH LANDRIEU WAS ELECTED to a second term—two days after opening arguments in Nagin's trial. Landrieu's chief challenger was a sixty-one-year-old black man named Michael Bagneris, a district court judge who relinquished his post to enter the race. Bagneris spoke often about the "forgotten New Orleans" and hammered at a police department where morale was so low, the city was nearly four hundred officers short of its hiring goals. The number of people murdered fell in 2012 and 2013, mirroring national trends, but the city's homicide rate was still nine times the national average and nearly four times higher than that of similar-size cities. Bagneris fared well in lower-income precincts and parts of New Orleans East, but Landrieu, who had been endorsed by Barack Obama, trounced his foe in the rest of the city. Landrieu captured 82 percent of the white vote and 44 percent of the black vote, allowing him to claim broad support in this majority-black city.

The African-American community was not without its victories in 2014. In that election season, blacks reclaimed the majority in the City Council, and Sheriff Marlin Gusman, one of the few African Americans to hold parishwide office, was reelected to another term. That summer, police chief Ronal Serpas resigned, allowing Landrieu to replace him with a black man, a popular district commander with twenty-three years on the force. WBOK's John Slade, however, was not impressed. "Lord Little Mitch decides to do something, finally, about a police chief he should've gotten rid of years ago?" Slade said. "And we're supposed to be happy?"

CONNIE UDDO LINGERED OVER coffee at a café in Lakeview a few days before the ninth anniversary of Katrina. She felt proud of all that she had accomplished, but mainly she felt at peace. Each year since the fifth anniversary, she had thought that would be the last she saw of the church groups and college kids who descended on New Orleans to help during spring break and the summer months. But even eight years after the storm, she was coordinating crews of sixty to eighty volunteers a day all that summer. "This is the first year we didn't get a huge influx of volunteers," she said in August 2014.

Uddo was playing tennis again. She chatted about the big trip she was taking with Mark to celebrate their twenty-fifth wedding anniversary. With a sense of wonder, she realized that her phone had not rung once in the two hours she had been sitting there. At 11:00 a.m. on a workday, there was no place she needed to be. Her eyes were bright, her face relaxed. "This is the first time I feel truly rested since the storm." Finally, nine years after Katrina, Uddo said, "I don't cry at everything."

Mack McClendon bought a 1959 Austin-Healey in August 2014. He still couldn't bring himself to attend an antique-auto show all these years after Katrina, but he was looking forward to tinkering on a car again. "My plan is to start working on it this week," he said four days before the ninth anniversary of Katrina. "It seems time." By then, the bank had seized the strange-shaped, multicolored building that had come to symbolize the Lower Ninth's struggle to rebuild. McClendon was living in a borrowed home a few blocks away. Where he would be living in a year wasn't clear.

McClendon seemed more resigned than angry with the approach of the ninth anniversary. Sitting in Café Dauphine, the Lower Ninth Ward's lone restaurant, he spoke with ambivalence about the newcomers who had discovered his corner of the city. New Orleans had always been a gumbo, he said, "a mix of everyone and everything." In a community only one-third occupied nearly a decade after the storm, how could he resent the smattering of whites who had moved there to help them rebuild?

Yet he thought of Bywater, which he still considered part of the Upper Ninth Ward, on the other side of the Industrial Canal. People he knew there had been priced out now that the modest-size cottage that was selling for $80,000 before Katrina cost more than $200,000. He said that more whites would inevitably cross the bridge in search of cheap housing and transform the Lower Ninth into a majority-white community. "I give it twenty years," he said.

McClendon, however, wouldn't live long enough to see whether he was right. He had lost his home through foreclosure and then his center. And at the end of 2014, he was told he had terminal brain cancer. He died less than three months later, in February 2015.

THE USUAL MEMORIALS, MASSES, and speeches marked the ninth anniversary of Katrina in August 2014. That morning the mayor spoke at a wreath-laying ceremony at a Hurricane Katrina memorial in Mid-City, where nearly a hundred unclaimed, unidentified bodies were entombed in a semicircle of black-marble mausoleums. There, Landrieu performed his usual balancing act, declaring New Orleans "America's greatest comeback story," while also noting that his administration had more work to do. At an event in the Lower Ninth Ward, a malfunctioning sound system forced the roster of speakers to shout. Their speeches were followed by a second-line parade to the site of the levee breach that had flooded the Lower Ninth, in honor of those who had lost their lives that day.

At 1:00 p.m., an advocacy group called the African American Leadership Project held a press conference in front of City Hall. Their purpose, two of its founders announced in an op-ed appearing in the previous day's *Times-Picayune*, was to challenge the city's "self-medicating illusion of progress." "We believe that insufficient attention is paid to the uneven outcomes of the city's so-called grand transformation," said Gail Glapion, the group's founding chairwoman. A doctor spoke of inequities in the health care system, a parent advocate decried a school system she believed was leaving too many black children behind. Nine years after the state's seemingly temporary takeover of New Orleans's failing schools, she noted, not a single one had been returned to local control. To help stir media interest, the organizers had also enlisted Oliver Thomas, the former City Council president, who, postprison, had reinvented himself as the drive-time morning host on WBOK.

Organizers had asked Thomas to talk for a few minutes about the growing disparity between black and white in a time of growth. Yet what struck Thomas when it was his turn to speak was the lack of local media. A single reporter had shown up for their press conference—an out-of-town author who was scheduled to eat lunch with him afterward. "Had this been a press conference about a young black boy or black girl doing something wrong, every news station in town would be here," Thomas said. "But when we hold a news conference about the state of things in black New Orleans? When we want to talk about what's going on with the majority of the population and that's not news? That, ladies and gentlemen, shows you how much they care about us."

ACKNOWLEDGMENTS

This book has been in the works for some years and therefore my debt load is high. My eternal gratitude is owed to those who gave so generously of their time, starting with Alden McDonald, who was harried and overburdened the first time I met him but nonetheless allowed me in his life in the midst of the chaos. Thanks as well to the Wall sisters, Mack McClendon, Connie Uddo, Jacques Morial, Bill Hines, and a long list of others I've gone back to so many times that I feared I was becoming a pest.

I'll be forever grateful to the *New York Times* for sending me to New Orleans post-Katrina. I want to thank Larry Ingrassia, Tom Redburn, and Kevin McKenna for the trust they showed in me, and Jill Abramson for making me part of the storm team. Paula Dwyer was a terrific editor who always made my copy smarter in those first crazy weeks after the levees broke, and I can't say enough about David Firestone, the storm editor and our fearless, implacable leader. The *Times* made an extraordinary commitment to the rebuilding story under executive editor Bill Keller. I feel lucky to have been enlisted in the cause.

I was fortunate to have found an ideal home post-*Times* with the Investigative Fund at the Nation Institute. The Investigative Fund was no stranger to the New Orleans narrative, having given A. C. Thompson the first rounds of funding he needed to report his extraordinary, groundbreaking piece, "Katrina's Hidden Race War." My editor at the Investigative Fund, Esther Kaplan, was wonderfully supportive even as this book intruded on other projects. Thanks as well to Joe Conason, Sarah Blustain, and Taya Kitman.

I'll love forever Lori Cobb of Lori Cobb Reporting in Baton Rouge for sharing with me the depositions that let me begin puzzling together what happened on the Crescent City Connection in those first few days after Katrina. I'm also indebted to Allison Plyer, executive director of the Data Center; Richard Campanella, the city's unofficial official geographer and a professor at Tulane; Lawrence Powell, an emeritus professor at Tulane and author who agreed to read the passages I had written about the city's history; and Edward E. Chervenak, a professor of political science at the University of New Orleans and director of UNO's Survey Research Center. Beverly McKenna, the publisher of the *New Orleans Tribune,* did me a great kindness by allowing me to spend long blocks of time inside the *Tribune*'s offices, going through archives. So, too, did marketing maven Bill Rouselle, when he made me copies of videotaped interviews with Alden McDonald and Norman Francis in anticipation of Liberty Bank's fortieth anniversary. Thanks, too, to Liberty's Ann Marie Allen.

Somewhere between the sixth and seventh anniversaries of Katrina, I wrote a fan letter to a political science professor named Caroline Heldman. In a single blog post, Heldman, who teaches at Occidental College, had seemed to capture the entirety of the New Orleans story post-Katrina. Heldman helped give shape to this book and then proved a careful and demanding reader after she generously agreed to read a draft manuscript. As if that were not contribution enough, she also recruited to the cause two of her more promising, New Orleans–loving students. Rebecca Cooper and Aaron Silvers proved great research assistants: smart, able, diligent.

I wish in the life of every writer an editor like Jon Karp—sharp-eyed, supportive, loyal. The two of us first began talking about a book about the rebuilding of New Orleans post-Katrina a few months after the storm—and rather than tire of the topic, Jon encouraged me to resurrect the idea for Simon & Schuster. He compounded this gift to me by assigning the book to Ben Loehnen, who has sometimes seemed more collaborator than editor in the three years we've been working together.

I couldn't have asked for a more talented, incisive, and committed editor. My watchwords throughout: In Ben I trust.

My thanks also to Steve Boldt, Brit Hvide, and Jonathan Evans for the care they showed in going through my manuscript. And thanks to my mother, Naomi Rivlin, whose boss considers her the best proofreader with whom he has ever worked. As always, she gave the book one last read to catch those pesky mistakes that somehow had gotten by the rest of us.

I was lucky early in my writing career to have teamed up with Elizabeth Kaplan, superagent. Elizabeth is wise, kind, and always there for me—even serving as occasional aunt when I've needed extra writing time. I also want to thank John Raeside, who has always played a special role in my writing life.

Geoff Sanborn played hero by giving my draft a speedy read at an anxious time—and then served as English professor with useful comments, suggestions, and corrections. This manuscript was also improved by suggestions from the two Mikes, Loftin and Kelly. I also want to thank others who helped me keep my moorings through this project: Jonathan Rabinovitz, Sue Matteucci, Mike Buchman, and Jeff Cohen. Thanks, too, to Jackie Stewart and Dina Harris, keeper of the cabin where large sections of this book were written. Thanks as well to Linda Santi, my sometime New Orleans landlord.

My two sons, Oliver and Silas, kept a smile on my face through the endurance test that is the writing of a book. And my spouse, Daisy Walker—this book wouldn't be possible without my Daisy. She picked up the slack when I needed more writing time. She provided the love and support when that was what I needed. And she also proved a terrific editor, if not a sometimes brutal one. For Daisy, who provided every kind of help I needed.

NOTES ON SOURCES

I conducted hundreds of interviews in the making of this book. I sat through more meetings than I care to count. Yet any work of nonfiction almost by definition builds on the work of others. Woven through this book are quotes, data points, and other jewels mined from a long list of books, documentaries, magazine and newspaper articles, radio reports, and Web-based pieces. I mention many by name in the body of the book but also felt protective of the narrative flow. Below is a more thorough rendering of all those works that enriched the tale I set out to tell.

Many books helped in the shaping of this narrative, starting with the first I read post-Katrina, *New Orleans: The Making of an Urban Landscape*. John King, the *San Francisco Chronicle*'s urban design critic, a friend and a former colleague, made sure I read this masterpiece by Peirce Lewis. That and the next book on my reading list, John M. Barry's splendid *Rising Tide: The Great Mississippi Flood of 1927 and How It Changed America*, probably made my early coverage a little geography-obsessed. But I couldn't have asked for two better primers. Two more recent works, Richard Campanella's *Bienville's Dilemma: A Historical Geography of New Orleans* and Lawrence N. Powell's *The Accidental City: Improvising New Orleans*, helped round out my understanding of the geography and history of New Orleans.

There have been any number of excellent books written about

New Orleans immediately after the flood. At or near the top of any list would be Douglas Brinkley's *The Great Deluge: Hurricane Katrina, New Orleans, and the Mississippi Gulf Coast,* a vivid snapshot of those first terrible days after Katrina that's as well written as it is insightful. I valued the brawling spirit of Jed Horne's *Breach of Faith: Hurricane Katrina and the Near Death of a Great American City,* which might be my personal favorite among this first batch of Katrina books. Also making my top tier: *Zeitoun,* by Dave Eggers, which tells the harrowing tale of Abdulrahman Zeitoun in the first couple of weeks after Katrina; *City of Refuge,* Tom Piazza's beautifully rendered novel about those first months after the storm; *Nine Lives: Death and Life in New Orleans,* by Dan Baum; and *1 Dead in Attic: After Katrina,* by Chris Rose.

Robert B. Olshansky and Laurie A. Johnson's *Clear as Mud: Planning for the Rebuilding of New Orleans* proves it's possible to fall in love with a book about urban planning. Valuable, too, was Kristina Ford's engaging book *The Trouble with City Planning: What New Orleans Can Teach Us.* Sarah Carr's evenhanded, clear-eyed account of school reform in post-Katrina New Orleans, *Hope Against Hope: Three Schools, One City, and the Struggle to Educate America's Children,* is an impressive work of journalism, as is *Disaster: Hurricane Katrina and the Failure of Homeland Security,* by Christopher Cooper and Robert Block. I also appreciated Michael Eric Dyson's incisive *Come Hell or High Water: Hurricane Katrina and the Color of Disaster;* Tom Wooten's heartfelt book *We Shall Not Be Moved: Rebuilding Home in the Wake of Katrina;* and Ivor van Heerden's engaging account of his pursuit of the truth in *The Storm: What Went Wrong and Why During Hurricane Katrina—the Inside Story from One Louisiana Scientist.*

Also deserving mention: *Resilience and Opportunity: Lessons From the U.S. Gulf Coast after Katrina and Rita,* edited by Amy Liu, Roland V. Anglin, Richard M. Mizelle Jr., and Allison Plyer; *A.D.: New Orleans After the Deluge,* by Josh Neufeld; *Unnatural Disaster,* a collection of articles from the *Nation* magazine edited by Betsy Reed; *The Fight for Home: How (Parts of) New Orleans Came Back,* by Daniel Wolff; *Floodlines: Community and Resistance from Katrina to the Jena Six,* by Jordan Flaherty; *The Shock Doctrine: The Rise of Disaster Capitalism,* by Naomi Klein; *There Is No Such Thing as a Natural Disaster: Race, Class, and*

Hurricane Katrina, edited by Chester Hartman and Gregory D. Squires; *Overcoming Katrina: African American Voices from the Crescent City and Beyond*, by D'Ann R. Penner and Keith C. Ferdinand; *City Adrift: New Orleans Before and After Katrina*, by the Center for Public Integrity; *The Ravaging Tide: Strange Weather, Future Katrinas, and the Coming Death of America's Coastal Cities*, by Mike Tidwell; and *Who Killed New Orleans? Mother Nature vs. Human Nature*, by Diane Holloway.

Spike Lee's sensational *When the Levees Broke: A Requiem in Four Acts* proved a much-needed jolt for the city when it premiered in August 2006. More high-quality documentaries followed, including Lee's sequel, *If God Is Willing and da Creek Don't Rise*. Tia Lessin and Carl Deal's *Trouble the Water* was a 2008 Oscar nominee that deserved all the praise it received and then some. Lolis Eric Elie's excellent *Faubourg Tremé* is a touching, poignant film that, true to its subtitle, offers "the untold story of black New Orleans." Other favorites that helped in the creation of this book: *The Big Uneasy*, by Harry Shearer; *Race*, by Katherine Cecil; and *Getting Back to Abnormal*, by Peter Odabashian, Andrew Kolker, Louis Alvarez, and Paul Stekler.

Any number of national media outlets remained committed to the Katrina story long after the hurricane was no longer headline news; all offered rich reserves of material for me to sift through. Any list would start with the *New York Times* and include CNN, NPR, the *Washington Post*, the *Los Angeles Times*, the *Houston Chronicle*, and the *Chicago Tribune*. I mention many of my *Times* colleagues by name within these pages, but a more thorough list includes Dan Barry, who deserved the Pulitzer in my eyes for the columns he wrote in those first days and months after Katrina, and also Deborah Sontag, Eric Lipton, Jennifer Steinhauer, Jeré Longman, and Leslie Eaton. The Associated Press also deserves a special shout-out for its commitment to covering post-flood New Orleans. When was the first jury trial post-Katrina? A search uncovered an AP article (carrying no byline) published in June 2006, ten months after Katrina, documenting jury selection for a man accused of stealing a car. The piece was short but included an estimate of the backload of cases (five thousand) and the approximate repair bill ($4 million) for the criminal court complex. Cain Burdeau, Michael Kunzelman, Becky Bohrer, Robert Tanner, and Michelle Roberts were the names I'd see most frequently on AP stories that carried a byline.

The *Times-Picayune* coverage of New Orleans post-Katrina was as impressive as it was invaluable to the writing of this book. Going through stacks of old clips and printouts, I'd see the same names over again: Gordon Russell, David Hammer, Laura Maggi, Katy Reckdahl, Frank Donze, Michelle Krupa, Mark Schleifstein, Brendan McCarthy, Bruce Nolan, Bruce Eggler, Bruce Alpert, Martha Carr, Sarah Carr, Trymaine D. Lee, Chris Kirkham, Brian Thevenot, Jeff Duncan, Kate Moran, Richard Rainey, Paul Purpura, Gwen Filosa, and Mark Waller. There were also the columnists I regularly read: Chris Rose, Lolis Eric Elie, Stephanie Grace, James Gill, and Jarvis DeBerry.

The pages of the *New Orleans Tribune* often offered a very different view than the *Times-Picayune* on the city's recovery. In the *Tribune* I'd read anything by Anitra D. Brown, J. B. Borders, or Beverly McKenna, who writes a regular publisher's note for the paper. Lance Hill is an occasional *Tribune* contributor, as is Bill Quigley, a Loyola law professor. The periodic post-storm updates that Quigley published in the *Trib* and also *CounterPunch* offered vivid snapshots that, along with the *New Orleans Index,* published jointly by the Brookings Institution and the Data Center (then the Greater New Orleans Data Center), allowed me to more accurately track the city's progress, or lack of it. The same is true of the series of articles the *New York Times* ran around both the first and second anniversaries of Katrina, and the anniversary pieces produced by any number of media outlets.

The *Gambit* often came through when I was looking to learn more about a subject. There were Clancy DuBos's entertaining columns about New Orleans politics and also the long features at which the paper's alternative weekly excelled. There was also the crew at the *Lens*, a local investigative news site, who always offered high-quality work whether on the schools, the coast, or city politics. I mention Karen Gadbois and Tyler Bridges within these pages, but other *Lens* staffers, past and present, deserve mention, including Jessica Williams, Mark Moseley, Charles Maldonado, and Jeff Adelson.

Dan Baum wrote "Deluged" and "The Lost Year," which might be my two favorite magazine pieces about New Orleans just after Katrina. Both appeared in the *New Yorker*, and both served as great sources while working on this book. I appreciated the occasional New Orleans dispatch Josh Levin filed for *Slate*, and I also found insights reading Robert Morris (the *Uptown Messenger*), Jeff Crouere, the *New Orleans Business Journal*, and the *Louisiana Weekly*.

The prologue to this book was based on a blend of interviews and depositions. An article appearing in the *Los Angeles Times* was my source for Blanco's quote expressing her frustration with the airlines.

I relied on numerous sources for the FEMA portions of this book. That includes an interview with Marty Bahamonde but also numerous books and articles. Cooper and Block's *Disaster* offered an invaluable history of FEMA along with a withering dissection of the federal government's many blunders after Katrina. Daniel Franklin, writing in the *Washington Monthly* in 1995 ("The FEMA Phoenix"), offered a vivid portrait of FEMA's earliest years and James Lee Witt's attempts to save the agency. So, too, did Jon Elliston in his excellent "FEMA: Confederacy of Dunces," appearing in the *Nation* a few weeks after Katrina. Also helpful were Spencer S. Hsu's reporting in the *Washington Post* and an Evan Thomas article appearing in *Newsweek*.

I interviewed Ray Nagin numerous times before he shut himself off from the media. Lucky for me, he wrote *Katrina's Secrets: Storms after the Storm*, his memoir about those first few weeks after Katrina. I was fortunate, too, that Sally Forman self-published *Eyes of the Storm: Inside City Hall During Katrina*. Sally set up several interviews with me and was generous with her time, but her well-written account of her time inside City Hall served as an additional source. Edward J. Blakely's memoir, *My Storm: Managing the Recovery of New Orleans in the Wake of Katrina*, also proved invaluable in offering Blakely's perspective on the recovery.

Any number of writers took on Nagin as a topic. I'm partial to Ethan Brown's terrific profile of New Orleans's then mayor in *Details* in 2008 and the pieces that Stephanie Grace, Mark Moseley, and Jarvis DeBerry wrote about the mayor over the years. And then there's that trio of locals—Gordon Rusell, Jason Berry, and David Hammer—whose reporting practically demanded that the US Attorney indict the former mayor on corruption charges. The Nagin trial itself was a good source for the crimes and misdemeanors Nagin committed in office.

Lolis Eric Elie's *Faubourg Tremé* gave me my first in-depth introduction to black history in New Orleans. Katy Reckdahl also deserves a shout-out for the moving piece she wrote for the fiftieth anniversary of the desegregation of the Orleans Parish schools.

I relied on a *Gambit* profile of Kathleen Blanco, written by Tyler Bridges, to fill out my portrait of the governor in these pages. An article written by the *New York Times'* Adam Nagourney and Anne E. Kornblut was my source for information on the "war room" the White House set up to combat criticisms of the president post-Katrina. Helping me to round out my portrait of the Bush administration: the *Washington Post's* Joby Warrick ("White House Got Early Warning on Katrina") and Paul Alexander's book *Machiavelli's Shadow: The Rise and Fall of Karl Rove*. Details about the "overly ornamented" Katrina bill that Senators Landrieu and Vitter introduced shortly after the storm were taken both from an article written by the *Washington Post's* Michael Grunwald and Susan B. Glasser and a James Gill column appearing in the *Times-Picayune*.

The *Advocate* in Baton Rouge broke the story of the state troopers from Michigan and New Mexico who felt they had been enlisted to intimidate rather than police in the days after Katrina. My account of the fight over the future of Charity was enriched by the work of my former colleague, Adam Nossiter, who wrote about disagreements between the state and the hospital's medical staff.

I learned from reading a Mark Schleifstein *Times-Picayune* article that 250 billion gallons of water covered the greater New Orleans area after Katrina. The story of evacuees who were made to feel unwelcome at their new school, including Dominique Townsend, was captured in *Education in Exile*, a short documentary by Lloyd Dennis. I found the Joe Canizaro quote about the city's lack of a plan for helping those of modest means return to New Orleans in an excellent AP story by Robert Tanner. I lifted the Ronald Lewis quote about the indignity of being cast as a poor person from Dan Baum's *Nine Lives*. *Nine Lives* was also my source for information on the search for someone—*anyone*—who might pick up the dead bodies scattered around New Orleans after the floodwaters receded.

The *New York Times'* Stephanie Strom was my source for reporting on the Red Cross's share of post-Katrina charitable giving. It was reading Olshansky and Johnson's *Clear as Mud* that revealed that the infamous green-dot map on the front page of the *Times-Picayune* was actually based on an obscure graphic meant to show generally where the city might add parkland if the residents of a community chose to allow low-lying parts of their neighborhood revert to wetlands. Ceci Connolly wrote movingly in the *Washington Post* about the spike in suicides after Katrina, which I allude to in the book. My depiction of the reopening of the Lower Ninth Ward three months after Katrina was aided by a report by NPR's Anthony Brooks and a Deborah Sontag article in the *New York Times.*

The *Times-Picayune*'s Jeffrey Meitrodt and the *Times'* Adam Nossiter wrote articles chronicling the city's decision to revise the damage estimates of most any homeowner choosing to rebuild. Both helped in the writing of that section of the book. A Nossiter article was also my source for a FEMA official's lament over the sheer scope of people seeking the agency's help after Katrina and Rita. I learned of the giant shredder the government dispatched to the Gulf Coast to help with the garbage problem in an entertaining report ("Katrina's Garbage Rates a Category 5") written by Andrew Martin, then of the *Chicago Tribune.*

Mike Davis, writing in *Mother Jones,* documented Louisiana's unsuccessful attempts to convince FEMA to help officials reach potential voters in New Orleans's pending municipal elections. Linton Weeks was the author of the *Washington Post*'s "A 20-Ring Political Circus: Strange Crew Populates New Orleans Mayoral Race." I picked up Stephen Bradberry's "whiter city" quote in an article by the *Post*'s Peter Whoriskey. Whoriskey also wrote a story about a criminal justice system in shambles that helped me tell that part of the story.

Anne Rochell Konigsmark reported on the return of crime to New Orleans for an article she wrote for *USA Today* sixteen months after Katrina. Around that same time, the *Christian Science Monitor*'s Patrik Jonsson wrote about the challenges still confronting the criminal justice system in a hobbled city. Pieces of the Doris Hicks/King Charter School story were gleaned from a terrific series written by *Education Week*'s Lesli A. Maxwell. I picked up details about UNOP's Community Congress–II in an article by the *Times-Picayune*'s Coleman Warner. Writing in the *Times-Picayune,* Gwen Filosa told the story of several locked-out public housing residents trying to move back home, even to units without utilities.

An article by the *New York Times'* Leslie Eaton was my source for the comparison of public dollars spent to help small businesses after September 11 and after Hurricane Katrina. Leslie's writing, too, provided me with the warning from Dr. David Myers not to bring sick people back to New Orleans, and data on the lack of hospital beds in New Orleans two years after Katrina. I plucked the Richard Campanella quote from another Leslie story. I picked up Alphonso Thomas's "90 percent suicidal" quote in a *Times* article written by Shaila Dewan. Albert Felton's quote about a lack of contractors working in Gentilly two years after Katrina was plucked from an Adam Nossiter article in the *Times*.

Leslie Eaton and Joseph B. Treaster wrote about homeowner dissatisfaction with their insurance carriers two years after Katrina in a long article that ran as part of the *Times'* "Patchwork City" series. That was my source for data about complaints with the state and lawsuits filed. Both the *Los Angeles Times* and Bloomberg reported on the record profits booked by private insurers in 2005.

I learned about Ed Blakely's hesitancy to take the job as recovery czar in reading J. B. Borders's profile of Blakely ("The Master of Disaster"), which appeared in the *New Orleans Tribune* a few months into his tenure. *Clear as Mud* is great in describing the press conference where Blakely first shared his rebuilding plan, as was a *Times-Picayune* article written by Gary Scheets.

David Hammer at the *Times-Picayune* led the pack with his vigorous reporting on the many shortcomings of the Road Home program. Also contributing to the cause were NPR's Steve Inskeep and PBS's Betty Ann Bowser, both of whom broadcast powerful reports about people's frustration with Road Home. It was in the *Shreveport Times* that I found the Pearson Cross quote after Blanco announced she would not seek a second term. Vincanne Adams tells the story of Anthony and Sylvia Blanchard in her book *Markets of Sorrow, Labors of Faith: New Orleans in the Wake of Katrina*, though she gives them the pseudonyms Henry and Gladys Bradlieu.

Patricia Jones was one of the few people who declined to talk with me for this book. Tom Wooten's *We Shall Not Be Moved* allowed me to tell the story of Jones and other dazed residents showing up at the Sanchez Community Center starting around six months after Katrina. Jones spoke at length to Wooten and also talked with NPR's Larry Abramson, who told her story in the "Gulf Coast's Everyday Heroes" series the radio station ran two and a half years after Katrina. Jones's story was also captured by a Tulane project called MediaNOLA, which bills itself as "a portal for histories of culture and cultural production in New Orleans."

The *Times'* Campbell Robertson arrived in New Orleans in 2009 and produced a number of stories that enriched the book's final set of chapters. An article he wrote about the significance of a Super Bowl win to the New Orleans psyche was beautifully written and also offered a bounty of anecdotes for a hungry author (churches that canceled evening mass on Super Bowl Sunday; schools that canceled class the next day). I picked up a quote from the Reverend Vien The Nguyen from another Campbell story.

Several people told me about the emotional meeting Mitch Landrieu held at the Household of Faith in New Orleans East shortly after taking over as mayor. I would attend a couple of Landrieu's "budgeting for outcomes" meetings myself. But my account of the Household of Faith gathering was based largely on the vivid writing of Justin Vogt, who wrote at length about that night in a *Washington Monthly* profile of Landrieu published in early 2011.

NPR's Alix Spiegel reported on the high rate of suicide five years after Katrina. An article by Richard Campanella taught me the term *gutter punks*. For a book he is apparently writing about gentrification, Peter Moskowitz interviewed Pres Kabacoff and posted a transcript on Gawker that helped in my portrayal of the controversial developer. And last but hardly least, there's the terrific article Nathaniel Rich wrote for the *New York Times Magazine* about the Southeast Louisiana Flood Protection Authority–East's attempt to save Louisiana's vanishing coastline by suing ninety-seven oil and gas companies. As the October 5, 2014, cover of the *Times* magazine asked, "Every Hour, An Acre of Louisiana Sinks into the Sea. Who Is to Blame?"

INDEX